GEOFF TIBBALLS is the author of the bestselling *Mammoth Book of Jokes* and *The Mammoth Book of Dirty Jokes* as well as many other books including *Business Blunders* and *Legal Blunders*. A former journalist and press officer, he is now a full-time writer who lists his hobbies as sport, eating, drinking and avoiding housework. He lives in Nottingham, England, with his wife and daughters.

★ ★ ★ ★ ★

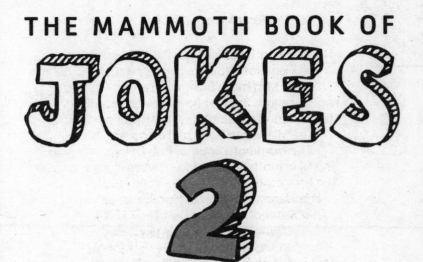

THE MAMMOTH BOOK OF
JOKES
2

Geoff Tibballs

ROBINSON

Constable & Robinson Ltd
55–56 Russell Square
London WC1B 4HP
www.constablerobinson.com

First published in the UK by Robinson,
an imprint of Constable & Robinson Ltd, 2012

A copy of the British Library Cataloguing in
Publication Data is available from the British Library

ISBN: 978-1-78033-484-4 (paperback)
ISBN: 978-1-78033-537-7 (ebook)

Printed and bound by CPI Group (UK) Ltd, Croydon, CR0 4YY

13 5 7 9 10 8 6 4 2

CONTENTS

★   ★   ★   ★   ★

INTRODUCTION

Recent research by an English academic has unearthed jokes dating back to Roman times. It seems that when the Romans weren't throwing Christians to the lions, they enjoyed nothing more than a good laugh. A third-century joke book written in Greek contains more than 250 Roman rib-ticklers, including probably the earliest ever doctor joke:

✳ "Doctor," asked the patient, "whenever I get up after a sleep, I feel dizzy for half an hour, then I'm all right."
The doctor replied: "Then wait for half an hour before getting up."

And if that didn't go down a storm at the forum, there was always this ancient version of the Monty Python dead parrot sketch:

✳ A man bought a slave who died soon after. When he complained, the slave seller replied: "Well, he didn't die when I owned him."

Fast forward 1,800 years and the ideas behind many modern jokes can be traced back to the basic principles instigated by the Romans. In fact, take a trip on a cruise ship and you'll hear the resident entertainer still telling many of the original gags. Meanwhile new jokes are constantly evolving. The cult of celebrity has brought about numerous jokes at the expense of the rich and famous while the fallout from the recession has meant that bankers have temporarily replaced lawyers as the people we most love to hate. Politicians come and go, but while comics have struggled to invent material on Barack Obama, happily there are still a few new George W. Bush jokes because where humorists are concerned, even though he is no longer in office, Dubya is the gift that just keeps on giving.

The vast majority of jokes in this book are brand new with the occasional classic thrown in, including the one about two nuns in a bath. I confess to having no idea how old that particular gem is. Who knows, it might originally have been a Roman bath.

Geoff Tibballs, 2009

★   ★   ★   ★   ★

ACCIDENTS

✳ A man called his wife from hospital and told her that his finger had been cut off on the building site where he worked.

"Oh my God!" cried the wife. "The whole finger?"

"No," he said, "the one next to it."

✳ A woman was driving along the road when the car in front braked suddenly and she ploughed into the back of it.

When the driver got out, the woman saw that he was a dwarf. He said: "I'm not happy."

The woman said: "Well, which one ARE you?"

✳ Why didn't the little boy tell his mother that he had been sucking a tube of glue?

Because his lips were sealed.

✳ A man was annoyed when his wife told him that a car had backed into hers, damaging the front bumper, and that she hadn't made a note of the licence plate number.

"What kind of car was he driving?" asked the husband.

"I don't know," she said. "I can never tell one make of car from another."

Hearing this, the husband decided it was time for her to learn and for the next few days, whenever they were out on the road, he made her name each car they passed until he was satisfied that she could identify every make.

It worked. A week later, she bounded in with a big grin on her face. "Darling," she said. "I hit a Pontiac G8!"

✳ What happened when two weathermen each broke an arm and a leg in an accident?

They were worried about the four casts.

✳   The telephone rang at dawn. "Hello, Señor Ralph? This is Alfredo, the caretaker at your country house."

"Hi, Alfredo. What can I do for you? Is there a problem?"

"Uh, I am just calling to tell you, Señor Ralph, that your parrot died."

"My parrot? Dead? The one that won the international competition?"

"Yes, Señor, that's the one."

"Damn! That's a pity. I spent a small fortune on that bird. What did he die from?"

"From eating rotten meat, Señor Ralph."

"Rotten meat? Who the hell fed him rotten meat?"

"Nobody, Señor. He ate the meat of the dead horse."

"Dead horse? What dead horse?"

"The thoroughbred, Señor Ralph."

"My prize thoroughbred is dead?"

"Yes, Señor Ralph, he died from all that work pulling the water cart."

"Are you insane? What water cart?"

"The one we used to put out the fire, Señor."

"My God! What fire are you talking about?"

"The one at your house, Señor. A candle fell and the curtains caught fire."

"What the hell . . . ? Are you telling me that my $5m mansion is destroyed because of a candle?"

"Yes, Señor Ralph."

"But there's electricity at the house! What was the candle for?"

"For the funeral, Señor Ralph."

"What bloody funeral?"

"Your wife's, Señor Ralph. She showed up one night out of the blue and I thought she was a thief. So I hit her with your new Tiger Woods' Nike driver."

There was a lengthy silence.

"Alfredo, if you broke that driver, you're in real trouble . . ."

✳ I walked into a blind man today. I didn't see him. I couldn't believe the irony.

> 66 I was in front of an ambulance the other day, and I noticed that the word 'ambulance' was spelled in reverse print on the hood of the ambulance. And I thought, 'Well, isn't that clever?' I look in the rear-view mirror, I can read the word 'ambulance' behind me. Of course, while you're reading, you don't see where you're going, you crash, you need an ambulance. I think they're trying to drum up some business on the way back from lunch.
>
> Jerry Seinfeld 99

✳ A woman was asked to give a talk on the power of prayer to her local women's group. With her husband sitting in the audience, she recounted how they had turned to God when her husband suffered an unfortunate accident.

"Three months ago," she began, "my husband Colin was knocked off his bicycle and his scrotum was smashed. The pain was excruciating and the doctors didn't know if they could help him. They warned that our lives might never be the same again. Colin was unable to get close to either me or the children and every move caused him enormous discomfort. It meant we could no longer touch him around the scrotum.

"So we prayed that the doctors would be able to repair him. Fortunately our prayers were answered and they were able to piece together the crushed remnants of Colin's scrotum and wrap wire around it to hold it in place. They said he should make a complete recovery and regain full use of his scrotum."

As the audience burst into spontaneous applause, a lone man walked up to the stage. He announced: "Good afternoon. My name is Colin, and I just want to tell my wife once again that the word is 'sternum'."

✳ Did you hear about the carpenter who accidentally sat on his electric drill and was bored to tears?

I drove past the fire department the other day, and they had a big public awareness sign that read: "Are your house numbers visible?" I thought: "Who cares? How about you just stop at the house that's on fire?"

＊ Driving home late one night, a man spotted a car on fire. He rushed over to help and saw that a beautiful woman was trapped inside, bleeding to death. He dragged her to safety from the flames, wrapped her in a blanket and drove her to the nearest hospital. Over the next six months, he regularly donated blood to keep her alive. It was touch and go whether she pulled through, but eventually she did recover and later that year they got married.

For two years they lived happily together, but then she grew restless and decided to leave him. As she came down the stairs one morning, carrying two large suitcases and a set of car keys, he challenged her: "Where are you going?"

"I'm leaving you," she said coldly.

"What are you doing with the car keys?"

"I'm leaving in the Mercedes."

"No, you're not. It's my car. I paid for that. You're not having it."

"Fine," she said, and threw the keys at him.

"And what's in those bulging suitcases?" he demanded.

"My clothes," she said.

"You mean the clothes I've paid for? They're not going anywhere!"

"Fine," she said, tipping out the cases before stripping off completely and hurling her clothes at him.

"And," he continued, warming to the theme, "what about the blood in your body? I sat with you for six months in the hospital. You know half of the blood is mine. You're not going anywhere."

With that, she whipped out her tampon and said: "I'll pay you back in monthly instalments!"

> **❝** Apparently 50,000 people died from driving last year, and 10,000 died from drinking. Yet only 500 died from drink-driving. Then again, only two people died from drink-driving and juggling. I think that's my safest way home then.
>
> Lee Mack **❞**

✳ A man phoned the fire department and said: "I have just had my front yard landscaped, I have nice new flowerbeds, a rose border, a new fish pond and a fountain."

"Very nice," said the fire chief, "but what does that have to do with the fire service?"

The caller said: "Because next door's house is on fire, and I don't want your men trampling all over my front yard!"

✳ A man returned to his parked BMW to find the headlights broken and considerable damage to the front end of the car. There was no sign of the offending vehicle, but he was relieved to see that there was a note stuck under the windshield wiper.

The note read: "Sorry I just backed into your car. The witnesses who saw the accident are nodding and smiling at me because they think I'm leaving my name, address and other particulars. But I'm not."

✳ Two paramedics arrived at the scene of a car crash. The driver of the car was sitting in his seat, screaming hysterically.

One of the paramedics tried to calm him. "Take deep breaths and pull yourself together. Be thankful that at least you haven't gone through the windshield like your passenger," and he pointed at a girl lying unconscious by the side of the road. "She looks in a really bad state."

Still crying uncontrollably, the driver yelled: "You haven't seen what's in her mouth!"

✳ A man was crossing the road when he was hit by a car, which then sped off. A police officer asked the injured man: "Did you get a look at the driver?"

"No," he said, "but I can tell you it was my ex-wife."

"How do you know that?" asked the officer.

"I'd recognize her laugh anywhere."

✳ The freeway near Los Angeles was blocked for three hours after a truck driven by a three-legged man crashed into a car driven by a bearded lady. Police described it as a freak accident.

★   ★   ★   ★   ★

ACCOUNTANTS

★ An accountant read a nursery rhyme to his young child. Afterwards he said: "No, son, when Little Bo Peep lost her sheep, that wouldn't be tax deductible. But I like your thinking."

★ What does an accountant say when you ask him the time? – "It's 10.12 and thirteen seconds . . . no, wait . . . fourteen seconds . . . no, wait . . . fifteen seconds . . ."

★ A businessman told his neighbour that his company was looking for a new accountant.

"Didn't your company hire a new accountant a few weeks ago?" asked the neighbour.

"Yes," replied the businessman. "That's the accountant we're looking for."

★ In preparation for starting a new office job, a young accountant spent a week with the retiring accountant whom he was replacing. He hoped to pick up a few tips from the old master and studied his daily routine intently.

Every morning the experienced accountant began the day by opening his desk drawer, taking out a frayed envelope and removing a yellowing piece of paper. He then read it, nodded his head sagely, returned the envelope to the drawer and started his day's work.

After the old man retired, the new boy could hardly wait to read for himself the message in the drawer, particularly since he felt somewhat inadequate about stepping into such illustrious shoes. Surely, he thought to himself, the envelope must contain the secret to accounting success, a pearl of wisdom to be treasured forever. The anticipation was so great that his hands were actually trembling as he opened the drawer and took out the mysterious envelope. And there, inside, on that aged piece of paper he read the following message:

"Debits in the column nearest the potted plant; credits in the column towards the door."

★ How do you know when an accountant is on vacation?

He doesn't wear a tie to work and comes in at 8.31.

★ Two accountants were in a bank when a gang of armed robbers burst in. While some of the robbers snatched bundles of cash from the tellers, others lined the customers up against the wall and relieved them of their wallets, watches and other valuables.

As the robbers moved down the line, one accountant pressed something into the hand of the other accountant.

"What's this?" said the second accountant without looking down.

His colleague replied: "It's that $100 I owe you."

★ A Martian landed on Earth to plunder, pillage and burn. He went up to the owner of the first house he saw and said: "I'm a Martian just arrived from the other side of the galaxy. We're here to destroy your civilization, pillage and burn. What do you think about that?"

The owner replied: "I don't have an opinion, I'm an accountant."

Why do accountants need pocket calculators? Surely they can count the number of pockets they've got.

★ An architect, an artist and an accountant were discussing whether it was better to spend time with a wife or a mistress. The architect said he enjoyed time with a wife, building a solid foundation for an enduring relationship. The artist said he enjoyed time with a mistress, because of the passion and mystery. The accountant said he liked both.

"Both?" chorused the others.

"Yes," said the accountant. "If you have a wife and a mistress, they will each assume you are spending time with the other woman, which means you can go to the office and get some work done."

★ If an accountant's wife has trouble sleeping, what does she say?

"Darling, tell me about your work."

★ What did the middle-aged accountant say by way of a chat-up line to the new girl in the office?

"You're the type of girl I could take home to my mother, which is just as well because I still live with her."

★   ★   ★   ★   ★

ACTUARIES AND INSURANCE

❖ An actuary was walking down the corridor at work when he felt a sudden twinge in his chest. Immediately he ran to the stairwell and hurled himself down.

His brother visited him in hospital and asked him why he had thrown himself down the stairs.

The actuary said: "Because the chances of having a heart attack and falling down the stairs are much lower than the chances of having a heart attack only."

❖ A man insured his car at great expense with a comprehensive plan that covered him against everything except acts of God. But when he tried to make a claim, the insurance company argued that he couldn't be sure that it wasn't Jesus who hadn't keyed the side of his car and smashed his windshield with a brick.

❖ **A man phoned to find out whether he could get insurance if the nearby volcano erupted. They assured him he would be covered.**

❖ An insurance agent was teaching his wife to drive when her brakes suddenly failed on a steep downhill gradient.

"I can't stop!" she screamed. "What should I do?"

"Brace yourself," he answered, "and try to hit something cheap."

❖ A company marketing officer asked an actuary why he was recommending selling more life insurance policies to ninety-eight-year-olds. The actuary said: "Because according to our figures, very few of them die each year."

❖ An actuary quoted an extremely low premium for an automobile "fire and theft" policy. When asked why it was so cheap, he replied: "Who'd steal a burnt car?"

❖ Two actuaries went duck hunting. They saw a duck in the air and both took aim. The first actuary's shot missed the duck by thirty feet to the left, and the second actuary's shot missed the duck by thirty feet to the right, but they gave each other high fives, because on average they shot it.

❖ A life actuary designed a new type of coverage called "Senility Insurance". When asked about its profitability by his company's CEO, the actuary confidently predicted low claims, because, "If you can remember that you have a policy, it is proof you're not senile."

❖ A husband and wife who were in the insurance business liked to get away from the stress of their job by renting a motor home in the country. Unfortunately their hopes of a peaceful vacation were wrecked by fellow campers repeatedly calling on them, asking whether they could borrow butter or sugar or even asking for directions to the nearest bar.

Finally they got so fed up with the interruptions that they decided to pin a notice to the door of the motor home which would guarantee their privacy. It read: "Insurance agent. Ask about our life-term package."

❖ A man with a wooden leg wanted to buy fire insurance for his limb. The first actuary he saw quoted an annual premium of $500, estimating that the leg would burn once in twenty years and that the value of the leg was $10,000. A second actuary quoted an annual premium of just $50.

When the second actuary was asked how he arrived at such a small figure, he replied: "I have this situation in the fire-schedule rating table. The object is a wooden structure with an upper sprinkler, right?"

❖ A man walked into an insurance office and asked two senior executives for a job.

"We're not taking on new staff," they said.

"But you can't afford to be without me," insisted the man. "I can sell insurance to anybody, anywhere, anytime."

"Okay," they said. "Prove it. There are two prospective clients who have resisted all our attempts to sell them a policy. If you can sell to just one of them, you're hired."

The guy was gone for around two hours, but when he returned he handed over two cheques – one for a $75,000 policy and another for a $50,000 policy.

"How in the world did you manage that?" asked the executives.

"I told you: I'm the world's best insurance salesman."

"There's just one thing," they said. "Did you get a urine sample?"

"Why?"

"It's company practice that if you sell a policy over $40,000, you have to get a urine sample from the customer. Take these two bottles and go back and get urine samples."

The guy was gone for four hours before he returned carrying two five-gallon buckets, one in each hand. He put down the buckets, reached inside his jacket and produced two bottles of urine. He said: "This one is Mr Brown's and this one is Mr Smith's."

"Very good," said the executives, "but what's in those two buckets?"

"Oh, I passed by the schoolhouse and they were having a state teachers' convention, so I sold them a group policy."

Carrying his policy, a man went to the office of his insurance company to ask if there was anything to collect on his wife, who had just died.

The insurance agent looked at the policy and then told him that it was not life insurance, but fire insurance.

"I know," said the man. "That's why I had her cremated."

❖ Three insurance salesmen were sitting in a restaurant boasting about their companies' speed of service.

The first said: "When one of our policyholders died suddenly on Monday, we got the news that evening and were able to process the claim for the wife so quickly that she received the cheque by Thursday morning."

The second said: "When one of our insured died on Monday, we were able to hand-deliver a cheque to his widow the same evening."

The third said: "That's nothing. Our office is on the eighteenth floor. One of our insured, who was washing a window on the seventy-third floor, slipped and fell on Monday. We handed him his cheque as he passed our floor!"

❖ One day at university, a fire broke out in a wastebasket in the dean's office. A physicist, a chemist and an actuary ran in to deal with the blaze.

The physicist immediately started to calculate how much energy would have to be removed from the fire in order to stop combustion.

The chemist worked out which reagent would have to be added to the fire to prevent oxidation.

Meanwhile, the actuary was setting fire to all the other wastebaskets in the office.

"What the hell are you doing that for?" asked the physicist and the chemist.

"Well," explained the actuary, "to solve the problem, obviously you need a large sample size."

★   ★   ★   ★   ★

ADULTERY

* A husband arrived home from work to find his wife in bed with his friend. Angered by the betrayal, the husband produced a gun and shot him dead. His wife shook her head in despair and said: "If you keep behaving like this, you'll lose all of your friends."

* A young wife, her boorish husband and a young handsome sailor were shipwrecked on a desert island. One morning, the sailor climbed a tall coconut tree and shouted: "Stop making love down there!"

  "What's the matter with you?" said the husband when the sailor climbed down. "We weren't making love."

  "Sorry," said the sailor. "From up there it looked like you were."

  Every morning from then on, the sailor scaled the same tree and yelled the same thing. Finally the husband decided to climb the tree and see for himself. With great difficulty, he made his way to the top and when he got there he looked down and said to himself: "Well, I never! He's right! It DOES look like they're making love down there!"

* A man went into a florist's and asked for a very big bunch of flowers.

  "How big exactly?" asked the florist.

  He replied: "Caught in bed with my wife's sister size."

* In the course of a blazing row, a wife yelled at her husband: "It just shows how much attention you pay to me; you don't even know that I've been sleeping with your brother for the past two months."

  The husband said: "You disgust me!"

  "As a matter of fact," she replied, "we didn't discuss you at all!"

✳ Jim lamented to his friend Larry that all the excitement had gone out of his marriage.

"That often happens when people have been married for ten years, like you," said Larry. "Have you ever considered having an affair? That might put a bit of life back into your relationship."

"No, I couldn't possibly do that," said Jim. "It's immoral."

"Get real," said Larry. "This is the twenty-first century. These things happen all the time."

"But what if my wife found out?"

"No problem. Be upfront. Tell her about it in advance."

Overcoming his initial misgivings, Jim plucked up the courage to break the news to his wife the next morning while she was reading a magazine over breakfast.

"Honey," he began hesitantly, "I don't want you to take this the wrong way . . . and please remember that I'm only doing this because I truly, truly love you, otherwise I would never dream of it . . . but I think maybe . . . just possibly . . . having an affair might bring us closer together."

"Forget it," said his wife, without even looking up from her magazine. "I've tried it, and it's never worked."

A husband was late home from work one evening. "I'm sure he's having an affair," said his wife to her mother.

"Why do you always think the worst?" said the mother. "Maybe he's just been in a car crash."

✳ A guy appeared in court for killing his wife after catching her in bed with another man. Passing sentence, the judge said: "Can I ask, why did you kill your wife instead of just killing her lover?"

The defendant replied: "But, your honour, is it not better that I just killed her rather than a different man each week?"

❋ A woman was going to Italy on a ten-day business trip. Before leaving, she asked her husband if there was a present he wanted her to bring back.

"How about an Italian girl?" he laughed.

The suggestion was met with stony silence.

Ten days later, she returned home and he asked her whether she'd had a good trip.

"Yes, it was surprisingly enjoyable," she replied.

"And where's my present?" he smiled.

"What present?"

"The one I asked for – an Italian girl."

"Oh, that! I did what I could; now we have to wait nine months to see if it's a girl."

❋ ## Why did the unfaithful husband fall over? He was on a guilt trip.

❋ Returning home a day early from an out-of-town business trip, a man caught a taxi from the airport shortly after midnight. On the cab journey, he confided to the driver that he thought his wife was having an affair. As they pulled up outside his house, the businessman asked the driver: "Would you come inside with me and be a witness?"

The driver agreed, and they both crept into the bedroom. The man then turned on the lights, pulled the blanket back and, sure enough, his wife was naked in bed with another man.

In a jealous rage, the businessman pulled out a gun and threatened to shoot his wife's lover. "Don't do it," she pleaded. "This man has been very generous. Who do you think paid for the new car I bought you for your birthday? Who do you think paid for our new boat? Who do you think paid for the deposit on this house? He did!"

His mind in turmoil, the husband looked over at the cab driver and asked: "What would you do in a case like this?"

The cabbie said: "I think I'd cover him up before he catches cold."

✳ A jealous husband hired a private detective to check on his wife's movements. The husband demanded more than just a written report – he wanted a video of his wife's activities.

A week later, the detective returned with a tape and sat down to watch it with the husband. As the tape played, he saw his wife meeting another man. He saw the two of them laughing in the park. He saw them enjoying themselves at an outdoor cafe. He saw them having a playful fight in the street. He saw them dancing in a dimly lit nightclub.

When the tape ended, the distraught husband said: "I can't believe this!"

"What's not to believe?" asked the detective. "It's right up there on the screen. The camera never lies."

The husband replied: "What I mean is, I can't believe my wife is so much fun!"

✳ A guy told his buddy: "Last night I confessed to my wife that I had cheated on her four times over the past year."

"Hey, that was a brave thing to do."

"Well, I believe that honesty is the most important thing in a relationship. Besides, now we won't have any secrets between us when she comes out of the coma."

✳ A man told a psychiatrist: "I was away on business last week and sent my wife a text message to say I'd be home a day early. But when I got home, I found her in bed with another man. How could she do this to me?"

"Don't be too hard on her," said the psychiatrist. "Perhaps she didn't have her cell phone switched on."

✳ Within two weeks of moving into a new house, the home-owner had to call an electrician, a plasterer, a carpenter and a roofer. One afternoon he returned home early from work and saw a plumber's van in the driveway.

"Lord," he pleaded. "Please let her be having an affair!"

★　　★　　★　　★　　★

AIRPLANES

★   How does the flight captain know the aircraft is safely at the ramp?

Both the engines and the co-pilot stop whining.

★   Two days before Christmas, Jim was flying from London's Heathrow Airport to Washington, DC, to visit his wife, who worked in the United States. He arrived at Heathrow to find the entire terminal decked in green and red, complete with tacky elves, Santas, reindeer, snowmen and Christmas trees wherever he looked. Meanwhile, between announcements of flight delays and cancellations, the loudspeakers blared out tinny renditions of Christmas carols.

As he checked-in his luggage, having queued for the best part of an hour, Jim noticed a sprig of cheap plastic mistletoe hanging over the conveyor belt. By now he had endured enough of the Heathrow experience and needed someone on whom to vent his frustration, so he said to the woman at the check-in desk: "I'm sorry, madam, but even if I were not married, I would not want to kiss you under such a ghastly mockery of mistletoe."

"Sir," she replied. "Look more closely at where the mistletoe is located."

"Okay," he said, "I can see that it's above the conveyor belt, which is where you'd have to step forward for a kiss."

"But that's not why it's there," she said. "It's there so that you can kiss your luggage goodbye."

> On the airlines they're confiscating tweezers and shaving equipment. What do they think you'll do – give someone a makeover?
>
> Ed Byrne

★ Pilot: "Control tower, what time is it?"
Control tower: "What airline is this?"
Pilot: "What difference does that make?"
Control tower: "Well, if it's United Airlines, it's 6 p.m.; if it's American Airlines, it's 18.00 hours; and if it's Alaska Airlines, the big hand is on the 12 . . ."

★ It was mealtime during a British Airways flight from London to New York. As the flight attendant moved down the plane, she asked one of the passengers: "Would you like dinner?"
    "What are my choices?" said the passenger.
    "Yes or no," replied the flight attendant.

> 66 You know you're in trouble when at the control tower, there's a note taped to the door that says, 'Back in five minutes.'
>
> Jeff Foxworthy 99

★ A man and his wife went to the check-in desk of a budget airline.
    "Do you have reservations?" asked the check-in clerk.
    "Of course we have reservations," said the man. "But we're flying with you anyway."

★ Back in the 1940s, two first-time flyers took a plane from New York to Los Angeles. When they made their first stop – at Philadelphia – a red truck arrived to put fuel in the plane.
    A little while later, they landed in Pittsburgh, and again a red truck pulled up to fill the plane's tanks with fuel.
    Each time they landed to discharge or take on passengers, a red truck would pull up and add fuel to the tanks. Finally, after landing in Kansas City and seeing the truck pull up again, one passenger said to the other: "We sure are making good time."
    "Yes, we are," said the other, "and so is that red truck!"

★ Before takeoff, an elderly lady passenger said to the pilot: "I've never flown before, and I'm very nervous. You will bring me down safely, won't you?"

"All I can say, ma'am," replied the pilot, "is that I've never left anyone up there yet!"

> 66 I went up to the airport information desk and asked the attendant: 'How many airports are there in the world?'
> Jimmy Carr 99

★ A pilot died at the controls of his airplane and went to Hell. The Devil took him to the "new arrivals" zone, where there were three doors marked one, two and three. The Devil said the pilot would be allowed to choose his own hell, but told him to stay where he was for a few minutes while the Devil disappeared to attend to some urgent business.

But the curious pilot couldn't help looking around in the Devil's absence. First he peered behind door number one and saw a pilot going through flight checks for all eternity. Then he looked behind number two and saw a pilot forever trying to resolve emergency situations. Finally he looked behind door number three and saw a flight captain being waited on hand and foot by scantily-clad stewardesses.

The Devil returned just as the pilot got back to his waiting position. He offered the pilot a choice between door number one and door number two.

The pilot said: "But I wanted door number three!"

"Sorry," replied the Devil. "That's flight attendants' hell."

★ When a passenger airplane encountered some turbulence, it started juddering and rocking noticeably from side to side. In a bid to keep the passengers calm, the flight attendant wheeled out the drinks trolley.

"Would you like a drink?" she asked a businessman.

"Why not?" he replied caustically. "I'll have whatever the pilot's been having."

★ *To combat the recession, a budget airline has introduced a wave of new passenger charges:*

Attendant: "Welcome aboard Cheapo Airlines, sir. May I see your ticket?"

Passenger: "Sure."

Attendant: "You're in seat 61C. That'll be $5 please."

Passenger: "What for?"

Attendant: "For telling you where to sit."

Passenger: "But I already knew where to sit."

Attendant: "Nevertheless we are now charging a seat-locater fee of $5. It's the airline's new policy."

Passenger: "That's the craziest thing I ever heard. I won't pay it."

Attendant: "Sir, do you want a seat on this flight, or not?"

Passenger: "Okay, I'll pay. But the airline is going to hear about this!"

Attendant: "Thank you. My goodness, your carry-on bag looks heavy. Would you like me to stow it in the overhead compartment for you?"

Passenger: "Yes, thank you."

Attendant: "No problem. That will be $10, sir."

Passenger: "What?"

Attendant: "The airline now charges a $10 carry-on assistance fee."

Passenger: "This is extortion. I won't stand for it!"

Attendant: "Actually, you're right, you can't stand. You need to sit, and fasten your seat belt. We're about to push back from the gate. But first I need that $10."

Passenger: "No way!"

Attendant: "Sir, if you don't comply, I will be forced to call the air marshal. And you really don't want me to do that."

Passenger: "Why not? Is he going to shoot me?"

Attendant: "No, but there's a $50 air marshal hailing fee."

Passenger: "Oh, all right, here, take the $10. I don't believe this!"

Attendant: "Thank you for your co-operation, sir. Is there anything else I can do for you?"

Passenger: "Yes, it's stuffy in here, and my overhead fan doesn't seem to work. Can you fix it?"

Attendant: "Your overhead fan is not broken, sir. Just insert two quarters into the overhead fan slot."

Passenger: "The airline is charging me for cabin air?"

Attendant: "Of course not, sir. Stagnant cabin air is provided free of charge. It's the circulating air that costs fifty cents."

Passenger: "I don't have any quarters. Do you have change for a dollar?"

Attendant: "Certainly, sir. Here you go."

Passenger: "But you've given me only three quarters for my dollar!"

Attendant: "Yes, there's a change-making fee of twenty-five cents."

Passenger: "For crying out loud! Now all I have left is a lousy quarter! What the heck can I do with this?"

Attendant: "Hang onto it, sir. You'll need it later for the lavatory."

In the course of his air test a young pilot flew through a rainbow. He passed with flying colours.

★ A pilot and co-pilot were in a light aircraft that was spiralling out of control. Starting to panic, the co-pilot said: "If it carries on like this, do you think we'll fall out?"

"Of course not," replied the pilot. "We've been mates for years."

★ A man phoned a budget airline to book a flight. The operator asked: "How many people are travelling with you?"

"How should I know?" said the man. "It's your plane!"

★ A pilot and co-pilot were descending for an emergency landing at an airport which they had never been to before. Suddenly the pilot looked out of the windshield and exclaimed: "Look how short the runway is! I've never seen one that short!"

At this, the co-pilot looked out and agreed: "Wow, you're right! Are you sure we can make it?"

"Well, we better had," said the pilot, "because we're almost out of fuel."

Trying not to betray his nerves, he went on the intercom and told the passengers to put their heads between their knees and prepare for an emergency landing. Then he set the flaps to full down and slowed the plane to a little over stall speed. The huge jumbo jet came screaming in to land, barely under control. The pilot was sweating profusely while the co-pilot said a silent prayer. After what seemed an age, they managed to touch down and came screeching to a halt just yards before the edge of the runway, tyres smoking.

"My God! That was close!" gasped the pilot, mopping the sweat from his brow. "That runway was SHORT!"

"Yeah!" said the co-pilot, "and WIDE too!"

★　★　★　★　★

ALIENS

❖ Two aliens in a spaceship were hovering above a golf course, watching a solitary golfer play. They had never witnessed this practice before but decided that it must be some form of game. They saw him mess up his tee shot, hit his second into a wood, take three more shots to get out of the trees, land in heavy rough, slice the ball into some bushes, end up in a bunker, take four more shots to get out of the sand and finally take three putts to put the ball in the hole.

As the ball disappeared down the hole, one alien turned to the other and said: "Now he's in trouble!"

❖ A spaceship crashed on Earth, but two glowing Martians survived the impact and set off to find a way home. They walked for miles through forests and fields before they finally arrived at a city.

Stopping at an intersection, they began to shake and moan at the mere sight of a green light. Suddenly the light turned from green to yellow, and then to red.

Turning to his travelling companion, one Martian said disgustedly: "Let's get out of here. If there's one thing I hate, it's a woman who's a tease."

❖ What did the alien say to the gas pump?

Don't you know it's rude to stick your finger in your ear when I'm talking to you?

❖ What do you call an overweight E.T.? Extra cholesterol.

❖ Two aliens were strolling around a small town in the US when they had a sudden urge to taste some Earth food. Having no Earth currency, they decided to steal two chocolate bars from a shop. So they walked into the shop and when they thought the shopkeeper wasn't looking, they slipped the chocolate bars into the pockets of their space suits and hurriedly left.

But they had only gone a few yards when they heard the shopkeeper shout: "Hey! You haven't paid for those!"

They ran back to their mothership as fast as their alien legs would carry them and just managed to climb through the doors of the craft before the shopkeeper could catch them.

In the sanctuary of the craft, one of the young aliens turned breathlessly to the other and said: "I don't know how that shopkeeper saw us stealing."

"Me neither," said the other. "He must have eyes in the front of his head."

❖ Why was the thirsty alien hanging around the computer?

He was looking for the space bar.

AMERICAN CITIES AND STATES

> " If you're black, America's like your uncle who paid your way through college and molested you at the same time.
>
> Chris Rock "

★ Alabama ★

✳ An Alabama state trooper pulled over a pickup truck on the highway.
  He said to the driver: "Got any ID?"
  The driver replied: "'Bout what?"

> " In Alabama and India, there are similar symbols for married women. In India, a red dot on the forehead means you're married. In Alabama, it's a black eye.
>
> Mark Saldana "

✳ An Alabama couple attended a school parents' evening. The teacher said: "Your son's marks are improving, but in future could you try using the naughty step instead of a whip?"

✳ A new law has been passed in Alabama. When a couple get divorced, they're still brother and sister.

✳ A guy in Alabama saw a sign in a public toilet that read: "Please leave this toilet in the condition that you would like to find it." So he left a can of beer and a girlie magazine.

★ **Alaska** ★

✳ A guy from Anchorage lived in a house with no indoor toilet, just an outhouse. And the older he got, the further away the outhouse seemed to get, so that eventually he grew lazy and started peeing off the front porch.

His wife was horrified and told him: "You do realize that the neighbours can you see when you're peeing off the porch!"

He promised not to do it again but a few nights later, on a typically cold Alaskan night, he could not face the trip to the outhouse and so he went off the porch. When he returned to bed, his wife was suspicious.

"You weren't gone long," she said.

"No," he replied, guilt written all over his face.

"You went off the porch again, didn't you?" she raged.

"Yes, I did."

"We talked about this, remember? How the neighbours can see you."

"Don't worry, they won't have seen me this time. I was squatting down."

> ❝ Some unusual laws went into effect in January 2008. In Alaska, it's illegal to give an alcoholic beverage to a moose. How lonely are the guys in Alaska? If you're with a moose, wouldn't you want to be the drunk one?
>
> Jay Leno ❞

★ **California** ★

★ A California family bought a ranch in Wyoming, where they planned to raise cattle. A friend came to visit one weekend and asked if the ranch had a name.

"Well," said the would-be cattleman, "to be honest we've had a few arguments over names. I wanted to call the ranch Bar-J; my wife favoured the Suzy-Q; one son liked the Flying-L; and my other son wanted the Happy-T. So as a compromise we've called it the Bar-J-Suzy-Q-Flying-L-Happy-T Ranch."

"Right," said the friend. "But tell me, where are all your cattle?"

"So far, none has survived the branding."

★ Two little girls – Chelsea and Harley – were in the lunchroom of a Beverly Hills elementary school.

"Guess what?" said Chelsea. "My mommy's getting married again, so I'm going to have a new daddy."

"Who's she marrying?" asked Harley.

"Brad Henderson," said Chelsea. "He's a famous Hollywood actor."

"Oh, you'll like him," said Harley. "He was my daddy last year."

★ **Florida** ★

66 I just had to fly down to Florida. But it was half business, half pleasure. I had to put my mother in a nursing home.
Dave Attell 99

You Know You're From Florida When . . .

The four seasons are: almost summer, summer, not summer but still hot, and February.

You're on first-name terms with the hurricane lists.

You can tell the difference between fire ant bites and mosquito bites.

Most of your neighbours are so old they referred to John McCain as "young man".

You have a drawer full of bathing suits but only one sweatshirt.

A mountain is any hill 100 feet above sea level.

You could swim before you could read.

You've never seen snow.

An alligator once walked through your neighbourhood.

A good parking place has nothing to do with proximity to the store, but everything to do with shade.

✳ A women's group from Miami Beach decided to go on a day trip to a working farm in the country. Since most of them had lived in the city all of their lives and had never been near a farm, they thought it would be a new and challenging experience.

Dressed for the part, they arrived in their minibus and were greeted by the farmer. As they looked around the various barns and outhouses, one woman was intrigued by an animal she spotted.

"Excuse me," she called to the farmer, "can you explain to us why this cow doesn't have any horns?"

The farmer cocked his head for a moment, and then explained patiently: "Well, ma'am, cattle can do a lot of damage with horns. So sometimes we keep 'em trimmed down with a hacksaw. Other times we can fix up the young 'uns by puttin' a couple of drops of acid where their horns would grow, and that stops 'em cold. Still, there are some breeds of cattle that never grow horns. But the reason this cow don't have no horns, ma'am, is because it's a horse."

★ Hawaii ★

✳ Hawaii vacationers are here today, gone to Maui.

★ Louisiana ★

❝ Louisiana has the best food on the planet if you don't really ask too much about what you're eating.

Jeff Foxworthy ❞

✳ A New Yorker was travelling in Louisiana around Christmas time. In a small town square he admired a nativity scene but was puzzled by one thing: the three wise men were wearing firemen's helmets. Unable to work out why, he decided to ask the old woman who worked at the store.

"Excuse me, ma'am," he said. "I'm not from these parts, and I don't understand why the three wise men are wearing firemen's helmets."

She snarled: "You damn Yankees, you never read your Bibles!"

"I do," he protested, "but I don't recall anything in the Bible about firemen."

She grabbed a Bible from beneath the counter and frantically leafed through the pages. Then waving the book under his nose, she barked triumphantly: "See, it says right here: 'The three wise men came from afar . . .'"

★ Maine ★

✳ A group of geological engineers surveying some land in New England found that in one particular area the border between New Hampshire and Maine had to be changed. They duly informed a farmer that his land was no longer in Maine but was now in New Hampshire.

"Thank heaven for that," said the farmer. "I don't think I could take another of these Maine winters."

★ Missouri ★

 I guess when you move to Missouri, they give you a trailer.

Christopher Titus

✳ A census-taker in Missouri went up to a trailer home and knocked on the door. When a woman answered, he asked her the names and ages of her children.

She said: "Let's see now, there are the twins, Billy and Bobby, they're fifteen. And the twins, Seth and Beth, they're fourteen. And the twins, Benny and Jenny, they're thirteen."

"Wait a minute!" said the census-taker. "Did you get twins every time?"

"Heck no," answered the woman. "There were hundreds of times we didn't get nothin'."

✳ Did you hear that the governor's mansion in Missouri burned down?

It almost took out the whole trailer park.

★ New York City ★

✳ Two New Yorkers were taking a lunch break at their soon to be opened store. One said: "I bet any minute some dumb tourist will walk by, put his face to the window and ask what we're selling."

Sure enough, a Texan happened to pass by and asked the pair: "What ya sellin'?"

The New Yorkers replied sarcastically: "We're selling assholes."

"You're sure doin' well," smiled the Texan. "You only got two left."

✳ A young New Yorker called directory inquiries. "Hello, operator," he said, "I would like the telephone number for Jane Jones in Los Angeles."

The operator said: "There are multiple listings for Jane Jones in Los Angeles. Do you have a street name?"

The young man said: "Well, my friends call me Bone Crusher."

> **"** I really want to leave New York City,
> but I just put $6,000 on my Metrocard.
> Zach Galifianakis **"**

✳ A woman from Chicago was visiting New York City. Her hostess was determined to make the Midwesterner feel cheap and unimportant.

"My dear," said the New York matron snobbishly, "here in the east we think breeding is everything."

"Oh, I don't know," replied the woman from Chicago. "Where I come from we think it's fun, too, but we try to have a few outside interests as well."

> **"** It's so cold in New York City today that
> Bernie Madoff is actually looking
> forward to burning in Hell.
> David Letterman **"**

Why did the New Yorker cross the road?
"What's it to you?"

✳ New York State ✳

✳ Did you hear about the chicken who knew the first leg of his journey would take him to Buffalo?

From there he decided to wing it.

⋆ **Seattle** ⋆

✳ A man died and found himself waiting in the long line of judgment. As he stood there, he noticed that some souls were allowed to march straight through the pearly gates into Heaven and others were led over to Satan, who then threw them into a burning pit. However he also observed that every now and again, instead of hurling poor souls into the fire, Satan would put them to one side on a separate pile.

After watching Satan do this several times, the man's curiosity got the better of him, so he strolled over to Satan and said: "Excuse me, Prince of Darkness, I'm waiting in line for judgment, but I couldn't help noticing that whereas you throw some people into the burning pit, you put others to one side."

"Ah, those," groaned Satan. "They're all from Seattle; they're too wet to burn."

⋆ **Texas** ⋆

✳ A Texan visitor to England asked an Englishman to show him the biggest building in town.

"There it is," said the Englishman. "It's quite impressive, I must admit."

"You call that big?" scoffed the Texan. "Back in Texas we have buildings just like that but over a hundred times bigger!"

"I'm not surprised," said the Englishman. "That's the local lunatic asylum!"

✳ A Texan was standing admiring the beauty of Niagara Falls when a New Yorker standing next to him said sarcastically: "I bet you don't have anything like this in Texas."

"No," said the Texan, "but we've got plumbers who could fix it!"

You Know You're in Texas When . . .

Hot water comes out of both taps.

You learn that a seat belt buckle makes a pretty good branding iron.

The temperature drops below ninety-five degrees, and you feel a little chilly.

You discover that in July it only takes two fingers to steer your car.

The cows are giving evaporated milk.

You realize that asphalt has a liquid state.

* A Scottish farmer was in his field digging up potatoes. An American tourist leaned over the fence and shouted out: "Back home in Texas we grow potatoes that are five times that size!"

   "Aye, laddie," replied the Scotsman, "but we only grow them to fit our own mouths."

* A man from Ireland was on a bus tour of the United States. As the bus travelled for miles and miles through desert landscape and oil fields, he asked the guide: "Where are we now?"

   The guide said proudly: "We're in the great state of Texas."

   "It's certainly big," mused the Irishman.

   "It's so big," added the guide, "that your County Kerry would fit into the smallest corner of it."

   "Yes," smiled the Irishman, "and wouldn't it do wonders for Texas!"

✴ As Hurricane Ike battered the east coast of America in 2008, people started wondering whether there was a town in Texas called Tina.

✴ A visitor to Texas asked a rancher: "Does it ever rain here?"

The rancher said: "Sure. We sometimes get rain. You know that part in the Bible where it rained for forty days and forty nights?"

"Yes," said the visitor, "I'm familiar with Noah's flood."

"Well, we must have had half an inch then."

★　★　★　★　★

ANIMALS

✴ Three old men – Bert, Arnie and Harry – were sitting on a park bench debating what the meanest animal in the world was.

Bert said: "The meanest animal in the world is the hippopotamus, because it's got such huge jaws. One bite and you're gone!"

Arnie shook his head and said: "No, the hippopotamus may be mean but he's a pussycat compared to an alligator. An alligator's got attitude, and one bite from those teeth, followed by the death roll, and you're gone!"

Harry thought for a moment before saying: "As a matter of fact, you're both wrong. The meanest animal in the world is a hippogator."

Bert and Arnie laughed. "What the hell's a hippogator?" they asked "There's no such creature."

"A hippogator", explained Harry, "has got a hippo head on one end and an alligator head on the other."

"Wait a minute!" interrupted Bert and Arnie. "If he has a head on both ends, how does he shit?"

"He doesn't," said Harry. "That's what makes him so mean."

> **66** What do you think you should do if you're attacked by a bear? Play dead? No, that's a lie promoted by the bears.
> Eugene Mirman **99**

★ A lion was becoming rather old and slow and was having trouble catching prey. He decided he needed a disguise so that other animals would not know he was a lion and would therefore not run away.

So he went into a fancy dress shop and bought a gorilla suit. He then headed for a watering hole to see if he could catch something with his cunning disguise. On the way to the hole, he came across two eagles sitting on a rock.

One eagle said: "Hi, Mr Lion."

The other eagle said: "Where did you get the gorilla suit?"

The lion was devastated. "How did you know I was a lion?" he asked.

The eagles then started to sing: "You can't hide your lion eyes . . ."

★ **Did you hear about the baby mouse that saw a bat?**

He ran home and told his mother he'd seen an angel.

★ Herds of elephants from all over Africa were summoned to a meeting in the jungle. As their national leader took his place on the stage, one of the African elephants trumpeted impatiently: "Come on, tell us what this is all about. We're all ears."

★ An elephant and a camel were chatting one day. The elephant asked: "Why are your tits on your back?"

"I don't know," said the camel. "Why is your dick on your face?"

★ Why have elephants got four feet?
Because they'd look silly with only three inches.

> 66 Scientists in Australia say they've discovered that kangaroos and humans shared a common ancestor. The scientists aren't sure who it was, but they are sure he must have been pretty drunk.
>
> Conan O'Brien 99

★ Two giraffes were in a race. They were neck and neck.

★ In ancient times in a far off land, three princes declared that they wanted to marry the king's beautiful daughter, but as a test to prove their worth, they first had to perform three difficult tasks: vanquish a giant, turn lead to gold and have sex with a sheep.

The first suitor was slain by the giant, the second failed to turn lead into gold, but the third successfully completed all three tasks.

"Congratulations," the king said to him. "You may now have my daughter's hand in marriage."

"Sod that," said the prince. "I want the sheep!"

★ What did the father buffalo say when he left his son?
Bison.

★ Six wise, blind elephants were discussing what humans were like. Failing to agree in any way, they decided to determine what humans were like by direct experience.

So using their sense of smell, the six blind elephants managed to locate a human who was tending to his crops on the outskirts of a village. The first blind elephant felt the human and declared: "Humans are flat." The other five blind elephants, after similarly feeling the human, agreed.

★ What did the polar bears say when they saw tourists in sleeping bags?

"Mmmm, sandwiches!"

★ When Noah lowered the ramp of the Ark for all the animals to leave, he told them: "Go forth and multiply."

All the animals left except for two snakes who lay quietly in the corner of the Ark.

"Why will you not go forth and multiply?" demanded Noah.

"We can't," said the snakes. "We're adders."

> My favourite animal is the manatee, the sea cow. The manatee is endangered, and I think it's because it's out of shape. It looks like a retired football player.
>
> Jim Gaffigan

★ In the heart of the jungle, two monkeys were sitting in a tree beneath which a lion was sleeping peacefully. One monkey said to the other: "I dare you to go down there and kick that lion in the butt!"

Feeling mischievous, the other monkey said: "Okay, I'll do it."

So he ran down the tree, kicked the lion as hard as he could in the butt, and then made his escape by racing off through the jungle. Roused from his slumbers, the angry lion immediately gave chase and was soon gaining fast on the monkey until he was only about fifty yards behind him. Realizing he had to act quickly to avoid being eaten by the lion, the monkey picked up a newspaper that was lying on the ground and sat on a tree stump pretending to read it.

A few moments later, the lion arrived on the scene. "Did you see a monkey pass this way just now?" asked the lion.

The monkey replied: "Do you mean the one that kicked the lion in the butt?"

"Damn!" said the lion. "Don't tell me it's in the papers already!"

★ Two cows in a field – which one's on holiday?
   The one with the wee calf.

★ A deer was trying to cross a busy road but the traffic was very heavy. After he had been trying unsuccessfully for five minutes, a bear walked past and said: "Excuse me, there's a zebra crossing a bit further along the road."
   The deer replied: "Well, I hope he's having better luck than I am!"

> " Have you ever seen a butcher unloading the delivery van? They get out the side of a cow. Where's the other side? Is there a cow still grazing in a field with a side missing?
>
> Lee Evans "

★ Like rabbits, hares mate prodigiously. One female used to mate with every hare in the field on a rota basis. One day she would mate with all the gentle, considerate hares, and on the next she would have sex with the rough, rude hares. This system continued throughout the year, but sometimes the animals would forget whose turn it was on a particular day, and this could lead to hurt feelings.
   One of the kind, sensitive male hares complained to a friend: "I don't know where I stand with her. All morning I've been trying to catch her eye, but she just doesn't want to know."
   "Don't worry," said the friend. "It's nothing you've done wrong. She's just having a bad hare day."

★ Mother rabbit to her small bunny: "A magician pulled you out of a hat. Now stop asking questions!"

★ What's white and goes "RRRRG! RRRRG!"?
   A polar bear walking backwards.

★ A couple were driving home late at night in the pouring rain when their car accidentally ran over a badger. They got out of the car to see whether it was still alive, and found that although it was very cold, the animal was still breathing.

"What shall we do?" said the wife.

"I know," said the husband. "Put it between your legs to warm it up."

"But it's all wet and it stinks!"

"Well, cover the badger's nose then!"

★ Did you hear about the skunk who went to church?
He had his own pew.

★ A humble crab fell in love with a beautiful lobster princess, but her father, the king, forbade the relationship on the grounds that the crab was of lowly stock. The unsuitable suitor was a crushed crustacean.

"Why does your father disapprove of me so?" he wailed.

The princess replied tearfully: "Daddy says you're not a well-dressed crab, but in truth, he doesn't care much for crabs anyway. He says they're common and, above all, they have that silly sideways walk. I'm so sorry, my darling, but it appears that we can never be together."

The crab was determined to prove the king wrong and win the claw of his fair daughter. The perfect opportunity to prove his worth was the forthcoming Grand Lobster Ball, an occasion that attracted lobsters from far and wide to feast, drink and dance. While the king sat on his throne, the lobster princess sat sombrely at his side, her heart longing for her absent lover.

Suddenly the huge double wooden doors flew open and in walked the crab. The music stopped and all eyes focused on him as he painstakingly made his way up the red carpet towards the throne, walking dead straight, one claw after another. Nobody had ever seen a crab walk straight before. Even the king was impressed.

Finally after fifteen minutes of straight walking, the crab reached the throne. There, he stopped, looked up at the king and said: "God, I'm drunk!"

★ A giraffe was visiting a waterhole in Africa when he spotted a frog. "Hey," he said to the frog, "you've got no neck!"

The frog said: "Why would I need a neck like yours?"

The giraffe replied: "With a neck like mine, you could enjoy life to the full. You see, when I eat something, it takes so long to go down that I can enjoy it all the way. I can savour every second. When I drink fresh water, I can feel it going from my lips to my stomach for ages. It adds a bit of extra quality to my life."

The frog said: "You've obviously never thrown up then!"

> " I visited the office of the RSPCA today. It's tiny; you couldn't even swing a cat in there!
>
> Tim Vine "

★ There were two bears in an airing cupboard. Which one was in the army?

The one on the tank.

And which one was Scottish?

The one on the pipes.

Who do bears have fur coats?
Because they'd look stupid in anoraks.

★ A man was walking along the street when he saw a crowd of people running towards him. He stopped one of the runners and asked: "What's happening?"

The runner replied breathlessly: "A lion has escaped from the city zoo."

"Oh my God! Which way is it heading?"

"Well you don't think we're chasing it, do you?"

★ An explorer in the jungle saw a monkey with a tin opener. He called out: "You don't need a tin opener to peel a banana."

"I know, stupid," replied the monkey. "This is for the custard."

★ What is the worst thing that can happen to a sleeping bat? Diarrhoea.

★ My hamster died today – he fell asleep at the wheel.

★ A police officer came across a terrible road accident where the driver and passenger had been killed. As he gazed at the wreckage, a little monkey emerged from the trees and started hopping around the crashed car.

"Gee," said the officer scratching his head and looking down at the monkey, "I wish you could talk."

The monkey looked up at the officer and nodded his head.

"You mean you can understand what I'm saying?" asked the officer.

Again the monkey nodded furiously.

"Well, did you see this accident?" asked the officer.

The monkey motioned in the affirmative.

"What happened?" said the officer.

The monkey mimed a drinking action.

"They were drinking?"

The monkey nodded his head.

"What else?" continued the officer.

The monkey pinched his fingers together, held them to his mouth and rolled his eyes.

"They were smoking marijuana?"

The monkey nodded.

"Anything else?" asked the officer.

The monkey mimed a kiss.

"They were kissing too?"

The monkey nodded his head.

"So," said the officer, "you're saying they were drinking, smoking and kissing before they crashed the car?"

The monkey nodded.

"And what were you doing while all this was going on?"

"Driving," mimed the monkey.

★   An explorer in the African jungle heard about a plan to capture the legendary King Kong. And sure enough, when he came to a clearing, there before him, imprisoned in a cage, sat the imposing figure of King Kong.

It occurred to the explorer that he could be the first person ever to touch the great ape and so, tentatively, he inched towards the cage. Since King Kong appeared quite passive, the explorer thought he would take a chance and reach through the bars to touch him. But as soon as he made contact with the gorilla's fur, King Kong went berserk. He immediately rose to his feet, began beating his chest and with an awesome display of strength, burst through the bars of his cage.

As the explorer ran for his life, King Kong set off in hot pursuit. Instinctively the explorer headed for the heart of the jungle, hoping that he might be able to hide from his manic pursuer, but wherever he tried to conceal himself, King Kong always managed to find him.

As night began to fall, the explorer prayed that he would be able to lose the gorilla in the darkness but no matter how fast he ran, the sound of King Kong's pounding footsteps was only ever about fifty yards behind.

For three long days and nights, the explorer ran through Africa with King Kong always close behind, occasionally letting out a menacing roar from his vast throat. Eventually the explorer reached the west coast. There were no ships in sight for an easy escape, so he realized the only option was to dive into the sea and hope that King Kong couldn't swim. But, to his horror, the gorilla jumped in straight after him and demonstrated an excellent front crawl.

On and on they swam across the Atlantic – rarely separated by more than thirty yards – until four months later the weary explorer arrived in Brazil. He scrambled ashore with as much energy as he could muster, only to see the mighty King Kong right behind him, still beating his chest ferociously and with steam billowing from his nostrils. Through the streets of Rio they stumbled, explorer and ape equally exhausted, until the explorer took a wrong turn and ended up down a dead end, his escape barred by a twenty-foot-high wall.

With nowhere left to run, he sank to his knees in despair and pleaded to King Kong: "Do whatever you want with me. Kill me, eat me, do what you like, but make it quick. Just put me out of my misery."

King Kong slowly stalked over to the cowering explorer, prodded him with a giant paw and bellowed with a terrifying roar: "You're it!"

One afternoon in the Arctic, a father polar bear and his polar bear son were sitting in the snow. The cub turned to his father and said: "Dad, am I 100 per cent polar bear?"

"Of course, son," replied the father. "You are 100 per cent polar bear."

A few minutes later, the cub turned to his father again and said: "Dad, tell me the truth, I can take it. Am I 100 per cent polar bear? No brown bear or black bear or grizzly bear?"

The father put a loving paw on his son's head. "Son," he said, "I am 100 per cent polar bear, your mother is 100 per cent polar bear, so you are definitely 100 per cent polar bear."

The cub seemed satisfied, but a few minutes later he turned to his father once more and said: "Look, Dad, I don't want you saying things just to spare my feelings. I have to know: am I 100 per cent polar bear?"

By now the father was becoming distressed by the continual questioning and said: "Why do you keep asking if you are 100 per cent polar bear?"

The cub replied: "Because I'm freezing!"

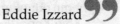

> Foxgloves: worn by foxes to avoid leaving fingerprints when killing chickens.
>
> Eddie Izzard

★ An elderly snake went to the doctor and told him: "Doc, my eyesight is so bad, I can't see to hunt any more. I think I need a pair of glasses."

So the doctor fixed the snake up with a pair of glasses and told him to come back if he still couldn't manage.

Two weeks later, the snake was back in the doctor's office. "I'm depressed," he complained.

"Why, what's the problem?" asked the doctor. "Haven't the glasses helped?"

"The glasses are fine," sighed the snake. "But I've discovered that I've been living with a garden hose for the past three years."

Why did the mother kangaroo jump up and down in pain?

She caught the kids smoking in bed.

★　★　★　★　★

APPEARANCE

❖ A woman went into hospital to have her wrinkles removed, but she woke up to find that the surgeon had given her breast implants.

"What have you done?" she demanded. "I came in here to have the wrinkles on my face removed, but instead you've given me these huge breasts."

"Yes," said the surgeon, "but at least nobody's looking at your wrinkles any more."

❖ A few days before his son was due to leave for his first semester at university, a father sat him down for a quiet chat.

"Son," he said, "in college you're going to be surrounded by beautiful girls, so I got you something from the chemist."

"Dad, you didn't need to. I've already got condoms."

"With a face like yours, you won't be needing condoms, son. I bought you some anti-depressants."

❖ A cosmetic surgeon was sitting in his consulting room chatting to a friend when a beautiful woman walked in, kissed the surgeon and said: "Thank you so much for everything you have done for me. I felt ugly before, but now you have turned me into a princess."

When the gorgeous lady left the room, the friend asked: "Wow, who was that? You've certainly done a good job on her."

The surgeon replied: "Oh, that was my mother." And they continued their conversation.

A few minutes later, another beautiful lady walked into the room. Even more stunning than the first, she, too, kissed the surgeon and said: "Thank you so much. You have made me look twenty years younger. The facelift and liposuction have done wonders for me."

As she left, the friend exclaimed: "Wow, she looks like a supermodel! Who was she?"

"Oh," replied the surgeon nonchalantly, "that was my wife." And they carried on with their conversation.

A few minutes later, a third beautiful woman walked in, this one even more gorgeous than the other two. She had a perfect body with breasts to die for. She walked over to the surgeon, slapped him hard around the face and yelled: "You bastard! Look what you have done to my body! You've ruined my life!"

As the woman stormed out, the friend looked at the surgeon in bewilderment.

The surgeon shook his head sadly and said: "Let's not talk about it. That was my father."

❖ A woman was waiting at a bus stop when a man arrived with envelopes and stamps plastered in a neat design all over his bare head.

She said: "If it's not a silly question, why have you got envelopes and stamps stuck all over your head in some sort of design?"

"Oh that," he replied. "It's mail pattern baldness."

❖ A young guy said to a conspicuously ugly girl: "What's your name?"

"Thursday," she replied.

"That's an unusual name."

"Yeah, when I was born my mom and dad looked in the cot and said, 'I think we'd better call it a day.'"

❖ A male charity collector knocked on a woman's front door and asked her if she had any old beer bottles.

She was highly indignant. "Do I look as if I drink beer?" she snapped.

The collector looked at her and said: "Okay, have you got any vinegar bottles?"

❖ **A completely unqualified man got a job as a cosmetic surgeon. I tell you, it raised a few eyebrows.**

❖ A country guy in a bar was becoming irritated by a flash city type with a vacuous blonde on his arm. Both had loud, braying voices and a seemingly endless supply of cash.

Eventually the country guy went up to him and said: "You know, you've got yourself a real trophy girlfriend there."

"Why do you think she's a trophy girlfriend?" said the city boy proudly. "Is it because she's got long blonde hair and lovely boobs?"

"No," said the country boy, "because she's got big ears."

❖ A small boy watched in fascination as his mother gently rubbed cold cream on her face.

"Why are you rubbing cold cream on your face?" he asked eventually.

"To make myself beautiful," replied his mother.

A few minutes later she began removing the cream with a tissue.

"What's the matter?" asked her son. "Giving up?"

❖ What happened to the pretty girl who lost her watch?

She became a timeless beauty.

❖ A guy was meeting a friend in a bar, and as he walked in, he noticed two pretty girls looking at him. He heard one girl say to the other: "Nine."

Feeling pleased with himself, he swaggered over to his buddy at the bar and told him that the girl in the corner had just rated him a nine out of ten.

"Sorry to spoil your evening," said his friend, "but when I walked in, they were speaking German."

❖ A wife who had seen better days posed in front of the bedroom mirror naked. "Tell me, honey," she said. "What turns you on more – my pretty face or my sexy body?"

Her husband replied dryly: "Your sense of humour."

❖ Two men were admiring a magazine photo of a famous actress. "Still," said one, "if you take away her fabulous hair, her magnificent breasts, her beautiful eyes, her gorgeous smile, her perfect features and her stunning figure, what are you left with?"

The other replied: "My wife."

A guy removed his new girlfriend's glasses and said to her: "Wow! You're stunning."

She said: "And so are you . . . suddenly."

ARMY

✳ A husband returned home after spending eight months on a solo posting with the US Army in Alaska. He told his wife: "Honey, I want you to know that I haven't wasted my time while I've been away. I've mastered the art of mind over matter. Watch this!"

He then dropped his pants and shorts and stood before her naked. "Now watch," he said.

"Dick, attention!" he barked, and his penis instantly sprang to full erection.

His wife was impressed.

Then he barked, "Dick, at ease!" and his penis immediately went soft.

"That's amazing," said his wife. "What a party piece! Hey, would you mind if I showed our neighbour Janice?"

The husband said he had no objections, and a few minutes later Janice – a pretty brunette wearing a short skirt and knee-high boots – called round to witness the trick. The husband could scarcely take his eyes off her long legs.

"Come on, darling," said his wife. "Show Janice what you can do."

Gathering himself together, he barked, "Dick, attention!" and his penis stood proud.

The two women roared with laughter.

Then he ordered, "Dick, at ease!" but nothing happened. It stayed hard.

"Dick, at ease!" he repeated, but still it refused to go down.

After two more fruitless attempts, the husband rushed embarrassed to the bathroom, leaving his wife to make excuses for him. After she had seen Janice out, she went into the bathroom and found him masturbating furiously.

"What are you doing?" she asked.

He gasped: "I'm giving this son-of-a-bitch a dishonourable discharge!"

✳ Two soldiers were chatting during their free time. The first asked: "Why did you join the Army?"

The second said: "I didn't have a wife and I loved war. So I joined. How about you? Why did you join the Army?"

"I had a wife and I loved peace. That's why I joined the Army."

✳ My uncle had his tongue shot off during the Vietnam War, but he doesn't talk about it.

✳ A general noticed one of his soldiers behaving oddly. The soldier would pick up any piece of paper he found, frown, say, "That's not it", and put it down again.

This went on for some time until the general arranged to have the soldier psychologically tested. The psychologist concluded that the soldier was deranged, and wrote out his discharge from the Army.

The soldier picked it up, smiled, and said: "That's it."

✳ Two brothers enlisting in the Army were undergoing their physicals. During the inspection, the doctor was surprised to see that both of the men possessed extraordinarily long penises.

"How do you account for this?" he asked the brothers.

"It's hereditary, sir," replied the older brother.

"I see," said the doctor, writing in his file. "Your father's the reason for your elongated penises?"

"No, sir, our mother."

"Your mother?" said the doctor. "Don't be so ridiculous! Women don't have penises!"

"I know, sir," replied the recruit, "but she only had one arm, and when it came to getting us out of the bathtub, she had to manage as best she could."

✳ A little boy said his ambition was to drive a tank. His father said: "Well, I won't stand in your way."

Murphy's Laws of Combat

If the enemy is in range, so are you.

Incoming fire has the right of way.

Don't look conspicuous, it draws fire.

There is always a way, but the easy way is mined.

Teamwork is essential – it gives them someone else to shoot at.

The enemy diversion you have been ignoring will be the main attack.

Never share a foxhole with anyone braver than you.

A "sucking chest wound" is nature's way of telling you to slow down.

If your attack is going well, you have walked into an ambush.

Never forget that your weapon is made by the lowest bidder.

＊ Three service veterans were boasting about the exploits of their ancestors.

One declared proudly: "At age thirteen, my great-grandfather was a drummer boy at Shiloh."

The second said: "Mine went down with Custer at the Battle of the Little Big Horn."

"I'm the only soldier in my family," confessed vet number three, "but if my great-grandfather was alive today, he'd be famous throughout the world."

"Why? What did he do?" asked the others.

"Nothing much, but he would be 177 years old!"

＊ As everyone sat around the table for a big family dinner, the youngest son announced that he had just signed up at an army recruitment office. There were audible gasps from the gathering, followed by laughter as his older brothers expressed their disbelief that he could handle army life.

"Oh, come on, quit joking," snickered one. "You haven't really signed up, have you?"

"You'd never get through basic training," scoffed another.

Finally his father spoke up. "It's going to take a lot of discipline. Are you ready for that?"

Coming under fire from all sides, the new recruit looked to his mother for help. But she said simply: "Are you really going to make your own bed every morning?"

> 66 The Afghan War has clearly reached a stage similar to that moment at your child's party where you realize you have forgotten to give the other parents a pick-up time.
>
> Jeremy Hardy 99

＊ The sergeant-major growled at the young soldier: "I didn't see you at camouflage training this morning."

"Thank you very much, sir."

＊ Fifty-four years ago, Elmer Harrison, a Montana mountain man, was drafted by the US Army.

On his first day in basic training, the Army issued him with a comb. That afternoon, the Army barber sheared off all of Elmer's hair.

On his second day, the Army issued him with a toothbrush. That afternoon, the Army dentist extracted seven of Elmer's teeth.

On the third day, the Army issued him with a jock-strap.

The US Army has been looking for Elmer for fifty-four years.

✳ "Well," snarled the sergeant-major to the young private, "I suppose after you get discharged from the Army, you'll just be waiting for me to die so you can come and piss on my grave?"

"Not me, sir!" replied the soldier. "Once I get out of the Army, I'm never going to stand in line again!"

★   ★   ★   ★   ★

ART

★ Two women visiting an art exhibition were staring intently at a painting entitled "Home for Lunch". The painting was of three naked black men sitting on a park bench. What puzzled the women was that the men on either end of the bench had black penises, but the man in the middle had a pink penis.

Just then the artist happened to walk by, so the women decided to ask him for an explanation.

"We don't quite understand the painting of the black men on the bench," they said. "Why does the man in the middle have a pink penis?"

"Oh, dear!" laughed the artist. "I'm afraid you have misinterpreted the picture. You see, the three men are not African Americans, they're coal miners, and the man in the middle went 'Home for Lunch'."

★ A man was standing in a gallery, studying two near-identical pictures by the same artist. Both showed a glass of wine, a basket of bread rolls, a bowl of salad and a plate of smoked salmon. Yet one painting was priced at $150, the other at $175. So he asked the gallery owner to explain why one was more expensive than the other.

"It's simple," said the gallery owner, indicating the more expensive painting. "You get two extra slices of smoked salmon in that one."

★ The artist tried to concentrate on his work, but the attraction he felt for his model finally become too great to resist. Suddenly he threw down his palette, took her in his arms and kissed her.

She pushed him away, saying: "Maybe your other models let you kiss them, but I'm different!"

He protested: "I've never tried to kiss a model before."

"Really," she said, softening. "How many models have there been?"

"Five," he replied. "A vase, a jug, two apples and a banana."

★ Homeowners in a neighbourhood were aware of a woman going around door-to-door carrying paint brushes, a tin of paints and an easel.

"Does anyone know what she's doing?" asked one.

"Yes," said another. "She's canvassing."

★ Pablo Picasso disturbed a burglar breaking into his chateau. Although the burglar got away, Picasso was able to draw a portrait of the suspect. As a result, police arrested a giant bar of Toblerone, a refrigerator and a grandfather clock.

★ What's green and smells like yellow paint? Green paint.

★ An artist asked the gallery owner if there had been any interest in his paintings that were currently on display.

"I've got good news and bad news," replied the gallery owner. "The good news is that a gentleman inquired about your work and wondered whether it would appreciate in value after your death. When I told him it would, he bought all fifteen of your paintings."

"That's great!" exclaimed the artist. "So what's the bad news?"

"The man was your doctor."

You Know You're an Artist When . . .

The only piece of new furniture you have in your home is a $2,000 easel.

You butter your toast with your fingers, just to feel its texture.

The highlights in your hair are from your palette and not Clairol.

You are more concerned about the colour of your car than its fuel consumption.

There are Prussian Blue fingerprints on your phone.

Your brushes are immaculate but your hair is unkempt.

Your family takes out a life insurance plan on you for less than $5,000.

Your "best" clothes are the ones with only small paint smears on them.

You clean your brushes in your coffee mug.

You refer to your relationship with your partner as "a work in progress".

A bowl of fruit is something to be painted rather than eaten.

You know the difference between beige, ecru, cream, off-white and eggshell.

The last five items of clothing you bought were all smocks.

You get excited about the football season because it means your partner will be sitting still on the sofa long enough for you to paint him.

You do judge a book by its cover.

AUTOMOBILES

❖ Before taking his family out for the day, a man called in at a gas station to put some air in his car's tyres, because he had noticed they were a bit flat.

"How much is that?" he asked the cashier.

"Ten dollars."

"Ten dollars! That's expensive! It's only air!"

The cashier said: "Well, that's inflation for you!"

❖ A motorist was driving along when he saw a police car behind, flashing him to stop. As he stepped out of the car, he threw up his hands in despair.

The officer said: "Sir, I'm afraid your rear lights aren't working properly."

"I don't believe this!" shouted the man. "I can't believe this has happened!"

"There's no need to get so worked up," said the officer. "You can easily get the lights fixed at a garage."

"Damn the lights!" yelled the driver. "Where's my caravan?"

> I masturbated in the car once. I wouldn't do it again, though, 'cause the cab driver got really pissed off. I said: 'I'm sorry, all I saw was the no smoking sign.'
> Mitch Fatel

❖ A wife drove her husband out for a meal, but just before they reached the restaurant, they realized they had neither cash nor credit cards with them. So he ordered her to pull alongside a parked car and then reverse into the space behind it.

"How is that going to help?" she asked.

He said: "Because you always make a meal out of parallel parking."

❖ I was sitting in traffic the other day, which was probably why I got run over.

Signs That the Car You Just Bought is an Old Wreck

As you leave the used car lot, you see the previous owner rush out and high-five the salesman.

You notice that the free car phone they threw in as part of the deal has a local breakdown company on speed dial.

The coat hanger that serves as a radio aerial is described by the salesman as a "feature".

You would take your car into the garage for repairs but it can't get up the ramp.

Priests cross themselves as you drive by.

The booster cables are not in the trunk but are permanently soldered to the battery.

Youths on the rampage in your street vandalize every car except yours.

As you drive up to a service station for gas, the mechanic automatically opens the big door to the service bay and waves you in.

In fifth gear, you are overtaken by a mobility scooter.

You get a "Good Luck" card from the previous owner.

Thieves thought about stealing your wheels but then realized that the bricks they were going to put in their place were actually worth more.

When you leave for work the next morning, you notice a tow truck parked in your street. As you drive off, it silently falls in behind you.

The steering wheel column appears to be held in place with Blu-Tack.

Whenever you signal to turn left, the windshield wipers start.

The front bumper has rope burns from being towed so much.

 I was going to get a BMW and rang my dad who knows a bit about cars. He said: 'You can't get a German car after what your granddad went through in the war.' I didn't know about this but apparently during the Second World War, my granddad had a succession of unreliable German cars. Which is embarrassing when you're an SS officer.

Jack Dee

❖ A woman was out driving when she stalled at a red light. Hard though she tried, she was unable to restart the engine and soon a long queue began to form. The male driver immediately behind her was particularly impatient, sounding his horn continuously.

Finally she got out of her car, went over to the driver behind and said: "I can't seem to get my car started. Would you be a sweetheart and see if you can get it started for me? I'll stay here in your car and lean on your horn for you!"

❖ A driver was heading the wrong way down a one-way street when a police officer pulled him over.

"Didn't you see the arrows?" asked the officer.

"Arrows?" repeated the driver. "I didn't even see the Indians!"

❖ A police officer pulled over a driver for speeding. "You were doing ninety miles an hour," said the officer. "What the hell were you playing at?"

"Well, you see," explained the driver, "my brakes failed about three miles back and I was rushing to get home before I caused an accident."

❖ **Did you hear about the guy who couldn't work out how to fasten his seat belt?**
Then it suddenly clicked.

❖ A woman driver caught speeding was told to pull over to the side of the road. Realizing she didn't have her seat belt on, she quickly buckled up before the police officer reached her window. After lecturing her about speeding, the officer said: "I see you are wearing your seat belt. Do you believe in wearing it at all times?"

"Most definitely, officer," she replied.

"I see. And do you always wear it looped through the steering wheel?"

> " Buying a used rental car is like going to a house of ill repute looking for a wife. Anything that's been driven that hard by that many people, you really don't want to put your key in it. "
>
> Jeff Foxworthy

❖ A motorist was furious at getting a ticket for speeding. "What am I supposed to do with this?" he said to the policeman.

"Keep it," said the officer. "When you collect four of them, you get a bicycle."

❖ Fearing that he would be late for an important business meeting in London, a motorist was beginning to panic because he couldn't find a parking space. Street after street was full, and growing ever more desperate, he decided to seek help from the Almighty.

Looking up to Heaven, he said: "Lord, please help me out here. If you find me a parking space, I'll give up drink and women and go to Mass every Sunday."

Then as he turned the corner, miraculously a parking space appeared.

He looked skyward again and said: "Never mind, I found one."

> " High gas prices leave a bad taste in people's mouths. That's mostly from the siphoning, but still . . . "
>
> Jay Leno

❖ Driving along a remote country road, a motorist saw a sign that said "Watch For Fallen Rocks".

A few miles later he spotted some small rocks by the side of the road and picked a few up and put them in his car. When he reached the next town, he took them to the highway maintenance office.

Placing them on the counter, he said to the official: "Here are your fallen rocks. Now where's my watch?"

> " Did you ever notice, when you are sitting at a red light, that when the person in front of you pulls up a couple of inches, you are compelled to move up too? Do we really think we are making progress toward our destination? 'Whew, I thought we'd be late, but now that I am nine inches closer, I can stop for coffee and a Danish!'
>
> Jerry Seinfeld "

★   ★   ★   ★   ★

BABIES

> " I went to see my friend's new baby today. She asked me if I'd like to wind it, but I thought that was a bit harsh, so I just gave it a dead leg.
>
> Tam Cowan "

✳ Two women sitting in the doctor's waiting room began discussing babies.

"I want a baby more than anything else in the world," said one. "But I guess it's impossible."

"I used to think that," said the other. "But then everything changed. That's why I'm here. I'm going to have a baby in three months."

"You must tell me what you did."

"I went to a faith healer."

"But I've tried that. My husband and I went to one for nearly a year and it didn't help at all."

The pregnant woman smiled and whispered: "Next time, try going alone."

✳ Gazing adoringly at his new son lying in the cot, a husband said with a cheeky grin: "He's quite big down there, isn't he?"

"Yes," said the wife. "But at least he's got your eyes."

✳ A new mother went to the doctor and said: "Doctor, since I had the baby, I can't sleep at night. When I'm in the next room I have this terrible fear that I won't hear the baby if he falls out of the crib at night. What should I do?"

"Easy," said the doctor. "Just take the carpet off the floor."

✳ Under intense parental questioning, a teenage girl admitted that she was pregnant but couldn't say for sure who the father was.

Her mother was furious. "Go to your room," she bellowed, "and don't come out until you can give us a definite answer!"

Later that night, the girl came downstairs apologetically. "Mom, I think I have an idea who the father might be now."

"I should think so, too!" exclaimed the mother. "The very idea that any daughter of mine could get pregnant so young, let alone not know the father!"

"Okay," said the girl, "I think I got it narrowed down to the band or the football team."

✳ A single guy was getting irritated because his friends preferred to hang out with their new kids rather than with him. "Where's the loyalty?" he protested. "I've known you for twenty-five years. How long have you known your baby? A month."

Did you hear about the guy whose wife asked him to go into town and buy a baby monitor?

He couldn't find one anywhere, so he bought her an iguana instead.

＊ A girl gave birth and told one of her ex-boyfriends that he was the father.

He was not convinced. "You were seeing plenty of men behind my back. How do I know this baby's mine?"

"He's got your characteristics," she said.

"Huh!" he scoffed. "Like what?"

"He was premature."

＊ One night a woman found her husband standing over their newborn baby's crib. Silently she watched him. As he stood looking down at the sleeping infant, she saw on his face a mixture of feelings: disbelief, doubt, delight, amazement, enchantment, scepticism.

Touched by his rare display of deep emotion, she felt her eyes grow moist. She slipped her arms around her husband. "A penny for your thoughts," she whispered tenderly in his ear.

"It's amazing," he replied. "A miracle almost. I just can't see how anybody can make a crib like this for only $49.95!"

＊ A mother was trying to explain to her little girl how she had recently become pregnant. She explained how a baby was growing in her tummy, and how it took an egg and a sperm to make the baby. Daddy made the sperm and Mommy made the egg.

Then the little girl asked: "Mommy, if it takes a sperm and an egg to make a baby and the egg is already in your tummy, then how does the sperm get in there? Does Mommy swallow it?"

The mother said: "She does, if she wants a new evening dress."

> A baby, if you really break it down, is just a tiny, shirtless, bald human being with a bag of its own crap tied around its waist.
>
> Patton Oswalt

* After a woman had given birth, the doctor appeared in the ward with a worried expression on his face and announced solemnly: "There's something I have to tell you about your baby."

The woman sat bolt upright in bed and demanded: "What's wrong with my baby, doctor?"

The doctor said: "Well, nothing's wrong exactly. It's just that your baby's a little bit different. You see, your baby is a hermaphrodite."

"A hermaphrodite?" repeated the woman. "What's that?"

"It means your baby has the . . . er . . . features of a male and a female."

The woman turned pale. "Oh my God!" she exclaimed. "You mean it has a penis AND a brain?"

* Jim was seconds away from having a vasectomy when his brother and sister-in-law barged in holding their newborn baby.

"Stop!" exclaimed the brother. "You can't go through with this!"

"And why not?" asked Jim.

"Don't you want to have a beautiful baby some day, like my wife and I have here?"

Jim said nothing.

The brother grew impatient. "Come on, Jim, I want a nephew. Make me an uncle."

Jim couldn't take any more of this. He gave his sister-in-law an apologetic look and asked his brother: "Are you sure you want a nephew?"

"Absolutely," said the brother.

"Well, congratulations," said Jim, "you're holding him!"

★   ★   ★   ★   ★

BANKING

★ A kindergarten had received a number of complaints from parents regarding the state of a hawthorn hedge that surrounded the school playground. It was so long and thorny in places that several people – including children – had received scratches. The town council had rejected all calls to trim the hedge, so the school decided to undertake the task themselves and proposed cutting back the hedge every three months to ensure that it stayed in shape and posed no danger.

To this end, the school formed a special committee of parent volunteers, each of whom took responsibility for a particular aspect of the operation. The key area was finance, and since one of the parents was an investment banker, the committee thought he would be the ideal person to set up an account from which money could be drawn to cover the costs associated with maintaining the hedge.

But when he was approached, the investment banker firmly declined, saying: "There's no way I'm getting involved in any more hedge funds."

★ What's the definition of optimism?
   A merchant banker ironing five shirts on a Sunday night.

★ What do you say to a hedge fund manager who can't sell anything?
   "A quarter-pounder with fries, please."

★ What's the difference between a no-claims bonus and a banker's bonus?
   You lose your no-claims bonus after a crash.

★ Why don't bankers like to talk about hedge funds?
   It's privet.

★ Two bankers were drowning their sorrows in a City of London bar. One turned to the other and said: "This credit crunch is worse than a divorce. I've lost half my net worth and I still have a wife."

> 66 The economy continues to spiral. I saw a bank robber today being held up by a teller. It's so bad, I went to my ATM machine and it gave me an IOU.
>
> Jay Leno 99

★ Worrying news from the Japanese financial markets. Following last week's disclosure that Origami Bank had folded, we hear that Sumo Bank has gone belly up and Bonsai Bank plans to cut back some of its branches. Meanwhile, shares in Kamikaze Bank were suspended after they nose-dived, 500 staff at Karate Bank got the chop and Karaoke Bank is up for sale and going for a song. Analysts also report that there is something fishy going on at Sushi Bank, where it is feared that staff may get a raw deal. But Samurai Bank is soldiering on after sharp cutbacks.

★ What's the difference between a banker and an asshole?
  An asshole does give a shit.

★ Why is a subprime RMBS (residential mortgage-backed security) like the sinking of the *Titanic*?
  The downside was not immediately apparent, it went underwater rapidly despite assurances that it was unsinkable and only a few wealthy people got out in time.

★ The problem with investment bank balance sheets is that on the left side nothing is right and on the right side nothing is left.

★ Two young investment bankers race their cars over a cliff to see who hits the bottom first. Who wins?
  Society.

★ Did you hear about the new credit crunch version of Monopoly?

There's no money in the banks and all the houses come with "For Sale" signs.

★ A man went to his bank manager and said: "I'd like to start a small business. How do I go about it?"

"Simple," said the bank manager. "Buy a big one and wait."

★ President Bush said that he was saddened to hear about the demise of Lehman Brothers. He said his thoughts went out to their mother as losing one son is hard but losing two is a tragedy.

★ A wealthy investor walked into a bank and told the manager: "I'd like to speak with Mr Rodney Wilson, a tried and trusted employee of yours."

The bank manager said: "He was certainly trusted, and he'll be tried just as soon as we catch him."

> What do you call a piece of meat that forecloses your house, causes a global recession and is marketed disproportionately to minorities?
> Subprime rib.

★ Employees at the British bank Bradford & Bingley complained that they had not been given prior notice of a takeover by Banco Santander. A British government spokesman said: "No one expected the Spanish acquisition."

★ The economy is in such a mess that the pen on the counter is now more valuable than the bank.

★ What's the difference between a guy who lost everything in Las Vegas and an investment banker?

A tie.

★ A blind rabbit and a blind snake were friends. One day the blind rabbit told the blind snake that he didn't know what he was, because he couldn't see. So he asked the snake for help in determining what he was.

The blind snake slithered up to the blind rabbit, felt it all over and said: "You have long, furry ears and a short little tail. You must be a rabbit."

The blind rabbit was delighted with the news, and agreed to repay the favour so that the blind snake could find out what he was.

The blind rabbit felt the blind snake all over and finally declared: "You're cold, you're slimy and you don't have any balls. You must be a banker."

★ **During the credit crunch, a guy went to an ATM and it said "insufficient funds". He wondered: "Is it them or me?"**

★ A director decided to award a prize of $100 for the best idea for saving the company money during the credit crunch. It was won by a young executive who suggested reducing the prize money to $10.

★ What's the difference between an investment banker and a large pizza?

The pizza can still feed a family of four.

★ The credit crunch is getting bad. I loaned my brother $10 last week, and it turns out I'm now America's third biggest lender.

★ A banker fell overboard while taking a cruise on a friend's yacht. The friend grabbed a lifebelt, held it up, and, not knowing whether the banker could swim, shouted: "Can you float alone?"

"Of course I can!" yelled the banker. "But this is a hell of a time to talk business!"

★ A new teacher was getting to know the kids by asking them their name and what their father did for a living.

The first little girl said: "My name is Mary and my daddy is a postman."

The next child, a little boy, said: "My name is Andy and my dad's a mechanic."

And so it went on until one little boy said: "My name is Johnny and my dad is a stripper in a gay bar."

The teacher gasped in shock and quickly changed the subject. Later in the school yard the teacher approached Johnny privately and asked if it was really true that his father danced naked in a gay bar.

Johnny blushed and said: "No, he's really a business development director at Lehman Brothers, but I'm just too embarrassed to tell anyone."

★ Did you hear what happened to the witch's house during the credit crunch?

It was re-possessed.

★ Why is a merchant bank like the model Jordan?

Both are institutions whose reputation is built on assets that, on closer inspection, turn out to be entirely artificial, vastly over-inflated and in danger of going through the floor at any moment.

★ What's the difference between an investment banker and a pigeon?

A pigeon is still capable of leaving a deposit on a new Ferrari.

★ A concerned customer asked his bank manager if the recent economic instability worried him.

"I've been sleeping like a baby," replied the bank manager.

"Really?"

"Absolutely," confirmed the bank manager. "I sleep for about an hour, wake up, and then cry for an hour."

★ A little old lady tried to phone her local bank but was put through instead to the bank's call centre in India.

"Is that the High Street branch?" she asked.

"No, madam," replied the voice at the other end. "It is now company policy to deal with telephone calls centrally."

"Well, I really need to speak to the branch," said the old lady.

"Madam, if you just let me know your query, I'm sure I can help you."

"I don't think you can, young man. I need to speak to the branch."

The call centre operator was adamant. "There's nothing that the branch can help you with that can't be dealt with by me."

"Very well then," sighed the old lady. "Can you just check on the counter? Did I leave my gloves behind when I came in this morning?"

★ **The Isle of Dogs Bank has collapsed. They've called in the retrievers.**

★ A woman with a $50 bill stuck in each ear went for a meeting with her bank manager.

"Mrs Fleming is waiting outside," the receptionist told the manager.

"Mrs Fleming?" he said, leafing through his files. "Ah, yes. She's $100 in arrears."

★ ★ ★ ★ ★

BARTENDERS

❖ A man with 3.1415927 eyes walked into a bar. The bartender said: "I'm sorry, sir, I can't serve you. You're already pi-eyed."

❖   A new bar manager at a country inn found two of his elderly regulars waiting on the doorstep at opening time.

"Good morning," they said, ordering a pint of beer. But as they stood at the bar, their faces fell. "Where's the snuff?" they asked.

"Snuff?" queried the bar manager.

They said: "Your predecessor always used to leave snuff on the bar in a big blue saucer for his most important customers. And that's us, because we're here every lunchtime, 365 days a year."

"Well, it's the first I've heard of it," explained the bar manager by way of apology, "but rest assured, there will be snuff on the bar for you tomorrow lunchtime. We always look after our customers."

The manager was so busy settling into his new post and getting to know the staff and regulars that he completely forgot about the snuff until he saw the two old men slowly walking up the lane the following lunchtime. He hurriedly put the big blue saucer on the bar and searched in the back room for the snuff. He rummaged through every cupboard in the place, but to no avail. Then he remembered that surplus stock was sometimes kept in an old building in the yard. So he looked there, too, but still had no luck.

On his way back across the yard, he spotted a dried up piece of dog poop in his path. In frustration, he kicked out at it and it crumbled into dozens of tiny pieces as it splattered against the wall. This gave him an idea. He dashed back into the pub, grabbed the blue saucer and, using a piece of paper towel, he picked up the remains of the poop and crumbled it into the saucer. He then went back into the pub and put the saucer on the bar just as his two old regulars entered.

"Morning," said one of the men, eyeing the saucer on the bar. "Glad to see you found some snuff."

"I said I would," said the bar manager, quietly keeping his fingers crossed as the old man helped himself to a large portion.

The man sniffed intently and said to the manager: "Can you smell dog shit?"

"No," mumbled the manager unconvincingly.

Then the second man, who had been hanging up his coat, wandered over and took a pinch from the saucer. "There's a smell of dog shit around here!" he exclaimed.

Again the manager mumbled that he couldn't smell anything.

Just then, a third elderly man entered. "Bill," the first man called, "come over here!"

Bill strolled over.

"Can you smell dog shit?" asked the first man. "Because I can and Bert can, but the bar manager can't."

Bill sniffed the air deeply, twice. "Can't smell a thing," he said. "But wait a minute." He then took two big pinches of the "snuff" – one in each nostril – from the saucer on the bar, and sniffed again. "Ah, I can smell dog shit now, right enough," he said. "This must be good snuff – it really clears your nose."

> David Hasselhoff walked into a bar and ordered a beer.
>
> The bartender said: "It's a pleasure to serve you, Mr Hasselhoff."
>
> "Just call me Hoff," said the actor.
>
> "Sure," said the bartender. "No hassle."

❖ A man walked into a bar and said to the bartender: "Do you serve women in this bar?"

"No," replied the bartender. "You have to bring your own."

❖ An eight-year-old girl walked into a bar and demanded of the bartender: "Give me a double scotch on the rocks."

"Do you want to get me into trouble?" asked the bartender, incredulous.

"Maybe later," said the girl. "Right now, I just want the scotch."

❖ A customer walked into a bar and said: "I'll have a pint of less, please."

"Less?" queried the bartender. "What's that?"

"I don't know either," said the customer, "but my doctor told me to drink less."

❖ Two men were standing at the crowded bar of a country club chatting in an animated fashion.

After a few minutes, the bartender interrupted them and said: "Excuse me, you're new members, aren't you?"

"Yes, we are," they said. "How could you tell among so many people?"

The bartender said: "You put your drinks down."

❖ The bartender asked a guy sitting at the bar: "What'll you have?"

The guy answered: "A scotch, please."

The bartender handed him the drink and said: "That'll be $5."

The guy said: "What are you talking about? I don't owe you anything for this."

A lawyer, sitting nearby and overhearing the conversation, said to the bartender: "You know, he's got you there. In the original offer, which constitutes a binding contract upon acceptance, there was no stipulation of remuneration."

The bartender was understandably unhappy, but said to the guy: "Okay, I'll let you off this time, but don't ever let me catch you in here again."

The next day, the same guy walked into the bar. The bartender said: "What the hell are you doing in here? I thought I told you to steer clear of this joint. I can't believe you've got the nerve to come back."

The guy said innocently: "What are you talking about? I've never been in this place in my life."

Fearing that he had made a mistake, the bartender backed down. "I'm very sorry," he said, "but the likeness is uncanny. You must have a double."

The guy replied: "Thanks. Make it a scotch."

❖ A snake slithered into a bar and asked the bartender for a beer. "I'm sorry," said the bartender, "but I can't serve you."

"Why not?" asked the snake.

"Because you can't hold your drink."

❖ A piece of gold walked into a Texas bar. The bartender said: "Au, get out of here!"

❖ The bartender said to one of his customers: "Do you always drink your whisky neat?"

The guy replied: "No, sometimes my shirt's hanging out."

❖ A man walked into a bar and said to the bartender: "Give me a beer before the arguments start."

The bartender poured him a beer.

A couple of minutes later, the man said again: "Give me a beer before the arguments start."

The bartender poured him another beer.

A few minutes later, the man said for a third time: "Give me a beer before the arguments start."

Thoroughly confused, the bartender said: "Excuse me, when are you going to pay for all these beers?"

The man said: "Now the arguments start."

❖ Jesus walked into a bar and asked for a glass of water, which he immediately turned into wine.

"Hey, what do you think you're doing?" yelled the bartender.

Jesus said: "Well, I'm not paying your prices for a glass of Chardonnay."

❖ A brain walked into a bar and said: "I'll have a beer please."

The bartender looked at the brain and said: "Sorry, I can't serve you."

"Why not?" asked the brain.

"Because you're already out of your head."

❖ A man walked into a bar and ordered a twelve-year-old scotch. Believing that the customer would not be able to tell the difference, the bartender poured him a shot of cheap three-year-old house scotch.

The man took a sip before spitting it out on the bar. "I'm not drinking this!" he complained. "This is cheap three-year-old scotch. Now give me the good twelve-year-old scotch that I asked for!"

Still looking to cut corners, the bartender poured him a shot of a moderate six-year-old scotch.

The man took a sip before once again spitting it out on the bar. "This is just a six-year-old scotch," he moaned. "I'm not paying for this! Now will you give me the twelve-year-old scotch I ordered?"

The bartender finally relented, and served the man his best quality twelve-year-old scotch.

The entire episode had been witnessed by an old drunk at the other end of the bar. He now walked up to the selective scotch drinker, put a glass down in front of him and asked: "What do you think of this?"

The scotch expert took a sip of the golden liquid and spat it out violently on the bar. "That's disgusting!" he said. "It tastes like piss!"

"It is," replied the old drunk. "Now tell me how old I am."

Charles Dickens walked into a bar. The bartender said: "Olive or twist?"

❖ A man walked into a bar with a banana on his head. As he served him, the bartender said: "Look, I don't know if you realize this, but you've got a banana on your head."

"That's okay," said the man. "I always wear a banana on my head on Tuesdays."

"But today's Wednesday," said the bartender.

"It's not, is it?" groaned the man. "Oh no! I must look a complete idiot!"

❖ Two vampires walked into a bar and called for the bartender.

"I'll have a glass of blood," said one.

"I'll have a glass of plasma," said the other.

"Okay," replied the bartender. "That'll be one blood and one blood lite."

*　　*　　*　　*　　*

THE BECKHAMS

✳ The England national soccer team were meeting ahead of a game in Germany. David Beckham asked the coach: "Where is Michael Owen?"

The coach replied: "He's gone to get a tetanus injection."

"Oh," said David. "I might just get a new car myself while I'm here."

> 66 If you asked David Beckham to recite the alphabet backwards, he'd turn around and recite the alphabet.
>
> Frankie Boyle 99

✳ Defending his wife, David Beckham said that Victoria is worth her weight in gold . . . which works out at around $7.50.

✳ David Beckham was flying out to the Beijing Olympics. A reporter asked him whether he was taking chopsticks.

David replied: "No, she's staying at home with the kids."

✳ Victoria and David Beckham were getting ready to attend a glittering awards ceremony when she turned to him and said: "This tampon. Does it make me look fat?"

> Victoria Beckham looks like she has a dump once every four years. That's probably how David knows that there's a World Cup coming up.
>
> Frankie Boyle

* Why is David Beckham like Ferrero Rocher?
  They both come in a posh box.

> Most of us have a skeleton in the cupboard. David Beckham takes his out in public.
>
> Andrew Lawrence

* David Beckham was walking down a Los Angeles street with his son Brooklyn when he passed a fast food outlet with a sign outside saying, "Free Big Mac."
  David turned to Brooklyn and said: "I wonder what he did?"

* Brooklyn was stuck with his math homework. "Dad," he yelled, "will you help me with my homework?"
  "I don't know, son," said David. "It wouldn't really be right, would it?"
  "Probably not," said Brooklyn. "But have a go anyway."

★   ★   ★   ★   ★

BIRDS

* How do we know that woodpeckers are smarter than chickens?
  Ever heard of Kentucky Fried Woodpecker?

★ A bird was flying south for the winter, but had left it too late to set off and found itself frozen solid in a blizzard. It dropped to earth in a field of cows, landing in a massive cow pat, just as it was being deposited by the fattest cow in the field. At first, the bird was disgusted until it realized that the pile of poop was actually thawing him out. As the ice melted and his feathers returned to normal, he tweeted joyously, but the sounds were heard by a nearby cat who promptly crept over and ate the bird.

There are three morals to this story:

1. Not everyone who gets you into shit is your enemy.
2. Not everyone who gets you out of shit is your friend.
3. If you are in shit, keep your mouth shut.

★ Old natural history books document the existence of a now extinct bird called the ono. From the same family as the albatross, it was a sea bird that roamed the Pacific until the late nineteenth century and was renowned for its huge wingspan and short legs. The male was particularly distinctive, possessing large, bright red testicles.

The ono bird was given its unusual name by American sailors who observed it coming in to land on desert island beaches. While the females of the species landed in silence, the males were heard to cry "Oh no, oh no, oh no" just before touching down on their short fifteen-centimetre legs – and large twenty-two-centimetre testicles.

★ Why do birds fly south in the winter?
Because it's too far to walk.

★ Two ducks were on honeymoon in a posh hotel. Just as they were about to make love, the male duck said: "Damn, we haven't got any condoms! I'll ring down to room service."

So he phoned room service and the woman there said: "Certainly, sir. Would you like them on your bill?"

"No," said the duck. "I'd suffocate."

★ What goes cluck, cluck, bang?
A chicken in a minefield.

★ Driving into work one morning, a man could only watch in horror as his car shuddered to a halt in the busy rush hour traffic. All his attempts at restarting the car failed and he was left to contemplate a lengthy wait until the vehicle breakdown service arrived.

Then from nowhere a pigeon landed on the hood and began looking inquisitively through the windshield. Soon it was joined by two dozen more pigeons. The driver had always considered pigeons to be particularly stupid birds but he looked on in amazement as they then produced a length of rope and began tying it around the car's front bumper. By now a hundred more pigeons had descended and each bird grabbed a section of rope in its beak and began to pull the car.

As more pigeons flew in to join the Herculean effort, the car slowly but surely began to edge forward. Soon they were clocking a respectable two miles per hour and within forty-five minutes these incredible birds were dragging the vehicle into the car park of the driver's office.

As he stepped out of his car, a female work colleague, who had witnessed the unorthodox arrival, said to him: "All these years and I never knew you were pigeon-towed."

★ Why did the rubber chicken cross the road?

To stretch her legs.

★ A chicken walked over to a duck that was standing at the side of a road. The chicken said: "Don't do it, pal. You'll never hear the end of it!"

★ A woodpecker was pecking a hole in a tree. Suddenly the tree was hit by a flash of lightning that sent the tree crashing to the ground.

The woodpecker looked bemused for a moment and then said: "Gee, I guess I just don't know my own strength!"

★ Night after night, a keen ornithologist stood in his backyard hooting like an owl. After weeks of getting no reply, he suddenly heard an owl hoot back at him. He was overjoyed at the response and for the next nine months man and bird kept up a regular dialogue of hooting. He was fascinated by his ability to relate to a wild creature and kept a detailed record of all their conversations.

Just when he was about to take his findings to the Natural History Society, his wife happened to be talking to a neighbour who lived four doors away.

"My husband spends his night calling to owls," she confided.

"That's funny," said the neighbour. "So does mine!"

★ ★ ★ ★ ★

BIRTH

❖ A man and a woman were discussing the worst pain that anyone could possibly experience. The woman said: "Without doubt, there is nothing more painful in life than childbirth."

"Nonsense," said the man, "a kick in the bollocks is much more painful. Ask any guy."

"You're so wrong," maintained the woman. "Childbirth is far more painful."

The man was not about to yield to her argument and announced: "I have proof that I am right."

"What proof?" she asked scornfully.

"Because," he continued, "a few years after giving birth a woman will say to her partner, 'Do you want to try for another baby?' But I have never, ever, ever heard a man say – even years later – 'You know what I'd really like? Another kick in the bollocks!'"

Pregnancy Q & A

Q. Should I have a baby after thirty-five?
A. No, thirty-five children is enough.

Q. When will my baby move?
A. With any luck, right after he finishes high school.

Q. Since I became pregnant, my breasts, butt and even my feet have grown? Is there anything that gets smaller during pregnancy?
A. Yes, your bladder.

Q. What is the most common pregnancy craving?
A. For men to be the ones who get pregnant.

Q. When is the best time to get an epidural?
A. Straight after you find out that you're pregnant.

Q. How long is the average woman in labour?
A. Whatever she says, divided by two.

❖ Two country doctors were discussing the population explosion. One said: "This crazy birth rate is getting so bad that soon there ain't gonna be room for everybody. It's gonna be standing room only on this here planet."

"Well," said his colleague, "that sure oughta slow 'em down a bit!"

❖ A young man walked into a drug store to buy condoms. The sales clerk persuaded him to buy some multi-coloured condoms, which were on special offer.

Nine months later, the young man returned to the drug store to buy a maternity bra.

"What bust?" asked the clerk.

"I think it was the blue one," said the young man.

Q. My childbirth instructor says it's not pain I'll feel
   during labour, but pressure. Is she right?
A. Yes, in the same way that a tornado might be called
   an air current.

Q. The more heavily pregnant I get, the more strangers
   smile at me. Why is that?
A. Because you're fatter than them.

Q. Is there anything I should avoid while recovering
   from childbirth?
A. Yes, pregnancy.

Q. Our baby was born last week. When will I begin
   to feel normal again?
A. When the kids are in college.

Q. My wife is five months pregnant and so moody
   that sometimes she's crazy and irrational.
A. So what's your question?

❖ A couple were attending their first pre-natal class. So
that the husband could get an idea of what it felt like to
be pregnant, the instructor strapped a bag of sand to his
stomach.

As he walked around with his new bulge, the husband
said: "This doesn't feel too bad."

Then the instructor deliberately dropped a pen and said
to the husband: "Now I want you to pick up that pen as if
you were pregnant."

"You want me to do it the way my wife would?" confirmed
the husband.

"Exactly the same," said the instructor.

The husband turned to his wife and said: "Honey, pick up
that pen for me."

❖ A young, heavily pregnant woman took a taxi to hospital
and asked to be given help, as she was about to have her
first child. A nurse escorted her to the maternity ward and
on the way asked: "Is the father with you at all?"

The young woman replied: "Actually, I don't know who
the father is."

"I'm very sorry," said the nurse. "It's none of my business
– it's just that it usually helps to have close family around
at times like this. Anyway let's get you a bed and bring this
baby into the world."

Two hours later, the baby boy was born, much to the
young mother's relief. But then she noticed that the nurse
looked a little concerned.

"What's the matter?" she cried. "Is my baby okay?"

Holding the baby just out of the mother's view, the nurse
said: "I'm just going to have to take the baby into the next
room for some tests, but it's nothing to be worried about.
You just relax, and I'll be back in a few minutes."

Twenty minutes later, the nurse returned without the
baby. "You've given birth to a perfectly healthy baby," she
said, "but there are one or two questions I'd like to ask,
particularly concerning the conception. For example, your
baby is black."

Looking slightly embarrassed, the mother said: "Let me
explain. At the time I was going through a rough period
in my life. I'd lost my job, I couldn't afford the rent on
my apartment, and so I'm ashamed to say I took part in a
pornographic film – just for the money – and my co-star was
a black man."

"I can understand that," said the nurse sympathetically,
"but it also appears that your baby has the facial features of
an Asian person."

Blushing visibly, the girl admitted: "Well, there was
another man in the film of Asian ethnicity who starred with
me."

The nurse nodded but continued: "And it also seems that
your baby has the most startling ginger hair I have ever seen
in a newborn child."

"I'm not altogether surprised," said the girl, shame-
faced. "Another co-star of mine in the film was a red-haired

gentleman." After a pause, she said: "May I see my baby now?"

The nurse went out of the room and returned a minute later with the black, Asian, ginger-haired baby. She handed the baby to the young mother, who immediately turned it upside down and smacked it firmly on the butt. The baby cried and the mother held it back in her arms.

Shocked, the nurse demanded: "What did you do that for?"

The girl replied: "Sorry, but I had to check if it barked too."

❖ **My wife's birth control pills also prevent acne. Ironically, when I was a teenager, acne was my form of birth control.**

❖ A young man was nervously pacing up and down the waiting room outside the maternity ward of a hospital. Meanwhile a middle-aged man was calmly reading a magazine. Sensing that the older man was not a first-time father, the young man asked him: "How long after the baby is born can you have sex with the mother?"

The older man lifted his head from his magazine and answered: "It depends on whether she's in a public ward or a private ward."

66 In Spain, a sixty-seven-year-old woman gave birth to twins, making her the world's oldest mother. The mother and babies are doing fine, but the doctor is still nauseous.

Conan O'Brien 99

❖ Why don't the wives of bus drivers get pregnant?
Because bus drivers have a habit of pulling out unexpectedly.

❖   A father-to-be was attending a pre-natal class. The nurse asked him if he had ever been present at a childbirth before.

"Just the once," he replied.

"What was it like?"

"It was very dark, then suddenly very light."

> 66 I've always looked young for my age, which was a bit creepy at birth.
> Matt Kirshen 99

★   ★   ★   ★   ★

BIRTHDAYS

✳   Two married men were drinking in a bar. One said to the other: "I got my wife a bag and a belt for her birthday. She wasn't happy, but the Hoover works fine now."

✳   Tom's wife had been dropping none too subtle hints about what she wanted for her birthday. She told him: "Tomorrow morning, I expect to find a gift in the driveway that goes from 0 to 200 in under six seconds."

So he got up early the next day, wrapped her gift, and left it on the driveway. It was bathroom scales.

He is due out of hospital any day now.

✳   A husband went to a florist to buy a dozen red roses for his wife's birthday. However the guy behind the counter said: "I'm sorry, sir, this isn't a florist – it's a male clinic specializing in circumcisions and vasectomies."

The husband was mystified. "So why have you got all those flowers in the window?"

The guy behind the counter replied: "And what do you suggest we put in the window?"

> My husband wanted one of those big-screen TVs for his birthday. I just moved his chair closer to the one we already have.
>
> Wendy Liebman

* A man met his neighbour over the garden fence. "It's your Leanne's birthday today, isn't it?" said the neighbour. "Wish her happy birthday from me. How old is she?"

  "She's twelve. And do you know what she said to me this morning? She said: 'Dad, don't worry, I won't have sex for another four years.' I tell you, she gets more like her mother every day!"

* "What did you get your wife for her birthday?" asked a work colleague.

  "Actually I bought her a new fan. She was blown away."

* A boss gave his personal assistant an expensive leather dress as a birthday present. As she admired herself in the mirror, he said: "Your panties are coming down."

  Embarrassed, she quickly looked down to check. "No, they're not," she said.

  "They are," he said, "or the dress goes back to the shop!"

For her birthday, a wife told her husband that she wanted him to take her somewhere expensive. So he took her to the local gas station.

* A guy was talking to his friend in a bar. "You might find this hard to believe, but I once went twelve years without sex, drugs or alcohol."

  "Really?"

  "Yeah. But my God, my dad knew how to throw a good thirteenth birthday party!"

✳ Waking up on the eve of her birthday, a woman said to her husband: "I just had a dream that you gave me the most beautiful diamond necklace. What do you think it means?"

"You'll know tomorrow," he said with a smile.

The woman could hardly think of anything else all day, and couldn't wait for the following morning to arrive. As she sat up in bed on her birthday, her husband handed a beautifully wrapped small package.

She opened it excitedly to find a book entitled *The Meaning of Dreams*.

✳ Alan and Mike were chatting at the bar. Alan said: "I don't know what to get my wife for her birthday – she has everything, and besides, anything she wants she knows she can buy. So I'm really stuck for an idea."

Mike said: "You need to come up with something original. I know, why don't you make up a certificate saying she can have great sex for sixty minutes anyway she wants it? She'll probably be thrilled."

Alan decided to take his friend's advice. The next day at the bar, Mike said: "Well? How did it go? Did she like the suggestion?"

"Oh, yes," replied Alan. "She jumped up, thanked me, kissed me on the cheek and ran out the door, yelling: 'I'll be back in an hour!'"

✳ A man asked his wife what she wanted for her birthday. She said: "Something to run around in would be nice."

So he bought her a tracksuit.

✳ A wife said to her husband: "Even though we've been married for eighteen years, because it's your birthday, you can go out tonight and pretend that we're not married yet."

He said: "No thanks. I don't want to think I've got eighteen years of this ahead of me!"

★   ★   ★   ★   ★

BLONDES

★ The guests at a dinner party were arguing whether men or women were more trustworthy.

One man was particularly outspoken, insisting: "No woman can keep a secret."

"That's not true," said the pretty blonde sitting opposite him. "I've kept my age a secret since I was twenty-one."

"You'll let it slip some day," said the man.

"No way," said the blonde. "When a woman has kept a secret for twenty-six years, she can keep it forever."

★ How can you tell if a blonde has been using your lawnmower?

Your green "WELCOME" mat is ripped to shreds.

★ A blonde got on an airplane and sat down in the first-class section, but the flight attendant told her she had to move because she didn't have a first-class ticket.

However the blonde refused to move, stating: "I'm blonde, I'm smart and I have a good job and I'm staying in first-class until we reach Jamaica."

Next, the senior flight attendant tried to persuade her to move, but the blonde remained defiant, repeating: "I'm blonde, I'm smart and I have a good job and I'm staying in first-class until we reach Jamaica."

Desperate to get the rest of the passengers seated so that the plane could take off, the cabin crew sought the help of the co-pilot to deal with the stubborn blonde. The co-pilot calmly walked over to the blonde, whispered in her ear, and she immediately got up and went to her seat in the standard-class section.

Impressed, the senior flight attendant asked him what he had said to the blonde to persuade her to move. He replied: "I told her the front half of the airplane wasn't going to Jamaica."

★ A blonde thought she might be pregnant, so her boyfriend went out and bought her a pregnancy-testing kit. He said: "Now take this into the bathroom, do your business on it and see if it changes colour."

Five minutes later, he called out: "Has it turned blue yet?"

"No," said the blonde. "It's still brown."

★ Three blondes were riding in an elevator when the lights suddenly went out and the elevator ground to a halt between floors. They tried using their cell phones, but to no avail.

After three-quarters of an hour, one said: "I think the best way to call for help is by yelling together."

The others agreed, so they all took a deep breath and yelled: "Together, together, together."

★ Two blondes were trapped in a dark cave. "I can't see anything," said one. "Have you got a match?"

The second blonde struck the match against the wall of the cave but nothing happened. "That's odd," she said. "This match worked okay this morning."

★ A blonde asked a brunette: "What does inexplicable mean?"

The brunette said: "I can't explain."

The blonde stormed off in a huff, complaining: "Well I'm so sorry I asked!"

★ A police officer saw a blonde crying in the street. "What's happened, ma'am?" he asked.

She sobbed: "A thief has just stolen $50 that I had hidden inside my panties."

"Did you try to stop him?" said the officer.

The blonde replied: "I didn't know he was after my money!"

★ A blonde pulled her car alongside a truck and shouted: "Driver, you're losing your load!"

"Go away!" yelled the truck driver.

Three miles further down the road, the blonde again drew alongside the truck and yelled across to the driver: "You're definitely losing your load!"

"Go to hell!" exclaimed the truck driver impatiently.

Three miles further on, the blonde pulled alongside the truck once more and shouted: "I'm not joking, driver. You really are losing your load!"

"For the last time, get lost!" yelled the truck driver. "I'm gritting!"

★ A blonde went to the doctor and said: "Doctor, I accidentally spilt a bottle of shampoo down the plughole and ended up swallowing a little. Will I die?"

The doctor smiled: "Well, everyone is going to die eventually."

"Oh my God!" shrieked the blonde. "Everyone? What have I done?"

A blonde was asked if she wanted molasses in a restaurant. She declined, saying that she wouldn't eat any part of a mole.

★ A blonde went into a sex shop and asked for a vibrator. The shop manager said: "Choose any one from our range on the wall."

After studying them for a few moments, the blonde declared: "I'll take the red one."

The manager said: "That's a fire extinguisher."

★ A blonde and a brunette went into a cafe and ordered two cups of tea. After a few minutes, the blonde complained: "Why does my eye hurt every time I take a sip of tea?"

The brunette said: "Try taking the spoon out."

★ A blonde went to see an optician. He directed her to read various letters with the left eye while covering her right eye, but she became so confused about which eye was which that the optician, in despair, took a paper lunch bag with a hole to see through, covered up the appropriate eye and asked her to read the letters.

As he did so, he noticed that she had tears streaming down her face. "There's no need to be upset about getting glasses," he said.

"I know," she sobbed, "but I had my heart set on wire frames."

★ A blonde got a scarf for Christmas, but she took it back to the shop because it was too tight.

★ For their first wedding anniversary, a blonde decided to cook her husband a special meal. She told him to go and sit in the lounge and relax watching TV while she prepared dinner.

Forty-five minutes passed and he started to get hungry. He called through to the kitchen: "Is everything okay, honey?"

"Yes," she replied, sounding a little harassed. "It won't be long."

He thought it best not to interfere and sat down again in front of the TV.

Another hour passed, and he was starting to feel light-headed.

"Any idea when dinner will be ready, honey?" he called out.

"Any minute now," replied the blonde, still sounding frantic.

Another half-hour passed, and he could stand it no longer. He barged into the kitchen to find the room in a terrible mess and the dinner not yet even in the oven.

"What's going on?" he demanded.

"Sorry it's taken longer than I thought," the blonde replied breathlessly. "But I had to refill the pepper shaker."

"How could that take over two hours?" he asked.

"Well," she said, "it's not easy stuffing the pepper through those dumb little holes."

★ A blonde went to the doctor and said: "It's been a month since my last visit, but I'm not feeling any better."

"I see," said the doctor, "and did you follow the instructions on the medicine I gave you?"

"I sure did," replied the blonde. "The bottle said: 'Keep Tightly Closed'."

★ A blonde walked into a bar holding a lump of dog poop. "How lucky was that!" she said to the bartender. "I very nearly stepped in this!"

★ A Minnesota factory that makes the Tickle Me Elmo toys – the toy laughs when you tickle it under the arms – took on a new blonde employee. But on only the blonde's second day at work, the foreman complained to the human resources manager that she was so slow, she was holding up the entire production line.

The HR manager decided to investigate for himself, and so the two men went down to the factory floor. There, they saw the blonde surrounded by dozens of Tickle Me Elmos while her fellow workers waited impatiently. The blonde had a roll of plush red fabric and a huge bag of small marbles, and the HR manager and the foreman watched in amazement as she cut a piece of fabric, wrapped it around two marbles and carefully sewed the little package between each Elmo's legs.

The HR manager suddenly burst out laughing and told the blonde: "I'm sorry, but I think you misunderstood the instructions I gave you yesterday. Your job is to give Elmo two test tickles!"

★ A husband arrived home to find his blonde wife reading his diary. Hurling it to the floor, she yelled: "Right. You've got five seconds to tell me: who the hell are April, May and June?"

★ A blonde went to the hospital to donate blood. The nurse asked her: "What type are you?"

   The blonde replied: "I'm an outgoing cat-lover."

★ Did you hear about the blonde *Friends* fan who tried to make her Internet password "JoeyChandlerRossRachelMonica" because she read it had to have at least five characters?

★ A blonde teenager went for a job interview at a major retail store. The woman conducting the interview said: "I see from your application form that under 'previous employment' you have put 'babysitter'. Would you mind telling me what your reason for leaving was?"

   "Yes," replied the blonde. "They came home."

★ A blonde rushed into a hospital emergency room late one night with the tip of her index finger shot off.

   "How did this happen?" asked the doctor.

   "I was trying to commit suicide," replied the blonde.

   "What?" gasped the doctor in disbelief. "You tried to commit suicide by shooting your finger off?"

   "No, silly!" smiled the blonde. "First I put the gun to my chest, and I thought: I just paid $5,000 for these breast implants, I'm not shooting myself in the chest."

   "So then what?"

   "Then I put the gun in my mouth, and I thought: I just paid $3,000 to get my teeth straightened, I'm not shooting myself in the mouth."

   "So what did you do?"

   "Then I put the gun to my ear, and I thought: this is going to make a really loud noise. So I put my finger in the other ear before I pulled the trigger."

★ A blonde was walking down the street when a car pulled up alongside her and the driver leaned over and asked: "Is there a B&Q in Northampton?"

   "Don't ask me," said the blonde. "I can't spell."

★ A brunette and a blonde were sitting in their office. The brunette said: "I see Christmas Day is on a Friday this year."

   The blonde said: "Well I hope it's not the thirteenth."

★ A blonde had grown sick of continually being labelled a dumb blonde. So she went to the hairdresser's to buy a brunette wig.

   "How much is this wig?" she asked the sales assistant.

   "A hundred and ten dollars plus tax."

   "Forget the tax," said the blonde, "I'll use glue."

★ A blonde, a brunette and a redhead took part in a swimming race across the English Channel to France. The brunette was first to arrive in Calais, the redhead came second, but the blonde was nowhere to be seen. Asked later why she didn't finish, the blonde explained: "I swam halfway but then I got really tired, so I swam back to England."

★ What's the definition of paralysis?
   Four blondes at a crossroads.

★ A blonde went to the doctor to complain of a sore throat. The doctor sat her down, got out his flashlight and said: "Open wide."

   "I can't," replied the blonde. "The arms on this chair get in my way."

★ A guy in an office saw a blonde standing next to a fax machine crying her eyes out.

   "What's wrong?" he asked.

   "It's this machine!" she wailed. "I can't get it to send a fax."

   Patiently he showed her how to do it and the sheet of paper was sent through successfully.

   "There!" he said. "There's nothing to it really."

   But when she lifted the lid and saw the piece of paper, she started crying again. "It hasn't worked at all! It's still there!"

★ A blonde went to check the mail that had just been delivered through her letterbox but immediately started wailing to her flatmate.

"What's the matter?" asked the flatmate.

The blonde cried: "There's a letter for me marked 'Do Not Bend'."

"So? What's the problem?"

"Well, how am I supposed to pick it up?"

★ In search of a Christmas tree, two blondes ventured deep into a Scandinavian forest. After hours of braving sub-zero temperatures and a biting wind, one blonde turned to the other wearily and said: "I'm chopping down the next tree I see. I don't care if it's decorated or not."

★ How did the blonde try to kill the fish?
By drowning it.

★ A flying saucer landed at a gas station on a lonely country road in New Mexico. The letters "UFO" were emblazoned in big letters on the side of the craft. Two bug-eyed aliens stepped out and while the gas station manager stood paralysed with shock, his young blonde assistant nonchalantly filled up the tank and waved to the aliens as they took off again.

As they disappeared into the sky, the station manager turned to the blonde and said: "Don't you realize what just happened?"

"Yeah," replied the blonde. "So what?"

"Didn't you see those two?" persisted the manager.

"Yeah," said the blonde, shrugging her shoulders. "So what?"

"But didn't you see the letters 'UFO' on the side of that vehicle?"

"Yeah. So what?"

"Don't you know what UFO stands for?"

The blonde rolled her eyes. "'Course I do, I've been working here five years. UFO stands for 'Unleaded Fuel Only'."

★   What do you call twenty blondes sitting in a circle?
    A dope ring.

★   Two blondes were away on an adventure weekend. The archery and rifle activities had passed off without incident but during the hunting expedition the pair became hopelessly lost. They were unable to get a signal on their cell phones and all their cries for help remained unanswered. So they sat down forlornly and discussed what to do next.

    Then, eyeing the weaponry, one said: "Didn't the guide say that we should shoot into the air to summon help if we got lost?"

    "You're right," said the other blonde and she grabbed the bag containing the weapons.

    But after another three hours and thirteen shots, still no one came.

    "Do you think anyone will find us?" asked the first blonde dejectedly.

    "I hope so," said the other. "We've only got two arrows left."

> Did you hear about the blonde who thought the world's most prolific inventor was an Irishman named Pat Pending?

★   Why did the blonde drive into a ditch?
    To turn the blinker off.

★   Two blondes were in a parking lot trying to unlock the door of their Mercedes with a coat hanger.

    One blonde complained: "I just can't seem to get this door unlocked."

    "Well, you'd better hurry up and try harder," urged the other blonde, "because it's starting to rain and the top is down."

★   How did the blonde know she'd been sleepwalking?
    She kept waking up in her own bed.

⭑ A movie at the cinema had just started when a blonde from the middle of the row suddenly stood up and said she needed to go. Everyone muttered their disapproval about having to stand up to let the blonde out and she apologized profusely as she clambered over people's legs and bags.

When she finally reached the end of the row, the guy in the last seat complained: "Couldn't you have done this earlier?"

"Sorry but no," said the blonde. "The 'Turn Off Your Cell Phone, Please' message only just flashed up on screen."

The man was mystified. "So why did you need to get up?"

The blonde said: "Because mine is in the car."

⭑ ## How can you tell which tricycle belongs to the blonde?
It's the one with the kickstand.

⭑ A boy was knocked out during a college football game. Immediately his blonde mom ran on to the field, grabbed his hand and said: "Son, can you hear me? Squeeze once for yes and twice for no."

⭑ Two all-female phone crews – one brunette, the other blonde – were putting up telephone poles in a Midwest town. At the end of the day, the company foreman asked the brunettes how many poles they had put in the ground.

"Eighteen," answered the leader of the brunettes proudly.

"That's pretty good," said the foreman. He then asked the blonde crew how many poles they had put in.

"Three," replied the leader of the blondes.

"Is that all?" yelled the foreman. "The others did eighteen. How come you only managed three?"

"Yes," said the leader of the blondes defiantly, "but look at how much they left sticking out of the ground."

★ Two blondes walked into a building – you'd think at least one of them would have seen it.

★ What do you call a brunette in a room full of blondes? Invisible.

★ The new blonde secretary asked her boss: "That letter you asked me to type double spaced, do you want the carbon copy double spaced as well?"

★ What's a blonde's favourite nursery rhyme? Humpme Dumpme.

★   ★   ★   ★   ★

BOOKS

❖ For several days, a husband was engrossed in a book on assertion entitled *Be the Man of Your House*. When he had finished it, he announced grandly to his wife: "From now on, things are going to be different around here. You will do exactly as I say; my every wish is your command. Tonight you will prepare me a gourmet meal and wash all of the dishes afterwards. When you have tidied up, we will have the kind of sex that I want. Then you will bathe me as I relax, towel me dry and massage my feet and back. And tomorrow, guess who will dress me and comb my hair?"

The wife replied caustically: "The funeral director would be my first guess."

> 66 My girlfriend got me this book on feng shui, but I didn't know where in my home to put it.
>
> Irwin Barker 99

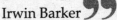

❖   Why did the surgeon rush out of the book signing?
    There was a problem with the appendix.

❖   A man went into a library and asked to borrow a book on
    suicide.
    "No way," said the librarian. "You won't bring it back."

> 66 A bit of advice: never read a pop-up
> book about giraffes.
>
> Sean Lock 99

❖   Eager to improve her computer skills, a woman borrowed
    a series of educational books from her local library over a
    period of a couple of months.
    Eventually the librarian remarked: "You must be getting
    really knowledgeable about computers by now."
    "Thanks," she replied. "What makes you say that?"
    "Well," said the librarian, "only one of the books you're
    taking out this week has 'For Dummies' in the title."

> 66 I bought a book on reincarnation
> yesterday. It was quite expensive, but I
> thought, 'You only live once.'
>
> Tim Vine 99

❖   A man went into a bookstore and complained: "I bought
    this book from you last week – *Cowards in History* – and all
    the pages fell out."
    The sales assistant said: "That's because it's got no
    spine."

> 66 I just found out we have a local library.
> They kept that quiet.
>
> Jack Dee 99

❖ While crossing a road, a man was knocked down by a mobile library van. As the man lay on the ground screaming in agony, the van driver went over to him and said: "Sssshhh!"

❖ Why did Miss Havisham no longer have Great Expectations of Nicholas Nickleby?
Because she saw his Little Dorrit.

❖ A female university librarian was suspended for having an inappropriate relationship with two male students. Now the kids are worried because the librarian is two weeks' overdue.

> ❝ My friend said you have to read this book, it's a page turner. Well, yes, I know how books work.
> Jimmy Carr ❞

❖ **A man walked into a bookbinding class. The teacher said: "Come in. Make yourself a tome."**

❖ A man wanted to carry out some home improvement. So he went to the library and asked the librarian if she had any books on shelves.

> ❝ I was in a bookstore the other day, and there was a third off all titles. I bought *The Lion, The Witch*.
> Jimmy Carr ❞

★　★　★　★　★

GEORGE W. BUSH

* In his last months as President, George W. Bush began to develop delusions of grandeur. He called in Vice-President Dick Cheney and announced: "Dick, I think I need a new title to reflect my position as leader of the free world. I'm going to call myself King."

  "You can't," said Cheney. "You don't have a kingdom."

  "Okay then," said Bush. "How about Emperor?"

  "Nope. You don't have an empire."

  "Maybe Prince?"

  "No. America isn't a principality."

  "Duke?"

  "No, it's not a duchy either."

  By now Bush was becoming exasperated. "So do you have any better ideas?" he demanded.

  Dick Cheney smiled. "It's obvious, George. You run a country."

> 66 Bush appeared at the Republican convention live via satellite, or as Bush calls it, 'Live via magic.'
>
> Conan O'Brien 99

* One day a small boy yelled out in public: "George W. Bush is the biggest asshole in the entire history of mankind!"

  A police officer overheard this outburst and immediately had the boy thrown into the county jail for two years. When he was finally released, the boy asked the officer why he had been jailed for so long.

  "I gave you one month for insulting the former President of the United States," said the officer, "and the other twenty-three months was for relaying confidential information."

* What do you get when you combine George W. Bush with O_2?

  An oxymoron.

> George Bush has gone. Well, he hasn't actually gone. He's still trapped inside the White House, tragically pushing on a door marked 'Pull'.
>
> Jonathan Ross

* George W. Bush arrived in Beijing for the 2008 Olympics. When a reporter asked him if he liked the decathlon, he said he preferred regular coffee.

> People say, 'Can you really imagine the United States of America having a black President?' And I say, 'Why not? We just had a retarded one.'
>
> Chris Rock

* Laura Bush said to Dubya: "We have the weekend free, darling. What would you like to do?"
    "Well now," he said. "Let's think . . ."
    "No," said Laura. "Let's do something you can do, too."

> Bush said he is leaving Washington with his head held high, because it is the best way to spot shoes that are coming at you.
>
> Jay Leno

* Shortly before the end of his term in office in 2009, George W. Bush was asked what he thought of the credit crunch. He replied: "It's my favourite candy bar."

* On his first-ever visit to a library, Bush asked for a book on the Iraq War. "No way," said the librarian. "You won't be able to finish it."

* Now that he is no longer in office, Bush has been asked to write his autobiography. His initial reaction was: "I don't really know much about cars."

> 66 If you think about it, Bush is at least partly responsible for us having our first black President, so never let it be said he didn't accomplish anything.
>
> Jimmy Kimmel 99

* Bush senior said to his son: "I made the same mistake with your mother that you did in Iraq – I didn't pull out in time."

* Which three little words do Americans like to hear the most?
    "Former President Bush".

* On a visit to Algeria, Bush was invited to address the nation. He began: "First of all I must apologize for speaking to you in English. I would love to address you in your native language but I'm afraid I was never very good at algebra."

> 66 Bush admitted – and it takes a big man to do this – that a couple of things didn't go according to plan. A couple of things went haywire: his first term and his second term. Those two things.
>
> David Letterman 99

* * * * *

CANNIBALS

★ A cannibal family had run out of tourists to eat and were forced to turn on each other in order to survive. At a formal family meeting, they decided that the father should be sacrificed first, partly because he was the oldest but also because there was enough meat on him to feed the wife and children for the rest of the week.

So they boiled him in a pot and started carving him up. For lunch on the first day, the children ate his ears and cheeks while their mother cooked his tongue. "Whatever you do," she told them, "don't let me forget to add salt to my dish."

But being kids they did forget and it was not until she took the first bite out of the tongue that she remembered the missing ingredient. "I knew I'd forget the condiment," she said.

"Why is it so important?" they asked.

"Because," she explained, "I have always made it a rule in life to take whatever comes out of your father's mouth with a pinch of salt."

Did you hear about the cannibal who was expelled from school for buttering up his teacher?

★ What is the most disappointing thing to a cannibal parent?
A spoiled child.

★ A cannibal son and his father were standing on a street corner looking for food. The son spotted a particularly plump woman, but the father said: "No, too fatty."

Then the son suggested a size zero model. "No, not enough meat on her," said the father.

Finally the son pointed out a very attractive woman. "Hmmm," said the father, licking his lips, "I think I'll take her home and eat your mother."

★ A cannibal king in a remote jungle territory had developed a particular taste for missionaries. Somehow their meat always tasted sweeter. Furthermore, he was an authority on good food, for there was nothing he enjoyed more than sitting down to a sumptuous banquet.

On one particular evening he was tucking in heartily to a huge platter of thinly sliced missionary. It was easy to see why he weighed over twenty-six stone. Whilst his people were happy to see the king enjoying himself – for he had a ferocious temper when roused – they were hoping that there would be a few scraps left over for them. For whereas the king was big and round, his subjects were thin from near-starvation. So with each slice of meat that he devoured, their hearts sank a little. It was beginning to look as if there would be nothing left.

The natives began to mutter amongst themselves. "It doesn't look good," said the cannibal underling who had killed the missionary in the first place. "He is going to eat the lot! It's always the same when we bring him back one of these religious types."

"He certainly has a liking for these men of God," agreed a fellow cannibal. "There's obviously something about their delicate skin."

"Well, it's just not fair," said the first subject, becoming increasingly angry. "It's about time we followed the example of the Mambawamba tribe across the river and refused to hunt until the king shows us more consideration and allows us a fair helping of his missionary meals."

"You mean," queried his fellow cannibal, "that we should ask him to implement some kind of prophet-sharing scheme?"

★ A cannibal returned from a family vacation with part of his leg missing.

"How was your holiday?" asked his friends.

"It was great," said the cannibal.

"Hey, but why is part of your leg missing?"

"Oh," said the cannibal, "we went self-catering."

＊ Two cannibals stumbled across a missionary in the jungle. After killing him, they decided to divide the body up evenly. The first cannibal said: "I'll start at the head, you start at the feet, and we'll meet in the middle."

So the two began to devour the missionary. After a while, the first cannibal called out: "How's it going down there?"

"I'm having a ball," replied the second cannibal.

"No!" shouted the first cannibal. "You're eating too fast!"

★ Why did the cannibal eat the tightrope walker?

He wanted a balanced meal.

＊   ＊   ＊   ＊   ＊

CATS

❖ Two female cats were sitting on a fence when a good-looking male cat walked past.

"Hey," purred one, "I wouldn't mind sharing a dead mouse with him!"

"Forget it," said her friend. "I went out with him once and all he did was talk about his operation."

> " Cats have a scam going – you buy the food, they eat the food, they go away; that's the deal.
>
> Eddie Izzard "

❖ A mother told her little boy: "Stop pulling the cat's tail!"

"I'm not," he protested. "I'm just holding it. The cat's doing the pulling."

Cat Commandments

Thou shalt not jump onto the keyboard while thy human is using the computer.

Thou shalt not pull the phone cord out of the back of the modem.

Thou shalt not sit in front of the television or monitor as thou art not transparent.

Thou shalt not walk in on a dinner party and start licking thy butt.

Thou shalt not lie down with thy butt in thy human's face.

Thou shalt not use thy human's legs as a climbing frame.

Thou shalt not pee over the side of thy litter tray.

Thou shalt not play with the Christmas tree decorations.

Thou shalt not unroll all of the toilet paper off the roll.

Thou shalt not hide dead mice behind radiators.

Thou shalt not leap from great heights onto thy human's lap.

Thou shalt not steal food from thy human's dinner plate while his back is momentarily turned.

Thou shalt not trip any humans even if they are walking too slowly.

Thou shalt not push open the bathroom door when there are guests in the house.

Thou shalt not secretly use thy human's shoes as a storage place for furballs.

Thou shalt not climb on garbage cans with hinged lids, as thou wilt fall in and trap thyself.

Thou shalt not breathe cat food breath in thy human's face.

Thou shalt not sit on thy human's pillow immediately after using thy litter tray.

Thou shalt not reset thy human's alarm clock by walking on it.

Thou shalt not climb curtains.

Thou shalt not jump onto a seat just as thy human is sitting down.

Thou shalt show remorse when being scolded.

❖ A tomcat was running all over the neighbourhood, down alleys, up fire escapes, into deserted buildings and down into cellars. Eventually a neighbour became so concerned that he called on the cat's owner.

"Your cat has been going crazy," said the neighbour. "He's been rushing around like mad."

"I know," said the owner. "He's just been neutered, and he's running around cancelling engagements."

> Cats are smarter than dogs. You can't get eight cats to pull a sled through snow.
>
> Jeff Valdez

❖ A man hated his wife's cat so much that he decided to get rid of it by driving it twenty blocks from home and dumping it. But as he got back home, he saw the cat strolling up the driveway.

So he drove the cat forty blocks away and dumped it. But when he arrived back home, there was the cat waiting for him at the front door.

In desperation, he finally drove the cat fifty miles out into the country and dumped it in the middle of a wood.

Four hours later his wife took a phone call at home. It was from her husband. "Darling," he said, "is the cat there?"

"Yes," said the wife. "Why?"

"Just put him on the line, will you? I need directions."

❖ A woman was out in her yard one afternoon when an elderly cat approached her. She stroked the cat, and it followed her indoors, where it proceeded to curl up on the most comfortable chair and fall asleep. Two hours later, the cat went to the door and the woman let it out.

The same thing happened the following day, and continued on and off for several weeks.

By then the woman was curious as to who owned the cat, and so she attached a note to its collar. The note read: "I would like to know who owns this lovely old cat and ask if you are aware that most afternoons your cat comes to my house for a nap."

The next day the cat arrived for its daily nap with a different note attached to its collar. It read: "He lives in a home with six children – two under the age of three. He's trying to catch up on his sleep. Can I come with him tomorrow?"

❖ A newly discovered chapter in the Book of Genesis has finally provided the answer to the eternal question: "Where do pets come from?"

Adam said: "Lord, when I was in the garden, you walked with me every day. Now I no longer see you. I am lonely here and it is difficult for me to remember how much you love me."

And God said: "No problem! I will create a companion

for you who will be with you forever and who will be a reflection of my love for you, so that you will love me even when you cannot see me. Regardless of how selfish, childish or unlovable you may be, this new companion will accept you as you are and will love you as I do, in spite of yourself."

And God created a new animal to be a companion for Adam. And it was a good animal. And God was pleased. And the new animal was pleased to be with Adam and he wagged his tail. And Adam said: "Lord, I have already named all the animals in the kingdom and I cannot think of a new name for this animal."

And God said: "No problem, because I have created this new animal to be a reflection of my love for you. Therefore his name will be a reflection of my own name, and I will call him Dog."

And Dog lived with Adam and was a companion to him and loved him.

And Adam was comforted.

And God was pleased.

And Dog was content and wagged his tail.

Soon it came to pass that Adam's guardian angel came to the Lord and said: "Lord, Adam has become filled with pride. He struts and preens like a peacock and believes he is worthy of adoration. Dog has indeed taught him that he is loved, but perhaps too well."

And the Lord said: "No problem! I will create for him a companion who will be with him forever and who will see him as he is. The companion will remind him of his limitations, so he will know that he is not always worthy of adoration."

And God created Cat to be a companion to Adam. And Cat would not obey Adam.

And when Adam gazed into Cat's eyes, he was reminded that he was not the Supreme Being. And Adam learned humility.

And God was pleased.

And Adam was pleased.

And the Dog was pleased.

And the Cat didn't give a damn one way or the other.

Feline Physics Laws

Law of Cat Inertia: A cat at rest will remain at rest unless acted upon by some outside force, such as a scurrying mouse or the opening of a tin of cat food.

Law of Cat Motion: A cat will move in a straight line unless there is a really good reason to change direction.

Law of Cat Sleeping: All cats must sleep with humans whenever possible, in the most uncomfortable position for the human and the most comfortable for the cat.

Law of Cat Elongation: A cat can make its body long enough to reach any counter top that has anything remotely edible on it.

Law of Energy Conservation: Cats know that energy can neither be created nor destroyed, and so they use as little energy as possible.

Law of Refrigerator Observation: If a cat watches a refrigerator long enough, someone will eventually come along and take out something worth eating.

❖ A man was sulking because Tiddles the family Persian Blue had eaten the ham-like cold meat that he was intending to have for his tea.

"What's the matter?" asked his wife. "Cat got your tongue?"

❖ While a little boy was away at school, his cat died. Worried about how he would take the news when he got home, his mother consoled him and said: "Don't worry, darling. Tiger is in Heaven with God now."

The boy looked at her and said: "What's God gonna do with a dead cat?"

Law of Cat Thermodynamics: Heat flows from a warmer to a cooler body, except in the case of a cat where all heat flows to the cat.

Law of Cat Stretching: A cat will stretch to a distance proportionate to the nap just taken.

Law of Electric Blanket Attraction: Turn on an electric blanket and a cat will jump onto the bed at the speed of light.

Law of Random Comfort Seeking: A cat will always seek – and usually take over – the most comfortable spot in any room.

Law of Obedience Resistance: A cat's resistance varies in proportion to a human's desire for it to do something.

Law of Cat Obstruction: A cat must lie on the floor in such a position as to obstruct the maximum amount of human foot traffic.

Law of Furniture Replacement: A cat's desire to scratch furniture is directly proportional to the cost of the furniture.

❖ A man was being driven crazy by his neighbour's cat. It kept him awake at night, left a mess on his driveway and dug up his plants. But worst of all, it peed on his prize tomatoes the night before the local fruit and vegetable show. The man burst into tears at the sight of his shrivelled specimens and vowed revenge on the cat.

So the next day, he killed the cat, cooked it and had it for dinner. But that evening he suffered such bad indigestion that he had to call out the doctor.

The doctor examined him and concluded: "It's nothing serious. I think you've just eaten something that's upset you."

❖ What's the difference between cats and dogs?
Dogs have owners, cats have staff.

> My friend Steve likes cats. People are always saying, 'Oh, Steve's really a cat person.' No he's not. If Steve were a cat person, it'd be, like, 'Hey, Steve never goes in the pool.'
>
> Demetri Martin

❖ What happened when the cat swallowed a coin?
There was some money in the kitty.

★   ★   ★   ★   ★

CELEBRITIES

★ Lindsay Lohan walked into a bank to withdraw some money. The bank clerk asked: "Can you identify yourself?"
Lindsay opened her handbag, looked in a mirror and said: "Yes, it's definitely me."

> Heard a report about Lindsay Lohan getting busted with coke in her car. That's a story? Call me when they find a book in her car.
>
> Dave Attell

> I can't believe Amy Winehouse self-harms. She's so irritating she must be able to find someone to do it for her.
>
> Zoe Lyons

✳ Anne Robinson, the Queen of Mean, went into a large store to buy a new enamel wash basin for her kitchen. Naturally, she wanted only the best, and insisted that the young sales assistant fill all three basins on display with water to test their efficiency. "And I want you to put a bucket beneath each one," she ordered, "so that I can make sure that you are not the only unwanted drip around here!"

The assistant dutifully obeyed, and Anne waited ten minutes before walking along the line to inspect the buckets with a view to deciding which basin to buy.

The bucket below the first basin was completely dry. Anne nodded approvingly. The second also showed no trace of water. "Good," muttered Anne. However, when she looked into the third bucket, there was nearly half an inch of water. "Oh dear," said Anne, looking at the basin accusingly. "Who is not up to the job? Who has no place in my kitchen? You are the leakiest sink. Goodbye."

Later that day, Anne went to a furrier's and, not one to be cowed by public opinion, announced that she wanted to buy a fur coat. "But I don't just want any fur coat," she told the store manager, "I want the most expensive you have."

"Certainly, madam," said the manager, producing five luxurious fur coats and laying them out on a large table for Anne to inspect.

"Would madam like to try them on?" he asked.

"All in good time," replied Anne. "But first I want to check the price tags."

"I can save you the trouble," said the manager. "The first four fur coats are all $6,500 and the fifth is $5,999."

"Oh dear," said Anne, examining the fifth coat. "Who is all fur coat and no knickers? Who would look more at home in a car boot sale? You are the cheapest mink. Goodbye."

> ❝ Apparently the guards put sperm in Paris Hilton's porridge when she was in prison. That's got to be horrible for her. 'Ugh! There's porridge in this!'
> Frankie Boyle ❞

★ A woman went into a tattoo parlour and asked the artist to tattoo a picture of Johnny Depp on her right upper thigh and Brad Pitt on her left upper thigh. The artist did so, and when he had finished he handed her a mirror so she could inspect the work.

She looked at the right thigh and said: "Wow! That's definitely Johnny Depp. Just look at those eyes." Then she examined her left thigh but complained: "That doesn't look like Brad Pitt."

The artist disagreed and suggested they settle the argument by seeking the opinion of an impartial judge. So they went to the bar next door and asked an elderly guy to identify the tattoos. The woman raised her skirt and dropped her panties, and the old man put his face up close. "Well, ma'am," he concluded, "the one on your right thigh is definitely Johnny Depp. You can tell by the eyes and the cheek bones. The one on your left I'm not sure about – but the one in the middle is definitely Willie Nelson."

> 66 Nicole Kidman is pregnant. Isn't that lovely? And here's the great news – she still has the little bed Tom used to sleep in.
> Craig Ferguson 99

✳ What's the difference between Paris Hilton and the *Titanic*? Fewer people went down on the *Titanic*.

> 66 Kirstie Alley says that she makes her new boyfriends wait six months before having sex with them. Of course, some of them insist on twelve months.
> Conan O'Brien 99

★ The Olympic opening ceremony featured representatives from 205 countries. Or, as Angelina Jolie calls it, one-stop shopping.

★ **Amy Winehouse was disappointed when it was explained to her that she had won five Grammys and not five grammes.**

★ Appearing on a TV chat show, Sean Connery boasted that despite his advanced years, he could still manage sex three times a night. Paris Hilton was a guest on the same show, and afterwards she made a beeline for Sean in the green room.

"I hope I'm not being too forward," she gushed, "but I've always had a thing about older men. I'd love to test your sexual prowess tonight. Would you like to come back to my place?"

So they went back to her house and had great sex. Afterwards Sean said: "If you think that was good, let me sleep for half an hour, and then we'll have even better sex. But while I'm sleeping, hold my balls in your left hand and my dick in your right hand."

Paris was a bit puzzled by the request, but agreed to go along with it. Half an hour later, he woke up and, as promised, they had even better sex.

Sean said: "Paris, my dear, that was wonderful. But if you let me sleep for an hour, we can have the best sex yet. But again while I'm sleeping, hold my balls in your left hand and my dick in your right hand."

Paris did as he asked, and when he woke up an hour later, they had truly fantastic sex.

As she basked in the afterglow, Paris turned to Sean and said: "Tell me, does holding your balls in my left hand and your dick in my right hand stimulate you while you're sleeping?"

"No," said Sean. "But the last time I had a one-night stand, the bitch stole my wallet."

> ❝ Sir Bob Geldof called his daughter silly, thoughtless and immature . . . before settling on Peaches.
>
> Jimmy Carr ❞

★   Amy Winehouse went to the Glastonbury Festival. Poor Amy had to wade through dirt, needles, rubbish and people lying around everywhere . . . just to get out of her flat.

★   A guy walked into a bar, and the bartender said: "Go on, Jed, tell them the Elvis Presley knock knock joke."

   "What's the Elvis Presley knock knock joke?" asked one of the regulars.

   Jed said: "Knock knock."

   "Who's there?"

   "Wurlitzer."

   "Wurlitzer who?"

   "Wurlitzer one for the money, two for the show . . ."

★   Why doesn't Amy Winehouse hide her syringe in her hair when she's on stage?

   Because it's like trying to find a needle in a haystack.

Jesus vs. Elvis

Jesus said: "Love Thy Neighbour." (Matthew 22:39)
Elvis said: "Don't Be Cruel." (RCA, 1956)

Jesus said: "Man shall not live by bread alone."
Elvis loved sandwiches with peanut butter and bananas.

Jesus is the Lord's shepherd.
Elvis dated Cybill Shepherd.

Jesus walked on water. (Matthew 14:25)
Elvis surfed. (*Blue Hawaii*, 1965)

Jesus lived in a state of grace in a near Eastern land.
Elvis lived in Graceland in a nearly eastern state.

Jesus was part of a trinity.
Elvis's first band was a trio.

66 Tom Cruise has got a creepy marriage, hasn't he? I reckon if you got invited round to his house for a dinner party, Katie Holmes would write 'Get help' in the peas.

Frankie Boyle 99

★ I wanted to follow in Tom Cruise's footsteps. But the judge called it stalking.

★ A little boy asked his father: "Is God a man or a woman?"
"Both," answered the father.
The child then asked: "And is God black or white?"
"Both," said the father.
The boy took in the information, thought for a moment, and then said: "Is God Michael Jackson?"

An important woman in Jesus's life, Mary, had an immaculate conception.
An important woman in Elvis's life, Priscilla, went to the Immaculate Conception Cathedral High School, Memphis, Tennessee.

Jesus's entourage, the Apostles, had twelve members.
Elvis's entourage, the Memphis Mafia, had twelve members.

Jesus was the Lamb of God.
Elvis had mutton chops.

Jesus's father is everywhere.
Elvis's father was a drifter and moved around quite a bit.

"Then they took up stones to cast at (Jesus)." (John 8:59)
Elvis was often stoned.

> 66 Thank God the Spice Girls reunion is over. The only way I want to see Geri Halliwell draped in a Union Jack again is if she dies in battle.
>
> Frankie Boyle 99

★　　★　　★　　★　　★

CHILDREN

❖ Little Johnny and his dad were walking through the park one day when Johnny noticed two dogs humping.

"What are those two dogs doing, Dad?" asked Johnny.

"They're making puppies," replied his father.

That evening at home, Johnny was awoken by noises coming from his parents' bedroom. He went to investigate and caught them having sex.

"What are you doing?" he asked.

His father replied: "We're making you a little brother or sister."

"Well, can you flip her over?" said Johnny. "Because I'd rather have a puppy."

❖ A father was trying to combine putting up some shelves with playing with his three-year-old daughter. At one point, she exclaimed excitedly: "Daddy, look at this!" and stuck out two of her fingers.

To keep her entertained, he playfully grabbed the fingers, put them in his mouth and said: "Daddy's gonna eat your fingers!" She shrieked with laughter, and he ran from the room.

When he returned moments later, the laughter had stopped. Instead she was looking glum.

"What's the matter, darling?" he asked.

She said: "Daddy, where's my booger?"

❖ A small boy came running out of the bathroom in tears.

"What's the matter, son?" asked his father.

"I dropped my toothbrush in the toilet."

"Okay, don't worry, but we'd better throw it out."

So the father fished the toothbrush out of the toilet and put it in the garbage. When he returned, the boy was holding another toothbrush.

"Isn't that my toothbrush?" asked the father.

"Yes," said the boy, "and we'd better throw this one out, too, because it fell in the toilet four days ago."

> 66 When I was a child, I asked my mum: 'What's a couple?' She said: 'Two or three.' Which probably explains why her marriage collapsed.
>
> Josie Long 99

❖ A father watched his young daughter playing in the garden, and smiled as he reflected on how sweet and pure the little girl was. Tears formed as he thought about her seeing the wonders of nature through such innocent eyes. Suddenly she just stopped and stared intently at the ground, so he went over to see what work of God had captured her attention. He found that she was watching two crane flies mating.

"Daddy, what are those two insects doing?" she asked.

"They're mating," replied her father.

"What do you call the insect on top?"

"That's a Daddy Longlegs."

"So the other one is a Mummy Longlegs?" suggested the little girl.

His heart soaring with the joy of such a cute and innocent question, he replied: "No, darling. Both of them are Daddy Longlegs."

Looking puzzled, the little girl thought for a moment, then lifted her foot and stamped the two insects flat, saying firmly: "We're not having any of that poofter shit in our garden!"

❖ A small boy turned to his Aunt Mildred and said: "My God, you're ugly!"

His mother overheard the remark and was appalled. She took him to one side and gave him a real telling-off before ordering him to go back and say sorry to Aunt Mildred.

Suitably chastened, the boy went over and said quietly: "Aunt Mildred, I'm sorry you're ugly."

❖ A small boy came home from school with a sofa slung across his back and armchairs under his arms. His father said angrily: "I told you not to accept suites from strangers."

❖ I've just found out I've got a three-year-old daughter. My wife says I need to be a bit more attentive around the house.

❖ A three-year-old boy was examining his testicles while taking a bath. "Mom," he asked, "are these my brains?"

"Not yet," she replied.

❖ A young boy was told by one of his friends that most adults are hiding at least one dark secret, and that this makes it very easy to blackmail them simply by saying: "I know the whole truth."

The boy decided to go home and put the theory into practice. Greeted by his mother, he announced: "I know the whole truth." She quickly handed him $20 and said: "Please don't tell your father."

Delighted with the result, the boy waited for his father to arrive home from work. Then he greeted him with: "I know the whole truth." The father promptly handed him $50 and said: "Please don't say a word to your mother."

Overjoyed with the profit he had made, the boy was on his way to school the next morning when he saw the mailman at the front door. Deciding to try out the plan again just for fun, he said to the mailman: "I know the whole truth."

The mailman immediately dropped his pile of letters, spread his arms wide and said: "Then come and give your father a big hug."

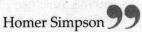

> **❝** Children are our future. Unless we stop them now.
>
> Homer Simpson **❞**

❖ A mother walked past her young son's room and saw him masturbating. Disturbed by what she had witnessed, she decided to have a gentle talk with him and told him that good little boys save it until they are married.

A few weeks later, she asked him: "How are you doing with that little problem we talked about?"

"Great," he answered. "So far I've saved nearly a quart!"

> **❝** I've sponsored a child in Africa. She's got a Jimmy Carr T-shirt, a Jimmy Carr hat. But I worry whether it's making any real difference, you know. I'm not getting any more bookings.
>
> Jimmy Carr **❞**

❖ With his wife out for the evening, a father was trying to watch the TV, but his young son kept coming in and asking for a glass of water.

After the seventh glass, the father lost his temper and yelled: "Go to sleep, I'm watching TV."

"But Dad," the boy protested, "my room's still on fire!"

❖ When his son asked for a lift in the car just to get to the end of their road, his father told him: "You should be ashamed. When Abraham Lincoln was your age, he used to walk ten miles every day to get to school."

"Really?" said the boy. "Well, when he was your age, he was president!"

> At the age of six I was left an orphan. What kind of idiot gives an orphan to a six-year-old?

❖ Little Johnny came into the house for dinner after playing with his little friend Wendy. His parents asked him what he had been doing all afternoon.

He said: "I played football for a while and then I proposed to Wendy."

His parents thought that was really sweet and, not wishing to make fun of him, went along with the idea. His father said: "But, Johnny, you know being married is an expensive business. How are you going to manage?"

"Well," said Johnny, "with the $5 I get each week from you and the $3 she gets from her mom and dad, we should be okay. I can always get a paper round."

Stifling a smile, his mother said: "That's all very well, darling. But how will you and Wendy manage if you have a baby?"

"Well," said Johnny, "so far – touch wood – we've been lucky."

> ❝ I don't like the girl scouts. I can't trust an adolescent female paramilitary organization that sells highly addictive baked goods.
>
> John Maclain ❞

❖ Little Johnny went over to Billy's house and rang the bell. Billy's mother answered the door.

Little Johnny said: "Can Billy come and play war in the street with his friends?"

Billy's mother replied: "You know Billy doesn't have any arms or legs."

"I know," said little Johnny, "but we want to use him as a sandbag."

❖ A frustrated father told a work colleague: "When I was a youngster, I was disciplined by being sent to my room without supper. But in my son's room, he has his own colour TV, computer, games console, cell phone and CD player."

"So what do you do?"

The father replied: "I send him to *my* room!"

❖ A woman was trying hard to get ketchup out of the jar. During the struggle the phone rang, so she asked her four-year-old daughter to answer it. The little girl said: "Mommy can't come to the phone to talk to you right now. She's hitting the bottle."

❖ Two brothers – one aged six, the other aged four – were hatching a plan in their bedroom. "You know what?" said the six-year-old. "I think it's about time we started cursing."

The four-year-old nodded his head in approval.

The older boy went on: "When we go downstairs for breakfast, I'm going to say something with 'hell' and you say something with 'ass'."

The four-year-old agreed enthusiastically.

When their mother walked into the kitchen and asked the six-year-old what he wanted for breakfast, he replied: "Aw, hell, Mom, I guess I'll have some Cheerios."

His mother gave him a resounding whack on his butt, sending him toppling from his chair. He then ran upstairs to his room in floods of tears.

Still fuming, the mother turned to the four-year-old and asked him sternly what he wanted for breakfast. "I don't know," he replied in a trembling voice, "but you can bet your fat ass it won't be Cheerios!"

❖ Grandpa was showing little Johnny around the farm and when they came to the corral, he explained: "That's a bull and a cow, and he's serving her."

Shortly afterwards, they saw two horses. Grandpa told Johnny: "That's a stud and a mare, and he's serving her, too."

That night at supper, after everyone was settled and grace was said, Grandma turned to Grandpa and said: "Will you please serve the turkey?"

Little Johnny jumped up and yelled: "If he does, I'm eating a hamburger!"

❖ A girl was given a tea set for her second birthday. It became one of her favourite toys, and when her mother went away for a few weeks to care for her sick aunt, the toddler loved to take her father a little cup of tea, which was just water really, while he was engrossed watching the news on TV.

He sipped each "cup of tea" he was brought and lavished generous praise on the taste, leaving the little girl immensely proud.

Eventually the mother returned home and the father couldn't wait to show her how his little princess had been looking after him. On cue, the girl took him his "cup of tea" and he sipped it before praising it to the heavens.

The mother watched him drink it and then said to him: "Did it ever occur to you that the only place that a toddler can reach to get water is the toilet?"

❖ A father asked his ten-year-old son if he knew about the birds and the bees.

"Don't tell me," pleaded the boy in some distress.

"Why not?" asked his father, puzzled.

"Because," explained the boy, "at seven years old I was told there was no Tooth Fairy, at eight I was told there was no Easter Bunny, at nine I was told there was no Father Christmas. So if you're now going to tell me that grown-ups don't get laid, there's nothing to live for."

✳ Little Johnny's mother decided it was time to sit him down and tell him about the birds and the bees. So she told him all about how babies are created. Afterwards he was uncharacteristically silent.

"Do you understand all the things I've told you?" asked his mother.

"Yes, I think so," said little Johnny.

"Any questions at all?"

"There is one thing. How are kittens and puppies made?"

"In exactly the same way as babies."

"Wow!" exclaimed little Johnny. "My dad will fuck anything!"

A woman took eight-year-old Johnny home and told his mother that he was caught playing doctors and nurses with Mary, her eight-year-old daughter.

Johnny's mom said: "Let's not be too harsh on them – they're bound to be curious about sex at that age."

"Curious about sex?" said Mary's mom. "He's taken her appendix out!"

❖ On a fine sunny day, a young brother and sister – Johnny and Susie – were playing naked in a sandbox. As they studied each other's bodies, they became increasingly curious as to why they had different bits.

So when Johnny went indoors, he asked their mother: "Why does Susie have a hole and I have a stick?"

Choosing a metaphor, his mother replied: "Susie has a garage, and you have a Ferrari. Men park their cars in the garage when they are ready."

"Oh," said Johnny.

Meanwhile Susie was upstairs asking their father the same question: "Why does Johnny have a stick between his legs and I have a hole?"

The father replied: "He has a Ferrari and you have a garage. You must never let him park his Ferrari in your garage."

"Okay," she said.

The next day, Johnny and Susie were playing naked again in the sandbox. Johnny suddenly said: "Please, Susie, let me park my Ferrari."

"No way!" said Susie.

"But I want to!" cried Johnny.

A couple of minutes later, Susie ran indoors. Her mother asked: "Susie, why is there blood on your hands?"

Susie said: "Johnny tried to park his Ferrari, so I pulled the back wheels off."

★　　★　　★　　★　　★

CHRISTMAS

✳ A man walked into a kebab shop and was surprised to see Father Christmas serving behind the counter.

"Santa!" he said. "What are you doing working here? Shouldn't you be up at the North Pole preparing for the big day?"

Santa let out a long sigh. He had really fallen on hard times. The red suit was splattered with chilli sauce and bits of lettuce, his apron was a mess, and he looked as if the last thing in the world he wanted to be doing was serving kebabs.

Eventually he admitted: "I'm afraid my business has gone belly up. What with the credit crunch and the recession, the toy industry took a hammering. I had to lay off some of the elves, the bank wouldn't give me a loan and we just lost our competitive edge. We wound up the delivery side and subcontracted out to UPS but none of these measures helped our profitability. Finally the receivers came in, asset-stripped the business and we went into liquidation."

"I'm really sorry to hear that," said the man. "It kind of takes the tradition out of Christmas."

"I know," said Santa, smiling weakly. "Anyway, enough of me, and my troubles. What can I get you?"

The man said: "I'll have a large Donner."

"Sorry," said Santa. "We're all out of Donner. Will Blitzen do instead?"

✳ A dad figured that at the age of seven his son would inevitably begin to have doubts about Santa Claus. Sure enough, one day the boy announced: "Dad, I know something about Santa Claus, the Easter Bunny AND the Tooth Fairy."

"Okay, son," said the dad, taking a deep breath. "Let's hear it. What do you know?"

The boy replied: "They're all nocturnal."

✳ Why are Christmas trees like people who can't knit?
They both drop their needles.

✳ A father said to his son: "Did you see Father Christmas this year, son?"

"No," replied the boy, "it was too dark to see him. But I heard what he said when he stubbed his toe on the edge of my bed."

> 66 I wrapped my Christmas presents early this year, but I used the wrong paper. The paper I used said 'Happy Birthday' on it. I didn't want to waste it, so I just wrote 'Jesus' on it.
>
> Demetri Martin 99

✳ A boy opened his Christmas present to find nothing but an empty shoe box. His parents told him it was an Action Man deserter.

✳ When a kindergarten student playing Joseph in the school nativity play forgot his lines, he was prompted from the side by a teacher. She whispered: "You have travelled a very long way, Joseph. You are hot and tired. What do you think you would say to the innkeeper?"

Joseph brightened up, wiped his brow and said loudly: "Boy, do I need a drink!"

> 66 Did you hear about the Al-Qaeda Christmas party? No dancing or music, but the fastest game of pass the parcel you've ever seen.
>
> Omid Djalili 99

✳ On Christmas morning, Rudolph was having a good moan to Prancer and Dancer. He said: "Santa has got me the wrong Christmas present – I'm beginning to think he must be dyslexic."

"What makes you think that?" they asked.

"Because he got me a Pony Sleigh Station!"

✳ A man went to the doctor complaining of a sore throat.

"Hmmm," said the doctor, examining him. "Your throat is very swollen. I wonder if it's an allergic reaction to something you've eaten. Have you eaten anything unusual lately?"

The man looked sheepish. "Well, doctor, I know it was a stupid thing to do, but two days ago I ate our Christmas decorations."

"Ah, that explains it!" exclaimed the doctor triumphantly. "You've got tinselitis."

✳ For her Christmas present last year, I plugged grandma into the mains. It was such a joy to see her face light up.

Things to Say When Receiving an Unwanted Christmas Gift

Gee, if I had not recently shot up four sizes this would have fitted me perfectly!

This will be great for wearing around the basement.

If the dog buries it, I'll be furious . . . won't I, boy?

I love it, but I fear the jealousy it will inspire.

I really don't deserve this.

To think . . . I've got this in the year I've promised to give all my presents to charity.

It's hard to put my feelings into words.

I hope this never catches fire. It is fire season, though. There are lots of unexplained fires.

＊ A woman was out Christmas shopping with her three young children. After hours of trailing around toy shops and hearing her kids asking for every item on the shelves, she was thoroughly fed up. Weighed down with bags, she squeezed herself and her kids into a crowded shopping mall elevator and sighed aloud, to nobody in particular: "Whoever started this whole Christmas thing should be arrested and strung up!"

A voice from the back of the elevator replied quietly: "Don't worry, ma'am, I believe they crucified him."

★　　★　　★　　★　　★

THE CLINTONS

★ A working man was at a Hillary Clinton campaign meeting in Maine, heckling her as she delivered a long, boring speech. Finally her frustration got the better of her and she rounded on the heckler, saying: "Would you like to stand up and tell the audience what you have ever done for the good of this country?"

"Sure," replied the heckler. "I voted against you in Massachusetts."

★ Why is Hillary Clinton particularly concerned about the threat of global warming?

She's afraid she's going to melt.

★ On the campaign trail, Hillary Clinton learned that a sandwich shop in a town she was visiting had named a sandwich after her.

Touched by this display of public affection, she asked the proprietor: "Tell me, what's in the special Hillary Clinton sandwich?"

He replied: "Mostly baloney."

> **"** All five living American Presidents had lunch together at the White House. The lunch went well – only three shoes were thrown. George Bush picked up the cheque, Bill Clinton picked up the waitress.
> David Letterman **"**

★ When he was still President, Bill and Hillary were invited to attend a baseball game. Before the start, an aide whispered something in Bill's ear, whereupon he suddenly picked up Hillary and hurled her down the stadium stairs.

The flustered aide said: "No, I think you misheard me, sir. I said throw out the first pitch."

★ Trying to make amends for past misdemeanours, Bill went to the shopping mall to buy Hillary a gift. "I'd like to buy some gloves for my wife," he said to the attractive salesgirl, "but I don't know her size."

"Will this help?" asked the salesgirl sweetly, placing her hand in his.

"Yes, thank you," said Bill. "Her hands are slightly larger than yours."

"Will there be anything else?" inquired the salesgirl as she wrapped the gloves.

"Now that you mention it," replied Bill, "she also needs a bra and panties."

★ Leaving Hillary back home, Bill went on a fact-finding trip to Europe. As his private plane approached London Heathrow, the captain made his customary announcement.

"Mr Clinton, would you please return the stewardess to the upright position and prepare to land?"

Hillary went to a fortune teller who revealed: "I have some bad news. Bill is going to die a horrible death."

Hillary said: "Just tell me one thing. Will I be acquitted?"

★ Chelsea Clinton had been on a date, so Hillary asked her if she had a good time.

"Yeah, it was great," said Chelsea. "I think I might be in love."

"You didn't have sex, did you?" asked Hillary.

Chelsea said: "Not according to Dad."

★　★　★　★　★

COLLEGE AND UNIVERSITY

❖ Instead of studying for their final college exam, four seniors spent the night partying in the house they shared off-campus. The next morning they waited until the exam would be nearing its conclusion and then made their way to class after first daubing their hands in grease to support the story they were going to tell the professor.

The exam was almost finished when the quartet burst into the room. "We're really sorry," their spokesman told the professor, "but we had a flat tyre and, as you can see from the state of our hands, we've been struggling to change it. I know we've missed the exam, but could we possibly retake it another time?"

The professor said that he was not an unreasonable man and would therefore reschedule the exam for the following week.

Making the most of their extra revision time, the four students studied diligently and by the day of the re-sit they thought they were ready for anything.

On arrival, each was placed in a separate classroom for the test, which consisted of two questions. The first question, worth five marks, was easy. The second question, worth ninety-five marks, simply read: "Which tyre?"

❖ Did you hear about the professor who discovered that his theories about earthquakes were on shaky ground?

❖ When a professor of mathematics noticed that his kitchen sink at home was leaking, he called a plumber. The plumber came out that same day, quickly fixed the leak and presented the professor with the bill. The professor was horrified to see that the bill for an hour's work amounted to one-third of his monthly salary.

Grudgingly he paid the bill after expressing his discontent to the plumber. "I do sympathize," said the plumber. "So why don't you apply for a plumber's position with our company? You will earn far more than you do as a professor. But remember, when you apply, tell them that you completed only seven elementary classes. They don't like educated people."

So the professor applied to the company and landed a job as a plumber. His salary improved beyond all recognition and he was generally happy with his life. Then one day the company decided that every plumber had to attend evening classes to complete the eighth grade.

The professor went along and it so happened that the first class was math. To check students' knowledge, the teacher asked for a formula for the area of a circle. The professor immediately jumped up and went over to the white board, only to realize that he had forgotten the formula. He tried to work it out and proceeded to fill the board with integrals, differentials and other advanced formulae. At the end he came up with "minus pi times r squared."

He didn't like the minus, so he started all over again, but struggled to remove it. Four times he tried, but each time he finished up with a minus.

In despair and frustration, he turned to the class and heard all the plumbers whisper: "Switch the limits of the integral!"

> ❝ One of my college friends has a stutter and a lot of people think that's a bad thing, but to me that's just like starting certain words with a drum roll. That's not an impediment, that's suspense.
> Demetri Martin ❞

❖ My daughter is doing her masters at university. Well, let's be honest, it's the only way she's going to get decent marks.

❖ ## What do you call somebody who pretends to be a college student?
An athlete.

❖ A history professor and a psychology professor were sitting outside at a nudist colony.
The history professor asked: "Have you read Marx?"
The psychology professor replied: "Yes. I think it's from the wicker chairs."

❖ Passing through his son's college town late one night on a business trip, a father thought he would pay him a surprise visit.
Arriving at the fraternity house, he knocked on the door and waited for an answer. Eventually a sleepy voice opened a second-floor window and called down: "What do you want?"
"Does Billy Mooney live here?" asked the father.
"Yeah," replied the voice. "Dump him on the front porch and we'll take care of him in the morning."

❖ When a university student returned home for Christmas, his mother asked: "How's your history paper coming along?"
"Well, my history professor suggested I use the Internet for research and it's been really helpful."
"Oh, that's good."
"Yes. So far I've located fourteen people who sell them."

❖ If the Bible had been written by college students, the Last Supper would have been eaten cold the next morning; and instead of God creating the world in six days and resting on the seventh, he would have put it off until the night before it was due and then pulled an all-nighter.

You're No Longer a Student When . . .

6 a.m. is when you get up, not when you go to sleep.

Mould isn't growing in the bottom of your coffee mugs.

You keep more food than beer in the fridge.

Your fantasies of having sex with three women with lesbian tendencies are replaced by fantasies of having sex with anyone at all.

Your underwear is clean on that day instead of that month.

You know where the Hoover is kept.

You don't volunteer for clinical trials at the hospital.

You know all the people sleeping in your house.

You carry an umbrella.

You hear your favourite song in the elevator at work.

A fire in the kitchen is not something to laugh about.

You don't consider Pot Noodle to be haute cuisine.

You haven't worn the same jumper every day for six months.

You realize that a bottle of wine costing less than four dollars isn't always the best.

Your house doesn't have sheets for curtains.

The heating in your house works.

You're the one calling the police because those damn kids next door won't turn down the stereo.

Tramps aren't kindred spirits.

You always know where you are when you wake up.

You get out of bed in the morning even if it's raining.

You are not addicted to daytime television.

Washing up is not an annual chore.

You don't know what time the kebab shop closes.

You don't have a strange attraction to road signs when you are drunk.

A poop left in the toilet is not hysterically funny.

❖ A teenage boy went off to university, but about a third of the way through the semester, he had foolishly squandered all the money his parents had given him. Desperate to get more money out of his father, he came up with a cunning plan.

Phoning home one weekend, he said: "Dad, you won't believe the educational opportunities that are available at this university! Why, they've even got a course here that will teach Rover how to talk!"

"They can teach a dog to talk? That's incredible!" said the gullible father. "How do I enrol him on the course?"

"Just send him down here with $1,000," said the son, "and I'll make sure he gets on the course."

So the father sent the dog and $1,000, but about two-thirds of the way through the semester, that money had also run out. The boy called his father again.

"How's Rover doing?" asked the father.

"Awesome, Dad. He's talking great. But you just won't believe this; they've had such amazing results with the talking dogs course that they're starting up a new one to teach the animals how to read!"

"Read?" echoed the father. "No kidding! What do I have to do to get him on that course?"

"Just send $2,500, and I'll get him on the course."

The father duly sent the money, but at the end of the semester, the boy was faced with a problem: how to conceal from his father the fact that the dog could neither talk nor read. So the son decided to take drastic action and shot the dog. When he arrived home for vacation, his father was waiting expectantly.

"Where's Rover?" asked the father. "I just can't wait to hear him talk or listen to him read something."

"Dad," said the boy solemnly, "I've got some bad news. This morning when I stepped out of the shower, Rover was in the living room reading the morning paper, like he usually does. Then suddenly he turned to me and asked: "So, is your dad still messing around with that little blonde at number fifty-three?"

The father's face turned red with rage and he yelled: "I hope you shot that lying dog!"

"I sure did, Dad."

"That's my boy!"

❖ In ancient Greece, the great philosopher and teacher Socrates was revered for his wisdom and common sense. One day, he bumped into an acquaintance who said excitedly: "Socrates, do you know what I just heard about one of your students?"

"Wait a moment," replied Socrates. "Before telling me anything, I would like you to pass a little test. It is called the Triple Filter Test."

"Triple Filter?"

"Yes," continued Socrates. "Before you tell me about my student, it might be advisable to take a minute and filter what you are going to say. The first filter is truth. Have you made absolutely sure that what you are about to tell me is true?"

"Well, er, not really," said the man. "I just heard about it and . . ."

"Very well," said Socrates. "So you are not really sure whether the story is true or not. Now let us try the second filter, the filter of goodness. Is what you are about to tell me concerning my student something good?"

"No, on the contrary . . ."

"So," continued Socrates, "you want to tell me something bad about him, but you are not certain that it is true. You may still pass the test, however, because there is one filter remaining: the filter of usefulness. Is what you want to tell me about my student going to be useful to me?"

"No, not really."

"Well," concluded Socrates, "if what you want to tell me is not true, good, or even useful, why tell it to me at all?"

And with that he walked off.

This is the reason why Socrates was a great philosopher and was held in such high esteem. It also explains why he never found out that Plato was shagging his wife.

★　★　★　★　★

COMPUTERS AND THE INTERNET

> Look at these kids today. We used to do crack, but they just drink Red Bull and go on the patio to smoke. The closest they've come to a fist fight is in a chatroom. 'You looking at my girlfriend? Well, I'm going to delete you from my MySpace friends list!'
>
> Doug Stanhope

✳   A truck driver, hauling a trailer-load of computers, stopped off at a roadside bar for a beer. As he entered, he noticed a large sign on the door that read: "COMPUTER NERDS NOT WELCOME! ENTER AT YOUR OWN RISK!"

No sooner had the truck driver sat down at the bar than the bartender began sniffing him and asking him what he did for a living. He explained that he was a truck driver, and that the smell was from the computers he was hauling that day. Serving him a beer, the bartender said: "That's okay. Truck drivers aren't nerds."

While he was sipping his beer, a skinny guy walked in wearing a pair of glasses held together with tape, plus a jacket, the breast pocket of which was lined with pencils and pens. Without saying a word, the bartender pulled out a rifle and shot the guy dead. When the truck driver asked him why he had done that, the bartender replied: "Don't worry. Computer nerds are in season because they are overpopulating Silicon Valley. You don't even need a licence to shoot them."

After finishing his beer, the truck driver set off on the highway once more but a few miles further on, he had to swerve to avoid an accident, and the sudden movement sent his load of computers spilling out on to the road. By the time he had climbed down from his cab to survey the damage, a crowd of computer geeks had formed – engineers, accountants and programmers, each wearing the nerdiest clothes he had ever seen. Fearing that they were about to steal the entire load of computers and remembering what had happened in the bar, he fetched his shotgun and began blasting away, killing several of them on the spot. But just then a highway patrol officer came roaring up and jumped out of his car, screaming at him to stop.

"What's the problem?" said the truck driver. "I thought computer nerds were in season."

"They are," replied the patrolman. "But you're not allowed to bait 'em!"

✳   Why was the computer in pain?
    It had a slipped disk.

✳ A pilot was flying a small, single-engine charter plane, carrying two leading business executives. He was approaching Seattle airport through thick fog when his instruments suddenly failed. In desperation, he began circling the area, looking for a landmark that would guide him to the airport runway, but after an hour or so, the plane was running low on fuel and his passengers were becoming increasingly edgy.

Finally, the visibility improved sufficiently for him to spot a tall building through a break in the fog. He could just make out one guy working alone on the eighth floor. Banking the plane, the pilot rolled down his window and shouted to the guy: "Hey, where am I?"

The solitary office worker replied: "You're in a plane."

The pilot then rolled up the window, made a 240-degree turn and proceeded to execute a perfect blind landing on the airport runway three miles away. As the plane came to a halt, the fuel ran out.

His relieved passengers were greatly impressed by his navigational skills. "How the hell did you do that?" they asked.

"Easy," said the pilot. "I asked the guy in that building a simple question. The answer he gave me was 100 per cent correct, but absolutely useless, and from that I deduced it must be Microsoft's support office, and I knew that from there the airport was just a few miles away."

Why are computers like air conditioners?
They work fine until you start opening Windows.

✳ A man bought a rug that was advertised on eBay as being "in mint condition". When it arrived, there was a big hole in the middle.

✳ What is a cursor?
Someone having problems with his computer.

✳ Bill Gates bumped into Hugh Grant at a Hollywood party. Gates said: "I've seen some fabulous pictures of Divine Brown lately, I'd really like to get together with her some time. Any chance you could fix me up?"

Grant said: "You have to remember that ever since that unfortunate incident with me, her prices have rocketed."

"Money's no object," said Gates. "Now, what's her number?"

So Gates phoned Divine Brown and set up a date. Afterwards, as they lay on the bed together, he turned to her and mumbled breathlessly: "Now I know why you chose the name Divine."

She replied: "And sadly now I know why you chose the name Microsoft."

❝ I'm just not good with computers. I had to call up the tech support guy to get some help with my home computer. He started asking me questions, 'What kind of operating system have you got there, sir?' 'Uh, electricity, I think. Yeah, I've been plugging into my wall. I've been having some luck with that.'
Jeff Caldwell ❞

❝ Twenty-five years ago there were no computers. Can you imagine your job without . . . solitaire?
Wendy Liebman ❞

✳ When I go on the Internet, I'm a totally different person. But that's ID theft for you.

✳ A boy computer mouse met a girl computer mouse. They clicked straight away.

✳ If you take a computer for a run, will you jog its memory?

Spell Checker Poem

I halve a spelling checker,
It came with my pea see.
It plainly marks four my revue
Mistakes I dew knot sea.

Eye strike a key and type a word
And weight four it two say
Weather eye am wrong oar write
It shows me strait aweigh.

As soon as a mist ache is maid
It nose bee fore two long
And eye can put the era rite
Its rarely ever wrong.

I've scent this massage threw it,
And I'm shore your pleased too no
Its letter prefect in every weigh;
My checker tolled me sew.

✳   A little girl asked: "Daddy, how was I born?"
Her father said: "I guess it's about time we told you, so
here goes. One day Mom and Dad got together in a chatroom on MSN. Dad set up a date via email with your mom
and we met at a cyber cafe. We snuck into a secluded room,
and then your mother downloaded from your dad's memory stick. As soon as Dad was ready for an upload, it was
discovered that neither of us had used a firewall. Since it
was too late to hit the delete button, nine months later the
blessed virus appeared. And that's the story."

✳   The day Microsoft makes something that doesn't suck is
probably the day they start making vacuum cleaners.

Reasons Why Computers Must Be Male

They carry plenty of data but are still clueless.

They look nice and shiny until you bring them home.

A better model is always just around the corner.

They are supposed to help you solve problems, but half the time they *are* the problem.

They'll do whatever you say if you push the right buttons.

The best part of having one is the games you can play.

The lights are on, but nobody's home.

The smallest virus can render them helpless.

In order to get their attention, you have to turn them on.

Big power surges knock them out for the night.

Size does matter.

Reasons Why Computers Must Be Female

They hear what you say, but not what you mean.

They correct you, even when you don't ask them to.

They respond well to being re-booted.

They have minds of their own.

Even the smallest mistakes are stored in long-term memory for possible future review.

They go down on you.

The language they use to communicate with other computers is incomprehensible to everyone else.

As soon as you make a commitment to one, you find yourself spending half your monthly salary on buying accessories for it.

Inserting a three-and-a-half-inch floppy can cause them to freeze.

They take half an hour to warm up in the morning.

You do the same thing for years, and suddenly it's wrong.

✳ Jesus and Satan were involved in an ongoing argument about who was the more accomplished on the computer. They had been niggling away at each other for days until God became tired of all the bickering. Finally God said: "Enough! I am going to set up a two-hour test to determine who is better on the computer. And I will be the judge."

So Jesus and Satan sat at their respective keyboards and typed away. They compiled spreadsheets, they wrote reports, they downloaded, and they sent emails with multiple attachments. In fact, they did just about every possible task.

But ten minutes before the end of the test, lightning suddenly flashed across the sky, thunder rolled and the power went off. Satan glared at his blank screen and screamed every swear word known to the underworld.

Jesus simply sighed. The power eventually flickered back on, and both restarted their computers. Satan began searching frantically for his work. "It's gone!" he screamed. "I lost everything when the power went off!"

Meanwhile Jesus quietly started printing out all his files from the past two hours. Seeing this, Satan was incensed.

"He must have cheated!" raged Satan. "How did he do it?"

God smiled and said: "Jesus saves."

✳ The world's most eminent scientists were preparing an elaborate experiment to ask the ultimate question. After spending months gathering all the different makes of computer in the world together in one place, they connected all the monitors and keyed in the one question that had been baffling humanity for centuries: "Is there a God?"

Suddenly there was a loud crash, a huge ball of smoke and flame, and all the screens went blank. Just one printer remained operational, and as it spluttered into action, one of the scientists ran over to read the answer.

The printout read: "There is now."

Officers at a military installation were being lectured about a sophisticated new computer. The training officer said it was able to withstand the most powerful nuclear and chemical attacks.

Just then he noticed that one of the officers was holding a cup of coffee. "Get out of here with that coffee!" he barked.

"Sure, but why?" asked the embarrassed officer.
"Because spilt coffee could ruin the keyboard."

CRIME

★ Two terrorists were making letter bombs. After they had finished, one said: "Do you think I put enough explosive in this envelope?"

"I don't know," said the other. "Open it and see."

"But it will explode."

"Don't be stupid! It's not addressed to you!"

★ Why are most serial killers men?

Because women like to kill one man slowly over many, many years.

★ A gunman burst into a convenience store and yelled at the assistant: "Hand over the money, or you're geography!"

The assistant said: "Don't you mean history?"

The robber shouted: "Don't change the subject."

❝ They say being a hostage is difficult, but I could do that with my hands tied behind my back.

Phil Nichol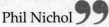

★ A husband wanted his eighty-three-year-old wife dead and asked a hitman how he would do it.

"I would shoot off her left nipple," said the hitman.

The husband threw up his hands in horror, exclaiming: "I want her dead – not kneecapped!"

★ A burglar broke into Bryan Adams' house, but while making his getaway he bumped into the singer himself in the street outside.

"Hey, Bryan!" said the burglar. "I've got all your records."

★ A teenage boy was stabbed to death outside the local Carpet Right store. Police think it might be rug related.

★ A pickpocket was found guilty and given the option of six months in jail or a $400 fine. The defence lawyer, knowing that his client could not pay the fine, pleaded with the judge: "Your honour, my client can only afford $75, but if you allow him a few minutes in the crowd . . ."

★ Did you hear about the thief who stole from a blood bank?

He was caught red-handed.

★ Did you hear about the men who were arrested for throwing bombs from a boat?

They dropped the charges.

★ The judge frowned at the defendant and said: "So you admit to breaking into the same store on three successive nights?"

"Yes, your honour."

"And why was that?"

"Because my wife wanted a dress."

The judge checked his records. "But it says here that you broke in three nights in a row."

"That's correct. She made me exchange it twice."

> **❝** I live in a neighbourhood so bad that you can get shot while getting shot.
> Chris Rock **❞**

★ A human heart was stolen from a hospital. Police later made a cardiac arrest.

★ A bank robber walked over to one of his hostages and said: "Did you see my face?"
"Yes," said the hostage.
And the robber shot him dead.
Then he turned to the next man and asked: "Did you see my face?"
"No," he said. "But I think my wife did."

★ Why can't a suspect take a second polygraph test?
Because they can't be re-lied upon.

★ Did you hear about the limbo dancer who had his pockets picked?
How could anyone stoop so low?

★ **Ten dozen computer screens were stolen from a factory. Police are monitoring the situation.**

★ Three guys were sitting at a bar complaining about the injustices of the legal system.
One said: "A friend of mine was taken to court for dropping a chocolate wrapper."
The other two shook their heads knowingly.
The second said: "A friend of mine has got a criminal record because he overfilled his garbage bin."
The other two shook their heads sadly.
The third said: "That's nothing. A friend of mine was prosecuted on account of his beliefs. He believed he could drive after nine pints."

★ Two verbs, three adjectives, three nouns and a conjunction appeared in court. They're due to be sentenced next week.

★ Did you hear about the woman who was mugged by an acupuncturist?

She was stabbed 147 times but the next morning she felt brilliant.

★ An armed robber held up a bank. The bank teller said: "This is your first robbery, isn't it?"

"What makes you think that?" he barked through the slit in his ski mask.

"Because you've sawn the wrong end off your shotgun."

I'd just like to say to the man wearing camouflage and using crutches who stole my wallet last week: "You can hide, but you can't run."

★ An elderly lady living alone surprised a burglar in her kitchen. He was weighed down with all the items he was planning to steal. With no weapon in reach, all she could think of doing was to quote scripture at him and so she held up her hand and shouted out: "Acts 2:38!"

The burglar instantly froze in fear, allowing the lady to get to the phone and dial 911. When the police arrived ten minutes later, the burglar was still quaking with terror. After arresting him, the officers were puzzled as to how an elderly woman with no weapon had managed to strike such fear into him.

She replied: "I simply quoted scripture at him. He must be a God-fearing boy."

While interviewing the burglar at the station, the officer asked him: "What was it about the scripture that had such an effect on you?"

"Scripture? What scripture?" demanded the burglar. "I thought she said she had an axe and two .38s!"

★ A man stole a joint of beef from a supermarket. As he ran out with the beef under his arm, a security guard spotted him and shouted: "What are you doing with that?"

   The thief shouted back: "Roast potatoes, carrots and Yorkshire pudding."

★ The judge asked the defendant: "What is your occupation?"

   "I'm a locksmith, your honour."

   "Then what were you doing in a jeweller's shop at three o'clock in the morning?"

   "I was making a bolt for the door!"

★ The defendant stood defiantly in the dock and said to the judge: "I don't recognize this court."

   "Why?" rapped the judge.

   "Because you've had it decorated since the last time I was here."

★ A man arrived home from the pub to find his wife in bed crying.

   "What's the matter, darling?" he asked.

   "We've had a burglar," she sobbed.

   "Did he get anything?" asked the husband.

   "Too right he did!" she wailed. "I thought it was you home early!"

★ A counterfeiter decided that the best way to pass off his phony $18 bills would be to unload them in some small rural town, so he drove until he found a tiny backwoods town with a solitary store.

   He entered the store, went up to the counter, and handed one of the bogus bills to the old man at the cash desk.

   "Could you change this for me, please?" he asked.

   The elderly clerk looked at the bill for a few seconds and then smiled: "Of course I can. Would you prefer two $9 bills or three $6 bills?"

★ My mate Sid was a victim of ID theft. Now he's just called S.

⋆ The other day I read in the paper, "A woman has been murdered in Los Angeles by a thirty-six-year-old man who has not been named." I thought: "Thirty-six years old and he still hasn't been named? What's everyone been calling him all these years?"

⋆ ## Do you know what would bring an end to knife crime overnight?
Guns.

⋆ Two terrorists were hired to assassinate a prominent politician as he arrived for work. They tracked his movements for several weeks and observed that the politician was extremely punctual, always arriving at his office at 9 a.m. precisely. Accordingly, on the day of the hit they made their way to the roof of a building opposite his office at 8.40 a.m. and waited for him to show.

But by 9.15, there was still no sign of him. The would-be assassins were growing anxious.

"I can't understand it," said one. "He's never been as much as a minute late before."

"Yes, it's strange," agreed the other. "I hope nothing's happened to him."

⋆ Police are on the lookout for a cross-eyed burglar. They have told members of the public: "If you see him peering in your front window, please warn the people next door."

⋆　　⋆　　⋆　　⋆　　⋆

DATING

❖ A girl said to her boyfriend: "You know, we would have less arguments if you weren't so pedantic."

He said: "Fewer arguments . . ."

❖ Wow, the girl I'm dating at the moment is unreal! I just hope she doesn't get a puncture.

❖ Did you hear about the couple who met in a revolving door?

They're still going round together.

❖ A guy was going out with a Siamese twin but she dumped him because she found out he was screwing her sister behind her back.

> 66 What would the world be like if people said whatever they were thinking, all the time, whenever it came to them?
> How long would a blind date last? About thirteen seconds, I think. 'Oh, sorry, your rear end is too big.' 'That's okay, your breath stinks anyway. See you later.'
>
> Jerry Seinfeld 99

❖ After five years without a relationship, Tom began dating again. Three weeks later, he met his pal Barney in the street.

"How's it going with your new girlfriend?" asked Barney.

"Yeah, it's okay," said Tom. "But there are so many things you have to get used to in a new relationship, things you forget about after five years of single life."

"Like what?"

"Well, like after sex, as we're lying there, I have to keep repeating to myself: "Don't hand her cash . . . don't hand her cash."

❖ Mike wanted to buy a motorbike. He struggled to find something he liked until one day he came across an affordable Harley for sale. Although it was ten years old, it was in immaculate condition, so he decided to buy it and asked the seller how he kept the bike looking brand new.

"It's quite simple, really," said the seller. "Whenever the bike is outside and it looks as if it's about to rain, rub Vaseline on the chrome. It protects it from the rain." And he handed Mike a jar of Vaseline.

That night, Mike's new girlfriend Suzy invited him over to meet her parents. Naturally, they travelled there on the Harley. Just as they were about to knock on the door, Suzy stopped him and said: "I have to tell you something about my family before we go in. When we eat dinner, we don't talk. In fact, the first person who says anything during dinner has to wash the dishes."

"No problem," said Mike, and in they went. But once inside, Mike had the shock of his life. There was a huge pile of dirty dishes in the living room and another in the kitchen. In fact, there were dirty dishes everywhere – in the hallway, up the stairs, even in the bathroom.

When they all sat down to dinner, sure enough nobody said a word. As the meal progressed, Mike decided to take advantage of the situation by leaning over and kissing Suzy. Nobody said a word, so then he reached over and fondled her breasts. Still there was silence.

Next he stood up, grabbed Suzy, ripped off her clothes, threw her on the table, and screwed her right there, in front of her parents. Suzy was a little flustered, her father was visibly furious, her mom horrified, but nobody said a word.

Then Mike looked at the mom, thinking to himself, "She's got a great body." So he grabbed her, bent her over the dinner table, and took her from behind. The mom was shaken by the ordeal, Suzy was furious and her dad was at boiling point, but still nobody said anything.

Suddenly there was a loud clap of thunder, and it started to rain. Remembering his bike, Mike pulled the jar of Vaseline from his pocket. Seeing this, the father backed away from the table and screamed: "All right, that's enough. I'll do the bloody dishes!"

> ❝ I just ended a long-term relationship.
> Don't worry, it wasn't mine.
>
> Jim Jeffries ❞

❖ A young couple were enjoying a romantic walk down a country lane. As they walked hand in hand, he grew increasingly amorous, but just as he was about to make a move on her, she announced: "Sorry, but I need a pee."

Slightly taken aback by her vulgarity, he suggested: "Why don't you go behind that hedge?"

So she disappeared behind the hedge. As he waited, he could hear the gentling rustling sound of lace knickers rolling down her smooth thighs and imagined what was being exposed in the warm summer breeze. Unable to contain his lust any longer, he reached a hand through the hedge and touched her leg. He quickly moved his hand up her thigh until, to his astonishment, he found himself gripping a long, thick appendage hanging between her legs.

He shouted: "My God, Mary! Have you changed sex?"

"No," she replied. "I've changed my mind. I'm having a shit instead."

❖ **A girl told her boyfriend: "You have to make sacrifices in a relationship."**

So he went out and slaughtered a goat.

❖ A jealous guy caught his girlfriend talking quietly on the phone and immediately confronted her over his suspicions.

"Who was that you were talking to?" he demanded. "Is there somebody else?"

"Of course not," she groaned. "Do you honestly think I'd be going out with a loser like you if there was somebody else?"

❖ I get very nervous on a first date, which is surprising as they are the only kind I have.

❖ Two men were discussing their girlfriends. One said: "I know all of my girlfriend's likes and dislikes – food, movies, music, everything."

"Well, I know every part of my girlfriend's body," said the other.

"Really?"

"Yeah, they're all neatly labelled in the freezer."

 When I leave a relationship I always like to burn the house down so there's no discussion about it later.
Ron Bennington

❖ A boy was brought up to lead a sheltered life by his very strict parents. They never allowed him to meet any girls, except his own relatives. He was so naive that when one day he saw a school friend kissing a girl, he went straight home to his mother and asked her what they were doing.

His mother told him: "It's called kissing, and any boy that does that to a girl will be instantly turned to stone!"

On the boy's twenty-first birthday, he was introduced by a friend to a sweet girl who knew that he had never been kissed before. When she got him alone, she tried to kiss him, but he resisted.

"Why won't you let me kiss you?" she asked. "There's nothing to be afraid of."

"There is!" he said. "My mother says that if I kiss a girl, I'll die that very minute!"

"That is nonsense," said the girl, and she proceeded to plant a full kiss on his lips.

He instantly recoiled in horror. "Oh no, I'm going to die!" he exclaimed.

"No, you're not."

"I am," he insisted. "I've only just kissed you and already one part of me has started to get stiff!"

❖ My girlfriend told me to perform an act that would show how much she meant to me. So I went down the pub.

❖ A young man took a girl out to dinner. They got on really well, and when he asked her if she wanted to come back to his apartment for a drink, she said yes.

After they had been in his apartment for a while, he asked her: "Do you mind if I give you an old-fashioned kiss?"

She replied: "At a time like this you want me to change positions?"

❖ Mike took Sue out on their first date. When he picked her up from her house, he was extremely attentive and chivalrous. At dinner in a smart restaurant, he made sure she had the best of everything and then afterwards they went to catch a movie. At the movie theatre, too, Mike attended to Sue's every need.

A few minutes into the movie, he asked her: "Can you see okay there?"

"Yes," she answered, "I can see fine."

A few seconds later, he asked: "Is your seat comfortable?"

"Yes," she replied, "it's very comfortable."

"You're not in a draught, are you?"

"No," she said, impressed by his attentiveness, "I can't feel a draught at all."

"Good," he said. "Let's switch seats."

❖ A girl took her boyfriend home late one night, and because her parents were already asleep in bed, she asked him not to make too much noise. So when he said that he was desperate to use the bathroom, rather than send him upstairs and risk waking her parents, she told him to use the kitchen sink instead.

A few minutes later, he put his head around the door.

"Have you finished?" she whispered.

"Yeah," he said. "Have you got any paper?"

> ❝ I went back to this girl's flat and she had an eight-foot light switch. I thought, 'That's a huge turn-off.' ❞
> Tim Vine

> ❝ I lived with a girl for a while. We worried about different things. One day, I said, 'What do you fear the most?' And she was like, 'I fear you'll meet someone else, and you'll leave me, and I'll be all alone.' And she said, 'What do you fear the most?' And I was like, 'Bears.' ❞
>
> Mike Birbiglia

A Guide to International Dating

English women
First date: You get to kiss her goodnight.
Second date: You get to grope her passionately.
Third date: You get to have sex, but only in the missionary position.

Irish women
First date: You both get blind drunk and have sex.
Second date: You both get blind drunk and have sex.
Third date: You both get blind drunk and have sex.

Italian women
First date: You take her to the theatre and an expensive restaurant.
Second date: You meet her parents.
Third date: You have sex, she wants to marry you and insists on a twenty-four-carat ring.

Romanian women
First date: You have great sex and she admires your physique.
Second date: You have great sex and she admires your passport photo.
Third date: You are too busy looking for your missing passport.

❖ A guy joined a dating agency but went on a series of unsuccessful dates. So he went back to the agency and said to its female proprietor: "Have you got someone on your books who doesn't care what I look like, isn't concerned about my personal hygiene and has a lovely big pair of boobs?"

The woman checked the computer database and said: "Actually we do have one. But it's you."

Jewish women
First date: You get great head.
Second date: You get even better head.
Third date: You tell her you'll marry her, and never get head again.

Chinese women
First date: You get to buy her an expensive dinner, but nothing happens.
Second date: You buy her an even more expensive dinner, but still nothing happens.
Third date: You don't bother with the third date.

Indian women
First date: You meet her parents.
Second date: You set the date of the wedding.
Third date: Wedding night.

Mexican women
First date: You buy her an expensive dinner, get drunk on tequila and have sex in the back of her car.
Second date: She's pregnant.
Third date: She moves in. A week later, her mother, father, his girlfriend, her two sisters, her brother, all of their kids, her grandma, her father's girlfriend's mother, her three cousins, her sister's boyfriend and his five kids also move in.

❖ A young man said to his friend: "I got a right goer back to my place last night."

   "Yeah?"

   "Yeah. She took one look at me naked and said, 'Right, I'm going.'"

❖ A guy asked for a goodnight kiss, but the girl rebuffed him haughtily, saying: "I don't do that sort of thing on my first date!"

   "Well," he said sarcastically, "how about on your last date?"

❖ A guy was sitting on the couch watching a romantic movie with his girlfriend. She was lying with her head in his lap.

   At the end of the movie, wiping back the tears, she said: "Give me a kiss."

   He said: "If I could reach down that far to kiss you, I wouldn't need you in the first place!"

> 66 My girlfriend was complaining last night that I never listen to her. Or something like that.
>
> Jack Dee 99

❖ On their first date, a guy took a girl to a city bar. "What would you like to drink?" he asked.

   "Champagne, I guess," she replied.

   He said: "Guess again."

❖ Ken's convertible slowed to a halt on a lonely country road.

   "I guess," said his pretty but reluctant date, "that you're going to pull the old 'out of gas' routine?"

   "No," said Ken, "I'm going to pull the 'here after' routine."

   "The 'here after' routine. What's that?" she asked.

   "If you're not here after what I'm here after, you'll be here after I'm gone."

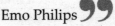

> I once got into trouble on a date. I didn't open her car door. Instead I just swam to the surface.
>
> Emo Philips

❖ A group of young men were talking about what their girlfriends were like in bed. One said: "My girlfriend snores really loudly."

"That's a bit of a turnoff," said the others.

"Yeah," he agreed. "Apparently she had her nose broken when she was younger. But it didn't teach her a lesson; she still snores loudly."

❖ A guy said to his mate in a bar: "I've been getting a little too close to my ex-girlfriend recently."

"Yeah?"

"Yeah. Bloody restraining order!"

> Monogamy is so weird: like when you know their name and stuff.
>
> Margaret Cho

❖ Ray and Eric were in a nightclub. They saw no action all evening, but then Eric came back from the bar with two girls.

Ray said: "They're like buses."

"Why?" queried Eric. "Because you wait for ages and then two come along at once?"

"No," said Ray. "They *are* like buses!"

❖ If you get a message from your boyfriend saying that he wants to "kick your puppy", don't call the animal welfare people. It just means that he's not very good at predictive text.

❖ Even my inflatable doll has dumped me – she said I kept letting her down.

> ❝ You know how you meet the right person, you know instantly? Why does it take a year and a half when it's the wrong one?
>
> Phil Hanley ❞

❖ A young man and his girlfriend were sitting in his apartment one evening when he turned to her and said: "I think it's time we named the day."

She immediately screamed with excitement, threw her arms around him, kissed him passionately on the mouth, jumped up and down, and, before he could say another word, phoned her mom and her best friend.

When she came off the phone, still bubbling over with joy, he said: "Sorry, I worded that badly. I meant 'call it a day'."

A girl said to her boyfriend: "They're not wrinkles, they're laughter lines."

He said: "Do you know, that's the nicest thing anyone has ever said about my scrotum?"

❖ A guy met a girl in a bar and asked: "Can I buy you a drink?"

"Okay," she said, "but it won't do you any good."

A little later he asked her: "Can I buy you another drink?"

"Okay," she replied, "but it won't do you any good."

At the end of the evening, he invited her back to his apartment. "Okay," she said, "but it won't do you any good."

They got to his apartment and he said: "You are without doubt the most beautiful girl I've ever seen. I want you for my wife."

The girl said: "Oh, that's different. Send her in."

❖ I've been with my girlfriend for eleven months now, although the first three months she didn't know it.

❖ A guy joined an Internet dating site. His first date was with a girl at a hospital. When he went to meet her, she said: "I don't know if the website told you, but I only have a few weeks to live."

He said: "That's okay. I don't know if the website told you, but I was only looking for a short-term relationship anyway."

❖ Steve finally plucked up the courage to tell his fiancée that he was breaking off their engagement so that he could marry another woman.

"Can she cook like I can?" asked the distraught fiancée.

"Not on her best day!" said Steve.

"Can she buy you expensive gifts like I do?"

"No, she's broke."

"Well then, is it sex?"

"No, nobody does it like you, babe."

"Then what is it? What can she do for you that I can't?"

Steve sighed: "She can sue me for child support."

★　　★　　★　　★　　★

DEATH

✳ Two lady guests at a funeral were chatting at the wake afterwards. One said: "I'll never forget my brother's funeral. His legs were too long to fit in the coffin, so the undertakers had to take drastic measures."

"Were they hacked off?" inquired her friend.

"Well, I certainly don't think they were too pleased."

✳ A funeral procession made its way down the road. Six close members of the family were carrying the coffin between them. On top of the coffin was a fishing line, a net and some bait.

A passer-by remarked: "He must have been a very keen fisherman."

"Oh, he still is," said another. "He's off to the river as soon as they've buried his wife."

✳ A man was walking past a cemetery when he saw four men carrying a coffin. Three hours later, he saw the same four men still wandering around carrying the coffin. He thought to himself: "They've lost the plot."

> ❝ I went to a funeral recently, and they handed out Kleenex *before* the funeral. Which I thought was cocky.
> Mike Birbiglia ❞

✳ A woman was at the undertaker's arranging her late husband's funeral.

"Do you have any special requests?" asked the undertaker.

"Well," said his widow, "he was bald and never went anywhere without his wig but every time I put it on his head, it slides off."

"No problem," said the undertaker. "I'll sort that out for you. Come back in an hour and a half."

Ninety minutes later she returned and, as promised, the wig was perfectly placed on the dead man's head.

"Oh, thank you so much," she said. "Now you must let me pay you something for your trouble – and I won't take no for an answer."

The undertaker said: "Well, just give me $2 for the nails then."

✳ The man who created the design for deckchairs died last week. It took five attempts before they got him in the coffin.

* A man was hiking up a mountain when he spotted a woman standing at the edge of a cliff, sobbing her heart out.

"What's the matter?" he called out.

"I'm going to kill myself," she replied.

"Well," he said, "if you're going to jump, how about giving me a blow job before you do it?"

"I suppose I might as well," wailed the woman. "My life's been nothing but misery."

After she had finished, the man said: "Wow! That was great! Why are you so depressed anyway?"

She replied: "My family disowned me for dressing like a woman."

> " I've noticed lately that there aren't always cards that suit the occasion. I was in a card shop a few days ago looking for a card for a mate who is terminally ill, so a 'Get Well Soon' card is not appropriate, as him getting well at all is a long shot. So I made my own. On the front I put 'Die With Dignity'. He's a funny guy and I'm sure he will find it funny and if he doesn't, it's not like I'll have to avoid him for long.
>
> Jimmy Carr "

* Two women got chatting in the street. One said: "I've had a terrible time of it lately, Maureen. My sister Joan committed suicide last month, because she had run up terrible debts on her credit card."

"Oh, I'm sorry to hear that, Helen," said the other. "A friend of mine was very depressed, too. He owed $1,000 to a loan shark, and his family were going to be thrown out on to the street the following day. He was so distraught he drove to the edge of a cliff and parked there, his head resting on the steering wheel. But all the nice people there had a whip-round and they got him his $1,000. It was a good job his bus was full that day."

✳ Just before the funeral service, the undertaker went over to the widow and asked: "How old was your husband?"

"Ninety-eight," she answered. "Two years older than me."

"So you're ninety-six," said the undertaker. "Hardly worth going home, is it?"

✳ A bunch of my mates were recently crushed to death when I dared them to lift a heavy seaside structure. Well, that's pier pressure for you.

✳ Did you hear about the guy who was chopping carrots with the Grim Reaper?

He was dicing with death.

> ❝ I got a cactus, and a week later it died. I got really depressed because I thought, 'Damn, I'm less nurturing than a desert!'
> Demetri Martin ❞

✳ A young man went into a bar and ordered a stiff drink. The bartender asked: "What's up?"

The young man said: "I went to a funeral this afternoon, but I'm never going to one again. It was terrible. When the music started playing, me and my mate were the only ones dancing."

> ❝ How come 'I'm sorry' and 'I apologize' mean the same thing, except if you say them at a funeral?
> Demetri Martin ❞

✳ Why did the kleptomaniac who lost both hands commit suicide?

He just couldn't take any more.

* A terminally ill man woke up in a hospital bed and called for his doctor. "Give it to me straight, doc," he said. "How long have I got?"

  The physician replied that he doubted whether the man would survive the night.

  So the man said: "Fetch me my lawyer."

  When the lawyer arrived, the man asked for the physician to stand on one side of the bed while the lawyer stood on the other. The man then closed his eyes.

  After a few minutes, the physician asked him what he was thinking about.

  The man replied: "Jesus died with a thief on either side. I thought I'd check out the same way."

* A wife was talking to her husband about reincarnation. "What exactly is reincarnation?" he asked.

  "It's when you die and come back as something completely different," she explained.

  "So," he suggested, "I could come back as a pig?"

  She sighed wearily. "You're not listening, are you?"

* **The other day I threw a boomerang at a ghost. I knew it would come back to haunt me.**

> 66 I decided I'm going to will my body to a bunch of necrophiliacs, so somebody can get some pleasure.
> David Cross 99

* Discussing the women they had known and lost, a man said to his friend: "My late wife was like an onion – that's not to say she had many layers as a person, but I did have a little sob when I was chopping her up."

* My mate and his other half separated last week. That'll teach him to fall asleep on railway tracks.

✳ An undertaker arrived home sporting a black eye. "What happened to you?" asked his wife.

"I've had a terrible day," he said. "I had to go to a hotel and collect a man who had died in his sleep. When I got there, the manager said they couldn't fit him into a body bag because he had this huge erection. Anyway, I found the room and, sure enough, there was this big, naked guy lying on the bed with a huge erection. So I did what I always do – I grabbed it with both hands and tried to snap it in half."

"I see," said his wife. "But how did you get the black eye?"

The undertaker replied: "Wrong room."

> ❝ My aunt died at precisely 10.47, and the old grandfather clock stopped at precisely the same time. It fell on her.
> Paul Merton ❞

✳ After losing one of his arms in an accident, a man became very depressed because he had previously been a keen sportsman.

One day, in the depths of despair, he decided to commit suicide. He got in an elevator and went to the top of a small office block with the intention of jumping off. He was standing on the ledge staring down at the street below when he saw a man skipping along, whistling and kicking up his heels. On closer inspection, he saw that this man didn't have any arms at all.

He started thinking, what am I doing up here, feeling sorry for myself when there are people much worse off than me? I still have one good arm to do things with. There goes a guy with no arms skipping down the sidewalk, so happy and just getting on with life.

So he abandoned his plans, hurried down and caught up with the man with no arms. He told him how, having lost one arm, he had felt useless and had been ready to kill himself, but that seeing him had been an inspiration. He thanked him for saving his life and said: "I now realize that I can survive with one arm if you can enjoy life with no arms."

The man with no arms began skipping and whistling and kicking up his heels again. The guy felt compelled to ask him: "Why ARE you so happy, anyway?"

The man with no arms said: "I'm not happy – my balls itch!"

✳ When my grandmother died, the funeral director said: "Bury her with something she liked."

As the coffin was lowered into the ground, all they could hear was granddad shouting for help.

✳ A woman was walking through a cemetery when she spotted a man hiding behind a gravestone.

"Morning," she called out.

"No," he said, "just having a shit."

✳ Drinking in a bar with his buddy, a guy said: "A little old lady down the end of my road got hit by a car this morning and was killed."

"Oh, that's sad."

"Yeah, it's such a shame – two days earlier and I could have got my wife some flowers for her birthday."

✳ Two guys were sitting at a bar. One said to the other: "You look a bit down. Everything okay?"

"You see," said the other, "my dear old grandmother died yesterday morning, God bless her. Still, at over ninety she'd had a good innings and she chose a lovely way to go. She just sat down in a chair, relaxed, closed her eyes and drifted off to sleep. She didn't wake up again. Mind you, she caused havoc in that dental practice."

> 66 If ever I saw an amputee getting hanged, I'd probably just start calling out letters.
>
> Demetri Martin 99

DIVORCE

★ After being granted a divorce on the grounds of her husband's infidelity, a woman was forced to move out of the house she had lovingly looked after for twenty-two years. She spent two whole days packing her belongings into boxes, crates and suitcases, and then on the third day the removal men came to collect her things. That evening, she sat alone in the house for the last time, preparing herself a final farewell meal of prawns and caviar, which she ate by candlelight at their beautiful dining room table. She was sad but bitter, too, and at the end of her meal she went into every room and placed a few half-eaten prawn shells dipped in caviar into the hollows of the curtain rods. She then tidied up the kitchen and left.

When the husband moved back in with his new girlfriend, all was bliss for the first few days. Then slowly the house began to acquire a strange smell. They tried everything to get rid of it – cleaning, mopping and airing the place out. Vents were checked for dead rodents and carpets were steam cleaned. Air fresheners were hung everywhere. Pest exterminators were called in to set off gas canisters, which made such a mess the couple had to move out for a few days and replace all their expensive wool carpets. But still nothing worked.

After a while, friends stopped coming to visit, repairmen refused to work in the house and the maid quit, fearing for her health.

Eventually they could bear the stench no longer and decided to put the house up for sale. But prospective buyers were immediately put off by the smell and, despite the price being greatly reduced, several months later they had still not managed to sell it. Things were so bad that they had to borrow a vast sum of money from the bank in order to purchase a new home.

Word of their misfortune reached the ears of his ex-wife who called to ask him how he was doing. When he relayed the saga of the rotting house, she listened politely and said that she missed her old home terribly. She suggested that she would even be willing to reduce her divorce settlement in exchange for getting her beloved house back.

The husband almost bit her hand off and the paperwork for the transaction went through quickly. He and his girlfriend congratulated themselves on finally finding a mug happy to take the horrible, stinking house off their hands and they smiled smugly as they watched the removal company pack up everything to take to their new home.

And just to spite his ex-wife, they even took the curtain rods!

✳ **Did you hear about the new Saturday night TV show for divorcees? – It's called *The Ex Factor*.**

★ The judge in a divorce case asked for the representatives to make their final statements.

The lawyer for the husband rose to his feet and said: "M'lud, may I just remind you once again that one of the key incidents in this case was, in actual fact, an act of chivalry. Since when has it been wrong for a husband to open a door for his wife?"

The lawyer for the wife stood up immediately and said: "I think my learned friend is overlooking the fact that the car was travelling at eighty miles an hour at the time."

★ "You're a male chauvinist pig," shrieked the wife. "You have no respect for women, and I want a divorce. And I'm going to take you to the cleaners!"

"That's so unfair," responded the husband. "I'm a new man. I've always treated women with the utmost respect. And anyway isn't cleaning your domain?"

★ When I got divorced, my wife said she would fight me for custody for the kids. I took her out with one punch.

★ Two newlyweds quickly realized that their marriage wasn't working and filed for divorce. The judge asked them what the problem was.

The husband replied: "In the five weeks that we've been together, we haven't been able to agree on a single thing."

The judge turned to the wife: "Have you anything to say?"

She answered: "It's been six weeks, your honour."

★ When a husband and wife appeared in a divorce court, the judge asked: "And what are the grounds for this divorce?"

The husband replied: "We live in a two-storey house."

"A two-storey house!" exclaimed the judge. "Since when has living in a two-storey house been suitable grounds for divorce?"

"Well, your honour," said the husband, "one story is 'I've got a headache' and the other story is 'It's that time of the month.'"

After lengthy discussions with the estranged husband, a divorce lawyer reported to his client: "Mrs Fletcher, I have agreed a settlement with your husband that is entirely fair to both of you."

"Fair to both of us?" Mrs Fletcher exploded. "I could have done that myself! Why do you think I hired a lawyer?"

★ Two guys were discussing their recent divorces. One said: "I suppose it was partly my fault really. I used to go out drinking all hours, leaving her to bring up the kids virtually single-handed."

The other said: "My ex-wife is profoundly deaf and she left me for a deaf friend of hers, and I blame myself."

"Why?"

"Well, I should have seen the signs."

★ "I can't believe that you and Claire are splitting up," said John to his friend Pete. "I've always thought of you as the perfect couple, that you'd be together forever. Surely you can sort things out. It can't be that bad."

"Well," explained Pete, "we were driving through a red-light district last night when Claire said: "Oh look, it's one of those hookers, or prossies, or whores or whatever you call them." And I said: 'It's Kelly. Her name is Kelly.'"

John fell silent for a moment, and then said: "So who do you think will get to keep the house?"

★ An old mountain man from Montana and his pretty young wife were locked in a bitter divorce case, the principal bone of contention being who should have custody of the children.

She maintained that because she had brought the children into the world, she ought to be granted custody. The judge listened patiently to her argument and then asked the old man why he thought he should be awarded custody of the kids.

Slowly the old man rose to his feet, thought for a moment and, addressing the judge, said: "Judge, when I put a quarter in a candy machine and a candy bar comes out, who does it belong to? Me or the machine?"

★ Following her divorce, a woman went to the local Department of Motor Vehicles and asked to have her maiden name reinstated on her driver's licence.

"Will there be any change of address?" asked the female clerk.

"No."

"Oh, good!" said the clerk. "You must have got the house!"

★ A man came home one day and said to his wife: "Honey, what would you do if I said I'd won the lottery?"

She sneered: "I'd take half, and then leave you."

"Excellent," he replied. "I had three numbers and won $10. Here's $5. Now get the hell out of here!"

★ A husband and wife were driving along the highway at fifty-five miles per hour when she suddenly announced: "I know we've been married for seventeen years but I want a divorce."

The husband said nothing but slowly increased the car's speed to sixty miles an hour.

His wife continued: "I don't want you trying to talk me out of it, I've made my decision. If you must know, I've been having an affair with your best friend, and he's a much better lover than you."

Again the husband said nothing, but increased the speed to sixty-five miles an hour.

His wife demanded: "I want the house; it's the least I deserve after giving up my career for you."

The husband remained silent but accelerated to seventy miles per hour.

"I want the kids, too," she added.

He put his foot down so that they were now doing eighty miles an hour.

"And," she went on, "I want the car, the yacht, the bank account and another $100,000 spending money."

He accelerated further and gradually started to steer the car toward a concrete bridge as she inquired: "Is there anything you want?"

Finally he spoke. "No thanks," he said. "I've got everything I need."

"What's that then?" she sneered.

Just before they hit the wall at ninety miles an hour, he replied: "I've got the airbag."

★   ★   ★   ★   ★

DOCTORS

❖ A man went to the doctor and said: "Doctor, I have terrible gas. It happens whenever I bend over."

"Okay," said the doctor, "I'd like you to stand up for me, please, and bend over that chair."

The man duly bent over and as he did so, he let out a loud farting sound, accompanied by the most awful stench.

"I see," said the doctor. He then reached for a long pole that was propped against the wall and said: "Right, this should do the trick."

The man's eyes widened in alarm. "What are you going to do with that?" he asked.

The doctor said: "I'm going to open the window to let some air into this room."

❖ Fed up with her husband's persistent snoring, a woman called on the family doctor to ask him if there was anything he could do to relieve her suffering.

"Well," said the doctor, "there is one operation I can perform that will cure your husband, but it really is rather expensive. It will cost $1,000 down, followed by payments of $1,500 every month for twenty-four months."

"What is it?"

"A new sports car."

"A new sports car? How will that help cure my husband's snoring?"

"Well, he won't be able to sleep at night for worrying about how he's going to pay for it."

❖ A meteorologist's wife went to the doctor and said: "Doctor, I just don't enjoy sex with my husband any more."

The doctor said: "That's because you've been under the weather."

❖ Worried about his performance in bed, a middle-aged husband went to see the doctor who had treated his family for years.

"Doctor," he said, "I've been having erectile problems lately. I'm worried that I may have a heart condition."

The doctor replied: "No, John, you don't have a heart condition. The reason you're having erectile problems is that you have a butt-ugly wife."

❖ A man went to the doctor and said: "Doctor, I've swallowed a bone."

"Are you choking?"

"No, I'm deadly serious."

> 66 An apple a day keeps the doctor away, but in my experience so does an air rifle and an open bedroom window.
>
> Harry Hill 99

Why did the doctor carry out blood tests on secretarial candidates?

So that he could eliminate type-Os.

❖ "Doctor! Doctor!" yelled the panic-stricken woman, rushing into his surgery. "My husband was asleep with his mouth open and he's swallowed a mouse! What shall I do?"

"Don't panic," said the doctor reassuringly. "You just tie a lump of cheese to a piece of string and lower it into your husband's mouth. As soon as the mouse takes a bite, haul it out."

"Oh, thank you, doctor," said the woman, relieved. "I'll go around to the fishmonger straight away and get a cod's head."

"What do you want a cod's head for?" asked the doctor.

"Oh, I forgot to tell you," said the woman. "I've got to get the cat out first!"

❖ A man had trouble with his left hand and wanted to show it to the doctor. Three fingers were willing to co-operate but the thumb and forefinger were opposed.

❖ "Doctor, doctor, you've got to help me. Some mornings I wake up and think I'm Donald Duck. Other times I think I'm Mickey Mouse."

"Hmmm. How long have you been having these Disney spells?"

❖ "What's wrong with me, doc?" asked the worried patient. "My balls have turned blue!"

The doctor examined him and told him that unless he had his testicles removed, he would die.

"You can't do that to me!" cried the patient. "My life won't be worth living!"

"If you don't have your testicles removed within the next forty-eight hours," replied the doctor, "you won't have a life anyway. Do you want to die?"

Left with no choice, the man glumly agreed to have his balls removed.

Two weeks later, the patient returned and announced: "Doc, now my penis has turned blue!"

The doctor examined him and came to the conclusion that unless the penis was removed within the next forty-eight hours, the man would die.

"But doc," protested the man tearfully. "How will I pee?"

"Simple," said the doctor. "We'll install a plastic pipe and that will do the job."

"Oh, I don't know," said the man. "Losing my penis is a terrible prospect."

"Do you want to die?" demanded the doctor brusquely.

Reluctantly, the man consented to the procedure for having his penis removed.

Two weeks later, he returned again. "Doc, the pipe has turned blue! What the hell is happening to me?"

The doctor scratched his head in bewilderment. "I'm not really sure," he said. "Wait . . . do you wear jeans?"

> ❝ I went to the doctor the other day. He told me there was something in my bladder. Whenever they tell you that, it's never anything good, like, 'We found something in your bladder, and it's season tickets to the Yankees!'
>
> Mike Birbiglia ❞

❖ I couldn't decide which of two physicians to see. It was a paradox.

❖ A man went to the doctor and said: "Doc, I keep calling out the names of characters from *The Lord of the Rings* and *The Hobbit* in the middle of the night. What's the matter with me?"

  The doctor said: "It sounds to me as if you've been Tolkien in your sleep."

❖ **"Doctor, doctor, I keep thinking I'm a clock."**

  "Try not to get so wound up."

❖ Racked with indigestion, a man was told by his doctor to drink warm water one hour before breakfast. However, there was no improvement in his condition – indeed when he went back to the doctor, he complained that he was actually feeling worse than ever.

  The doctor said: "Did you drink warm water an hour before breakfast each day?"

  "I tried," replied the patient. "But all I could manage was twenty minutes."

❖ A man went to the doctor and said: "Doc, I bought some steroids, and they've had nasty side effects. I've grown an extra penis."

  "Anabolic?"

  "No, just a penis."

❖ After examining a male patient, a doctor took the man's wife to one side.

"I must be honest with you," said the doctor in an ominous tone, "I don't like the look of your husband."

"Me neither," said the wife. "But he brings home a good wage and he's great with the kids."

❖ A man told the doctor: "I've got AIDS, syphilis, herpes and gonorrhoea."

"Ah," said the doctor, "you're what we call an incurable romantic."

❖ A young woman wasn't feeling very well and asked her boss to recommend a physician. "I know a good one in the city," said the boss, "but he is very expensive. He charges $500 for the first visit and $100 for each one after that."

So when the woman went to the doctor's office, she cheekily tried to save herself $400 by announcing: "It's me again!"

Not fooled for a second, the doctor quickly examined her and said: "Very good. Just continue the treatment I prescribed on your last visit."

❖ "Doctor, can you cure my sleepwalking?"

"Try these."

"Are they sleeping pills?"

"No, they're tintacks. Sprinkle them on the floor."

❖ A newspaper proprietor went to the doctor and said: "Doc, I'm really worried. My paper has lost 50,000 readers over the past year."

"Right," said the doctor. "I'll prescribe you some tablets."

"What use will they be?"

"Well, they'll help improve your circulation."

❖ "Doctor, doctor, I think I may be suffering from déjà vu."

"Didn't I see you yesterday?"

❖   A dwarf woman went to the doctor and said: "Doctor, every time it rains my vagina gets sore."

   The doctor was at a loss to know how to treat her, so he suggested that she came back and saw him when it was raining and then he would see what he could do.

   A couple of days later, it was pouring with rain and the dwarf woman returned to the doctor. "Okay," he said, "stand on the chair and I'll take a look at you."

   So she stood on the chair and he examined the sore area. Producing his scalpel from his desk, he said: "Right, I just need to make a couple of cuts here and there."

   "Yes, anything, doctor, just to relieve the soreness around my vagina."

   A couple of minutes later, he told her to climb down from the chair. "There. How does that feel now?"

   "That's wonderful, doctor. What did you do?"

   "Oh, I just took a couple of inches off the top of your gumboots."

❖   A doctor received a call from a concerned female patient. "I'm diabetic," she said, "and I'm afraid I've had too much sugar today."

   "Are you light-headed?" asked the doctor.

   "No," the caller answered. "I'm a brunette."

❖   A man went to the doctor and said: "Doctor, I keep having visions of the future."

   "When did these start?"

   "Next Thursday."

❖   A woman went to see her doctor for a check-up. Afterwards he said: "I have some good news and some bad news."

   "Okay," said the woman apprehensively. "Tell me the bad news first."

   "Well," said the doctor, "I'm afraid you have a brain tumour and have only two months to live."

   "Oh my God!" cried the woman. "What's the good news?"

   "Congratulations! You're three months pregnant."

A man told the doctor: "I don't know what's wrong with me. My right ear is always warmer than my left one."

"I see the problem," said the doctor. "You need to adjust your toupee."

❖ A flat-chested young woman went to the doctor about having her tiny breasts enlarged. Dr Harrison told her: "Every morning after your shower, rub your chest and say, 'Scooby doobie doobies, I want bigger boobies.'"

So she did this for several months, and amazingly it worked. She grew magnificent D-cup boobs. Then one morning she was running late and in her haste to catch the train, she realized that she had forgotten her morning ritual. Fearing that she might lose her lovely breasts if she didn't recite the rhyme, she stood in the middle of the crowded train and said: "Scooby doobie doobies, I want bigger boobies."

Hearing this, the guy standing next to her said: "Excuse me, are you by any chance a patient of Dr Harrison?"

"Why yes," she replied. "How did you know?"

He leaned closer, winked and whispered: "Hickory dickory dock . . ."

❖ An elderly doctor visited a woman patient at her home. "Could you fetch me a hammer from the garage?" he asked the woman's husband.

The husband fetched the hammer.

"Right," said the old doctor a couple of minutes later. "Now I'd like you to get me some pliers, a screwdriver and a hacksaw."

The husband became alarmed at the last request and asked anxiously: "Just exactly what are you going to do to my wife?"

The old doctor replied: "Nothing until I can get my medical bag open."

❖ A man went to the doctor and said: "Doctor, I think I'm a moth."

The doctor said: "You think you're a moth? Well instead of coming to me, why didn't you go to a psychiatrist?"

The man said: "Your light was on."

❖ A guy went to his lady doctor for an annual check-up. She told him: "You've got to stop masturbating."

"Why?"

"Because I'm trying to examine you."

★　　★　　★　　★　　★

DOGS

✳ A man walked into a restaurant with his dog. The manager quickly intercepted them, saying: "I'm sorry, we don't allow dogs in here."

"But this is a special talking dog," said the man.

"I've heard it all before," said the manager. "People are always coming in and claiming to have talking dogs. But I'm a fair man: if that dog can speak, you can both eat here for free."

"Okay," said the dog owner. "Ask him a question."

"Right, dog, what's above this restaurant?"

The dog growled: "Rrrrooof!"

"I thought so!" said the manager. "He's a fraud. Now get out, the pair of you!"

On their way out, the man and dog looked up. "Oh, sorry!" said the dog. "I didn't realize there was a hairdresser's above the restaurant."

✳ **What do you call a poodle with no legs? A sponge.**

> Dogs have no money. They're broke their entire lives. But they get through. You know why dogs have no money? No pockets.
>
> Jerry Seinfeld

* An eight-year-old boy went into a grocery store and picked out a large box of laundry detergent. The grocer walked over and asked him if he had a lot of laundry to do.

"Oh no, I don't have any laundry to do," said the boy. "I'm going to wash my dog."

"You shouldn't use this stuff on your dog," advised the grocer. "It's very powerful. If you wash your dog in this, he'll get sick. In fact, it might even kill him."

But the boy refused to listen and bought the detergent anyway.

A week later, he was back in the store buying some biscuits. The grocer asked him how his dog was doing.

"Oh, he died," said the boy.

"I'm sorry to hear that," said the grocer, "but I did try to warn you about using that detergent on your dog."

"I don't think it was the detergent that killed him," said the boy.

"Oh," said the grocer. "What was it, then?"

"I think it was the spin cycle."

* Did you hear about the dog that ate nothing but garlic?
His bark was much worse than his bite.

* The best place to smuggle drugs is up a dog's butt. That way, if the sniffer dog suspects anything, the customs officers will think he's just being frisky.

* A man said to his friend: "I took our dog for a walk the other day and played Frisbee with him, but he was useless. I really need to get a flatter dog."

✳ Did you hear about the dog that gave birth to puppies near the road and was ticketed for littering?

✳ Two dog owners were talking in the park. One said: "I'm fed up with my dog – he'll chase anyone on a bike."

"What are you going to do?" asked the other. "Have him put down?"

"No, I think I'll just take his bike away."

✳ In the winter, my dog wears his coat but in the summer he wears his coat and pants.

✳ To prove that a dog is truly man's best friend, lock your dog and your wife in the trunk of your car for three-quarters of an hour. When you open the trunk, which one is really happy to see you?

Dog Property Rules

If I like it, it's mine.

If it's in my mouth, it's mine.

If I can take it from you, it's mine.

If I had it a little while ago, it's mine.

If I'm chewing something up, all the pieces are mine.

If I saw it first, it's mine.

If it just looks like mine, it's mine.

If you are playing with something and you put it down, it automatically becomes mine.

If it's broken, it's yours.

✳ A woman saw an advert in the newspaper that read: "Purebred police dog for sale, $20." Thinking it a bargain, she rang the number and bought the dog. But when it was delivered, she found that she had bought nothing but a mangy-looking mongrel.

So she phoned the man who had placed the ad to complain. "How can you possibly call that scruffy mutt a purebred police dog?"

"Don't let his looks deceive you," said the man. "He's working undercover."

✳ A man was reported to the animal welfare authorities for feeding Viagra to his pet Labrador. The man is now banned from keeping any pets. And the Labrador is now a pointer.

✳ Three handsome male dogs – a German Shepherd, a Labrador and a Chihuahua – were walking down the street when they saw a beautiful female poodle. The three males fell over themselves to be the first to reach her, but ended up arriving in front of her at the same time. They were rendered speechless in the face of her style and elegance and were immediately reduced to slobbering wrecks.

Aware of the effect she was having on her three suitors, the poodle decided to set them a little test to win her heart. She told them: "The first one who can use the words 'liver' and 'cheese' together in an imaginative sentence gets to go on a hot date with me."

The muscular German Shepherd stepped forward and said: "I love liver and cheese."

"Oh dear!" sighed the poodle. "That's not very imaginative at all."

So the sleek black Labrador stepped forward and said: "I hate liver and cheese."

"That's just as bad as the first one," groaned the poodle. "You'll have to do better than that."

Finally the little Chihuahua stepped forward and, turning to the other two with a sly smile, said: "Liver alone. Cheese mine."

＊ A keen duck hunter was looking to buy a new bird dog. His search ended when he found a dog that could actually walk on water to retrieve a duck. Amazed by his discovery, he was sure none of his friends would ever believe him.

He decided to try and break the news to a friend of his, an eternal pessimist who steadfastly refused to be impressed by anyone or anything. In the hope that even he would be impressed by a dog that could walk on water, the pessimist was invited to join the hunter and his dog on a trip to the country. However, the hunter deliberately refrained from mentioning the dog's special talent – he wanted his friend to see for himself.

The two men and the dog made their way to a good hunting lake and as they waited by the shore, a flock of ducks flew overhead. The men fired, and a duck fell. The dog responded and jumped into the water, but instead of sinking, it walked across the water to retrieve the bird, never getting more than its paws wet. This continued throughout the day. Each time a duck fell, the dog walked across the surface of the water to retrieve it.

The pessimist watched carefully, observing everything, but did not say a word. Then on the drive home, the hunter finally casually asked his friend: "Did you notice anything unusual about my new dog?"

"Sure did," replied the pessimist. "He can't swim."

> Why are all the dogs at dog shows really nice dogs? You never see a pitbull with a ribbon around his head, going, 'If you say one fucking word . . .'
> Lee Evans

＊ I bought a new dog yesterday. I've named him Rolex. He's a watchdog.

A Dog's Diary

8 a.m.: Dog food! My favourite thing!

9 a.m.: A car ride! My favourite thing!

9.20 a.m.: A walk in the park! My favourite thing!

9.45 a.m.: Dived in the lake! My favourite thing!

10.30 a.m.: Got rubbed and petted! My favourite thing!

12.15 p.m.: Lamb bones! My favourite thing!

1 p.m.: Played in the yard! My favourite thing!

2.30 p.m.: Saw another dog! My favourite thing!

4.10 p.m.: Chased a car! My favourite thing!

5 p.m.: Dinner! My favourite thing!

7 p.m.: Played ball! My favourite thing!

8 p.m.: Watched TV with the people! My favourite thing!

11 p.m.: Sleeping on the bed! My favourite thing!

DRINK AND DRUNKS

★ Two men were drinking in a bar. One of the men, who was very drunk, said: "I bet you $100 that I can bite my eye."

The second guy thought it would be easy taking money from a drunk, so he said: "Okay, you're on."

The drunk then took out his glass eye and bit it. And the second guy had to pay the $100.

A while later, the drunk said: "I bet you $100 I can bite my other eye."

Knowing that the drunk couldn't possibly have two glass eyes, otherwise he wouldn't have been able to see, the second guy accepted the challenge, confident that he would win back his money.

The drunk promptly took out his false teeth and bit his other eye.

★   Phil arrived home from the pub late one Friday evening drunk as usual, and crept into bed beside his wife, who was already asleep. He kissed her gently on the cheek and fell asleep. When he awoke, he found a strange man standing at the end of his bed. "Who the hell are you?" asked Phil, "and what are you doing in my bedroom?"

The mysterious man answered: "I am St Peter and this is not your bedroom."

Phil was stunned. "You mean I'm dead? I can't be, I have so much to live for, and I haven't said goodbye to my family. You have to send me back straight away."

St Peter replied: "Yes, you can be reincarnated, but there is a condition. We can only send you back as a dog or a hen."

Phil was devastated, but knowing there was a farm not far from his house, he asked to be sent back as a hen. A flash of light later, he was covered in feathers and clucking around, pecking the ground.

"This isn't so bad," he thought until he experienced a strange feeling welling up inside him.

The farmyard rooster strolled over and said, "So you're the new hen. How are you enjoying your first day here?"

"It's okay," said Phil, "but I have this strange feeling inside like I'm about to explode."

"You're ovulating," explained the rooster. "Don't tell me you've never laid an egg before!"

"Never," replied Phil.

"Well just relax," advised the rooster, "and let it happen."

So he did and after a few uncomfortable seconds, an egg popped out from under Phil's tail. An immense sense of relief swept over him and his emotions got the better of him as he experienced motherhood for the first time. When he then laid his second egg, the feeling of happiness was overwhelming and he knew that being reincarnated as a hen was the best thing that had ever happened to him.

The joy kept coming but just as he was about to lay his third egg, he felt an enormous smack on the back of his head and heard his wife shouting: "Phil, wake up, you drunken bastard! You've shit the bed!"

> There are these machines now that tell you when to stop drinking. They're called cashpoint machines.
>
> Harry Hill

★ A man woke up one morning to find his wife cooking in the kitchen. He saw one of his socks in the frying pan. "What on earth are you doing?" he cried.

   She said: "I'm doing what you asked me to do last night when you came to bed drunk."

   Puzzled, he thought to himself, "I don't remember asking her to cook my sock . . ."

★ Staggering home from the pub, a drunk was desperate for a pee, and so decided to relieve himself up against a wall.

   Just then, a police car pulled up, lights flashing, and a policewoman called out: "If I wasn't on my way to a burglary, I'd put you inside."

   "You're not missing much," shouted the drunk. "I can never get it up after ten pints."

★ She was only a whisky maker but he loved her still.

★ A guy said to his drinking partner: "I got so drunk last night that someone put me in the recovery position. This morning I woke up in the back of a breakdown truck."

> My local's rough as anything. I went to the pub quiz the other night. The first question was, 'What the fuck are you looking at?'
>
> Jack Dee

★ A man confided to a bartender: "I got really drunk last night and ended up snogging my best friend. It was so embarrassing – I couldn't even face taking him for a walk this morning."

> Starbucks announced that they are laying off a thousand workers and closing more stores. Experts predict that by the end of the year, we could wind up with just two Starbucks on every corner.
>
> Jay Leno

★ Did you hear about the guy who got drunk and collapsed in a heap beside the bar?

It caused a major delay in the gymnastics competition.

★ A drunk was walking through a park when he saw a woman in the lake, flapping her arms about and screaming: "Help me, I can't swim!"

He shouted back: "Neither can I, but I don't go around making a great fuss about it!"

★ A guy walked into a bar and saw Van Gogh sitting on a stool.

"Hi, Vince," he said. "Can I get you a drink?"

"No, you're okay," said Van Gogh. "I've got one 'ere."

> What I don't get is that women will accept a drink from you in a bar. But when I stand on my front doorstep with a can of Kestrel, see a female and ask, 'D'you want a swig?' they run away.
>
> Sean Lock

★ A drunk staggered out of a bar, swaying and stumbling all over the place, barely able to put one foot in front of the other. He eventually managed to reach his car, but just as he was about to try and open the door, a police officer tapped him on the shoulder and said: "I hope you're not thinking of driving tonight, sir?"

"Of course I am," replied the drunk. "I'm in no fit state to walk!"

★ Did you know that there are female hormones in beer?

  If you drink too much, it makes you talk garbage and drive badly.

★ Arriving home drunk one night, a husband cut himself when he walked into an overhanging shelf in the garage. With blood trickling down his face, he went straight upstairs to the bathroom to carry out repairs on his wounds.

  The next morning his wife said: "You came home drunk last night, didn't you?"

  "No," he replied, mustering all the sincerity at his disposal.

  "Then perhaps you can explain to me why there are plasters all over the bathroom mirror?"

> " Eggnog, who thought that one up? 'I wanna get a little drunk, but I also want some pancakes.'
>
> Dave Attell "

★ Betty, the self-appointed moral guardian and general busybody of a small town, publicly accused a local man, Ted, of being an alcoholic purely because she had seen his pickup truck parked outside the town's only bar one afternoon.

  A man of few words, Ted stared at her for a moment and then walked off without saying anything. Later that evening, he parked his pickup truck in front of Betty's house and left it there all night.

★ An old drunk was wandering around an airport terminal with tears streaming down his face.

  "What's the problem?" asked an airline employee.

  "I've lost all my luggage," sobbed the drunk.

  "How did that happen?"

  "The cork fell out."

★ A man was staggering home drunk in the early hours of the morning when he was stopped by a police officer.

"What are you doing out at this time of night?" asked the officer.

"I'm going to a lecture," said the drunk.

"And who's going to be giving a lecture at this hour?"

"My wife."

★ A man walked into a bar sporting a black eye.

"What happened to you?" asked his friend.

"Well, I was drinking in here last night when this big burly guy deliberately barged into me, spilling all my beer. I'd had a few by then, so feeling brave, I told him: 'Right, we'll sort this outside!' 'Chill out, man,' he said. 'I'm a lover, not a fighter.' So in an act of forgiveness, I gave him a playful kiss. It turned out he *was* a fighter . . ."

★ A drunk walked into a bar and started staring at the barmaid's cleavage. Then he leaned over the bar and started kissing her. She was stunned by his behaviour but when she had pulled herself together, she slapped him very hard across the face, and he apologized immediately.

"I'm sorry," he said, "but I thought you were my wife – you look just like her."

"You worthless, wretched, no good drunk!" she exclaimed. "Don't you ever lay your grubby little hands on me again!"

"Well I'll be damned," said the drunk. "You even sound just like her, too!"

★ A drunk staggered into a Catholic church, sat down in the confession box and said nothing. The bewildered priest coughed to attract his attention, but still the drunk remained silent. The priest then knocked on the wall three times in a final attempt to get the man to speak.

"No use knocking, pal," said the drunk. "There's no paper in this one either."

★ An attractive woman in her forties was standing at the bar when she turned to the man next to her and purred: "I love the strong silent type."

Thinking he was being chatted up, he replied: "You mean a man like me?"

"No," she said moving away, "Farts – like the one I've just done."

A man went to the doctor with a mystery ailment.
The doctor asked: "Do you drink to excess?"
The man replied: "I'll drink to anything."

★ A woman and her husband were out having a few drinks in a bar. As they were discussing different drinks, she remembered a new cocktail she had heard about and begged her husband to try one.

After a little persuasion, he relented and allowed her to order the drink for him. The bartender subsequently placed the following items on the bar: a salt shaker, a shot of Baileys, and a shot of lime juice.

The husband looked at the ingredients quizzically and the woman explained: "First you put a bit of salt on your tongue. Next you drink the shot of Baileys and hold it in your mouth. Then finally you drink the lime juice."

So the husband, trying to please her, went along with it. He put the salt on his tongue – it was salty, obviously, but okay. He drank the shot of Baileys – smooth, rich, cool, very pleasant. He thought it was quite a good drink – until he drank the lime juice.

At one second, the sharp lime taste hit. At two seconds, the Baileys curdled. At three seconds, the salty, curdled taste and mucous-like consistency hit. At four seconds, it felt as if he had a mouth full of catarrh. This triggered his gag reflex, but being manly and not wanting to disappoint his wife, he swallowed the now foul-tasting drink.

After finally choking it down, he turned to his wife and said: "My God, what do you call that drink?"

She smiled at him and answered: "Blow Job Revenge."

★ A woman yelled at her husband as he stumbled through the front door: "What's the big idea coming home half drunk?"
"Sorry, honey," he slurred. "I ran out of money."

★ A hardened drinker took his sixteen-year-old son to his local bar for the first time and ordered beers for them both. Several drinks later, the boy had given up but his father was blind drunk, became involved in a fight and ended up being thrown out into the gutter, where he was violently sick.
Wiping the vomit from his mouth, he said to his son: "See? And all these years you and your mother thought I came here to enjoy myself!"

★ Did you hear about the man who called his father-in-law "the Exorcist" because every time he came to visit he made the spirits disappear?

★ A drunk stumbled into the back of a taxi. He leaned towards the driver and said: "Excuse me, have you got room for a lobster and three bottles of wine on your front seat?"
"I think so," said the driver.
"Good," replied the drunk, and he threw up.

★   ★   ★   ★   ★

ENGINEERS

❖ Most people believe that if it ain't broke, don't fix it. Engineers believe that if it ain't broke, it doesn't have enough features yet.

You Know You're an Engineer If . . .

You have ever removed the back of your TV set just to see what's inside.

Your wristwatch has more buttons than a telephone.

You have a pet named after a scientist.

You can type seventy words a minute but can't read your own handwriting.

You always explain things by drawing on a napkin.

You own one or more white short-sleeved dress shirts.

You have more toys than your children.

You can understand sentences containing four or more acronyms.

You have ever saved the power cord from a broken appliance.

At traffic lights, you try to figure out the synchronization pattern between your car's windscreen wipers and those of the car next to you.

You take along a printout of the schedule of your family vacation.

Your IQ is bigger than your weight.

You can remember nine computer passwords but not your wedding anniversary.

❖ A physicist, a mathematician and an engineer were out in the woods on a scouting expedition when an animal suddenly darted through the bush.

The physicist observed that it behaved like a deer, so it must have been a deer. The mathematician asked the physicist what it was, thereby reducing it to a previously solved problem. The engineer was in the woods to hunt deer. Therefore it was a deer.

❖ Three engineers boarded a crowded bus and somehow managed to work their way to the middle of the vehicle where they found three girls willing to exchange their seats for a place on the guys' laps.

After travelling like that for several minutes, the first girl asked the man on whose lap she was perched: "Are you by any chance an electrical engineer?"

"Yes, I am," he replied, surprised. "How did you know?"

"Easy," she said cheekily. "I'm getting shocked by your soldering iron."

A few minutes later, the second girl asked her guy: "Do you happen to be a mechanical engineer?"

"Why yes," he said. "How did you know that?"

"Simple," she smiled. "Your piston is scraping my cylinder."

Shortly afterwards, the third girl turned to her guy and asked: "Are you a civil engineer?"

"I certainly am," he answered. "How could you have known that?"

"Well," she said, "I figured it out as soon as your dam burst and flooded my village."

❖ Scientists at NASA built a gun specifically for launching dead chickens at the windshields of civilian airplanes, jet fighters and the space shuttle, all travelling at maximum velocity. The idea was to simulate the frequent collisions with airborne fowl and to test the strength of the windshields in such situations.

British engineers heard about the special gun and were eager to test it on the windshields of their new high-speed trains. So it was arranged that one of the guns should be sent to the British engineers.

When the gun was fired, the British engineers stood shocked as the chicken hurtled out of the barrel, crashed through the supposedly shatterproof shield, smashing it to pieces, blasted through the control console, snapped the engineer's backrest in two and embedded itself in a wall.

The horrified British sent NASA the disastrous results of the experiment, along with the designs of the windshield, and begged the US scientists for suggestions.

NASA responded with a one-line memo: "Thaw the chicken."

★　　★　　★　　★　　★

ESKIMOS

✳ Three Inuit were talking about how cold it was. One said: "I don't ever remember it being this cold. Come to my igloo and I'll show how cold it is."

So the three men trooped off to his igloo, where they found a can of beer frozen solid.

The second Inuit said: "My igloo is colder than this. Come with me and I'll show you what I mean."

So they headed for the second man's igloo, where they watched as a fresh pot of hot coffee froze as it was poured into a cup.

The third Inuit said: "That's not cold! My igloo is much colder than this. Come over and see."

So they trekked through the snow to the third igloo, where the third Inuit pulled down the furs on his bed. The other two stared in amazement at three frozen balls that lay on the bed. The third Inuit then lit a match and held it under the frozen balls. As they heated up, they burst with a "fart, fart, fart."

* What's the difference between a eunuch and an Eskimo?

    A eunuch is a massive vassal with a passive tassel, while an Eskimo is a rigid midget with a frigid digit.

* Two Eskimos were chatting. One said: "Where did your mother come from?"

    "Alaska."

    "Don't bother, I'll ask her myself!"

> What do you get when you cross an Eskimo and a Mexican?
>
>   A snowblower that doesn't work.

* An Eskimo was fishing on the polar ice cap at a time of year when there were twenty-three hours of sunshine a day. After eighteen hours, his butt was numb with cold, so he packed up his gear and headed back to his igloo. There, he hung up his sealskin coat and was just tucking into his seal steak dinner when his wife said: "Ingit?"

    "What?" he said without changing his expression.

    "I've got some news for you."

    "What?" he said through clenched teeth.

    "Your mother-in-law has slipped on the ice and broken her hip."

    Again his expression didn't change, but he picked up a frozen herring from the table and smacked his wife on the head with the fish.

    "Ow!" she yelled. "What did you do that for?"

    "I've told you before: don't make me laugh when I've got chapped lips."

★   ★   ★   ★   ★

FAMILIES

❝ I come from a very traditional family. When I was seven, my Uncle Terry hanged himself on Christmas Eve. My family didn't take his body down until the 6th of January.

Nick Doody ❞

★ A man went to his wife's family for Sunday lunch for the first time. As he sat down at the table, his mother-in-law asked him: "How many potatoes would you like?"

"Just one," he replied.

"It's okay," she said, "there's no need to be polite."

"Very well," he said. "I'll have one, you fat old cow!"

★ A little boy greeted his grandma with a hug and said: "I'm so happy to see you, Grandma. Now maybe Daddy will do the trick he has been promising us."

"What trick's that?" she asked.

"Well," said the little boy excitedly, "I heard Daddy tell Mommy that he would climb the walls if you came to visit us again."

❝ My grandfather once killed a bear. It was looking the other way so he pushed it off a cliff.

Mark Watson ❞

★ Two small boys were arguing over whose dad was the coolest. "My dad's really cool," boasted one. "He works in Hollywood and he gets to hang out with all the famous movie stars. How cool is that?"

"Well, my dad's more than cool," countered the other. "He's cold; he's dead."

> ❝ What my mom used to do to punish me, because she couldn't hit me, was to iron a crease into the front of my pants. So then the other kids at school would hit me. ❞
>
> Josh Thomas

★ Tom was plagued by his spiteful mother-in-law who, much to his dismay, lived with the family. Each morning, just as he was about to leave for work, the mother-in-law would take him to one side and hiss: "If you don't treat my daughter right after I'm dead, I'll dig up from the grave and haunt you!"

It was the same when Tom came home for lunch. The mother-in-law would sidle up to him and whisper menacingly: "If you don't treat my daughter right after I'm dead, I'll dig up from the grave and haunt you!"

And at night, she would collar him on his way to bed and snarl: "If you don't treat my daughter right after I'm dead, I'll dig up from the grave and haunt you!"

He had recounted his awful life with the old woman to a friend. Later, after not seeing Tom for a few months, the friend asked him how his mother-in-law was feeling.

"She isn't feeling anything," said Tom gleefully. "She died three weeks ago."

"Aren't you worried about her ominous threat?" asked the friend.

"Not really," replied Tom, "but, just to be sure, I had her buried face down. So let her dig!"

★ When I left home, my mother said: "Don't forget to write." I thought, "That's unlikely. After all, it's a fairly basic skill."

★ Father: "Did Paul bring you home last night?"
Daughter: "Yes, it was late, Dad. Did the noise disturb you?"
Father: "No, it wasn't the noise. It was the silence."

★ Two small boys were talking on their way home from school. One said: "I'm really worried. My dad works sixty hours a week to give us a lovely home, plenty of food and great vacations. And my mom spends half her time keeping the house clean and washing and ironing my clothes, and the rest of her time doing a part-time job to earn us extra little luxuries."

"Wow!" said his friend. "You sound really lucky. So why are you worried?"

The first boy said: "What if they try to escape?"

★ Two young men were discussing their fathers. One said: "I recently split up with my girlfriend, and my dad really helped me get through it."

"Yeah?"

"Yeah." He said: "Forget about her, son. She wasn't even any good in bed."

★ I decided to trace my family tree because I'm not very good at drawing.

★ A couple's marriage nearly broke up because of the presence in their household of old Aunt Jessie. For nineteen long years, she lived with them, always bad-tempered, always demanding. Then finally she passed away.

On the way back from the cemetery, the husband confessed to his wife: "Darling, if I didn't love you so much I don't think I could have put up with having your Aunt Jessie in the house all those years."

His wife looked at him aghast. "My Aunt Jessie?" she cried. "I thought she was your Aunt Jessie!"

★ Two married men were sitting in a bar discussing their respective mothers-in-law. One said: "They say if you look at your mother-in-law, you can see your wife in thirty years."

"That's rubbish," said the other. "I looked at my mother-in-law today and I saw my wife fifteen minutes later."

★ A married couple were celebrating their golden wedding anniversary. Their three sons, all extremely successful and wealthy, agreed to a Sunday lunch to mark the occasion, but as usual they were all late and came up with a variety of excuses.

The first son turned up fifteen minutes late. "Happy anniversary," he said. "Sorry I'm a bit late. I had a flat tyre this morning and as a result I'm afraid I haven't had time to get you a present."

"Not to worry," said the father. "The important thing is that you made it here okay."

Five minutes later, son number two showed up. "Happy anniversary," he said. "Sorry I'm late, but my flight from Paris was delayed, and so I haven't had time to buy you a present."

"Never mind," said the father. "It's the thought that counts."

Ten minutes later, the third son arrived. "Happy anniversary," he said breathlessly. "Really sorry I'm late, but it's been manic at work. I even had to go into the office this morning, which left me with no time to buy you a present."

"It's not important," said the father. "All the matters is that the five of us are here together today."

They enjoyed a convivial meal, at the end of which the father stood up and made a little announcement: "Listen, you three, there's something your mother and I have wanted to tell you for a long time. We came to this country penniless but by working hard we were able to save enough to send the three of you to university and lay the foundations for your glitteringly successful careers. The thing is, we worked so hard that we never actually got round to getting married . . ."

The three sons gasped in shock. "You mean we're bastards?"

"Yeah," said the father. "And cheap ones too!"

I remember the same year that my uncle went to prison for forgery was when I stopped getting a birthday card from Pamela Anderson.

* A man said to a friend at work: "I went to see my grandma last night. I held her hand and watched her slip away."

  "Oh, that's really sad."

  "Not really. I might even take her tobogganing again next week."

* When he saw how astronomically high his latest phone bill was, the head of the house called a family meeting.

  "This is unacceptable," said the father. "You have to limit the use of the phone. I never use this phone – I always use the one at the office."

  The mother said: "Same here. I hardly ever use the home phone, because I use my work phone."

  The son said: "Me, too. I never use the home phone. I always use the company's mobile."

  "So what is the problem?" asked the maid. "We all use our work telephones."

* A butcher lived in an apartment above his shop. One night he was woken by strange noises from below. So he crept downstairs and there he quietly observed his eighteen-year-old daughter sitting on a chopping board and pleasuring herself with a liverwurst. Without saying a word, the butcher sighed knowingly and tiptoed back up to bed.

  The next day, a customer came into the shop and asked for some liverwurst.

  "I'm afraid we're clean out of liverwurst," replied the butcher. "There's none left."

  "What do you mean?" snapped the customer. "What's that hanging on the hook over there?"

  The butcher leaned forward and said: "That, sir, is my son-in-law."

★ I went to the zoo with my family today. In the afternoon, I was watching the gorillas with my gran when they suddenly started mating. It hurt at first, but I think gran enjoyed it.

★ A couple were admiring their garden from the kitchen window. The wife said: "Sooner or later, we're going to have to make a proper scarecrow to keep the birds off the flowerbeds."

"What's wrong with the one we've got?" asked the husband.

"Nothing. But mother's arms are getting tired."

> 66 I had all my grandchildren together and they still fight. It's like nature's way of saying, 'You should have given head.'
>
> Thea Vidale 99

★ A man outlined his father's philosophy to his teenage sons. "Grandpa strongly believes that you should live every day as if it were your last – which is why for the past twenty-two years he has been in the intensive care unit wearing an oxygen mask and with a tube up his butt."

★ Wanting to take his children to the movies, a father reserved three tickets over the phone.

"How much are the tickets?" he asked.

"Eight dollars," said the ticket advisor.

"How much for the children?"

"The same price, eight dollars."

"But the airlines only charge half fare for children."

"Well, why don't you put your kids on a plane to somewhere and you come to the movie? You'll probably enjoy it a lot more that way."

★ A guy waiting in a bank line kept shaking his head in sorrow.

"Are you all right?" asked the woman behind him.

"Yeah, I've just had my dreams dashed, that's all. You see, I thought I was made for life when my dad died and I inherited his estate. But apparently 1997 Volvos aren't worth much these days."

★　★　★　★　★

FARMERS

❖ A farmer's young son ran into the house and said: "Mommy, Mommy, the bull is shagging the cow!"

"Timmy, please!" cried his mother, aghast. "Don't use language like that. You must be polite. You have to say the bull is 'surprising the cow'."

Twenty minutes later, the boy ran in again. "Mommy, Mommy, the bull is surprising all the cows!"

"He can't be surprising *all* the cows, Timmy."

"He is. He's shagging the horse!"

❖ Two farmers were standing in a field. One said: "Have you seen my flock of cows?"

The other corrected him: "Herd of cows."

"'Course I've heard of cows. I've got a whole flock of them!"

❖ A farmer was in a bar talking to villagers about his animals. "I've just been informed that a lot of my sheep have blue tongue."

"That must have come as a shock," said one of the villagers.

"Indeed it has," said the farmer. "I didn't even know my sheep had cell phones."

❖ Two brothers inherited a farm, where the livestock consisted of a herd of cows and one horny bull. On their first morning in charge, the brothers went outside to find that the bull had escaped from his pen and run amok with the cows. When the brothers found him, his eyes were crossed.

Not knowing what to do for the best, they called the local veterinary. He came out that afternoon, stuck a tube in the bull's rear, blew really hard on the other end of the tube, and the bull's eyes went back to normal. He charged the brothers $180.

On the second morning, the brothers woke to discover that the bull was back out with the cows and his eyes were crossed again. With money tight, they decided against calling the vet, reasoning that if they could find a tube, they could do it themselves.

One brother said to the other: "I'll blow on the tube, you watch his eyes."

After a series of unsuccessful attempts, the brothers decided they should switch roles. The one who was originally watching the eyes walked round to the rear of the bull, pulled out the tube, and stuck the other end in.

"What did you do that for?" asked his brother.

"Well, you don't think I want to blow on the same end as you, do you?"

❖ **Did you hear about the farmer who called his pig Ink because it was always running out of the pen?**

❖ A man, a woman and their three sons lived on a farm in the country. Early one morning, the farmer's wife awoke and looking out of the window, saw that the family's only cow was lying dead in the field. Fearing that with the cow dead she would no longer be able to feed her family, the poor woman went to the barn and hanged herself.

A few minutes later, the farmer awoke. Finding both the cow and his wife dead, he saw no reason to continue living and shot himself dead.

Then the eldest son woke to find both of his parents and the cow dead. In the depths of despair, he ran to the river and decided to drown himself. When he reached the river, he found a small mermaid sitting on the bank. She said: "I've seen what has happened and know why you are so sad, but if you will have sex with me five times in a row, I will bring your parents and the cow back to life."

The son agreed to try, but after four times, he was simply unable to satisfy her again. So the mermaid drowned him in the river.

Next the middle son woke up and, discovering what had happened, he, too, elected to throw himself into the river. The mermaid said to him: "I have seen the tragedy that has befallen you, but if you will have sex with me ten times in a row, I will restore your family and your cow to you."

The son tried his best, but could not get beyond eight. So the mermaid drowned him in the river.

Finally the youngest son woke up. He saw the cow dead, his parents dead, and his brothers gone. Deciding that he no longer wished to live, he ran down to the river with the intention of drowning himself. When he got there, the mermaid said: "I have seen all that has happened, but if you have sex with me fifteen times in a row, I will make everything all right again."

The youngest son replied: "Is that all? Why not twenty times in a row?"

The mermaid was taken aback by the suggestion.

Then the youngest son said: "Hell, why not twenty-five times in a row, or even thirty?"

"Okay," said the mermaid, scarcely able to believe her good fortune. "If you have sex with me thirty times in a row, I will bring everybody back to perfect health."

The youngest son was just about to drop his pants when he said: "Wait! How do I know that thirty times in a row won't kill you like it did the cow?"

❖ Did you hear about the farmer who found hundreds of phallic-shaped toadstools growing on his land?

Unfortunately he's now having trouble with squatters.

❖   A farmer was helping one of his cows to give birth when he noticed his young son watching wide-eyed from behind the fence. "Oh dear," thought the farmer, "I'm going to have to explain the birds and bees to him."

So when he had finished, he asked the boy: "Well, have you got any questions about what you've just seen?"

"Just one," said the boy. "How fast was that calf going when it hit the cow?"

❖   A farmhand went to church one Sunday, but when he entered he saw that he and the preacher were the only ones present. The preacher asked the farmhand if he wanted him to go ahead and preach.

"Well," said the farmhand, "I'm not too smart, but if I went to feed my cattle and only one showed up, I'd still feed him."

So the minister began his sermon. An hour passed, then two hours, then two and a half hours. Finally the preacher finished, and asked the farmhand whether he had enjoyed the sermon.

"Well," said the farmhand, "I'm not too smart, but if I went to feed my cattle and only one showed up, I sure wouldn't feed him all the hay."

❖   On a hot summer afternoon, a beautiful young woman came across a secluded pool, largely hidden from view by a row of bushes. After checking that nobody was around, she took off all her clothes, but just as she was about to jump in, a man appeared from behind the bushes.

"I've been watching you!" he yelled, "This is private farm land, and I'm the owner. Swimming in this pool is strictly prohibited."

"You could have told me that before I undressed!" she said.

The farmer replied: "Swimming is prohibited; undressing isn't."

❖ A farmer was giving his wife last-minute instructions before going into town on business. He said: "That fellow will be along this afternoon to impregnate one of the cows. I've hung a nail by the correct stall so you'll know which one I want him to impregnate."

Satisfied that his wife understood, the farmer left for town.

That afternoon, the inseminator arrived, and the wife, who knew virtually nothing about farming, dutifully led him out to the barn and directly to the stall with the nail.

"This is the cow right here," she said.

"What's the nail for?" asked the inseminator.

She shrugged and replied: "I guess it's to hang up your pants."

❖ A farmer was pulling a cartload of horse manure down the lane.

"What are you going to do with that?" asked his dim-witted farmhand.

"I'm going to put it on my strawberries," said the farmer.

"That's odd," said the farmhand. "We put cream and sugar on ours."

> Why did the farmer plough his field with a steam-roller?
>
> He wanted to grow mashed potatoes.

❖ A farmer was distraught because his faithful sheepdog had gone missing. His wife suggested: "Why don't you put an advert in the paper to get him back?"

"That's a good idea," said the farmer. So he placed the ad, but a month later there was still no sign of the dog.

The farmer's wife said: "I really thought that advert would work. What did you write in it?"

The farmer replied: "Here, boy."

FASHION

✳ A young man kept pestering a tailor about giving him a job selling suits.

Eventually the tailor agreed that if the young man could sell a particularly hideous green suit, he would take him on.

"But don't get your hopes up," he warned. "That suit has been in this shop for more than two years. Nobody has been able to sell it – not even me. So I doubt you'll fare any better than the others."

Two hours later, the tailor returned from lunch to find the young man bleeding, his face covered in scratches and his clothing torn, but wearing a big smile.

"I sold the green suit," grinned the young man.

"Congratulations," said the tailor. "The job is yours. Nobody has come close to selling that old, ugly green suit. But tell me, what on earth happened to you?"

The young man replied: "Well, the customer loved the suit, but as for my injuries, unfortunately he had a really sensitive seeing-eye dog."

> ❝ If you have a choice of selling shoes to ladies or giving birth to a flaming porcupine, look into that second, less painful career.
>
> Richard Jeni ❞

> ❝ Some people arrange the clothes in their wardrobe according to colours; I arrange mine according to stains.
>
> Sean Lock ❞

✳ A guy bought a jacket from a charity shop. The only thing wrong with it was one sleeve was slightly longer than the other two.

✳ A guy walked into the office wearing a horribly loud shirt and tie.

"Do you like my new shirt?" he asked a colleague. "It's made of the finest silk and has got loads of cactuses all over it."

"Cacti," said the colleague, correcting him.

"Never mind the tie! Look at my shirt!"

> 66 I think that when you get dressed in the morning, sometimes you're really making a decision about your behaviour for the day. Like if you put on flip-flops you're saying, 'Hope I don't get chased today.'
> Demetri Martin 99

✳ A woman said to her friend: "Whenever I'm down in the dumps I buy myself a dress."

"Really?" said the friend. "I've always wondered where you got them."

> 66 I saw a transvestite wearing a T-shirt that said 'Guess'.
> Demetri Martin 99

> 66 You know it's time to do the laundry when you dry off with a sneaker.
> Zach Galifianakis 99

✳ My daughter said she wanted to get lots of body piercings. So to save on money, I made her bath the cat.

> 66 I used to file my nails, but I thought, 'What's the point in keeping them?'
> Tim Vine 99

* Getting ready for a night out, a young woman appeared wearing a low-cut top, tight black leather mini skirt and thigh-length boots.

  "You look like you're going to a brothel!" scoffed her boyfriend.

  "Well, what if I am?" she said defiantly.

  He replied: "You could give me a lift."

> ❝ Men want the same thing from their underwear that they want from women: a little bit of support and a little bit of freedom.
>
> Jerry Seinfeld ❞

* I went to a shoe shop and they had a special offer: "Buy one, get one free." Then I thought, "Aren't all shoes sold that way?"

* A man walked into a shoe shop and asked for a pair of shoes, size eight.

  The sales assistant said: "Are you sure, sir? You look like a size twelve to me."

  "Just bring me a size eight," insisted the customer.

  So the assistant fetched a pair of size eight shoes, and the man squeezed his feet into them with obvious discomfort. He then stood up in the shoes, but with considerable pain.

  "Are you absolutely sure you want these shoes?" repeated the assistant.

  "Listen," said the man. "I've lost my house to the bank, I live with my mother-in-law, my daughter ran off with my best friend and my son just told me he's gay. The only pleasure I have left is to come home at night and take my shoes off!"

> ❝ I like what mechanics wear, overall.
>
> Stewart Francis ❞

Euphemisms for "Your Flies Are Open"

The cucumber has left the salad.

I can see the gun of Navarone.

The beast is asleep, but the gate is open.

You've got Windows in your laptop.

Your soldier isn't so unknown now.

Paging Mr Johnson . . . Paging Mr Johnson . . .

Elvis Junior has left the building.

The Buick is not all the way in the garage.

I thought you were crazy; now I see your nuts.

You need to bring your tray table to the upright and locked position.

You've got your fly set for Monica instead of Hillary.

You've got a security breach at Los Pantalones.

Quasimodo needs to go back in the tower and tend to his bell.

Sailor Ned's trying to take a little shore leave.

* ### The designers of jeans are always looking at the bottom line.

* Struggling to make ends meet on his meagre salary, a young pastor was horrified to find that his wife had spent $300 on a new dress.

   "How could you do it?" he demanded.

   She explained apologetically: "I was outside the store looking at the dress in the window, and the next thing I knew, I was trying it on. It was like Satan was whispering in my ear: 'You look fabulous in that dress. Buy it!'"

   "Well," replied the pastor, "you know how I deal with that kind of temptation. I say: 'Get thee behind me, Satan!'"

   "I did," replied the wife, "but then Satan said: 'It looks fabulous from back here, too!'"

* My wife is very big in fashion – size twenty!

* Elias Howe, the inventor of the zip fastener, is to be honoured with a posthumous peerage. From now on, he will be known as the Lord of the Flies.

> **“** Am I the only one who's always tempted to light the wick on the top of a beret?
>
> Paul Merton **”**

* Two men were enjoying a long evening drinking at the bar. After about five hours, one turned to the other and said: "I've got to get out of here. I have to go home and take my wife's panties off."

   The other man looked at him and said: "What made you suddenly think of that?"

   The first guy replied: "Because they're too damn tight and they're cutting off my blood circulation."

*   *   *   *   *

FISH AND FISHING

★ A small boy was looking after his baby sister while his parents went shopping in town. He decided to go fishing, so he took her with him.

But that evening when his parents were back home, he was in a bad mood. "I'm never taking my sister fishing again," he told his mother. "I didn't catch a thing!"

"Never mind," said his mother. "Next time I'm sure she'll be quiet and not scare the fish away."

"It wasn't that," said the boy. "She ate all the bait!"

> Interesting fact: a shark will only attack you if you're wet.
>
> Sean Lock

★ A husband crept out of bed early one Saturday morning to go fishing. He packed his fishing equipment in the trunk of the car, hooked up the boat on a trailer and set off. The weather was terrible – driving sleet and a howling gale – so after a couple of miles he stopped the car to listen to the weather forecast in the hope that conditions would improve as the morning wore on. When it was obvious that the bad weather was set in for the day, he decided to turn around and go home.

Having parked the car in the garage, he crept back up the stairs and slid into bed, cuddling up to his wife's back. "The weather out there is terrible," he whispered.

"I know," she said. "And to think my stupid husband is out fishing in it!"

★ My uncle used to own a fishing shop. Every morning, he made sure he had a fifty-pound float. I don't know why; nobody ever wanted to buy one.

★ How do you tune a fish?
Adjust its scales.

★ A small-town doctor was famous in the area for always catching large fish. One day while he was out on one of his frequent fishing trips, he received a call to say that a woman at a neighbouring farm was giving birth. He rushed to her aid and delivered a normal-sized, healthy baby boy.

The farmer had nothing with which to weigh the baby, so the doctor used his fishing scales. They showed that the baby weighed 34lb 10oz.

★ It was a quiet day on the Ark and Noah was getting bored, so he told his wife that he was going to relieve the tedium by going off on a fishing expedition.

"That's a good idea," she said. "You could do with a break."

Noah collected all his equipment and set off, but thirty minutes later he was back and still complaining that he was bored.

His wife said: "I didn't expect you back so soon. If you're that bored, why did you stop fishing after only half an hour?"

Noah said: "I only had two worms."

★ **What's the difference between a fish and a mountain goat?**
One mucks about in fountains . . .

★ After returning from a fishing trip with her husband, a wife told her neighbour: "I did everything wrong again today. I talked too much and too loud, I used the wrong bait, I reeled in too soon, and I caught more than he did."

> 66 I don't eat fish because that's disgusting. How do you know when fish has gone bad? It still smells like fish. 'Hey, this smells like a dumpster, let's eat it.'
>
> Jim Gaffigan 99

★ A man marched into a pet shop and complained: "That goldfish you sold me last week is epileptic."

"What do you mean? Epileptic?" said the pet shop owner.

"Oh, I grant you he's okay when he's in the bowl, but the moment I take him out to play fetch, he has a seizure."

★ I wanted to be a sea fisherman, but I couldn't live off my net income.

★ Driving home from a fishing trip in northern Michigan with his boat in tow, a man had engine trouble a few miles inland from Lake Huron. He didn't have a cell phone with him, so he decided to use his marine radio to get help. Climbing into his boat, he broadcast his call sign and asked for assistance.

A coastguard officer responded: "Please state your location."

The man said: "I'm on Interstate-75, two miles south of Standish."

The officer paused. "Could you repeat that?"

"Interstate-75, two miles south of Standish."

There was a longer pause. Then the officer asked: "Just how fast were you going when you hit shore?"

★ A little girl won two goldfish at a fair. When the family arrived home, her mother asked her what she was going to call them.

"I think I'll call them One and Two," said the little girl.

"They're unusual names for goldfish. Why have you chosen them?"

"Because if One dies, I'll still have Two!"

★ Two fish were swimming in the sea. One said: "I had a terrible shock last week. Someone came and ripped out all my insides."

The other fish said: "I bet that made you unhappy."

"Unhappy? I was completely gutted."

★ Two friends were recounting their most recent dreams.

"I dreamed I was on vacation," said one man fondly. "It was just me and my fishing rod and this big beautiful lake. What a dream!"

"I had a great dream, too," recalled the other. "I dreamed I was on a date with two gorgeous women and having the time of my life."

"Hey!" cried his friend, hurt. "You dreamed you were with two gorgeous women, and you didn't call me?"

"I did," said the other. "But your wife said you'd gone fishing."

★ A regular customer at Elliott's Food Store marvelled at the proprietor's quick wit and intelligence. "Tell me, Elliott," he said. "What makes you so smart?"

"I wouldn't share my secret with just anyone," answered Elliott, lowering his voice so the other shoppers wouldn't hear, "but seeing as how you have been a loyal customer here for about a decade, I'll tell you: it's fish heads. You eat enough of them, you'll be positively brilliant."

"Do you sell them here?" asked the customer eagerly.

"Sure," said Elliott. "Just $4 each."

"Great," said the customer. "I'll take three."

A week later, the customer returned to the store to complain that the fish heads were disgusting and he wasn't feeling any smarter.

"That's because you didn't eat enough," said Elliott.

So the customer bought another twenty fish heads.

Two weeks later, the customer was back in the shop and this time he was really angry. "Hey, Elliott!" he barked. "You've been selling me fish heads for $4 apiece when I can buy the whole fish for $2. You've been ripping me off!"

"See?" said Elliott. "You're smarter already!"

Did you hear about the dyslexic angler?
He landed a giant crap.

FOOD

❖ A pretty young woman loved to grow vegetables in her garden, but she could never get her tomatoes to ripen. Admiring her elderly neighbour's garden, which had beautiful, bright red tomatoes, she asked him his secret.

"It's simple," said the old man. "Twice a day – in the morning and evening – I expose myself in front of the tomatoes and they turn red with embarrassment. You should try it."

So the young woman took his advice and exposed herself to her plants twice daily. Two weeks later, her neighbour asked her how she was doing.

"Any luck with your tomatoes?" he inquired.

"No," she replied excitedly, "but you should see the size of my cucumbers!"

❖ Kids these days really are obsessed with food. When I'm watching a violent film with my kids, I have to say, "Don't worry, it's not really tomato ketchup, it's only blood."

❖ **What is the best way to make an apple crumble?**
   Torture it for ten minutes.

❖ A man went into a fish and chip shop but was dismayed to receive only a small portion of chips. He asked the girl behind the counter: "Are you sure this fish is cooked properly?"

"Yes. Why?"

"Because it's eaten all my chips!"

 When you eat a lot of spicy food, you can lose your taste. When I was in India last summer, I was listening to a lot of Michael Bolton.

Jimmy Carr

How a Real Woman Interprets Handy Hints From British TV Cook Delia Smith

Delia's Way: Stuff a miniature marshmallow in the bottom of a sugar cone to prevent ice cream drips.

The Real Woman's Way: Just suck the ice cream out of the bottom of the cone, for God's sake! You are probably lying on the couch with your feet up eating it anyway.

Delia's Way: If you accidentally over-salt a dish while it's still cooking, drop in a potato slice.

The Real Woman's Way: If you over-salt a dish while you are cooking, tough shit! Remember the Real Woman's motto: "I made it, and you will eat it, and I don't care how bad it tastes."

Delia's Way: Wrap celery in aluminium foil when putting in the refrigerator and it will keep for weeks.

The Real Woman's Way: Let it keep forever. Who eats celery anyway?

Delia's Way: Brush some beaten egg white over piecrust before baking to yield a beautiful glossy finish.

❖ A wife served some homemade cinnamon rolls for breakfast and waited eagerly for her husband's reaction. When none was immediately forthcoming, she said: "If I baked these commercially, how much do you think I could get for one of them?"

Without looking up from his newspaper, he replied: "About ten years."

The Real Woman's Way: Tesco's frozen pie directions do not include anything about brushing egg white over the crust, so we don't do that.

Delia's Way: To keep potatoes from budding, place an apple in the bag with the potatoes.
The Real Woman's Way: Buy a packet of instant potato and keep it in the cupboard for a year.

Delia's Way: Cure for headaches. Take a lime, cut it in half and rub into your forehead. The throbbing will go away.
The Real Woman's Way: Cure for headaches. Take a lime, cut it in half and drop it in eight ounces of vodka. Drink the vodka. You might still have the headache, but at least you will be happy.

Delia's Way: If you have a problem opening jars, try using latex dishwashing gloves. They give a non-slip grip that makes opening jars easy.
Real Woman's Way: Forget the gloves, use that gadget you keep in front of the TV – that's what he's there for, isn't it?

Delia's Way: Freeze leftover wine into ice cubes for future use in casseroles and sauces.
Real Woman's Way: Leftover wine???? . . . Hello!!!!

❖ A young man went into an ice cream parlour and asked: "What flavour ice creams do you have?"

The young girl who was serving replied in a hoarse voice: "Chocolate, vanilla and strawberry."

"Do you have laryngitis?" he said.

"No," she answered. "Just chocolate, vanilla and strawberry."

❖ A woman went into a butcher's and said: "I'd like an oxtail please."

   The butcher said: "Certainly, madam. Once upon a time there was an ox . . ."

❖ What do you call a melon that's not allowed to get married?

   Can't elope.

> " I have finally found what the best thing *before* sliced bread was – massive sandwiches.
>
> Jimmy Carr "

> " We don't eat dolphins because they're cute and intelligent. If a dolphin was ugly and tasted good, we'd be eating it by the truckload. No one would care. The only negative thing that ever happened to a tuna was that it was born butt ugly and it mixes well with mayo.
>
> David Cross "

❖ Two young guys were standing at a bar. One said: "I went for a vindaloo last night, and my arse is really sore today."

   "Yeah?"

   "Yeah. I can't believe some of the things I do for a free curry."

❖ How do you stop sandwiches from curling?

   Take away their brooms.

❖ If you cook alphabet soup on the stove and leave it unattended, it could spell disaster.

❖ "Waiter, what is that bug doing in my salad?"

   "Trying to find its way out, sir."

❖ Did you hear about the new factory that Kraft Foods is building in Israel?

It's called Cheeses of Nazareth.

 Pizza is like a lady's breasts. There's good pizza. And there's great pizza. But there isn't bad pizza.

Richard Jeni

❖ A man walked past the refrigerator and heard two onions singing a Bee Gees song. When he opened the fridge door, it was just chives talking.

❖ Did you hear about the new Chinese diet?

You put as much food as you want on the plate, but you only get one chopstick.

❖ A wife was preparing a breakfast of fried eggs for her husband when he suddenly burst into the kitchen.

"Careful!" he said. "Careful! Put in some more butter! Oh, my God! You're cooking too many at once! Too many! Turn them! Turn them now! Now! We need more butter! Oh, my God! They're going to stick! Slow things down a bit! Careful! Careful! I said be careful! You never listen to me when you're cooking! Never! Right, turn them! Hurry up! Turn them now! Are you crazy? Have you lost your mind? Don't forget to salt them. You know you always forget to salt them. Use the salt. USE THE SALT! USE THE SALT! USE THE SALT!"

The wife stared at him in disbelief. "What the hell is wrong with you? Do you think I don't know how to fry a couple of eggs?"

The husband replied calmly: "I just wanted to show you what it feels like when I'm driving."

❖ Did you hear about the guy who cooked a casserole from hyena meat and Oxo cubes?

He made himself a laughing stock.

> ❝ I love restaurants, but they always
> boast about home cooking. I don't want
> home cooking. That's why I'm here,
> 'cos I don't like the shit at home! ❞
>
> Lee Evans

❖ What did the lettuce say to the celery?
"Are you stalking me?"

❖ After a night drinking in various bars around town, a young man ended the evening in a Chinese restaurant. He was just about to eat a plate of food when he suddenly shrieked: "I can see a pair of eyes staring at me from the plate!"

The waiter came over to see what was causing the commotion.

"Waiter!" he said, "I know I've had a few drinks, but I definitely saw two eyes peering at me from beneath the noodles."

"Not to worry, sir," said the waiter. "It's only the Peeking Duck."

❖ A hippie walked into a bar and grill. When the waiter came over to take his order, the hippie said: "I want a cheeseburger – not too rare, not too well done, but right in the groove."

"And would you like anything to drink?" asked the waiter.

"Yeah," said the hippie. "A cup of tea – not too strong, not too weak, but right in the groove."

The waiter was becoming irritated by the hippie's manner and feared the worst when, a little while later, he asked him whether he wanted any dessert.

"Yeah," said the hippie. "I'll have ice cream – not too chocolate, not too vanilla, but right in the groove."

"I tell you what," said the waiter, finally losing his cool, "you can kiss my ass – not the right cheek, not the left cheek, but right in the groove!"

❖ "What a delicious meal," said the husband to his wife as he cleared his plate. "Did you thaw it yourself?"

> ❝ Sex and pizza, they are similar. When it's good, it's good. When it's bad, you get it on your shirt.
> Mike Birbiglia ❞

❖ What do you call a gingerbread man with one leg?
Limp Bizkit.

❖ A sausage and an egg were sizzling in a pan. The sausage looked at the egg and said: "It's hot in here."
The egg said: "Fancy that, a talking sausage!"

❖ I went into a cafe where they were serving all-day breakfasts. They looked great, but I couldn't spare that much time.

> ❝ I wouldn't touch a hot dog unless you put a condom on it! You realize that the job of a hot dog is to use parts of the animal that the Chinese can't figure out how to make into a belt.
> Bill Maher ❞

❖ "How were your sandwiches today, darling?" asked the wife as her husband returned home from work.
"They were fine," he replied.
"Are you sure they tasted okay?"
"Yeah, they were great."
"You don't feel ill at all?"
"No, never felt better. Why?"
"Oh, nothing. By the way, tomorrow you're going to have to clean your shoes with fish paste."

> Did you hear about the man who went for a meal in a German restaurant?
>
> The sauerkraut starter was bad enough but the wurst was yet to come.

❖ A tramp said to a businessman in the street: "Mister, I haven't tasted food for a week."

"Don't worry," said the businessman. "It still tastes the same."

❖ A customer was ordering food in an Indian restaurant. Studying the menu, he asked the waiter: "What's the Chicken Tarka?"

The waiter said: "It's the same as Chicken Tikka, but a little 'otter."

★　★　★　★　★

GAMBLING

✳ Harry was a compulsive gambler who would bet on anything – cards, horses, roulette, dogs, football, baseball, dice, basketball. One day after a run of bad luck, he said to his best friend: "Buddy, I hate asking you this, but I need $3,000 urgently. We've got no food in the house, I owe three months' rent, the kids need new clothes and my wife is too ashamed to go out because we have bad cheques at every store in town. Is there any way you can help me out?"

The friend thought for a moment before writing Harry a cheque for $4,000 so that he could get back on his feet. "But there's one condition," he said. "I don't want you using the money for gambling."

"No worries," said Harry. "I've got money put aside for that."

* A priest, a minister and a rabbi were playing poker when the police raided the game.

  Addressing the priest, the lead officer said: "Father O'Reilly, were you gambling?"

  Turning his eyes to Heaven, the priest whispered: "Lord, forgive me for what I am about to do." And then he told the policeman firmly: "No, officer, I was not gambling."

  The officer then asked the minister: "Pastor Jackson, were you gambling?"

  The minister whispered an apology to God before answering: "No, officer, I was not gambling."

  Turning finally to the rabbi, the officer asked: "Rabbi Goldblum, were you gambling?"

  Shrugging his shoulders, the rabbi replied: "With whom?"

* On a visit to the zoo, a hatchet-faced woman tapped the keeper of the monkey house indignantly on the shoulder. "Those wretched animals of yours," she raged, "appear to be engaged in shooting dice. It's immoral! I demand that you break the game up at once."

  "Listen, ma'am," said the keeper, "they're staying strictly within the law. They're only playing for peanuts."

* A blackjack dealer and a player with a thirteen count in his hand were debating whether or not it was appropriate to tip the dealer.

  The player said: "When I get bad cards, it's not the dealer's fault. Similarly when I get good cards, the dealer isn't responsible. So why should I tip him?"

  The dealer countered: "When you eat out, do you tip the waiter?"

  "Er, yes."

  "Well, he serves you food, and I'm serving you cards, so you should tip me."

  "Fair enough," said the player, "but the waiter gives me what I ask for. I'll take an eight . . ."

✳   Jim had spent the evening in a casino playing pontoon. He'd suffered a miserable run of bad luck and had lost almost everything. "Surely my luck must change," he thought to himself. "I'll give it one last go." He then pulled from his jacket pocket the deeds to his house – his last remaining possession in the whole world.

The croupier dealt the cards and Jim picked them up. First a jack – it looked hopeful. Then a six, damn! "Sixteen!" he said to himself. "What the hell am I going to do?"

As Jim gazed into the distance pondering his next move, a leprechaun suddenly appeared on his shoulder, looked at the cards and then looked at Jim. The leprechaun started jumping up and down saying, "Twist, twist." Jim was startled by the noise and looked disbelievingly at the leprechaun.

"Who are you?" asked Jim.

"Twist, twist," repeated the leprechaun.

"But I've got everything riding on this," said Jim. "I've already lost all my money and my car. If I lose this, I'll lose my house as well."

"Twist, twist," cried the leprechaun.

Jim looked at the leprechaun and thought perhaps he should trust it after all. Following a further moment's consideration, Jim said, "Twist," to the croupier.

He turned the card offered. It was a two. Jim breathed a huge sigh of relief. "Great," he thought, wiping the perspiration from his brow. "I reckon I'll be okay."

"Twist, twist," said the leprechaun, jumping up and down again.

"But it's eighteen," said Jim. "That's a good score. I've got a good chance with that."

"Twist, twist," insisted the leprechaun.

"Are you sure?" asked Jim.

"Yeah, trust me. Twist, twist."

Jim agonized for a few seconds and eventually reasoned that because the leprechaun was right last time, he would go for it. "Twist, please," Jim said to the croupier. The croupier drew another card – an ace.

"Wow!" thought Jim. "Now I can win back everything I lost earlier." He was just about to place his cards face down when the leprechaun jumped up and down, saying: "Twist, twist."

"What?" said Jim in disbelief. "But I've got nineteen. If I twist I'll almost certainly go bust."

"Twist, twist. Go on."

Against his better judgment, Jim had to admit that the leprechaun hadn't let him down yet, so he decided to go for it one last time. "Twist, please," he said to the croupier.

The croupier drew the card. Hardly daring to turn it over, Jim took it slowly and pulled it up to his chest. Finally he summoned up the courage to look at the card. A two. Twenty-one, a five-card trick. He had done it, he'd hit the jackpot. He'd kept his house, won back his car, all of his money and a few grand more besides.

"Yeeesss!" he cried out jubilantly.

The leprechaun had stopped jumping up and down and was now motionless, staring at the cards. Then it turned to Jim and said: "You jammy bastard!"

Two dog owners were boasting about the intelligence of their pets.

"The smartest dog I ever had," said one, "was an Afghan hound that could play cards. He was amazing at poker, he could beat anyone, even professionals. But I had to have him put down."

"You had him put to sleep?" said the other. "You must be crazy. A bright dog like that could be worth a million dollars."

"I had no choice. I caught him using marked cards."

66 Gamblers Anonymous: how do they know where to send your winnings?
Harry Hill 99

✳ An anxious father said to his son's school principal: "I want you to stop my son gambling. All he ever seems to want to do all day is bet, bet, bet."

"Leave it to me," said the principal.

A week later, the principal phoned the father and said: "I think I've cured him."

"How?" asked the father.

"Well, I saw him looking at my beard and then he said, 'I bet that's a false beard.' 'How much do you want to bet on it?' I asked him. And he said, 'Five dollars.'"

"What happened?" asked the father.

"Well, he tugged my beard, which is perfectly real, and I made him give me the five dollars. I'm sure that's taught him a lesson and he won't be gambling any more."

"I wouldn't be so sure," said the father. "He bet me ten dollars this morning that he'd pull your beard with your permission by the end of the week!"

✳ Did you hear about the young gambler who bet his girlfriend that she wouldn't marry him?

She not only called his bluff but she raised him five.

✳ Tony had a serious gambling problem, and whenever he came home his wife would ask him how much he had lost at the casino. Then one night, Tony didn't come home at all. Instead it was ten o'clock the following morning when he finally walked through the door. His wife was furious.

He smiled at her and said: "Honey, I have a confession to make. I was at the bar last night, got drunk, and went home with the barmaid. I stayed overnight and we had the most fantastic sex ever."

"Don't give me that rubbish," snapped his wife. "Come on, tell me, how much did you lose last night?"

✳ A man was passing a pet shop when he saw a talking monkey advertised for sale. He was so impressed by its vocabulary that he bought it on the spot.

That evening he took it to his local bar and bet everyone $10 that the monkey could talk. A dozen people accepted the challenge but despite its new owner's coaxing, the monkey refused to say a word and the man had to pay up, When he got it home, the man was puzzled to hear the monkey chatting away merrily.

The next evening, the man returned to the bar and bet everyone $20 that the monkey could talk. Again there were plenty of takers but, to the man's fury, the monkey remained silent. After paying up, the man took the monkey outside.

"I'm taking you back to the shop," he raged. "You're a complete waste of money!"

"Chill out," said the monkey. "Think of the odds we'll get tomorrow."

★　　★　　★　　★　　★

GAY AND LESBIAN

★ The Pope was addressing the masses in Rome and finished his sermon with the Latin phrase "*Tutti Homini*" – "Blessed be Mankind."

The sermon seemed to have been well received but the next day a women's rights group asked the Pope why he had not mentioned womankind in his conclusion. Not wishing to offend, the Pope ended his next sermon by saying, "*Tutti Homini et Tutti Femini*" – "Blessed be Mankind and Womankind."

But the following day a gay rights group took exception to the Pope's words and asked him why he had not included gays in his blessing. Eager to please, he duly amended his text, concluding his next sermon with "*Tutti Homini, et Tutti Femini, et Tutti Fruiti*."

★ A businessman was propositioned in a bar by a guy who had one leg much shorter than the other. Turning down his offer of sex, the businessman told him he wasn't that way inclined.

★ Why did the Englishman start cruising gay bars?

Because government health officers told everyone they had to have five fruits a day.

★ An airline's passengers were being served by a flamboyantly gay flight attendant who entertained them by cracking jokes while handing out the food and drinks.

As the plane prepared to descend, he came swishing down the aisle and announced to passengers: "Captain Kenny has asked me to tell you that he'll be landing the big scary plane shortly, lovely people, so if you could just put up your trays that would be super."

On his trip back up the aisle he noticed that a well-dressed, sophisticated woman hadn't moved. He said to her cheerfully: "Perhaps you didn't hear me over those big brute engines. I asked you to raise your trazy-poo so the main man can pitty-pat us on the ground."

She slowly turned to face him and replied haughtily: "In my country I am called a princess. I take orders from no one."

To which the flight attendant answered: "Well, in my country I'm called a queen, so put your tray up, bitch."

> ❝ I'm all for gay adoption. Gay men would make brilliant dads. They know where all the best parks are. And they know how to apply talcum powder to sore bottoms.
>
> Frankie Boyle ❞

★ A gay guy was told by his doctor that he had AIDS. "Is there anything I can do?" he asked.

"Yes," said the doctor. "I want you to go home and eat five pounds of spicy sausage, a hot curry, twenty Jalapeno peppers, a bowl of chilli, and wash it all down with a gallon of prune juice."

"And will that cure me, doc?"

"No, but it will make you realize what your ass is for."

★ Three gay men were in an internet chatroom boasting about the size of their dicks.

The first said: "My dick is so huge I have to drop my pants to take it out!!"

The second said: "Mine is so huge I can turn my monitor on and off with it while I'm sitting in my chair!!!"

The third said: "Well, mine is so huge that if I laid it out on my keyboard, it would stretch all the way from A to Z!!!! No, wait . . ."

Did you hear about the bisexual pride parade?
It went both ways.

★ A gay man was worried about his lack of chest hair, which he thought made him less attractive to his partner. So he decided to visit a doctor to see if anything could be done.

The doctor suggested that the man smother Vaseline all over his chest once a day in the hope that the skin there would be stimulated sufficiently to produce hair.

So the guy went home and smothered his chest in Vaseline. When his partner came home and jumped into bed with him, he was alarmed by the feel of his friend's chest.

"What the hell have you done?" he asked.

"It's Vaseline."

"But why?"

"Because the doctor said that rubbing it on my chest might encourage hair to grow."

"Deary me! Don't you think if that was true you'd have a ponytail coming out of your ass by now?"

★ How can you tell if your young son is gay?
  He tries to push the cylinder shape into the star-shaped hole.

★ Two gay men – Derek and Nigel – went to a fairground. Derek said he wanted to go on the Ferris wheel but Nigel said he had a sore butt so he declined. The wheel went round and round, but then suddenly the cart Derek was sitting in crashed to the ground, landing near Nigel's feet.
  "Are you hurt?" asked Nigel, rushing over to his friend.
  "Of course I am," snapped Derek. "Three times I went round and you didn't wave once!"

★ Two elderly lesbians were having sex on a park bench. One said: "Take your glasses off, you're scratching my leg."
  The other one said: "Put your glasses on, you're licking the bench."

★ An article claimed that over 70 per cent of bishops are gay. Imagine if they changed the rules of chess to acknowledge this fact – the bishops would still move in the same directions but could only be taken from behind.

★ A guy explained to a gay colleague at work: "I'm not homophobic in the same way that I'm not arachnophobic. I'm not scared of gays and I'm not scared of spiders. But if I were to walk in and find one in my bed, I'd be a little worried."

 I say no to gay marriage. It'll end up leading to gay divorce, and that'll be bitchy.

Jimmy Carr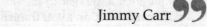

★ How many nails are used to make a lesbian's coffin?
   None: it's all tongue and groove.

★ A young woman went to the doctor after noticing two small circular rash marks, one on each side of her inner thigh. The doctor asked her to remove her pants, sat her in a chair and, kneeling down to position himself between her legs, examined the marks.
   Eventually he asked her: "Are you by any chance a lesbian?"
   "Yes, I am," blushed the woman.
   Standing up, the doctor said: "Well, don't worry, your rash will go away."
   "Is there anything I need to do?"
   "Yes, go home and tell your girlfriend her earrings aren't real gold."

★ What do you call a lesbian with long fingernails?
   Single.

★ A lesbian walked into a whorehouse and said: "I want a fourteen-year-old girl."
   The madam said: "Sorry, but we don't serve minors to lickers here."

★ ★ ★ ★ ★

GENIES

❖ A genie went to a psychiatrist, and said: "Doctor, I have a problem."
   "I can see," said the psychiatrist. "Your emotions are all bottled up."

❖ A married couple were playing golf when the wife sliced her tee shot through the window of a house that adjoined the course. Apprehensively, they walked over to the house and, finding the back door open, called out: "Is anyone at home?"

"Yes, come in," replied a voice.

So they entered the house and saw glass everywhere, a broken bottle on the floor and a man sitting on the couch.

"Are you the people who broke my window?" asked the man.

"Yes, we're really sorry . . ." began the husband.

The man cut him short. "There's no need to apologize. On the contrary, you've done me a favour, so I want to thank you. You see, I'm a genie who was trapped in that bottle until your wayward shot released me. As a fully paid-up member of the genies' union, I'm allowed to grant you three wishes, so I'd like to grant you one wish each and, if you don't mind, keep the last wish for myself as recompense for being stuck in that bottle for the past ten years."

"Great," said the husband. "My wish is to have $5 million a year for the rest of my life."

"No problem," said the genie. "And you, madam?"

"My wish," said the wife, "is to own a house in every state in America."

"Consider it done," said the genie. Turning to the husband, he continued: "And now for my wish. Because I've been trapped in that wretched bottle, I haven't had sex for ages. So if you don't mind, I'd like to sleep with your wife."

The husband gave the idea a moment's thought and replied: "Why not? It seems only fair. After all, we are going to be getting all that money and those houses. Is that okay with you, darling?"

"Yes, I suppose so," agreed the wife.

So the genie took her upstairs and ravished her for three hours. When he was finally satisfied, he rolled over, looked at her and asked: "How old is your husband?"

"Thirty-eight," she replied.

"And he still believes in genies?"

❖ A bear and a racoon were walking through the woods one day when they came across a genie who was lost. The genie was so happy with the directions the animals gave him that he promised them: "I will give you three wishes each."

First he turned to the bear. The bear thought for a moment and said: "I wish all the bears in this forest were female, except me."

His wish was granted.

The genie turned to the racoon. The racoon thought for a minute before saying: "I wish I could have a motorcycle."

The bear thought he was crazy, but the genie granted his wish.

Then it was the bear's turn to make his second wish. "I wish," said the bear, "that all the bears in the next forest were female, too!"

His wish was granted.

The racoon pondered his second wish, and then said: "I wish I could have a motorcycle helmet."

"You idiot!" yelled the bear. "You could ask for all the money in the world and be able to buy those things! You're wasting your wishes on junk!"

The racoon just shrugged, and his wish for a motorcycle helmet was granted.

Now it was time for the bear's final wish. He didn't have to think long about it. "I wish," he announced, "that all the bears in the whole world were female, except for me."

His wish was granted.

The bear and the genie looked at the racoon expectantly. The racoon got on his motorcycle, strapped on the helmet, and turned the engine on. He revved the engine, said, "I wish the bear was gay," and rode off.

An Irishman found an old lamp in his garden shed and started to polish it. Suddenly a genie appeared and granted him three wishes.

"Well now," mused the Irishman, "I've always liked my Guinness in bottles. So I'd like a bottle of Guinness that will never, ever be empty."

No sooner had he spoken than a bottle of Guinness appeared, as ordered. He opened the bottle and took a swig. "Oh, that's beautiful," he purred. "Did you say I get three wishes?"

"Yes, that's right," said the genie.

"Well, in that case, I'll take two more of these."

❖ While trying to escape through Pakistan, Osama Bin Laden found a bottle on the sand and picked it up. Suddenly a genie emerged from the bottle and with a smile said: "Master, may I grant you one wish?"

"You ignorant, unworthy daughter of a dog!" snarled Bin Laden. "Don't you know who I am! I don't need any common woman giving me anything!"

The shocked genie said: "Please, I must grant you a wish or I shall be returned to that bottle forever."

Bin Laden thought for a moment, grumbled about the impertinence of women, and then thought of a suitably twisted fantasy which would keep the genie happy. "Very well, then. I want to wake up tomorrow morning with three American women in my bed. Now do it, and be off with you!"

Irritated by his attitude, the genie said, "So be it!" and vanished.

The next morning, Bin Laden woke in bed with Lorena Bobbitt, Tonya Harding and Hillary Clinton. His penis was gone, his knees were broken, and he had no health insurance.

❖ A golfer was thrilled to hit a hole in one at the first hole. As he picked his ball out of the cup, a genie popped out and announced: "I am the genie of the first green. For getting a hole in one, I shall grant you one wish."

The man thought for a moment before answering: "My wish is for a big dick."

The genie promised that his wish would be granted, and sure enough after each hole the golfer noticed that his dick had grown by half an inch, so that by the time he finished the eighteenth, it was so long he had to tuck it in his sock.

"This is crazy," he muttered to himself. "I've turned into a freak. I can't carry on like this."

So he went back to the first hole and hit another hole in one. The genie immediately appeared and offered him another wish.

The golfer replied: "My wish is for longer legs."

❖ A man was walking through the woods when he came across a lamp. Hoping that there might be a genie inside the lamp, he picked it up and rubbed it, and, sure enough, out popped a genie who immediately granted him three wishes.

"For my first wish," said the man, "I'd like $5 million."

And POOF! Five million dollars appeared.

"What is your second wish?" asked the genie.

"I'd like a new Ferrari," said the man.

And POOF! A gleaming new Ferrari suddenly appeared.

"And for your third wish?" inquired the genie.

The man thought for a moment. "Well, I've got the money and the car, so I guess I'd like to be irresistible to women."

And POOF! He was turned into a box of chocolates.

★　　★　　★　　★　　★

GLOBAL WARMING

> " Global warming isn't real? Excuse me,
> there are Scottish people with suntans! "
> Adam Hills

* A guy went into a shop to complain about his recent purchase. "I don't think much of these energy-saving lightbulbs," he said. "I still have to get up and switch them on."

> " A group of scientists warned that
> because of global warming, sea levels
> will rise so much that some parts of
> New Jersey will be under water. The bad
> news? Parts of New Jersey won't be under
> water.
> Conan O'Brien "

* Some experts say that it is global warming that is making the seas rise, causing flooding. Others believe that if Americans were to stay out of the water, the problem would go away.

* How many climate sceptics does it take to change a lightbulb?
  None. It's too early to say if the lightbulb needs changing.

> " Attempting to recycle Marmite jars
> while Alaska is being drilled for oil –
> it's like turning up at an earthquake
> with a dustpan and brush.
> Sean Lock "

* A woman was going round the neighbourhood door-to-door, trying to make homeowners aware of the threat from climate change.

   At one house, she said to the man who answered the door: "Do you have any idea of the size of your carbon footprint?"

   "I don't have a carbon footprint," he answered. "I drive everywhere."

> 66 Al Gore says that global warming is more serious than terrorism. Unless the terrorist is on your plane, when that extra half a degree doesn't bother you so much.
>
> Jay Leno 99

* A man received a phone call at work from his wife asking him to pick up some organic vegetables on his way home for that night's dinner.

   The husband arrived at the store and searched everywhere for organic vegetables. Eventually he had to ask a young member of staff where they were.

   "Organic vegetables?" said the store worker. "What do you mean by organic?"

   Exasperated, the husband explained: "These vegetables are for my wife. Have they been sprayed with poisonous chemicals?"

   "No, sir," replied the store worker. "You will have to do that yourself."

* George W. Bush said he was amazed by the speed of global warming, until an aide took him to one side and pointed out that it was springtime.

> 66 Clean coal is a bit like wearing a porous condom – at least the intention was there.
>
> Robin Williams 99

Some Benefits of Global Warming

No one will ever face a long drive to the coast.

Winter will only last twenty-four hours.

The hotter it is, the colder beer will taste.

Due to the lack of ice, hockey will finally become the sport it was meant to be – a bunch of guys hitting each other with sticks under water.

It will take a lot less time to boil water.

The Olympic torch will never go out.

After decades of segregation, polar bears might finally get to find out what penguin tastes like.

The ark-building industry will flourish.

* My wife left me because of my views on the environment. I tried conserving water by showering with our neighbour's daughter.

* Moses was praying to God to free his people when the voice of God rang out from the heavens.
    "Moses," he said, "I have good news and bad news."
    "What's the good news?" asked Moses.
    God said: "If Pharaoh will not let my people go, I will send down a rain of frogs, a plague of locusts and a plague of flies, and I will turn rivers to blood. And if Pharaoh pursues you, I shall open a path for you in the Red Sea but then close it again to drown his army."
    "That would be really helpful," said Moses. "But tell me, what's the bad news?"
    God said: "Before I can do all this, you have to prepare an environmental impact statement."

❝ Lots of stuff's bad for the environment. And 4x4s are just too big. Often when I'm out dogging, I have to stand on someone's shoulders just to get my balls in the windshield.

Frankie Boyle ❞

★   ★   ★   ★   ★

GOLF

★ A golf professional at a country club was notoriously rude to the club members. Not only did he take their money after beating them but he pointed out the faults in their game in no uncertain terms. One member became so annoyed at this that he trained a gorilla to play golf and challenged the professional to take on the mighty ape over eighteen holes, with the winner pocketing $1,000. Naturally the professional, sensing easy money, readily agreed to the match.

The first hole was a par five of 575 yards. The pro drove first and sent his shot 290 yards down the fairway. He then confidently stood aside, ready to mock the gorilla's swing and stance.

The gorilla lumbered up to the tee, placed the ball on the ground and with a huge swing of the club sent the ball soaring off into the distance – 100 . . . 200 . . . 300 . . . 400 . . . 500 . . . 575 yards, the ball eventually coming to rest three inches from the hole.

The pro went white as a sheet. If this was the gorilla's standard of play, he knew he was in for an afternoon of total humiliation. Unwilling to prolong the agony, he immediately settled the bet, made his excuses and prepared to leave.

As the pro headed for the clubhouse, he turned to the gorilla's trainer and asked: "One thing. How does he putt?"

The trainer said: "Same as he drives – 575 yards."

★   A marine drill sergeant fancied a game of golf one afternoon and so set off to play on his favourite course. Waiting on the first tee, he noticed an air force commander, and since both were alone and in the armed forces, they decided to play together.

They soon started talking about work. They shared boot camp stories, war memories and jokes about new recruits. They carried on like this until the fifth hole, when the marine sergeant concluded a story about a runaway tank by saying: "It's a fact that the marines are the bravest of all the armed forces."

The air force commander dropped his putter. "What do you mean by that?" he demanded.

"Well," the sergeant went on, "who do you send to take new territory? Who do you send in when you're outnumbered? Who gets the call for the most covert operations?"

The air force commander putted out before snapping back: "While you lot are hiding in the bushes, who is a clear target in the sky? Who do you call for support when you're losing? No, sir, the men of the air force are the bravest."

This argument lasted for the rest of the round, with both men insisting that their men were the bravest and producing stories of outstanding bravery to back up their claims.

After finishing, they headed up to the clubhouse for a beer, still debating the matter. Finally the marine sergeant said: "I must get back to camp. Do you want to play again next week?"

Hearing this, the air force commander said: "I must apologize, it seems I was mistaken. Anyone who played like you did today and is willing to come back to the same golf course is a much braver man than me!"

★   A golfer was on the green, a few feet from the hole, and was just about to putt when someone came up and told him: "Your father's just died."

The golfer stared solemnly at the ground for a moment, then picked up his putter, addressed the ball and announced: "This is for pa."

★ A guy was lining up his drive when a voice from the clubhouse called out: "Will the gentleman on the ladies' tee please move back to the men's tee!"

The golfer ignored the request and continued with his practice swings. The voice called out again: "Sir, will you please move back to the men's tee now!"

The golfer carried on regardless and was just addressing the ball when the voice called out for a third time: "This is your last warning! You are violating club rules. Move back to the men's tee immediately or I will have you thrown off the course."

The golfer turned angrily in the direction of the clubhouse and shouted back: "Do you mind shutting up while I play my second shot!"

★ **What's the difference between a bad golfer and a bad skydiver?**
A bad golfer goes WHACK . . . "Damn!"; a bad skydiver goes "Damn!" . . . WHACK.

★ What are the worst four words you can hear during a game of golf?
"It's still your turn."

★ George and Dave were playing golf when George sliced his shot into a deep wooded gully. Taking his eight-iron, he clambered down the embankment in search of his ball. After spending ten minutes hacking at the undergrowth, he suddenly spotted something glistening among the leaves. As he got closer, he could see that it was an eight-iron in the hands of a human skeleton.

George immediately called up to Dave: "Hey, Dave, I've made a shocking discovery!"

"What's up?" shouted Dave.

"Bring me my wedge," yelled George. "You can't get out of here with an eight-iron."

> **"** What's the deal with golf? People play
> it wearing one glove. You wouldn't
> play it wearing one shoe, would you?
> They say it's for grip, but you know what
> would give more grip? Two gloves!
>
> Lee Evans **"**

★ An American was playing golf in India on a remote country course. The local people had not seen many Americans before, so his presence soon attracted a sizeable crowd who watched his progress enthusiastically.

He seemed to respond to the attention, making a succession of low scores, which his new-found fan club applauded warmly.

On the eleventh hole, he surpassed himself by holing a thirty-foot putt for a birdie. As the ball went in, the crowd shouted: "Tiger Woods! Tiger Woods!"

He thought such adulation was a little over-the-top but when he turned to acknowledge them, they had all vanished. That's when he saw the tiger come out of the woods.

A father phoned the doctor. "Doctor, come quick, we've got an emergency! My little boy has swallowed my golf tees!"

"Okay," said the doctor, "I'll be with you as soon as I can."

"Tell me what to do till you get here."

The doctor said: "Practise your putting."

★ After a wayward shot landed among a group of players, two golfers came to blows. One started lashing out with a six-iron, repeatedly hitting his adversary over the back with the club. Soon the police arrived to break up the fight.

"Right," said the police officer to the aggressor. "I want all the details. How many times did you hit him with that golf club?"

"Eight," he replied. "But put me down for five."

⋆ A golf professional said to the student: "Your trouble is that you're not addressing the ball correctly."

The student replied: "Well, I've been polite to the bloody thing for long enough!"

⋆ A minister went to his local golf course in the hope of finding someone to play with. As luck would have it, there was a member in the professional's shop looking for a game, so they were introduced and went to the first tee.

The member asked: "What's your handicap?"

"I'm a twelve," said the minister.

"Me, too," said the member. "Would you like to bet a dollar a hole?"

The minister agreed, and when they had finished their round, they retired to the clubhouse, where the minister solemnly handed over $18. As he parted with his cash, the minister said: "Say, I'd like you to come along to the church some time."

The member replied: "Sure. I'd like that."

Then the minister added: "And bring your mother and father. I'd like to marry them."

⋆ Sam had a real zest for life, but he was beset by bad luck. He loved poker, but poker did not love him. He played the stock market, but always sold at the wrong time. He invested heavily in property, but just as the market crashed. His first three wives left him for close friends of his.

The one constant in his life was golf. He wasn't much of a player – only occasionally did he break 100 – but come rain or shine, he was out there every weekend. Then one day, he was taken ill and died. In accordance with his wishes, he was cremated and his ashes were to be scattered just off the fairway on the fifteenth hole of his local course.

A small gathering of friends turned up at the fifteenth to witness the ceremony. It was a beautiful, sunny day but then just as the ashes were being strewn, a sudden gust of wind sprang up and blew Sam out of bounds.

⋆ A golf professional, hired by a big store to give lessons, was approached by two women.

"Would you like to have lessons?" he asked one of the women.

"Oh, no," she replied. "It's my friend here who's interested in learning. I learned last Wednesday."

⋆ A golfer was enduring the most miserable round. Every shot he tried seemed to end in disaster. He and his caddie had trailed in and out of woodland, deep rough, a lake and countless sand traps. On the seventeenth hole he was left with a shot of 180 yards to the green.

"Do you think I can get there with a five-iron?" he asked his caddie.

The caddie sighed: "Eventually."

⋆ What is the definition of a handicapped golfer?
One who plays with his boss.

⋆ A man was playing his first ever round of golf. Standing on the tee with the club professional, he asked: "Right. What do I do?"

Pointing into the distance, the professional said: "See that flag 350 yards over there?"

"Yes," said the beginner.

"Well, just try and hit the ball towards the flag."

The beginner wound himself up and with a mighty backswing, launched the ball unerringly in the direction of the flag. In fact, his drive was so accurate that the ball actually hit the flag before dropping on to the green less than two feet from the hole.

When they reached the green and the professional saw where the ball had finished, he was speechless.

"Now what do I do?" asked the beginner, unfazed.

"Well, uh, you hit into the hole," said the professional.

"Oh great! *Now* you tell me!"

★ Larry and Ken were playing golf together, but as they stood on the first tee, Ken looked distracted.

"What's the problem?" asked Larry.

"It's that new golf pro," said Ken. "I can't bear the man. He's just been trying to correct my stance."

"He's only trying to help your game."

"Yeah, but I was using the urinal at the time."

★ Harry was sitting in the clubhouse bar, thinking about his latest extra-marital affair. Absent-mindedly, he began thinking aloud: "Not worth it, never as good as you hoped. Expensive, it messes with your mind and it's not fair on the wife."

Overhearing this, a friend sitting nearby leaned over and said: "Come on, Harry, you knew what to expect when you took up golf."

★ A golfer had such a terrible round that when he reached the eighteenth hole and spotted a lake beside the fairway, he said to his caddie: "I've played so badly today, I'm going to drown myself in that lake!"

The caddie looked at him and said: "Do you think you'll be able to keep your head down that long?"

★ A keen golfer was in the middle of a round when he was suddenly struck by lightning and dropped down dead. When the man reached Heaven, St Peter confessed that the lightning bolt had been meant for his playing partner, but because he didn't want word to get around that God made mistakes, the man would have to return to Earth as someone else.

"So," said St Peter, "what do you want to be?"

The man gave the matter brief thought before answering: "I'd like to go back as a lesbian."

"A lesbian?" queried St Peter. "Why would a macho guy like you want to go back to Earth as a lesbian?"

"Well," replied the man, "that way I can still make love to women, and I get to play from the ladies' tee!"

★ After a long evening drinking in the golf club bar, a man set off for home but half a mile down the road his car was pulled over by a police officer.

The officer did not need a breathalyser to see what the problem was. "You're too drunk to drive," he said.

"Too drunk to drive?" repeated the golfer. "I'm too drunk to putt!"

★ A man came home from his game of golf, threw his arms around his wife and smiled: "Darling, I'm so relieved. I thought I'd lost you."

The wife was bewildered. "What do you mean? Lost me?"

He said: "Well, I had to sink a thirty-footer on the final green to win my bet."

★ Kevin took his golf very seriously – so much so that it was jeopardizing his marriage to Samantha because he was off playing golf seven days a week. In an attempt to save their crumbling marriage, she suggested that she should go to the course with him and take some lessons.

"Okay," he said reluctantly, "but remember golf is a serious game. I don't want you ruining the one perfect thing in my life."

So they went to the course and Samantha signed up to take a course of lessons with the local pro. Meanwhile Kevin played his round and she never bothered him.

After a few weeks, a friend at the golf club asked Kevin how his marriage was faring. "Much better," said Kevin. "Since Samantha's been taking lessons from the pro, she lets me play all the golf I want and she never gives me any hassle."

"Oh," said the friend glumly. "So I guess you don't know that she's been screwing around with the pro?"

Kevin threw his clubs to the ground in a fit of rage. "I knew it wouldn't last! I knew she'd make a mockery of the game!"

"Mildred!" cried the golfer to his nagging wife. "Be quiet, or you'll drive me out of my mind!"

"That wouldn't be a drive," she argued. "It would be a putt!"

★ A golfer ran screaming hysterically into the clubhouse. "I think I've just killed my wife!" he wailed. "I didn't see her. She was standing behind me, and when I started my backswing I must have hit her right between the eyes with the club. I'm sure she's dead! It's awful!"

"What club were you using?" asked a concerned bystander.

"A two-iron," sobbed the man.

"Hmm. That's the club that always gets me into trouble, too."

★ A hapless golfer said to his caddie: "Do you think my game is improving?"

"Oh yes, sir," replied the caddie. "You don't miss the ball by as much as you used to."

★ Standing on the tee of a 300-yard, par four hole, a super-confident golfer said to his caddie: "Looks like a four-wood and a putt to me."

The caddie handed him the four-wood, but, taking an almighty swing, the player hopelessly topped his shot so that the ball trickled just fifteen yards from the front of the tee.

The caddie immediately handed him his putter and said: "And now for one hell of a putt . . ."

★ After another wayward shot, a golfer and his caddie were searching in deep undergrowth when they finally came across a ball.

The golfer picked it up but said: "That can't be my ball. It's far too old."

"Don't forget," said the caddie, "it has been a long time since we started . . ."

★ A businessman persuaded his wife to join him in a game of foursomes against two customers. The wife had only ever played a few times and was understandably nervous, but the husband assured her: "I'll drive on the first hole, so by the time you play the second shot, our opponents will be the other side of the fairway. Nobody will be watching you."

As good as his word, the husband teed off and hit a 300-yard drive down the left side of the fairway, leaving his wife with a simple twenty-yard chip to the pin. He handed his wife a nine-iron and told her just to aim for the middle of the green. Instead she sliced her shot horribly along the ground almost at right angles and the ball rolled into a greenside bunker.

From there, the husband played a superb recovery shot to leave the ball on the green six feet from the hole. But the wife hit that fourth shot way too hard and sent the ball scurrying off the green into light rough. Again he played a fine shot to leave the ball close to the pin, but she read the putt all wrong and sent the ball into another bunker. Six.

Faced with a horrible lie in the sand trap, the husband did brilliantly to leave the ball on the apron of the green with their seventh shot, but the wife's attempt at a putt rolled no more than an inch. Eight.

With their ninth shot, the husband left the ball only six inches from the hole, but the wife somehow missed the next putt, sending it four feet away down the hill. Ten.

Showing great fortitude, the husband sank the uphill putt for an eleven. Meanwhile their opponents got down in four.

Unable to hide his disgust, the husband then stomped angrily off the green, threw his clubs in his bag, ripped up the scorecard and, shaking his fist at his wife, marched off to the clubhouse. The wife turned to their opponents and said: "I don't know what he's so mad about. After all, he took six shots; I only had five!"

★ As Bill and Jack headed off for their weekly round of golf, Bill suggested: "To make the game more interesting, why don't we have $10 on the lowest score for the day?"

Jack agreed, and they enjoyed a really close game. With one hole to play, Bill led by a single stroke, but then on the eighteenth he cut his ball into the rough.

"Help me find my ball," he called to Jack. "You search over there, I'll look around here."

After five minutes of fruitless searching, Bill, knowing that he was facing a disastrous penalty for a lost ball, sneakily pulled a ball from his pocket, dropped it on the ground and called out triumphantly: "Hey, I've found my ball!"

Jack looked across at him in disgust. "After all the years we've been friends," he said, "how could you cheat on me at golf for a measly few bucks?"

"What do you mean – cheat?" protested Bill. "I found my ball sitting right there!"

"And a liar, too!" exclaimed Jack in disbelief.

"What makes you think I'm lying?" yelled Bill.

"Because," said Jack, "I've been standing on your ball for the last five minutes!"

★ A hack golfer was enduring a particularly torrid round. His tee shot on the first hole sailed out of bounds, his fourth shot ended up in the woods and his sixth landed in the lake. In total, he lost three brand new golf balls on that hole.

Teeing off at the second hole, he hooked his drive wildly onto an adjoining railway track. "Damn!" he cursed. "There goes another new ball!" His next shot fared no better, flying into a corn field. "That's yet another new ball I've lost!" he groaned. "This round is costing me a fortune!"

Watching his struggles, a player in the group behind suggested: "In view of the number of balls you lose, why don't you play with an old ball?"

"Because," replied the hack golfer sourly, "I've never had one!"

Golfing Truths

Golf balls are like eggs. They're white, they're sold by the dozen, and every week you have to buy more.

It's amazing how a golfer who never helps out around the house will replace his divots, repair his ball marks and rake sand traps.

It's much easier to get up at 6 a.m. to play golf than at 11 a.m. to mow the lawn.

A good golf partner is one who is slightly worse than you.

Playing with your spouse on the golf course runs almost as great a marital risk as getting caught playing with someone else's spouse anywhere else.

A good drive on the eighteenth hole has stopped many a golfer from giving up the game.

Golf is the perfect thing to do on a Sunday because you always end up praying a lot.

No matter how badly you play golf, it is always possible to get worse.

If your opponent has trouble remembering whether he shot a six or a seven, he probably shot an eight.

★ A fourball watched a lone golfer play up short of the green they were on. As they moved on to the next tee, they saw him hurriedly chip on to the green and putt out. He then ran to the tee where the fourball were.

"Excuse me," he said breathlessly. "Would you mind if I played through? I've just heard that my wife has been involved in a terrible accident."

★ An elderly couple were competing in their golf club's annual seniors' tournament. On the final hole, the wife had to make a six-inch putt to tie with the leading score, but she missed and they lost out on their chance of victory.

In the car on their way home, the husband was still angry about the miss. "I can't believe you didn't hole that putt," he snapped. "It was no longer than my willy!"

"Yes, dear," she replied. "But it was much harder!"

★ Terry received a call from the coroner, who wanted to talk about his wife's recent death. Terry told him the sad story: "We were on the fourth hole, and Lily, my wife, was standing on the ladies' tee about thirty yards ahead of the men's tee when I hit my drive. From the sound when the ball hit her head and the way she dropped like a stone, I knew instantly that she was dead. God knows where the ball ended up!"

"I see" said the coroner. "Well that explains the injury to her head but what about the ball that was wedged up her rectum?"

"Oh," explained Terry. "That was my provisional."

★ ★ ★ ★ ★

HAIR

❖ "My, you look different today, Ellen!" said Patti to her co-worker. "Your hair is extra curly, and you have this wide-eyed look. What did you use – special curlers and some dramatic eye make-up?"

"No," replied Ellen. "My vibrator shorted out this morning!"

❖ A middle-aged guy who was bald bought a hairpiece in the hope that it would make him more attractive to women. That night he took it for its first outing to a singles bar, where he picked up a pretty young woman and took her back to his apartment.

To get her into the mood, he switched off the lights but as they started fumbling passionately in the dark, he realized to his horror that his toupee had fallen off. He began groping frantically for it, hoping to put it back on his head before the girl saw that he was really bald.

In the zeal of the search, he inadvertently ran his hands up the girl's legs.

"Oh! That's it!" she gasped in ecstasy.

"No, it isn't," he said, momentarily forgetting himself. "Mine's got a side parting."

> ❝ I was going to buy a book on hair loss,
> but the pages kept falling out.
> Jay London ❞

❖ A man was a quarter of an hour late back to work after his lunch break.

"Where have you been?" asked the boss.

"Getting a haircut."

"On company time?"

"It grew on company time."

"Not all of it."

"I didn't get it all cut off."

❖ A man went into a barber's. The barber said: "Shall I cut your hair round the back, sir?"

The man said: "What's wrong with doing it in the shop?"

❖ A balding man went into a barber's shop and asked how much it would be for a haircut.

"Twenty-five dollars," said the barber.

"Twenty-five dollars, that's crazy!" exclaimed the man. "I've hardly got any hair. How can it be that expensive?"

The barber explained: "It's $5 for the actual cut, and $20 for the search fee."

❖ A bald man had a real hang-up about his lack of hair. He had tried all types of treatment, but without success. Then one day he passed a barber's shop with a sign in the window that read: "Bald Men. Your Problems Solved Instantly. You Too Can Have a Head of Hair Like Mine For Five Hundred Dollars." And beneath the sign was a photo of the barber with his flowing mane of hair.

So the bald men went into the shop and asked the barber: "Can you guarantee that for $500 my hair will instantly look like yours?"

"Certainly," said the barber. "It will take no more than a few seconds for us to look exactly alike."

"Okay then," said the bald man, handing over the money. "Let's go for it."

The barber took the money and shaved his own hair off.

❖ A woman getting her hair cut asked the hairdresser when would be the best time to bring in her two-year-old son for his first haircut. The hairdresser replied: "When he's four."

❖ I'll never forget that terrifying moment I saw my first grey pubic hair. It was on a kebab.

How to Shower Like a Woman

Take off clothing and place it in sectioned laundry basket according to whites and coloureds.

Walk to bathroom wearing long dressing gown.

If you see husband along the way, cover up any exposed areas.

Look at your womanly physique in the mirror – make mental note to do more sit-ups.

Get in shower. Use face cloth, arm cloth, leg cloth, long loofah, wide loofah and pumice stone.

Wash hair once with cucumber and sage shampoo with forty-three added vitamins. Wash hair again to make sure it is clean.

Condition hair with grapefruit mint conditioner enhanced with natural avocado oil, and leave on hair for fifteen minutes.

Wash face with crushed apricot facial, scrub for ten minutes until red.

Wash rest of body with ginger nut and jaffa cake body wash.

Shave armpits and legs.

Turn off shower. Squeegee off all wet surfaces in shower, spray mould spots with liquid detergent.

Get out of shower. Dry with towel the size of a small country. Wrap hair in super absorbent towel.

Return to bedroom wearing long dressing gown and towel on head. If you see husband along the way, cover any exposed areas.

How to Shower Like a Man

Take off clothes while sitting on the edge of the bed.
Leave in a crumpled pile.

Walk naked to the bathroom. If you see wife along the
way, shake knob at her making "wha-hey" sound.

Look at manly physique in the mirror, admire size of
knob and scratch your ass.

Get in the shower.

Wash your face. Wash your armpits. Blow your nose
in your hands and let the water rinse it off.

Fart loudly and laugh at how loud it sounds in the
shower.

Spend majority of time washing privates and
surrounding area. Wash your butt, leaving four pubic
hairs stuck on the soap.

Shampoo hair. Make shampoo Mohawk.

Pee.

Rinse off and get out of the shower. Partially dry off.

Fail to notice water on the floor. Admire knob size
in mirror again. Leave shower door open, leave wet
mat on the floor, leave light and fan on.

Return to bedroom with towel around waist, leaving
trail of wet footprints behind you. If you pass wife,
pull off towel, shake knob at her and make "wha-
hey" noise. Again.

Throw wet towel on bed.

> Two adjoining barber's shops were in fierce competition. One put up a sign advertising haircuts for $7. So the other shop put up a sign that read: "We repair $7 haircuts."

❖ Not many people know it, but the Devil actually wears a wig. It has been a closely guarded secret for years and even some of those closest to him had no idea because it is a remarkably good fit. But down in the world of fire and brimstone one guy did find out, and he decided to play a practical joke. So one night he sneaked past the guardian demons, crept into Satan's bed chamber, stole the hairpiece and made good his escape.

When the Devil discovered that his wig had vanished, he was furious. He immediately summoned his demons and demanded to know which of them had allowed an outsider to break into the Satanic sleeping quarters. Nobody owned up, which merely made him madder still.

So he called a general meeting of the entire underworld, ordering everyone to attend. The meeting took place in a giant cavern, and as Satan stepped up to speak, there were stifled giggles from the audience as people saw for the first time that their leader was follically challenged. As the giggling turned to peals of laughter, Satan roared impatiently: "Be quiet!"

A deathly silence descended. "Whoever stole it," bellowed Satan, jabbing his finger angrily, "had better return it at once!" And here he paused for effect . . .

"Or else there'll be Hell toupee!"

★　　★　　★　　★　　★

HEALTH

* A mother said to her grown-up daughter: "Honey, I don't want you to think I have diabetes because I'm fat. I have diabetes because it runs in our family."

  The daughter shook her head in despair. "No, Mom," she replied, "you have diabetes because no one runs in our family."

> The only time it's cool to yell, 'I have diarrhoea!' is when you're playing Scrabble.
>
> Zach Galifianakis

* A man rang up the incontinence helpline and told the adviser: "I've got an incontinence problem. Before I go into details, is all the information I give you confidential."

  "Of course," said the adviser. "Now, where are you ringing from?"

  "The waist down."

* Why do bulimics love KFC?
  ## Because it comes with a bucket.

* Did you hear about the international Frisbee player who died after catching something that was going around?

* A brown paper bag went to the doctor complaining of feeling unwell. The doctor took a blood sample and told the bag to come back the following week.

  When the bag arrived for his follow-up appointment, the doctor said: "I'm afraid I have some bad news. The results of your blood tests indicate that you have haemophilia."

  "How can I possibly have haemophilia? I'm a brown paper bag!"

  "Yes," replied the doctor, "but it seems your mother was a carrier."

✱ Feeling stressed out, a man decided to take a long hot bath, but just as he had made himself comfortable, the doorbell rang. The man climbed out of the tub, wrapped a large towel around his waist, wrapped his head in a small towel, put on his slippers, and went to the door. It was a salesman trying to sell him brushes. Slamming the door, the man returned to his hot bath.

No sooner had he climbed back into his hot bath than there was another ring at the doorbell. The man climbed out of the tub, wrapped a large towel around his waist, wrapped his head in a smaller towel, put on his slippers, and trudged downstairs to answer the door. It was an energy company trying to persuade him to change his power supply. Slamming the door, the man returned to his hot bath.

Five minutes later, the doorbell rang again. On went the slippers and towels as before, but as he tottered towards the bathroom door, he slipped on a wet patch of floor and hurt his back in falling against the hard porcelain of the tub.

Cursing under his breath, the man struggled into his street clothes and, with every movement causing a stabbing pain, he drove to the doctor's surgery. After examining him, the doctor said: "You know, you've been lucky. There are no bones broken. But you need to relax. Why don't you go home and take a long hot bath?"

✱ Wife: "How can you sleep knowing you're killing yourself by smoking?"
Husband: "Easy, because I know I'm killing you through passive smoking."

> ❝ I hate not being able to smoke in pubs. People say to me: 'Think of the money you'll save by not smoking.' But actually I won't save any money at all, because I'll live longer.
>
> Sean Lock ❞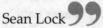

✳ Did you hear about the man who was kicked out of a Tourette's Society meeting for using good language?

✳ A small boy was playing with a balloon around the house, flicking it in the air with his hand. His mother told him to stop in case he broke an ornament, but he paid no attention. Finally after incessant nagging, he stopped.

"Right," she said, "I'm just going to the shop for some groceries. I'll only be twenty minutes, so I want you to stay here and behave yourself."

As soon as she was gone, he started playing with the balloon again, flicking it from room to room until, to his dismay, it landed in the toilet bowl. He left it there and went off to play with something else.

Shortly afterwards his mother returned home in a state of high anxiety. Hurriedly dumping the groceries in the kitchen, she ran to the toilet and proceeded to unleash a torrent of diarrhoea. Relieved when it was all over, she turned to inspect the damage and couldn't believe her eyes. There in the toilet bowl was this big brown thing.

She immediately called her doctor, who could offer no obvious explanation but promised that he would come straight round. When he arrived, she led him to the toilet, where he got down on his knees and took a long, hard look at the thing. Perplexed, he took out his pen and prodded it in the hope of finding out what it might be. And POP! The balloon exploded, showering poop everywhere – all over his clothes, up the walls and on the floor.

"Doctor, are you all right?" she asked.

Wiping the poop from his eyes, he said: "Do you know, I've been a doctor for twenty-five years, and this is the first time I've ever actually seen a fart!"

✳ My cavity wasn't fixed by my regular dentist but by a guy who was filling in.

* On a visit to the health centre, a man saw his neighbour looking extremely worried.

"You look really gloomy," he said. "What's the matter?"

"I've got the big C."

"What, cancer?"

"No, dyslexia."

> Apparently over-thinking or worrying about things may actually keep your brain healthier. You know what that means? If you're not a worrier, you should be worried about that.
>
> Jay Leno

* My uncle's in a coma – he's living the dream.

* A boxer went to a doctor for treatment for insomnia.

"Have you tried counting sheep?" suggested the doctor.

"It doesn't work," replied the boxer. "Whenever I get to nine, I stand up!"

* Smoking seriously damages your health. Smoking for fun is fine.

> My friend was told by her doctor that she is morbidly obese . . . as if she doesn't have enough on her plate.
>
> Jimmy Carr

* Two men at work were discussing the dangers of smoking. The first said: "Just one cigarette killed my mate."

"Really?"

"Yes. He was fixing a gas leak at the time."

* Being crushed by large objects can be very depressing.

✳ A man suffered from terrible constipation. The doctor asked him about his diet, and the man admitted that the only vegetable he ever ate was peas.

"That's almost certainly the cause of your constipation," said the doctor. "All those peas you've been eating have clogged up your system. I'm afraid you'll have to give them up for good."

A few years later, the man was sitting in a restaurant with his boss and the boss's wife. The boss's wife said: "If there's one thing I miss in life, it's a nice piece of cheese. But I had to give it up for health reasons."

The boss said: "It's the same with me and beer. I'd love a pint, but the doctor has warned me not to."

"I know how you feel," said the man. "I haven't had a pea in six years."

The boss immediately jumped to his feet and screamed: "Right, anyone who can't swim, grab a table!"

✳ Did you hear about the man who was addicted to going on TV chat shows?

He had Parkinson's disease.

✳ Having gone to the hospital for a routine check-up, a man was devastated to learn that he had the rare deadly disease B55. The doctor told him that he had just one week to live.

Determined to make the most of his last week rather than mope around feeling sorry for himself, he decided to take his wife out to bingo. He even entered the prize draw game. First, he got one line and won $10,000; then he got two lines and won a car; and finally he got a full house and won a holiday for two in the Seychelles.

At the end of the round, the bingo caller went over to him and said: "You must be the luckiest man in the world! You have just won $10,000, a car and a fantastic luxury holiday in just one game!"

"I'm not that lucky," replied the man. "I've got B55."

The bingo caller's face turned to shock and he said: "You lucky bastard! You've won the raffle as well!"

> ❝ It should not be an act of social disobedience to light a cigarette. Unless you're actually a doctor working at an incubator.
>
> Dylan Moran ❞

* The Colour Blind Association are holding a social night next week – they're going to paint the town grey.

* Seeing a man with no feet, a guy suddenly went over and kicked him.
  "What did you do that for?" asked the victim.
  "Because I'm lack-toes intolerant."

* A man with Tourette's witnessed a road accident and was asked to testify in court. All went well until he was asked to swear on the Bible.

* A guy was woken in the night by the bulimic who lived in the apartment above him. So he banged on the ceiling and shouted: "Keep it down, love!"

* A guy picked up a hot girl and took her back to his house. There, they proceeded to rip each other's clothes off until she noticed scars on his knees.
  "What are those?" she asked.
  He explained: "Oh, when I was a kid I contracted kneesles."
  "You mean measles?"
  "No, kneesles."
  Unfazed, they continued undressing each other until she noticed his crooked toes.
  "Ah, I also contracted toelio," he said.
  "Don't you mean polio?"
  "No, I got toelio."
  She dismissed his denials as a peculiar quirk until he dropped his underpants. Surveying the scene before her, she said: "Ah, let me guess: smallcox."

> **❝** I saw a shop window displaying 'essential oils'. I didn't have any of them. I'm lucky to be alive!
>
> Ardal O'Hanlon **❞**

* A woman who had enrolled in nursing school was attending an anatomy class. The subject of the day was involuntary muscles. The lecturer, hoping to capture the students' interest, asked the woman if she knew what her asshole did when she had an orgasm.

   "Sure," she replied, "he's at home taking care of the kids."

* Snow White was in the bath feeling sleepy. He got out, so she felt dopey instead.

> **❝** It's not only breasts that drop. Vaginas do, too. I woke up eight years ago and asked myself why I was wearing a bunny slipper. And why it was grey.
>
> Joan Rivers **❞**

* A young woman went into a pet shop one morning and mumbled: "Do you sell large white bears?"

   "No, I'm afraid we don't," said the sales assistant.

   And the woman left.

   The next day, she was back again. "Do you sell large white bears?" she asked.

   "No, I'm afraid we don't," said the same assistant.

   And the woman left.

   The next day she was back again. "Do you sell large white bears?" she asked.

   "No, we don't," said the sales assistant. "And this is the third day you've come in and asked me that."

   "I'm so sorry," said the young woman, "but I can't help it. You see, I have buy polar disorder."

* If smoking is so bad for you, how come it cures salmon?

Your Health Questions Answered

Q. I've heard that daily exercise can prolong life. Is this true?

A. Your heart is only good for so many beats, and that's it. Don't waste them on exercise. Everything wears out eventually. Speeding up your heart will not make you live longer – that's like saying you can extend the life of your car by driving faster. If you really want to live longer, take a nap.

Q. Should I improve my diet by cutting down on meat and eating more fruits and vegetables?

A. You need to understand the chain of nutrition. What does a cow eat? Hay and corn. And what are these? Vegetables. So a steak is simply an efficient mechanism for delivering vegetables to your system. Pork and lamb are equally productive sources of vegetables, and if you want to increase your grain intake, eat chicken.

Q. Is swimming good for your figure?

A. If it is, explain whales to me.

✳ A man took time off work because he was feeling sick. On the third day, he said to his girlfriend: "Call the doctor, I'm dying here! I've got a fever and a sore throat and I ache all over!"

She said: "Oh, stop making such a fuss and feeling sorry for yourself! It's just Man Flu."

She was right, and a few days later he felt fine again.

The following week, it was his girlfriend's turn to feel unwell. She said to him: "Call the doctor, I'm dying here! I've coughed up a pint of blood, I've gone blind and I'm paralysed down my left side!"

Her boyfriend said: "Oh, stop making such a fuss and feeling sorry for yourself! It's just Bird Flu!"

Q. How can I calculate my body/fat ratio?
A. Well, if you have a body and you have body fat, your ratio is one to one. If you have two bodies, your ratio is two to one, etc.

Q. Should I reduce my alcohol intake?
A. Certainly not. Wine is made from fruit while brandy is distilled wine, which means they take the water out of the fruity bit so that you get even more of the goodness.

Q. Are fried foods bad for you?
A. These days, foods are fried in vegetable oil. How can getting more vegetables be bad for you?

Q. Is chocolate bad for me?
A. Helloooo! Cocoa beans . . . another vegetable!

Q. Will doing sit-ups help me get a flat stomach?
A. On the contrary, when you exercise a muscle, it gets bigger. You should only be doing sit-ups if you want a bigger stomach.

> I hope we find a cure for every major disease, because I'm tired of walking 5k.
>
> Daniel Tosh

* A married couple were participating in a blood donor scheme, and as part of the pre-screening process, an elderly female volunteer was asking them a series of questions.

    The volunteer asked the husband: "Have you ever paid for sex?"

    Glancing wearily over at his wife who was trying to calm a new baby as well as tend to several other children milling around her, he sighed: "Every time."

❋ A young newlywed couple had a number of disagreements about the wife's refusal to give up smoking.

One afternoon, when she again lit up following sex, he told her: "You really ought to quit."

Getting tired of his nagging, she responded: "I really enjoy a good cigarette after sex."

"But they stunt your growth," he replied.

"Have you ever smoked?" she asked.

"No," he said.

Lifting her gaze to his groin, she laughed: "So what's your excuse?"

❋ An Indonesian man has won a freaky features competition thanks to his twenty-three-inch fingernails. He's apparently using the $20,000 prize money to invest in property, enjoy a holiday and find a cure for haemorrhoids.

> My girlfriend has crabs, so I bought her fishnet stockings.
>
> Jay London

> I did think about giving up smoking, but I decided not to, because I'm not a quitter. And I know that every cigarette I smoke takes five minutes off my life, but I also know it takes ten minutes to smoke it. That's a clear five-minute net gain, I reckon.
>
> Ed Byrne

> My sister was diagnosed with multiple personalities. She phoned me the other day, and my caller ID exploded.
>
> Zach Galifianakis

✳ Two old guys, aged eighty and eighty-seven, were sitting on their favourite park bench one morning. The eighty-seven-year-old had just finished his morning jog and wasn't even short of breath. The eighty-year-old was amazed at his friend's stamina and asked him what he did to have so much energy.

The eighty-seven-year-old said: "Well, I eat rye bread every day. It's a well-known fact that it keeps your energy level high, and that it will give you great stamina with the ladies."

So on the way home, the eighty-year-old stopped off at the bakery. As he was looking round, the female sales clerk asked him if he needed any assistance.

"Do you have any rye bread?" he asked.

"Yes," she said. "There's a whole shelf of it. Would you like some?"

"Sure. I'd like five loaves."

"My goodness, five loaves!" she exclaimed. "By the time you get to the fifth loaf, it'll be hard."

He replied: "I can't believe it! Everyone knows about this stuff except me!"

> According to a recent study, it seems that men and women tend to gravitate to different areas in health clubs. For example, women tend to head to the exercise bikes whereas men tend to head to the area right behind the exercise bikes.
>
> Jay Leno

✳ A doctor remarked on a new patient's extraordinarily ruddy complexion.

"It's high blood pressure, doc. It comes from my family."

"Your mother's side or your father's?" asked the doctor.

"Neither. It's from my wife's family."

"I'm sorry, but I don't see how you can get high blood pressure from your *wife's* family."

"You should try spending a weekend with them!"

＊ In the beginning, God created Heaven and Earth and populated the Earth with broccoli, cauliflower and spinach, green and yellow vegetables of all kinds, so that Man and Woman would live long and healthy lives.

Then using God's great gifts, Satan created Ben and Jerry's Ice Cream and Krispy Crème Donuts. And Satan said: "You want chocolate with that?"

And Man said, "Yes", and Woman said, "While you're at it, add some sprinklies." And they gained ten pounds. And Satan smiled.

And God created the beautiful yogurt so that Woman might keep the figure that Man found so fair. And Satan brought forth white flour from the wheat and sugar from the cane and combined them. And Woman went from size six to size fourteen.

So God said, "Try my fresh green salad." And Satan presented Ranch Dressing, buttery croutons and garlic toast on the side. And Man and Woman unfastened their belts following the repast.

God then said, "I have sent you healthy vegetables and olive oil in which to cook them." And Satan brought forth deep-fried fish and fried chicken steak so big it needed its own platter. And Man gained more weight and his cholesterol went through the roof.

God then created a light, fluffy white cake, named it "Angel Food Cake" and said, "It is good." Satan then created rich, dark chocolate cake and named it "Devil's Temptation."

God then brought forth running shoes so that His children might lose extra pounds. And Satan gave cable TV with a remote control so Man would not have to toil changing the channels. And Man and Woman laughed and cried before the flickering blue light and gained pounds.

Then God brought forth the potato, naturally low in fat and brimming with nutrition. And Satan peeled off the healthy skin and sliced the starchy centre into chips and deep fried them. And Man gained pounds.

God then gave lean beef so that Man might consume fewer calories and still satisfy his appetite. And Satan created

McDonald's and its ninety-nine-cent double cheeseburger. Then Satan said, "You want fries with that?" And Man replied, "Yes! And super size them!" And Satan said, "It is good." And Man went into cardiac arrest.

God sighed and created quadruple bypass surgery.

Then Satan created the National Health Service.

* A pregnant woman was waiting in line at a bank when three masked robbers burst in waving guns. As they peppered the place with gunfire, the woman ended up getting shot three times in the stomach. Happily, she pulled through, and in hospital asked the doctor whether her baby was safe.

The doctor said: "Actually you're having triplets. And they're all fine, but each one has a bullet lodged in its stomach. But don't worry, the bullets will pass through their systems through normal metabolism."

The woman went on to give birth to two girls and a boy. Thirteen years later, one of the girls said to the mother: "Mom, I've done a really weird thing. I've just passed a bullet into the toilet."

Her mother comforted her and explained about the bank robbery.

A few weeks later, the other daughter ran in with tears streaming down her face. "Mom," she cried, "I've done something really freaky!"

"Let me guess," said the mother. "You passed a bullet into the toilet?"

"Yes," replied the daughter. "How did you know?" And the mother comforted her and explained about the bank robbery.

A month later, the son announced: "Mom, I've done a very bad thing."

The mother said: "You passed a bullet into the toilet, right?"

"No," said the boy. "I was masturbating and I shot the dog!"

> **❝** British scientists have demonstrated
> that cigarettes can harm your children.
> Fair enough. Use an ashtray.
>
> Jimmy Carr **❞**

★　　★　　★　　★　　★

HEALTH: MENTAL

★ The Queen was on a visit to a mental hospital. She talked to a
male patient tending the hospital flowerbeds and asked him
why he was there. In a calm and orderly manner, he told her
his life story, adding that he had been in the institution for
more than twenty years. The Queen was greatly impressed
by his manner and hinted that she might be able to secure
his release as he seemed completely cured and ready to
resume his place in society. The man was extremely grateful
and returned to his gardening as the Queen departed.

Her Majesty was just about to leave the hospital grounds
when a brick hit her on the back of the head. With blood
oozing from the wound, she turned groggily to see the man
standing there.

He said: "You won't forget, will you?"

> **❝** People say there's a fine line between
> genius and insanity. I don't think
> there's a fine line, I actually think
> there's a yawning gulf. You see some poor
> bugger scuffling up the road with balloons
> tied to his ears, he's not going home to invent
> a rocket, is he?
>
> Bill Bailey **❞**

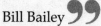

★ All day a patient in a mental hospital would put his ear to the wall and listen. The doctor watched him do it day after day. Curious as to what the patient was listening to, one day the doctor decided to put his own ear to the wall, but heard nothing.

So he turned to the patient and said: "I don't hear anything."

The patient said: "Yeah, I know. It's been like that for months!"

★ A woman was visiting her elderly mother in a mental hospital when a guy entered the ward, waving his arms about and making beeping noises.

"Excuse me," said the woman. "What are you doing?"

"I'm driving my car," he replied cheerily. "Beep, beep!"

"But you're in a mental hospital," she tried to explain. "You're not in a car."

"Don't tell him that," cried one of the other patients. "He pays me $20 a week to wash it."

★ On an official visit to a state asylum, a US senator observed a patient reaching up and then putting something invisible into a basket on the ground.

"What are you doing?" asked the senator.

The patient replied: "I'm taking the stars from the sky."

Puzzled, the senator moved on to the next patient, who appeared to be taking something invisible from the same basket and then reaching up high.

"What are you doing?" inquired the senator.

The patient explained: "I'm putting the stars back in the sky."

More mystified than ever, the senator moved on to the next patient, who was sitting in the middle of the floor making a rowing movement with both arms and shouting out, "Ahoy to starboard!"

"And what are you doing?" asked the senator.

The patient answered: "Trying to get away from those two nutters!"

A schizophrenic passed a poster advertising a rock gig. He thought to himself, "I've half a mind to go to that."

★ The condition of a man who had been in a mental home for some years finally seemed to have improved to the point where he was being considered for release. Before allowing him to be freed into the outside world, however, the hospital chief wanted to ascertain how he would be able to cope with it.

"Tell me," said the medic, "if we release you – and all the reports indicate that you are now completely sane – what do you intend to do with your life?"

The patient said: "It would be wonderful to return to leading a normal life and if I do, I will certainly refrain from making the same mistakes as before. I was a nuclear physicist, you know, and it was the stress of my work in weapons research that helped put me here. If I am released, I shall confine my work purely to theory, where I trust the situation will be less stressful."

"Excellent," said the hospital chief.

"Or alternatively," continued the patient, "I might teach. There is a lot to be said for devoting one's energies to bringing up a new generation of scientists."

"Absolutely," echoed the chief enthusiastically.

"Then again, I might write. There is a considerable need for books on science that can be understood by ordinary members of the public. Or I might even write a novel based on my experiences in this fine institution."

"An interesting possibility," agreed the hospital chief.

"Or, if none of these things appeal to me," mused the patient, "I can always carry on my life as a teapot."

★ A schizophrenic bumped into me in the bank today. Who the hell does he think he is?

★ For a day out, a doctor at an asylum took a dozen of the inmates to a baseball game. For weeks in advance, he had prepared them for the outing by coaching them to respond to his commands so that they could behave perfectly on the day of the game.

Inside the stadium as soon as the national anthem started, the doctor shouted, "Up nuts!" And the inmates all stood up obediently.

When the anthem finished, he shouted, "Down nuts!" And the patients all sat down.

Later, after a home run, he shouted, "Cheer nuts!" And they clapped and cheered on cue.

In fact, the doctor was so pleased with how smoothly the day out was going that he decided to head off for a beer and a hot dog, leaving his young assistant in charge. But when he returned twenty-five minutes later, the place was in uproar.

He asked his assistant: "What's gone wrong?"

She replied: "Everything was just fine until some guy walked by and shouted, 'Peanuts!'"

★ ★ ★ ★ ★

HOLLYWOOD

❖ Did you hear about the leper who went into a video shop and said: "Have you got *My Left Foot*?"

❖ Browsing around a video shop, a man spotted a sale of old titles. Among them was Walt Disney's *Bambi*.

"How much is *Bambi*?" he asked the sales assistant.

"Twenty-five dollars."

"That's a little dear."

Classic Hollywood Remakes

Captain Corelli's Mandarin – Instead of fighting the Second World War, an Italian officer becomes obsessed with fruit on a Greek island.

Madame Ovary – A nineteenth-century woman controversially leaves her husband and family to rent herself out as a freelance surrogate mother.

Mend It Like Beckham – Soccer player David Beckham shows his flair for needlework and darning.

The Sound of Mucus – An Austrian singing family fear their phlegm-filled throats will betray them to the Nazis.

Low Litre – A promiscuous young barmaid is accused of giving short measures.

Pilates of the Caribbean – A gang of seafaring scoundrels take time off from looting ships around Jamaica to improve their posture.

Lady Chatterley's Plover – An aristocratic siren shows her tender side by taking a sea bird under her wing.

Saving Ryan's Privates – A US soldier finds himself in a tricky situation when tortured by the Germans in war-torn France.

Foetal Attraction – A psychotic woman develops an unhealthy obsession with unborn babies.

The Liceman Cometh – Assorted barflies in a 1912 saloon await a visit from the nit inspector.

The Umpire Strikes Back – A Wimbledon tennis official exacts a bloody revenge for years of abuse from John McEnroe.

The Mancunian Candidate – A tense political thriller in which suspicions are aroused when Liam Gallagher is a surprise nominee for the post of Vice-President of the United States.

Little Seizure – A mobster's ambition to become an underworld big shot are hampered when he suffers a petit mal.

The Nuns of Gavarone – A Second World War action drama in which Allied soldiers capture the German fortress of Gavarone by posing as the residents of a convent.

Bridget Jones' Dairy – A thirtysomething woman abandons her chaotic and unrewarding city life to start a new career in the country producing butter.

Donny and Clyde – Tired of life with the Osmonds, one of their number joins up with a notorious bank robber on a crime spree across the United States.

Turban Cowboy – A Sikh seeks his fortune in the Wild West.

Last Traction Hero – A boy's hopes of Hollywood fame are wrecked when the star of the movie ends up in hospital following a serious road accident.

How Green Was My Valet – The moving story of a naive Welsh butler.

❖ Why did the actor turn down a movie role as a juggler?
   He didn't have the balls to do it.

❖ **I saw a movie about a beaver last week. It was the best dam movie I've ever seen.**

❖ A guy said to his pal: "Did you see that horrific movie last night? It was about a little boy who accidentally knocked over a kettle and scalded himself with hot tea. To be honest, it shouldn't have had a PG rating."

❖ Did you hear about the guy who watched *The Lord of the Rings* over and over again?
   It was just force of Hobbit.

❖ A Hollywood movie producer was lying beside the pool at the Beverly Hills Hilton when his business partner showed up in a state of high excitement.
   "How did the meeting go?" asked the first guy.
   "Great," said his associate. "Tarantino will write and direct for ten million, Tom Hanks will star for nine million, and we can bring in the whole picture for under fifty million."
   "That's fantastic news!" said the guy by the pool.
   "There's just one snag," warned the associate.
   "What's that?"
   "We have to put up two thousand in cash."

> ❝ The best thing about buying illegal DVDs is that you don't have to sit through the warning not to buy illegal DVDs at the start. It just goes straight into the film.
>
> Dara O'Briain ❞

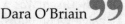

❖ A man went into a video store and said: "Have you got that movie that features Long John Silver?"
   "Sorry," said the sales clerk, "we don't sell pirate videos."

❖ There was disappointment in Hollywood last week when the Sylvester Stallone Movie Festival got off to a rocky start.

❖ On a visit to a movie theatre, a man was struggling to hear the dialogue above the chatter of the two women sitting directly in front of him. Unable to bear it any longer, he tapped one of the women on the shoulder.

"Excuse me," he said, "I can't hear."

"I should hope not," replied one of the women sharply. "This is a private conversation."

❖ A man went into a video store and complained: "I bought this video of a famous movie about the Allies' defeat at Arnhem in the Second World War, but it has been cut so much that a lot of the key scenes are missing. It's impossible to follow the story. I want the original full-length version."

The sales clerk said: "Ah, yes. I know the movie you mean. It's been abridged too far."

★　★　★　★　★

HOOKERS

✳ A naive young man plucked up the courage to visit a New York City whorehouse. There, a girl dragged him upstairs and wasted no time in taking off her pants and panties.

Peering between her legs, the young man asked shyly: "What's that?"

"It's my lower mouth," said the hooker.

"What do you mean, your lower mouth?"

"Well, it's like a mouth. It's got a beard, it's got lips . . ."

"Has it got a tongue in it?"

The hooker pulled him towards her and said: "Not yet!"

✳ A stranger in town knocked on the door of a house where a taxi driver had told him he could be sexually accommodated. An eye-level panel slid open and a female voice asked what he wanted.

"I want to get screwed," said the man.

"Okay, mister," replied the voice, "but this is a private club. So you've gotta slip fifty bucks as an introduction fee through the mail slot."

The man put in his $50 and the panel was closed. He then waited for several minutes but nothing happened. Eventually he banged on the door until the panel slid open again.

"I want to get screwed," said the man.

"What?" said the voice. "Again?"

✳ A young US sailor was on shore leave in Korea for the first time. While the rest of the guys were enjoying the attractions of the city's red-light district, he was too shy to come right out and ask the hookers what they charged for sex. After enduring two nights of frustration, on the third night he hatched a cunning plan to get laid. So when one of the local girls approached him and asked him his name, he answered: "Rick Peanus."

"Lick Peanus?" she queried.

"Sure," said the sailor. "How much?"

✳ It was my regular dominatrix's birthday last week. All her clients had a whipround for her.

✳ A blind man went to a brothel and because he couldn't see what he was getting, he was given the roughest old whore in town.

They went upstairs and she undressed, but when he started to run his hands over her spotty butt, he recoiled.

"Don't worry," she said. "It's just a touch of acne."

"Thank God!" said the blind man. "I thought it was the price list!"

✳ On a bitterly cold night, a young man called in at the town brothel.

The madam said: "You'll have to wait."

"But there are lots of girls who aren't busy right now," said the guy.

"I know," she said, "but several of the rooms are closed for repairs."

"Listen," he persisted, "I'm really desperate. I don't need a room, I'll do it anywhere."

So she took his money and he went upstairs with one of the girls. Looking for a suitable place, they decided to do it on the roof. But it was such a cold night that they froze to death halfway through having sex and fell to the sidewalk below. A passing drunk looked them over, staggered to the brothel door, and knocked.

"Clear off!" yelled the madam. "We don't allow drunks in here."

"I don't want to come in." said the drunk. "I just wanted to tell you that your sign fell down."

I rang up a girl I used to date and asked if she was free Friday night. She said no, but her prices were reasonable.

✳ On his way to school each day, a boy had to walk past a whorehouse. One of the hookers always sat outside and when the boy passed by, she would call out, "Hiya, kid" while wiggling her pinky at him.

After this had happened a few times, he asked her why she always wiggled her little finger at him.

"Well," she laughed, "that's about the size of your privates, isn't it?"

The next day the boy walked by and once again the hooker shouted out, "Hiya, kid" and wiggled her pinky.

Putting his fingers in his mouth to stretch his lips as wide as they would go, he called back: "How you doing, lady?"

✳ What's the difference between a hooker and a wife?
   One is contract, the other is pay-as-you-go.

✳ A man was walking through the streets of Bangkok when a small girl approached him for sex.
   "No," he said. "You're far too young."
   The girl said: "How do you know my name?"

✳ Did you hear about the guy who was such a failure with women that even a hooker told him she had a headache?

✳ A hooker went to a doctor complaining of morning sickness.
   The doctor confirmed: "You are pregnant. Do you know who the father is?"
   The hooker laughed: "If you ate a tin of beans, would you know which one made you fart?"

✳ A girl who led a secret life as a hooker was arrested by police during a raid on a sex party at a hotel. The police then put the hookers in a line outside the hotel so that they could get their names and details. Just then the girl's grandmother happened to pass by and spotted her granddaughter standing in the line.
   "Why are you standing in line here, darling?" she asked.
   The girl, anxious to keep the truth from her grandmother, said: "The police are handing out free oranges, and I'm just lining up for some."
   "That's very generous of them," said the grandmother. "I think I'll get some for myself." And she joined the line at the back.
   A police officer passed down the line, asking for information from all of the hookers. When he reached the grandmother, he was shocked and exclaimed: "Wow! Still going strong at your age! How do you do it?"
   She said: "I just take my dentures out, rip the skin back and suck them dry."
   The officer fainted.

* Jerry thought he would be ashamed of having a sister who was a hooker until he learned that she gave family discount.

* A madam answered the door of her brothel to find a distinguished looking man in his late forties standing there.

"Can I help you?" she asked.

"I want to see Carrie," he replied.

"Sir, I have to tell you that Carrie is one of our most expensive ladies," said the madam. "Perhaps you would prefer someone else."

But the man was adamant. "No, I must see Carrie."

So Carrie was summoned, and she told the man that she charged $1,000 a visit. Without hesitation, he pulled out ten $100 bills, gave them to Carrie and they went upstairs. After his allotted hour was up, he left.

The next night, the man visited the brothel again and insisted on seeing Carrie. The madam was amazed and explained that nobody had ever come back to Carrie two nights in a row because she was simply too expensive. When Carrie appeared, she reminded the man that she charged $1,000 an hour – and no discounts. Again he pulled ten $100 bills from his wallet, handed the money to Carrie and they went upstairs. An hour later he left.

The following night the man was there again, demanding to see Carrie. Nobody at the brothel could believe that he was back for a third successive night but, as before, he paid Carrie $1,000 in cash and they went upstairs.

After their session was over, Carrie said to him: "Nobody has ever been with me three nights in a row. Where are you from?"

The man replied: "West Virginia."

"Really?" said Carrie. "I have family in West Virginia."

"I know," said the man. "Your father died last month, and I am your sister's attorney. She asked me to give you your $3,000 inheritance."

﹡ What did the sign say on the door of the whorehouse?
Beat it. We're closed.

﹡ Three guys visited a hooker. As it was a slow night, she told
them they could pay by the inch. When the first guy came
out, the others asked him how much he had paid.
"Seventy-five dollars," he replied.
Then the second guy went in and when he came out, he
told them he had paid $85. Finally the third guy came out.
"How much did you pay?" asked his two pals.
"Twenty dollars," he answered.
"Only $20? How come?"
"I ain't stupid," he said, "I paid on the way out instead of
on the way in!"

﹡ Did you hear about the man who filled his escort up with
diesel?
It nearly killed her.

★ ★ ★ ★ ★

HOSPITALS

★ A nurse was walking down a hospital corridor when she was
spotted by her supervisor. The supervisor couldn't believe
what she was seeing. The nurse's hair was unkempt, her
skirt was crumpled, and to round things off, her left breast
was hanging out of the open front of her uniform.
"Nurse Philpott!" boomed the supervisor. "What is
the meaning of this? Why are you walking around the
hospital not only looking like a tramp, but with your breast
exposed?"
"Oh," said the nurse, stuffing her breast back into her
uniform. "It's those damn interns! They never put anything
back when they're through using it!"

★ When a trick went wrong, an amateur magician accidentally turned his wife into a couch and his two children into armchairs. He tried everything he knew to reverse the trick but when all attempts failed, he took them to hospital.

He paced up and down in casualty for hours until finally a junior doctor came out to see him.

"My wife is a couch and my two children are armchairs," said the magician. "I need to know how they're doing."

The doctor glanced at his notes and said: "They're comfortable."

> I told the ambulance men the wrong blood type for my ex, so he knows what rejection feels like.
>
> Pippa Evans

★ A female punk rocker was brought into a hospital emergency department to undergo surgery for acute appendicitis. The young woman had a green Mohican hairstyle and when she was undressed on the operating table, the theatre staff discovered that she had also dyed her pubic hair green. And above it was a tattoo reading: "Keep off the grass."

After the operation was successfully completed, the surgeon added a small note to the dressing which read: "Sorry, had to mow the lawn."

★ A patient who had just undergone a very complicated operation kept complaining that he could feel some sort of bump on his head and that he had a pounding headache. Since the operation had been on his stomach, these were not the type of side effects that the nursing staff had anticipated. Fearing that he might be suffering from post-operative shock, one of the nurses mentioned the symptoms to the surgeon who had carried out the operation.

"Don't worry," said the surgeon, "it's not shock. He really does have a bump on his head. Halfway through the operation we ran out of anaesthetic."

★ What's the difference between a haematologist and a urologist?

The haematologist pricks your finger.

★ A renowned cardiologist died and was given an elaborate funeral. To commemorate his life's work, a huge heart covered in flowers was placed behind the coffin during the service. At the end of the eulogy, the heart opened and the casket slid inside. The heart then closed, sealing the doctor inside the beautiful heart forever.

At that point, one of the mourners suddenly started laughing. As heads turned to glare at him, he said: "I'm sorry, I was just thinking of my own funeral. You see, I'm a gynaecologist."

Meanwhile the proctologist fainted.

★ A man ended up in hospital, covered in wood and hay, with a toy horse lodged in his butt. Doctors described his condition as "stable".

★ A woman went to a hospital to visit a friend. She hadn't been inside a hospital for several years and felt very ignorant about all the new technology. A technician followed her into the elevator, wheeling a large, intimidating-looking machine with numerous tubes, wires and dials.

She looked at it and smiled: "I certainly wouldn't want to be hooked up to that!"

"Neither would I," replied the technician. "It's a floor-cleaning machine."

★ A man was lying in a hospital bed with virtually his entire body wrapped in a cast. One of the nurses inserted a rectal thermometer and said: "Don't move, I'll be right back."

When she returned a minute or so later, she was alarmed to see that the thermometer was now in his mouth. "How did you get that in your mouth?" she asked. "You can barely move."

He said: "I hiccupped."

★ The transplant patient was wheeled into the operating theatre, and then he had a change of heart.

★ A man was lying in hospital, covered in bandages from head to toe. The guy in the next bed said: "What do you do for a living?"

The bandaged man replied: "I used to be a window cleaner."

"Oh, when did you give it up?"

"About halfway down."

★ Who are the most decent people in a hospital?
The ultra sound department.

★ A man went to the hospital out-patients' department and said to a nurse: "A wasp has given me a nasty sting. Is there something you can give me?"

"Whereabouts is it?" asked the nurse.

"I don't know," said the man. "It'll be miles away by now!"

★ A man lost both ears in an accident and was distraught at the prospect of being unable to hear ever again.

The surgeon said to him: "There are no human transplant ears available at present but we do have a dog's ear and a pig's ear that are ready to transplant. Would you consider those?"

"Yes, okay," replied the patient. "I'll try anything to save my hearing."

So the transplants went ahead and a month later the man returned to the hospital for a check-up.

"How have things been?" asked the surgeon.

"Well, doctor, the dog's ear is brilliant – I can hear for miles – but with the pig's ear, I seem to be getting a bit of crackling in it."

★ A guy was lying in his hospital bed, wired up with drips and monitors, breathing with the aid of an oxygen mask. A young woman was going round the ward with the tea trolley and when she reached his bed she asked him: "Is there anything you would like?"

"Yes," he answered. "Could you tell me if my testicles are black?"

"I'm sorry, but I'm not medical staff," she replied. "I can't help you with that."

"Oh, please have a look for me," he begged. "I'm really worried. Are my testicles black?"

Taking pity on his obvious distress, the girl glanced around the ward and, seeing no sign of any medical staff, said: "All right, I'll have a look for you." So she pulled back the bedcover, lifted his dick out of the way and, cupping his balls in her hand, told him: "No, they look fine to me."

In some agitation, the patient immediately pulled off his oxygen mask and shouted: "I asked, 'Are my test results back?'"

> 66 I went to the emergency room recently. I don't want to say the wait was long, but the guy in front of me was being treated for a musket wound.
>
> Nick DiPaolo 99

★ Two small boys were sitting outside a clinic. One was crying very loudly.

"What's the matter?" asked the other boy.

"I came here for a blood test."

"So? That's nothing to be afraid of."

"You don't understand. For the blood test, they cut my finger."

Hearing this, the second boy started to cry, too.

"Why are you crying?" sobbed the first boy.

"Because I'm here for a urine test."

★ Two women were bemoaning the state of the National Health Service. One said: "Do you know, my ninety-three-year-old mother has been waiting over a year for her operation?"

"That's appalling," said the other woman. "What a terrible way to treat someone of that age."

"I know," said the first woman. "It got so bad that at one point I even said to her, 'Mum, do you really need bigger boobs?'"

★ Pacing the hospital corridor, a man was getting really anxious about his imminent operation.

His wife asked him: "What's the matter? Why are you getting so worked up?"

He replied: "I heard one of the nurses say, 'It's a very simple operation, don't worry, I'm sure it will be all right.'"

"She was just trying to comfort you," said his wife. "What's so frightening about that?"

"She was talking to the surgeon!"

My Auntie Marge has been in hospital for seven months.

I Can't Believe She's Not Better!

★ A man was visiting a friend in hospital. He had recently quit smoking and was chewing on an unlit cigar when he stepped into the elevator. But a woman who was already in the elevator told him firmly: "Sir, there is no smoking in this hospital!"

"I'm not smoking, lady," replied the man.

"But you have a cigar in your mouth!"

"Yes, and I'm wearing Jockey shorts, but I'm not riding a horse!"

★ Did you hear about the woman who had to have a canister of perfume removed from her rectum? – It was Chanel No. 2.

★   Two medical students were walking along the street when they noticed an old man walking with his legs spread wide apart. One of the students said to his friend: "I bet he has Wallinsky Syndrome. That's how people with that condition walk."

The other student disagreed. "No, I reckon he has Perkins Syndrome. Remember, we learned about it in class? That's how those people walk – a classic case if ever I saw one!"

Since they were unable to agree, they decided to ask the old man. "We're medical students," they said, "and we couldn't help noticing the distinctive way you walk. But we can't agree on what syndrome you have. Could you tell us what it is, please?"

The old man said: "I'll tell you, but first you must let me know what you think it is."

The first student said: "I think it's Wallinsky Syndrome."

The old man said: "You thought, but you are wrong."

The second student said: "I think it's Perkins Syndrome."

The old man said: "You thought, but you are wrong."

"So what do you have?" they asked.

The old man said: "I thought it was wind, but I was wrong."

★   When a patient regained consciousness after an operation, the surgeon told her: "I'm really sorry, but I'm afraid we're going to have to open you up again. You see, unfortunately I left my rubber gloves inside you."

The patient said: "Well, if that's all it is, I'd prefer you to leave me alone and I'll buy you a new pair."

★   A man walked into a hospital carrying a Tupperware container. He handed it to a nurse who, to her horror, found that it contained an enormous hard poop.

"Why have you brought this in?" she asked.

"Because I need to see an optician," he replied.

"Don't you mean a dietician?"

"No, I need an optician, because every time I do one of these, my eyes start to water."

★ A worried man asked a hospital doctor: "How is my elderly aunt, Mrs Charles – she was admitted yesterday?"

"Ah yes," said the doctor. "Since she has been here, she has done nothing but complain. She has complained about her bed, she has complained about the food and she has complained about the nurses."

The man frowned. "So you mean . . .?"

"Yes," interrupted the doctor. "She's critical."

★　★　★　★　★

HOTELS

✳ A penguin walked into a hotel and asked the receptionist: "Has my wife been in yet?"

"I don't know," said the receptionist. "What does she look like?"

❖ Away from home on a business trip, a man arrived at a city hotel around midnight and booked a single room. As the clerk filled out the paperwork, the man noticed a sexy young woman sitting alone in the lobby. He told the clerk to wait while he went over and talked to her. Moments later, he returned with the girl on his arm.

Lying to the clerk, he said: "Fancy meeting my wife here! I'll need a double room instead."

The next morning, he went to settle the bill and was horrified to see that it came to $3,500.

"What's the meaning of this?" he yelled at the clerk. "I've only been here one night!"

"Yes," said the clerk, "but your 'wife' has been here for three weeks."

❖ After inspecting his Mexican hotel room, an American tourist marched straight down to the hotel reception to complain. Wiping the sweat from his brow, he said: "My room has got a large fan at the back, and two huge grills from wall to wall. It's like an oven in there!"

> 66 A hotel mini-bar allows you to see into the future and what a can of Pepsi will cost in 2020.
>
> Rich Hall 99

A man asked the hotel receptionist for a wake-up call. Next morning, she rang and said: "What are you doing with your life?"

❖ A businessman travelling through rural England decided to stop the night at a picturesque country inn, the George and Dragon.

Checking-in at reception, he asked the lady co-owner whether meals were still being served at the bar.

"No," she replied forcefully. "Last meals are 8 p.m. sharp. It is now 8.10 p.m."

"Not even a sandwich?" he asked sheepishly.

"No, not even a sandwich. The chef has packed up, and I'm certainly not going to start slaving away in the kitchen at this time of night just because you haven't thought things out very well."

"Very well," he said resignedly. "Is there any chance of having breakfast in my room in the morning?"

"Certainly not," she snapped. "All breakfasts are served in the dining room at 7.30 a.m. prompt. Any more questions?"

"Yes. Do you think I might have a word with George?"

❖   A drunk staggered down to hotel reception and demanded a change of room. He was so insistent that the receptionist was forced to call the manager.

"What seems to be the problem?" asked the manager.

"I want another room," said the drunk.

"But I see you're in room 341. That's one of the best rooms in the hotel."

"I don't care. I want another room."

"Very well, sir. If you're adamant, we can move you from 341 to 362. But would you mind telling me what you don't like about your room?"

"Well," said the drunk, "for one thing, it's on fire."

❖   Staying the night in a cheap hotel in a dead-end town, a businessman was bored out of his skull. The hotel bar – always his first port of call – was closed for renovations, there were no restaurants nearby and the TV in his room was broken. He resorted to looking in the bedside table drawer for some reading material, but all he could find was a Bible. He opened the first page and a note fell out.

It read: "My son, if you are troubled by the demons of alcohol and seek help in your darkest hour of need, you can always call on me and I will be there to ease your pain and anguish. Don't be afraid to pick up the phone and call me. I will happily listen to your temptations and be as supportive as possible."

The note struck a chord, so, close to tears, he picked up the phone and called the number given. After a few seconds, a voice at the other end answered: "Harry's Liquor Store . . ."

> 66 Why is sex always better in a hotel? Is it because you're with a hooker?
>
> Jimmy Carr 99

❖   As a guest checked into a cheap hotel, the receptionist said: "I hope you have a good memory for faces."

"Why?"

"Because there's no mirror in the bathroom."

❖ A husband and wife in their late twenties were on vacation in Spain at the same hotel as an attractive blonde. The husband was flirting with the blonde, much to his wife's annoyance.

One day while the three were sitting around the hotel pool watching the children splashing about, the blonde said: "I love kids."

"We'll get on really well then," said the husband.

"Why?" asked the blonde. "Is it because you have got children?"

"No," said the wife. "It's because he's hung like a four-year-old."

❖ A family man checked into a hotel. At the front desk, the businessman in front of him said curtly to the receptionist: "I hope the porn channel is disabled."

The family man thought to himself, "It's unbelievable what some people are into."

★　★　★　★　★

INSECTS

✳ A group of boy scouts from the city were on a camping trip. The mosquitoes were so fierce that the boys had to hide under a blanket to avoid being bitten.

Then one of the boys saw some fireflies and said to his friend: "We might as well give up. They're coming after us with flashlights."

✳ A couple's house was plagued by an invasion of flies in hot weather. After the husband went round with the fly swatter, his wife asked him whether he had managed to kill any.

"Yes," he said. "Four males and two females."

"How can you tell?" she asked.

"Four were on a beer can and two were on the phone."

✳ The world expert on wasps and the sounds that they make was strolling through a town in America's Midwest when he stumbled upon an old record shop that sold vinyl classics. Flicking through the racks of LPs, his attention was caught by an album entitled "Wasps of the World – and the Sounds They Make."

Intrigued, he asked the young sales assistant if he could listen to the album. "Certainly, sir," said the assistant. "Step into the booth, put on the headphones, and I'll put the LP on for you."

So the world expert on wasps and the sounds that they make stepped into the booth, put on the earphones and listened to the LP. Five minutes later, he came out of the booth and announced: "I am the world expert on wasps and the sounds that they make, but I did not recognize any of those."

"I'm very sorry, sir," said the young assistant. "If you'd like to step back into the booth, I'll play you another track."

The world expert on wasps and the sounds that they make re-entered the booth and put the headphones back on. But five minutes later, he came out of the booth again, shaking his head. "I don't understand it," he said. "I am the world expert on wasps and the sounds that they make, and yet still I am unable to recognize any of those."

"I really am sorry, sir," said the young assistant. "Perhaps if you would like to step back into the booth, I could play you another track."

Eager to salvage his reputation, the world expert on wasps and the sounds that they make went back into the booth, only to emerge five minutes later in a state of considerable agitation. "I am the world expert on wasps and the sounds that they make, and yet I have recognized none of the wasps on this LP."

"I really am terribly sorry," said the young assistant, blushing. "I've just realized I was playing you the bee side."

What do bees say in summer?
Swarm.

* Two flies from Liverpool were sitting on a poop. One turned to the other and said: "I haven't seen you around for a while."

  "Yeah," said the other. "I've been on the sick."

* An elephant was walking through the jungle, but with each step he took he trampled dozens of ants under his huge feet. The ants became so angry that they started crawling up the elephant's body, hell-bent on revenge.

  As the elephant felt their presence, he shook his body, causing all of the ants except one to plunge to the ground. This one ant clung on bravely to the elephant's neck while all the ants on the ground started to yell: "Strangle him! Strangle him!"

* A boy asked his father if he could have a pet spider for his birthday. So the father went down to the pet shop and asked how much it would cost to buy a spider.

  "Fifty dollars," said the pet shop owner.

  "Forget it!" replied the father. "I can get one cheaper on the web."

* * * * *

JEWISH JOKES

* A Catholic wanted to convert to Judaism. After studying the faith for six months, he was ready to convert but his local rabbi informed him: "Before you can become a fully-fledged Jew, you have to pass a test. I conduct the test and my fee for doing so is $3,000."

  "Three thousand dollars! That's a lot of money just for a test. How about $300?"

  "Congratulations!" said the rabbi. "You've passed!"

★ Two beggars – one Jewish, the other Catholic – were sitting side by side in a street in Rome. One had the Star of David in front of him; the other had a cross. A number of people passed by and looked at both beggars, but only put money into the hat of the one sitting behind the cross.

Among the crowds was a priest who paused and watched dozens of people giving to the beggar behind the cross while completely ignoring the one behind the Star of David. Eventually he felt so sorry for the beggar behind the Star of David that he went over to offer him a little advice.

"My dear fellow," said the priest, "don't you understand? This is a Catholic country; this city is the home of Catholicism. People aren't going to give money if you sit there with a Star of David in front of you, especially when you're sitting beside a beggar who has a cross. In fact, people who might not ordinarily give to beggars are probably giving him money purely to spite you."

The beggar behind the Star of David listened to the priest, then turned to the beggar behind the cross and said: "Morrie, look who's trying to teach the Rosenberg brothers about marketing!"

★ Why do Jewish mothers make great parole officers?
   They never let anyone finish a sentence.

★ Two Jewish mothers met up for their regular weekly chat. One said: "Before we go any further, I have good news and bad news to impart."

"Tell me the bad news," said the other.

"My Joshua phoned last night to tell me he's gay."

"Oh my! How terrible for you – and after all that you've done for that boy! But you mustn't blame yourself, you've been a wonderful mother. Now tell me the good news."

"He's marrying a doctor."

★ An astronaut landed on the moon, and to his surprise he saw ahead of him a small shop with the name above it: "Morris Cohen, Bespoke Tailors." Out of curiosity, he went into the shop.

As he entered the shop, a little Jewish man appeared behind the counter with a tape measure wrapped around his neck.

"Who are you?" asked the little Jewish man.

"I'm an astronaut," replied the visitor. "I've come all the way from Earth."

Hearing this, the little Jewish man closed his eyes and slapped himself on the cheek with one hand. "Cutters, I asked for," he groaned. "Instead they send me astronauts!"

> Sushi must have been created by two Jews thinking: 'How can we open a restaurant without a kitchen?'
>
> Jackie Mason

★ A Jewish man moved into a Catholic neighbourhood. Every Friday, the Catholics complained bitterly among themselves because while they had to eat bland fish, the Jew was outside barbecuing delicious, aromatic steaks.

Insanely jealous of his superior menu and fearing that they might be tempted to lapse by the smell of the steaks, they decided the only solution was to convert him to Catholicism. It took a sizeable bribe but the Jew eventually agreed and was taken to a priest who sprinkled him with holy water and told the Jew to chant: "Born a Jew, raised a Jew, now a Catholic."

The Catholics were thrilled, convinced that they would no longer have to put up with the maddening smells every Friday evening. But the next Friday, the scent of barbecue once again wafted through the neighbourhood. The Catholics immediately rushed to the Jew's house to remind him of his new diet.

They found him sprinkling water over a steak and chanting: "Born a cow, raised a cow, now a fish."

★ The international financial crisis is so bad that Jewish women are starting to marry for love.

★ When their local rabbi died, dozens of Jews filed into the synagogue to lend their respect.

★ A Jewish woman said to her mother: "I'm divorcing Sheldon. All he ever wants is anal sex, and so my asshole is now the size of a fifty-cent piece when it used to be the size of a ten-cent piece."

Her mother said: "You're married to a multi-millionaire, you live in a nine-bedroom mansion, you drive a Porsche, you get a $5,000 weekly allowance, you get six holidays a year! And you want to throw all that away for forty cents?"

Two Jewish mothers were sitting in a restaurant. After a while the waiter came over and asked: "Is *anything* all right?"

★ A woman phoned her local newspaper to ask if she could put a notice in the obituary column.

"Certainly, ma'am," said the operator.

"How much do funeral notices cost?" asked the woman.

"Five dollars per word."

"Good, do you have a paper and pencil handy?"

"Yes, ma'am."

"Write this then: 'Cohen died.'"

"Sorry, ma'am, I forget to tell you: there's a five-word minimum."

"Huh!" said the woman testily. "You certainly did forget to tell me that!" She thought for a moment and then said: "Okay. Got your pencil and paper?"

"Yes, ma'am."

"Right. Print this: 'Cohen died. Cadillac for sale.'"

★   An elderly Jewish tailor owned a shop next door to a smart French restaurant. Every day at lunchtime, the tailor would go out to the back of his shop and eat his black bread and herring while smelling the wonderful odours coming from the restaurant kitchen.

Then one day the tailor was surprised to receive an invoice for $30 for "enjoyment of food over a nine-month period". So he went to the restaurant to point out that he had not actually bought anything from them.

But the restaurant manager said: "You're enjoying our food, so you should pay us for it."

The tailor refused to pay, and so the restaurant manager sued him. At the hearing, the judge asked the restaurant to present its side of the case. The manager said: "Every day, this man comes and sits outside our restaurant and smells our food while eating his. It is clear that we are providing added value to his poor food and we deserve to be compensated for it."

The judge then turned to the tailor and asked: "What do you have to say to that?"

The tailor didn't say anything, but instead put his hand in his pocket and rattled the coins inside.

"What is the meaning of that?" demanded the judge.

The tailor replied: "I'm paying for the smell of his food with the sound of my money."

★ Have you heard about the new Jewish game show on TV?
It's called *The Price Is Too Much*.

★   A little Jewish boy went up to his dad and asked: "Dad, can I have five dollars?"

The father said: "Three dollars? What do you want two dollars for? I ain't got a dollar! Here's fifty cents, share it with your sister."

★ The only cow in a small town in Poland stopped giving milk. The people did some research and found that they could buy a cow from Moscow for two thousand roubles or one from Minsk for one thousand roubles. Being frugal, they bought the cow from Minsk.

The cow was wonderful. It produced lots of milk, and the people were so happy that they decided to acquire a bull to mate with the cow and so produce more cows like it. Then they would never have to worry about their milk supply again.

So they bought a bull and put it in the pasture with their beloved cow. But whenever the bull came close to the cow, the cow would move away. No matter what approach the bull tried, the cow didn't want to know.

The people were very upset and decided to ask their wise rabbi for his advice. They told the rabbi what had been happening. "Whenever the bull approaches our cow, she moves away," they said. "If he approaches from the back, she moves forward. When he approaches her from the front, she backs off. An approach from the side and she just walks away to the other side."

The rabbi thought about the problem for a minute and then asked: "Did you buy this cow from Minsk?"

The people were amazed, because they had never mentioned where they had bought the cow. "You are truly a wise rabbi," they said. "How did you know we got the cow from Minsk?"

The rabbi replied sadly: "My wife is from Minsk."

★ A Jewish guy was up a ladder cleaning a window when a coin fell out of his pocket. He climbed down to get it and it hit him on the head.

★ The doctor called Mrs Goldstein to tell her that her cheque came back.

She replied: "So did my arthritis!"

★ Old Moishe was on his deathbed with his three sons around him.

"Shimon, are you here?" he asks.

"Yes, father, I am by your side," said Shimon.

"And you, Daniel?"

"Yes, father," said Daniel. "Have no fear, I am here with you."

"And Abraham, have you come as well?"

"Yes, father," replied Abraham. "I am here, too."

Moishe threw up his arms in horror. "Then who is minding the shop?"

★ A man called on his Jewish friend one evening and found him removing the wallpaper from the walls of his lounge.

"Doing some decorating, are you?" inquired the man.

"No," said the Jewish guy. "We're moving."

★ Solly was walking through town one day when he bumped into Hymie, an old school friend whom he hadn't seen for years. As they started chatting, they realized they had a lot of catching up to do, so Solly invited Hymie to visit him at his apartment.

"I have a wife and three kids," said Solly, "and it would be great if you came to see us."

"Yes. Why not?" said Hymie. "Where do you live?"

"The address is 76 Parkside Mansions," said Solly. "There's plenty of parking space behind the apartment. Park there and come round to the front door, kick it open with your foot, go to the elevator and press the button with your left elbow, then enter. When you reach the seventh floor, go down the hall until you see number 76. Then press the doorbell with your right elbow and I'll let you in."

"Right, that's fine," said Hymie. "But tell me, what is all this business of kicking the front door open, then pressing the elevator button with my left elbow and your doorbell with my right elbow?"

"Well, surely you're not coming empty-handed?"

The Words of Famous Jewish Mothers

Mona Lisa's Jewish mother: "After all that money your father and I spent on braces, that's the biggest smile you can give us?"

Christopher Columbus' Jewish mother: "I don't care what you've discovered, you could still have written!"

Michelangelo's Jewish mother: "Can't you paint on walls like other children? Do you have any idea how hard it is to get that stuff off a ceiling?"

Napoleon Bonaparte's Jewish mother: "All right, if you're not hiding your report card inside your jacket, take your hand out of there and show me."

Thomas Edison's Jewish mother: "Of course I am proud that you invented the electric light bulb. Now turn it off – the bill will cost us a fortune."

Albert Einstein's Jewish mother: "But it's your senior picture. Couldn't you have done something about your hair?"

Abraham Lincoln's Jewish mother: "Again with the hat? Why can't you wear a baseball cap like the other kids?"

Moses' Jewish mother: "That's a nice story. Now tell me where you have really been for the last forty years."

★ A wealthy Jew owned a company that manufactured nails. His only son had just graduated from college and the father wanted to get him involved in the family business. At first he sent the young man to learn the ropes in various different departments – research and development, then manufacturing, and then sales, but in each the son proved a major disappointment. Determined to find a place for his offspring, the father decided that his son needed his own project.

So the father put him in charge of the firm's new advertising campaign. He told him that he would have no supervision and that all of the resources he needed would be placed at his disposal. In effect, he was his own boss. The son was delighted by the faith his father was showing in him and vowed to repay his confidence.

A month later, the son informed his father that he had devised an advertising campaign and took him to a site in town to look at the billboard. As they drove to the location, the son explained how he had been struggling for ideas until having a sudden flash of inspiration. They turned the corner and to the father's horror, the giant billboard depicted Christ on a cross with the caption: "Even Then They Used Goldstein Nails."

The father explained to his son that they couldn't portray Christ on a cross because it might offend their Christian clients. Dejected, the son said he would rethink the campaign and report back in due course.

A week later, the son phoned his father to tell him that he had resolved the problem and drove him out to see the billboard. Sure enough, in accordance with his father's instructions, Christ was no longer on the cross; instead he was lying at the base.

The caption read: "This Wouldn't Happen With Goldstein Nails."

★ What is the definition of a genius?
An average student with a Jewish mother.

★ Three Jewish mothers met for lunch.

The first wailed: "What a terrible week I've had! You wouldn't believe it! On Monday, my daughter's husband of fifteen years, the father of my three grandchildren, announced that he's leaving her for another woman!"

"You think you've got problems?" exclaimed the second. "My son the lawyer has a terminal disease. He may only have weeks to live!"

"That's nothing!" declared the third. "I've lost my cleaning woman!"

★　　★　　★　　★　　★

JUDGES AND JURIES

❖ The judge asked a surly defendant if he had anything to say before passing sentence.

The defendant muttered: "Fuck all!"

"What did he say?" inquired the judge.

The clerk of the court turned to the judge and replied: "The defendant said 'Fuck all', your honour."

"Really?" said the judge. "I could have sworn I saw his lips move."

❖ The jurors in a multi-billion dollar lawsuit against the tobacco industry were ordered by a judge not to watch a new movie called *Smoking Kills* in case it influenced their verdict. He also told them not to watch *The House on Haunted Hill*.

The prosecutor was mystified. He said to the judge: "I can understand why you have instructed the jurors not to watch *Smoking Kills*, but why have you told them not to watch *The House on Haunted Hill*?"

The judge leaned forward and said: "Because I got it on video last week, and it sucks!"

❖ Tried in a hostile town, a man didn't think he had any chance of getting off a murder charge, so shortly before the jury retired, he bribed one of the jurors to find him guilty of the lesser crime of manslaughter.

The jury were out for over three days before eventually returning a verdict of manslaughter. The relieved defendant sought out the bribed juror and said: "Thanks. How ever did you manage it?"

"It wasn't easy," admitted the juror. "All the others wanted to acquit you."

❖ **What did the judge say when the skunk entered the courtroom?**
Odour! Odour in court!

❖ It was Christmas, and the judge was in a benevolent mood as he questioned the defendant.

"What exactly is it you're charged with?" he asked.

"Doing my Christmas shopping early," replied the defendant.

"That's not an offence," said the judge. "How early were you doing this shopping?"

"Before the store opened."

❖ Before a high-profile trial, the long process of jury selection took place. On this occasion it was particularly protracted as both sides repeatedly objected to potential jurors on the grounds that they had probably made up their minds about the case after reading sensational pre-trial stories in the newspapers.

One man was called forward for his interrogation.

"Are you a property owner?" asked the judge.

"Yes, I am, your honour."

"Married or single?"

"Married for twenty-seven years, your honour."

Then the judge said: "Formed or expressed an opinion?"

The man replied: "Not in twenty-seven years, your honour."

❖ A man was forced to take a day off work to appear in court on a minor charge. After waiting all day for his case to be heard, he was finally called before the judge late in the afternoon. But no sooner had the defendant stood in the dock than the judge announced that the court would be adjourned until the following day.

"This is an outrage!" shouted the defendant.

Tired at the end of a long day, the judge rapped back: "Twenty dollars, contempt of court!"

Then, noticing the defendant checking his wallet, the judge softened and said: "It's all right. You don't have to pay right now."

"I wasn't going to," replied the defendant. "I was just seeing if I'd got enough money for two more words!"

The judge looked at the defendant brought before him and said: "Haven't I seen you somewhere before?"

"Yes, your honour. I taught your son to play the drums."

"Twenty years!"

❖ Brought before the judge at night court, the defendant was asked to state his name, occupation and charge.

He said: "I'm Sparks, I'm an electrician, and I'm charged with battery."

The judge ordered: "Bailiff! Put this man in a dry cell!"

❖ In a murder trial, the judge asked the expert witness, a doctor: "Tell me, how many autopsies have you performed on dead people?"

The doctor replied: "All my autopsies are on dead people."

> The judge said to the defendant: "I thought I told you I never wanted to see you in here again."
>
> The defendant replied: "That's what I told the police, but they wouldn't listen!"

❖ To the irritation of the judge, a man was trying to be excused jury service. "Tell me," rapped the judge, "is there any good reason why you cannot serve as a juror in this trial?"

The man replied: "I don't want to be away from my job that long."

"Can't they do without you at work?" demanded the judge.

"Yes," admitted the juror. "But I don't want them to realize it."

★　★　★　★　★

KNIGHTS

✳ A knight went off to fight in the Holy Crusades but before leaving he made his wife wear a chastity belt. After tightly securing her nether regions, he handed the key to his best friend with the instruction: "If I do not return within seven years, unlock my wife and set her free to lead a normal life."

The knight then rode off on the first leg of his journey to the Holy Land, but he had travelled barely half an hour when he was suddenly aware of the sound of pounding hooves behind him. He turned to see that it was best friend.

"What is the problem?" asked the knight.

His best friend replied: "You gave me the wrong key."

✳ Sir Lancelot was a high-ranking official in the court of King Arthur. His greatest ambition was to suck the voluptuous breasts of Arthur's queen, Guinevere, whose very presence caused him enormous sexual frustration.

One day he revealed his secret fantasy to the king's chief adviser, Merlin the magician, and begged him to do something about it. After due deliberation, the wily Merlin agreed to help . . . in return for 1,000 gold coins.

The following day Merlin prepared a concentrated itching lotion and poured it into the queen's bra, which she had left out while she was taking a bath. Soon the queen's breasts started to itch with great intensity and the worried king summoned Merlin to find a solution. Merlin's diagnosis was that the condition could be cured only by a special saliva, which needed to be applied vigorously for four hours. The saliva in question, added Merlin, could be found only in the mouth of Sir Lancelot.

Arthur summoned Sir Lancelot, who, acting on the king's orders, enthusiastically sucked the queen's breasts for four hours. Lancelot's every fantasy was being fulfilled.

Afterwards, Merlin asked for the agreed payment but Lancelot, having got what he wanted, reneged on the deal, reasoning that the magician could never report the matter to the king.

But Lancelot had underestimated Merlin. The next day, Merlin put the same itching lotion in King Arthur's underpants. Lancelot was again summoned by the king . . .

✳ Sir Gwilym and his men returned to the king's castle bearing bags of gold and half a dozen slave women, the fruits of plundering the land for a week.

"Where have you been all this time, Sir Gwilym?" asked the king.

"I have been robbing and pillaging on your behalf all week, sire, burning the villages of your enemies in the north."

"But I don't have any enemies in the north," protested the king.

"You have now, sire."

✳   After years of renting, King Arthur wanted to buy his castle, Camelot, outright but the bank was wary about lending him the money, fearing that he might default on payments. To persuade the bank that he was a safe risk, he offered the blade of his famous, priceless sword, Excalibur, as collateral.

The bank agreed to these terms but a year later, with financial markets in disarray, it began to get twitchy and demanded the whole of Excalibur as collateral.

King Arthur was distraught. "You can't suddenly change the terms of our agreement," he said, "so that the whole of my trusty sword is now at risk. I'm already mortgaged up to the hilt."

✳   The great wizard Merlin was showing King Arthur his latest invention. It was a chastity belt, except that it had a rather large hole in the most obvious place.

"This is no good, Merlin!" exclaimed the king. "Look at this opening. How is this supposed to protect Queen Guinevere?"

"Observe, sire," said Merlin. He then picked up one of his old wands and inserted it in the chastity belt's gaping aperture. As he did so, a small guillotine blade came down and sliced the wand in two.

"Merlin, you are a genius!" said the grateful monarch. "Now I can depart on my expedition to find the Holy Grail, safe in the knowledge that my dear queen is fully protected." After putting Guinevere in the belt, King Arthur set off on his great adventure.

It was six long years before he returned to Camelot. Immediately he assembled all of his knights in the courtyard and ordered them to drop their pants so that he could see whether any had violated Guinevere in his absence. Sure enough, every one of his knights had been amputated in some way – all except Sir Galahad.

"Sir Galahad," beamed King Arthur, throwing his arms around the knight. "Only you have remained loyal to me: my one trusted knight. Anything in my power I will grant you. Name it and it is yours."

Alas, Sir Galahad was speechless.

* Which knight of the Round Table was appointed Camelot's official chef?
  Sir Loin.

* * * * *

LAWYERS

* A woman went to her doctor for advice. She told him that her husband had developed a liking for anal sex, but she wasn't sure it was such a good idea.

  The doctor asked her: "Does it hurt you?"

  She said: "No."

  "Well then," he continued, "there's no reason why you shouldn't practise anal sex if you don't mind it, so long as you take care not to get pregnant."

  The woman was puzzled. "You mean you can get pregnant from anal sex?"

  "Of course," smiled the doctor. "Where do you think lawyers come from?"

> " To me, a lawyer is basically the person that knows the rules of the country.
> We're all throwing the dice, playing the game, moving our pieces around the board, but if there is a problem, the lawyer is the only person who has read the inside of the top of the box.
>
> Jerry Seinfeld "

* What's the difference between a good lawyer and a bad lawyer?

  A bad lawyer can let a case drag on for several years. A good lawyer can make it last even longer.

★ Walking past a courthouse, a man spotted his friend sitting on the steps, sobbing loudly, his head buried in his hands.

"What's the problem?" he asked. "Did your lawyer give you bad advice?"

"No, it's worse than that – he sold it to me."

★ Two lawyers met at a cocktail party.

"How's business?" asked one.

"Lousy," said the other. "Yesterday, I chased an ambulance for twenty-five miles. When I finally caught up with it, there were already two other lawyers hanging on to the bumper."

> What's the difference between a lawyer and a herd of buffalo?
> A lawyer charges more.

★ A lawyer was walking down the street when he spotted a woman with spectacular breasts. He immediately offered her $100 if she would let him bite them.

"No way!" she exclaimed indignantly.

"What about for $1,000?" he persisted.

"No, certainly not. What kind of woman do you think I am?"

"You wouldn't even do it for $10,000?" he asked.

The woman looked astounded. "You'll pay me $10,000 if I let you bite my breasts?"

"That's right."

"Okay, let's go over to that dark alley."

Once there she took off her blouse, and the lawyer began caressing her breasts, kissing them, sucking them and fondling them.

She was beginning to get impatient. "Are you gonna bite them or what?" she snapped.

"No," he said. "Too expensive."

★ A lawyer called his client to tell him about the schedule for his fee payments.

"Right," said the lawyer, "you owe me $1,000 up front, and then $509.55 each month for the next thirty-six months."

"What!" exclaimed the client. "That sounds like the payment schedule on a new car!"

"You're right," said the lawyer. "It's mine."

★ A lawyer was talking to his teenage son about his future career. "Why do you want to be a doctor instead of a lawyer?" he asked. "What's wrong with lawyers?"

"Well, Dad," explained the boy, "I really want to help people. And when was the last time you heard anybody stand up in a crowd and shout frantically: 'Is there a lawyer in the house?'"

★ A businessman received a call urging him to go to his lawyer's office immediately. When he arrived, his lawyer greeted him gloomily with the question: "Do you want the bad news or the terrible news?"

The businessman said: "If you put it like that, I guess I'll take the bad news first."

"Okay," said the lawyer. "Your wife found a picture worth half a million dollars."

"That's the bad news?" queried the businessman. "If you call that bad, I can't wait to hear the terrible news!"

"The terrible news is the picture is of you and your secretary."

★ The lawyer stood before the appeals court judge and declared: "Your honour, I wish to appeal my client's case on the basis of newly discovered evidence."

"And what is the nature of this new evidence?" asked the judge.

The lawyer replied: "I discovered that my client still has $1,500 left."

★ Arriving at hospital, a man saw two doctors down on their hands and knees in one of the flowerbeds.

"Can I help?" asked the man. "Have you lost something?"

"No, it's okay," said one of the doctors. "We're about to perform a heart transplant on a lawyer and we're looking for a suitable stone."

Actual Courtroom Exchanges

Attorney: "What was the first thing your husband said to you that morning?"
Witness: "He said, 'Where am I, Cathy?'"
Attorney: "And why did that upset you?"
Witness: "My name is Susan."

Attorney: "So the date of conception was 8 August?"
Witness: "Yes."
Attorney: "And what were you doing at that time?"
Witness: "Getting laid."

Attorney: "Are you sexually active?"
Witness: "No, I just lie there."

Attorney: "Do you recall the time that you examined the body?"
Witness: "The autopsy started around 8.30 p.m."
Attorney: "And Mr Denton was dead at the time?"
Witness: "If not, he was by the time I finished."

Attorney: "Do you know if your daughter has ever been involved in voodoo?"
Witness: "We both do."
Attorney: "Voodoo?"
Witness: "We do."
Attorney: "You do?"
Witness: "Yes, voodoo."

★ An airplane was experiencing engine trouble, and the pilot instructed the cabin crew to have the passengers return to their seats and prepare for an emergency landing.

A few minutes later, the pilot asked the flight attendants if everyone was buckled in and ready.

"All set back here, captain," came the reply, "except the lawyers are still going around handing out business cards."

Attorney: "Now, doctor, isn't it true that when a person dies in his sleep, he doesn't know about it until the next morning?"
Witness: "Did you actually pass the bar exam?"

Attorney: "Can you describe the individual?"
Witness: "About medium height with a beard."
Attorney: "Was this a male or a female?"
Witness: "Unless the circus was in town, I'm going with male."

Attorney: "The youngest son, the twenty-year-old, how old is he?"
Witness: "He's twenty, much like your IQ."

Attorney: "How was your first marriage terminated?"
Witness: "By death."
Attorney: "And by whose death was it terminated?"
Witness: "Take a guess."

Attorney: "She had three children, right?"
Witness: "Yes."
Attorney: "How many were boys?"
Witness: "None."
Attorney: "Were there any girls?"
Witness: "Your honour, I think I need a different attorney. Can I get a new attorney?"

★   After graduating from college, a lawyer's son was pondering his future. Unsure about his career path, he asked his father whether he might be permitted to observe his work from a chair in the corner of the office to determine whether the law appealed to him as a profession. The father thought it was an excellent idea, and so the son joined him in the office the following morning.

The first client was an impoverished tenant farmer who proceeded to outline his case. "I work for the Henderson farm on the north side of town. For many years, I have tended their crops and animals, including some cows. I have raised the cows, fed them and generally looked after them. And I was always led to believe that I was the owner of these cows. Now old Mr Henderson has died and his son has inherited the farm. He believes that since the cows were raised on his land and ate his hay, the cows are his. In short, we are in dispute over who owns the cows."

"Thank you," said the lawyer. "I have heard enough. I will take your case. Don't worry about the cows."

The next client was a wealthy landowner. "My name is Henderson," he said by way of introduction, "and I own a farm on the north side of town. We have a tenant farmer who has worked for my family for many years, tending crops and the animals, including some cows. I believe the cows belong to me because they were raised on my land and were fed my hay, but the tenant farmer believes they are his because he raised them and cared for them In short, we are in dispute over who owns the cows."

"Thank you," said the lawyer. "I have heard enough. I will take your case. Don't worry about the cows."

After the client left, the lawyer's son could not help but express his concern. "Father, I know very little about the law, but isn't there a conflict of interest here? It seems we have a very serious problem concerning these cows."

"Don't worry about the cows," said the lawyer. "The cows will be ours."

★ A judge was hearing a drink-driving case but the defendant, who had a history of driving under the influence, demanded trial by jury. It was nearly four o'clock in the afternoon and getting a jury would take some time, so the judge called a recess and went out in the hall to recruit anyone available for jury duty. In the main lobby, he found a dozen lawyers and told them that they were to be the jury. The lawyers thought this would be a novel experience and followed the judge back into the courtroom.

The prosecution and defence cases were heard in little over twenty minutes, and it was obvious that the defendant was guilty. The jurors retired to their room, and the judge, thinking that they would return with their verdict in a matter of minutes, prepared to go home. But after three days and nights, the jury of lawyers was still out. The judge was furious and eventually sent the bailiff into the jury room to find out what was delaying the verdict.

When the bailiff returned, the judge said impatiently: "Well, have they reached a verdict yet?"

The bailiff shook his head and said: "Verdict? They're still arguing over who should be foreman!"

★ A chief executive was interviewing ambitious young lawyers for a company post.

"I'm sure you can understand," said the chief executive to the first applicant, "that in a business such as this, our personal integrity must be beyond question. So what I really need to know is, are you an honest lawyer?"

"Honest?" replied the young lawyer. "Let me tell you something about honest. I'm so honest that my father lent me $15,000 for my education, and I paid back every last cent the minute I tried my very first case."

"That's very impressive," said the chief executive. "And what sort of case was it?"

The lawyer squirmed in his seat and admitted: "My father sued me for the money."

★ A lawyer was walking along the street when he saw an automobile accident. He rushed over, started handing out business cards, and said: "I saw the whole thing. I'll take either side."

★   ★   ★   ★   ★

LOVE AND MARRIAGE

❖ On their weekly night out, three girlfriends were discussing their respective relationships. One was engaged, the second was a mistress, and the third was married. They decided that to surprise their men, all three would dress up in a leather S&M-style bodice, red stilettos and a black eye-mask.

The following week, they met up again and compared their experiences.

The engaged girl said: "When my fiancé came home and found me wearing the leather bodice, stilettos and eye-mask, he immediately grabbed me, told me how much he loved me and carried me upstairs, where we made passionate love for the rest of the evening."

The mistress said: "I went up to my lover's hotel room where he was waiting for me. I was wearing the leather bodice, the red stilettos and the black eye-mask, with a long leather coat on top. When I entered the room, I dropped my coat to the floor to reveal my outfit. He went "Wow!" and we had fantastic sex all night."

"Huh!" said the married girl tetchily. "I got myself dressed up the same as you two – leather bodice, red stilettos and black eye-mask – and waited for my husband to get home from work. He opened the door, came in and said: 'Evening, Batman, what's for dinner?'"

❖ A man congratulated his elderly neighbour on his hundred-and-second birthday. "Actually," whispered the old man, "I'm really only eighty-one but since my wife died three weeks ago, it feels like every day is my birthday!"

❖ A girl turned to her fiancé and said: "When we get married, I want to share all your troubles and worries."

"That's very kind of you, darling," he replied, "but I don't have any troubles or worries."

She said: "Well, that's because we aren't married yet."

❖ A wife complained to her husband: "You never let me go out any more."

He said: "That's because last time you made a run for it."

> ❝ My wallet was full, my balls were empty. And I asked myself: how can I reverse these two things? So I got married.
>
> Nick DiPaolo ❞

❖ A woman walked into a gun shop and asked for help in choosing a rifle. "It's for my husband," she said.

"Okay," said the sales clerk. "Did he say what calibre he wanted?"

"No, he didn't," said the woman. "In fact, he doesn't even know I'm going to shoot him yet!"

❖ What's the difference between a heavily pregnant woman and a supermodel?

Nothing, if the husband knows what's good for him.

❖ Wife: "You make love like you decorate."
Husband: "What, very slow and professional?"
Wife: "No, fast and sloppy, and I have to finish the job myself!"

❖ A married couple slept in adjoining rooms during the week because both had to be up early for work in the morning. This arrangement usually ruled out sex on weekdays but one night the husband started feeling frisky. So he called out to his wife: "My darling little honey bunch, would you like to join your hubby-wubby in a spot of hanky-panky?"

The wife got out of her bed and entered her husband's room but then tripped on his carpet and fell flat on her face.

"Oh!" he cried, full of concern. "Did my honey-woney fall on her little nosey-wosey?"

The wife picked herself up and climbed into her husband's bed. They had great sex, and afterwards she got out to return to her own bed. But on the way she again tripped on the same piece of carpet and fell flat on her face.

He looked at her lying on the floor and muttered: "Clumsy bitch!"

❖ Before marriage, a man yearns for the woman he loves. After marriage, the "y" becomes silent.

❖ A woman confided to her girlfriend: "My ex-husband wants to marry me again."

"How flattering!" said the friend.

"Not really. I think he's after the money I married him for."

 Marriage is like a coffin and each kid is another nail.

Homer Simpson

❖ A woman was taking her time browsing through the various items at a friend's yard sale. She said: "My husband is going to be really angry that I stopped off at a yard sale."

"I'm sure he'll understand when you tell him about the bargains you found," said the friend.

"Normally, yes. But he's just broken his leg, and he's waiting for me to take him to hospital to have it set."

❖ Desperate to use a payphone, a visitor to town searched high and low, and when he eventually found one, it was already occupied. Hoping that the man inside the kiosk wouldn't be long, the visitor waited impatiently outside, constantly looking at his watch. In an attempt to convey a sense of urgency, the visitor kept staring at the man on the phone but soon noticed that he wasn't actually saying anything. As the minutes passed, the visitor kept looking, nodding, and pointing to his watch, but the guy inside paid no attention and just stood there with the phone in his hand, saying nothing into the receiver.

After a quarter of an hour, the guy inside had still not said a word into the phone. Thinking that he was being deliberately obstructive and just wasting time, the visitor finally lost his cool. Opening the door of the box, he tried to snatch the phone from the other man's hand.

"Do you mind!" said the guy with the phone. "I'm talking to my wife!"

A man and his wife tried to spice up their marriage by buying a water bed, but instead they started to drift apart.

❖ My wife came home from work yesterday and asked me to console her. So I hit her over the head with my Xbox.

❖ What is a husband?
An attachment you screw on the bed to get shelves put up.

❖ A wife was a less than fastidious housekeeper. One evening, her husband returned home from work and teased her: "You know, honey, I can write my name in the dust on the mantel."

She turned to him and replied sweetly: "Yes, darling, I know. That's why I married a college graduate."

❖ After celebrating their twenty-fifth wedding anniversary with a romantic dinner in a restaurant, the wife thanked her husband for a wonderful evening.

"It's not over yet," he said, and once back at their house, he presented her with a little black velvet box. She opened it in eager anticipation, but found nothing more than two pills inside.

"What are these pills?" she asked, puzzled.

"Aspirin."

"But I don't have a headache."

"Gotcha!" he cried triumphantly.

> We were into different things, you know. I like life, and she likes sucking it out of me.
>
> Daniel Townes

❖ Trapped in an unhappy marriage, a guy decided he needed some companionship. So he went to a pet store with a view to buying a dog or a cat.

He explained his situation to the pet store owner who said: "I've got the ideal pet for you – a toothless hamster."

"No, I don't think so," said the man.

"But," insisted the store owner, "it gives great head."

So the guy bought the hamster and took it home. His wife took one look at it and screamed: "What the hell is that thing?"

"Never mind what it is!" said the husband. "Just teach it to cook, and pack your bags!"

❖ I found out today that my marriage isn't legal because her dad didn't have a licence for that shotgun.

❖ A wife told her husband that she wanted more freedom. "No problem," he said. "I'll extend the kitchen."

Mafia Valentine Verses

My love for you, it came and went
So your feet are now in wet cement.

> The string of my heart you know how to pull it
> So be my Valentine or take a bullet.

I'm here to fulfil your fondest wishes
Now that your husband sleeps with the fishes.

> Violets are blue, roses are red,
> I blew up your car – so why ain't you dead?

I picked up this card from a slim selection
But that's all they offer here in witness protection.

> Your family are dead, you have nothing to lose
> So let me make you an offer you can't refuse.

If only you'd have let me share your bed
You wouldn't have woken up next to a horse's head.

> Lust is fleeting, true love lingers
> Be my Valentine and you'll keep your fingers.

When a goon makes you die
'Cos you told him goodbye – that's amore!

❖ A guy was telling one of his colleagues at work: "You know, I never realized just how much my wife loved me until I was off sick last week. When the milkman and the postman walked down the drive, she ran out and shouted excitedly: 'My husband's home!'"

❖ A woman came home and told her husband: "Remember those headaches I've been suffering from all these years? Well, they're finally gone."

"That's great," said her husband. "How did you manage to get rid of them?"

She replied: "My friend suggested I try visiting a hypnotist. I didn't tell you about it because I thought you'd laugh. But he gave me really good advice. He told me to stand in front of a mirror, stare at myself and repeat: "I do not have a headache, I do not have a headache, I do not have a headache." And it worked. The headaches are all gone."

"Hey, that's amazing!" said the husband. "I'm really pleased for you."

The wife continued: "I don't want to be unkind, but you haven't exactly been a tiger in the bedroom these last few years. Why don't you go to the hypnotist and see if he can do anything about your sex drive?"

Reluctantly the husband agreed to try it.

After his first appointment with the hypnotist, the husband arrived home, tore off his clothes, picked up his wife, carried her into the bedroom, put her on the bed and ripped off her clothes, saying: "Don't move. I'll be right back."

He then went into the bathroom and when he re-emerged a few minutes later, he jumped into bed and made wild, passionate love to her, the like of which she had never experienced in their previous thirty-three years of marriage.

Afterwards she flopped back on the bed and said: "That was fantastic!"

The husband then said: "Don't move. I'll be right back."

And again he went into the bathroom for a couple of minutes before returning to have mind-blowing sex with her that was even better than the first time.

By now her head was spinning. Whatever the hypnotist had said to her husband had obviously done the trick. So much so that for a third time he told her: "Don't move. I'll be right back."

This time when he dived into the bathroom, she quietly followed him. She saw him standing there in front of the mirror, repeating: "She is not my wife, she is not my wife, she is not my wife . . ."

> ❝ I read about a ninety-year-old man who married a ninety-three-year-old woman. I thought to myself, 'That's not going to last.'
>
> Jimmy Carr ❞

❖ To many girls, the word "marriage" has a nice ring to it.

❖ After twenty-five years of marriage, a husband took a long look at his wife one day and said: "Twenty-five years ago, we had a cheap apartment, a cheap car and slept on a sofa bed, but I got to sleep every night with a sexy twenty-six-year-old blonde. Now, we have a nice house, nice car and a big bed, but I'm sleeping with a fifty-one-year-old woman. It seems to me that you're not pulling your weight."

She replied calmly: "Then why don't you go out and find yourself a sexy twenty-six-year-old blonde? And if you do, I'll make sure that once again you'll be living in a cheap apartment, driving a cheap car and sleeping on a sofa bed."

❖ Why do married men hang strobe lights from their bedroom ceilings?

To create the optical illusion that their wives are moving during sex.

❖ **A psychic showed me the girl I was going to marry. It was love at second sight.**

❖ I shouldn't joke about my wife, because she is attached to a machine that keeps her alive – the refrigerator.

❖ A wife told her husband that he put football before their marriage.

"That's not true," he said. "After all, this is our fourth season together."

❖ A husband and wife were sitting at a table at her fiftieth high school reunion. The husband kept staring at a drunken guy sitting alone at a nearby table and eventually he asked his wife: "Do you know him?"

"Yes," she replied. "He's my old boyfriend. I understand he started drinking right after we split up all those years ago, and apparently he hasn't been sober since."

"My God!" exclaimed the husband. "Who would think a person could go on celebrating that long!"

> 66 I've never understood why some people beat their wives. I mean, that's like keying your *own* car.
>
> Jimmy Carr 99

❖ A woman was about to settle down to a bridge evening with her lady friends when her husband announced that he was going to the pub. She calmly walked over to him, unzipped his pants, kissed him on the head of his dick, zipped him back up, said goodbye and sat down to play cards.

Her friends were dumbfounded and after he had gone, one of them felt obliged to ask: "Why do you kiss your husband goodbye on his thing?"

The wife replied: "Obviously you've never smelled his breath!"

❖ One morning at breakfast a husband was intently reading the newspaper when his frustrated wife said: "I wish I were your newspaper, because then you'd give me your undivided attention."

"Come to think of it," he replied, "I wish I could have a wife like a newspaper."

"Why, so you could run your hands over me all day?"

"No, because I could throw the old one out every night and pick up a nice, fresh, new one every morning."

❖ My wife and I have an open marriage. I just haven't told her yet.

❖ Seeing her husband poring through the contents of a shoe box, his wife asked him: "What are you looking for?"

"Nothing," he said.

"Nothing? You've been reading our marriage certificate for half an hour."

"If you must know, I was just looking for the expiry date."

> 66 The longer you're married, the more you learn. When I was a single guy, I thought I could dress myself.
> Simon Cotter 99

❖ A wife said to her husband: "Did you hear about Tony at number ninety-four? He died last night. And they'd only been married for ten weeks."

The husband said: "Well, at least he didn't suffer for too long then."

There's one thing I really hate about my new Thai bride – she keeps leaving the toilet seat up.

❖ A husband was sitting in his back yard looking rather sad. His neighbour called over the fence to ask what the problem was.

"I fell for one of those crazy questions women ask," said the husband. "Now I'm in the doghouse."

"What kind of question?" asked the neighbour.

"My wife asked me if I would still love her when she was old, fat and ugly."

"That's easy. You just say, 'Of course I will.'"

"Yeah," sighed the husband, "that's what I meant to say. But what came out was, 'Of course I do.'"

❖ Did you hear about the leper whose wife left him?

He was in pieces.

A Conversation Before Marriage:

Him: "Yes. At last. It was so hard to wait."
Her: "Do you want me to leave?"
Him: "No. Don't even think about it."
Her: "Do you love me?"
Him: "Of course. Over and over!"
Her: "Have you ever cheated on me?"
Him: "No. Why are you even asking?"
Her: "Will you kiss me?"
Him: "Every chance I get."
Her: "Will you hit me?"
Him: "Are you crazy? I'm not that kind of person."
Her: "Can I trust you?"
Him: "Yes."
Her: "Darling!"

For a conversation after marriage, simply read this in reverse.

❖ Show me a man who is greeted with smiles and compliments every evening, has his jacket hung up and his shoes taken off, has cushions arranged for him before he sits down, is made to feel comfortable and welcome in every way and is then served a delicious meal – and I'll show you a man who is a regular in a Japanese restaurant.

❖ A husband arrived home from work excitedly. "Hey, honey," he called out, "I've discovered a new position we can try to spice up our sex life."

   "Really?" said his wife. "What?"

   "Back to back."

   "Back to back?" she queried. "That's impossible. It can't be done."

   "Sure it can," insisted the husband. "And I've persuaded another couple to come over and help us."

❖ A guy said to his friend in a bar: "There really is no pleasing some women. I recently put up a bird table, but my wife went mad. I don't know why – I gave her six out of ten, which is more than fair."

❖ A woman was enjoying a game of bridge with her friends one afternoon. But then suddenly she noticed the time and exclaimed: "Oh no! I have to rush home and fix dinner for my husband! He'll be furious if it's not ready on time."

When she got home, she realized she didn't have enough time to get to the supermarket and found that all she had in the cupboard was a wilted lettuce leaf, an egg, and a can of cat food. In a panic, she opened the can of cat food, stirred in the egg, and garnished it with the lettuce leaf just as she heard her husband's car pull up outside. She greeted him lovingly and then watched in apprehension as he sat down to the improvised meal.

To her amazement, he really enjoyed it. "Darling, this is the best dinner you've made me in ages! We must have it again!" Needless to say, she kept quiet about the ingredients.

So every bridge afternoon from then on, she made him the same dish of lettuce, egg and cat food. She told her bridge friends about it and they were all horrified. "You'll kill him!" they said.

Then two months later, her husband died.

At the next bridge gathering, one of the women lost her temper. "I said you'd end up killing him," she told the wife, "feeding the poor man cat food every week! How can you just sit there so calmly playing bridge knowing that you murdered your husband?"

"I didn't kill him," the wife protested. "He fell off the window ledge while he was licking himself."

❖ "It's too hot to wear clothes today," said the husband stepping out of the shower. "What do you reckon the neighbours will think if I mow the grass like this?"

"Probably that I married you for your money," answered his wife.

MADONNA

* When Madonna first moved to England she said she wanted to feel more English. She is now an unmarried, single mother with four kids from different fathers, two of them black. Job done.

* ## What's the difference between a Madonna video and a porn video?
  The music is better in a porn video.

* Due to a mix-up on Grammy night, Christina Aguilera and Madonna were forced to share a private jet in order to arrive in time for the ceremony. Once up in the air, Christina pulled out a $1,000 bill and announced: "I'm going to throw this $1,000 bill out the window and make someone down below very happy."

  Not to be outdone, Madonna pulled out a $1,000 bill, ripped it in half and threw it out of the window, gushing excitely: "Look, I just made two people really happy."

> ❝ Madonna's brother has come out with a book, *Life With My Sister Madonna*.
> Madonna's brother claims she's a self-obsessed egomaniac who thinks she's the only person in the universe. Of course, Madonna was shocked by this. She said: 'What? I have a brother?'
>
> Jay Leno ❞

* How is Madonna similar to breakfast pastries?
  They're both pop tarts.

* What's the difference between Jesus and Madonna?
  Jesus has only been resurrected once.

* A wife said to her husband: "Do you want to go and see the new Madonna movie tonight?"

   "I'm a little tired, honey," he replied. "How about we go tomorrow night?"

   "Are you kidding?" said the wife. "This is a Madonna movie we're talking about. It might not be on tomorrow!"

> 66 Madonna gives millions to charity, she's done lots of benefits, given a lot of money away. Her greatest gift, of course, to mankind is that she's promised never to do another movie.
> Craig Ferguson 99

* The recession has hit so hard that even Madonna got rid of one of her personal assistants, Guy Ritchie.

> 66 Guy Ritchie's now making a film about Sherlock Holmes, where a man in a tweed coat and hat is trying to get the better of some mad dog. No idea why Guy feels such an affinity with the story.
> Frankie Boyle 99

★ ★ ★ ★ ★

MEMORY

★ My uncle came out of the closet yesterday. He's not gay, but he's got Alzheimer's, and he thought it was the car.

★ When I was younger my fairy godmother told me I could either have a long memory or a long penis. I forget my response.

★ A man went to the doctor for his annual physical. He told the doctor: "I'm getting really forgetful. I forget where I live, I forget where I've parked my car, and I go into shops and I can't remember what it is that I want. And when I do get to the checkout, I find I've forgotten my wallet. It's getting pretty bad, doc. What can I do?"

   The doctor thought for a moment and said: "Pay me in advance."

★ Two old men were sitting down to breakfast. One said to the other: "Do you know you've got a suppository in your left ear?"

   "Really?" said his friend, removing the suppository. "I'm so glad you pointed that out. Now I think I remember where I put my hearing aid."

★ One of the best things about memory loss is that you're always surprised to find out what's in your sandwiches – if only you could remember where you left your lunchbox.

★ A man collecting in a shopping mall asked a woman for a donation to Alzheimer's.

   She said: "But I've already given just now. Don't you remember?"

> ❝ I was thinking to myself the other day: 'Why does a Frisbee look bigger and bigger the closer it gets?' And then it hit me!
>
> Tim Vine ❞

★ An elderly couple were struggling to remember things, so they decided to go to the doctor to make sure there was nothing medically wrong with them. After checking them out, the doctor said they were healthy but added that they might be able to improve their memory by writing things down. The couple agreed that it sounded a good idea.

Later that night while watching TV, the old man got up from his chair. His wife asked: "Where are you going?"

"To the kitchen," he replied.

"Will you get me a bowl of ice cream?"

"Sure."

Then his wife asked him: "Don't you think you should write it down so you can remember it?"

"No," he said confidently. "I can remember that."

"Well, I would also like some strawberries on top," continued the wife. "You had better write that down because I know you'll forget that."

"I can remember that," insisted the old man. "You want a bowl of ice cream with strawberries."

She then said: "Well, I would also like whipped cream on top of the strawberries. You'd better write that down because you're sure to forget that."

With irritation in his voice he said: "I don't need to write it down. I can remember it." Then he went into the kitchen.

Twenty minutes later, he returned from the kitchen and handed her a plate of bacon and eggs.

The old woman stared at the plate for a moment and said: "You forgot my toast!"

★ Did you hear about the man who was always getting confused between cayenne pepper and KY jelly? He could never remember which went where.

★ A boy confided to his school friend: "My poor grandmother has had Alzheimer's for several years now. But I guess I should be grateful for the $10 I get for my birthday every week."

★   ★   ★   ★   ★

MEN

❖ A wife said to her husband: "The trouble with men is that they can't multi-task: they can't do two things at once."

"Actually I can," replied the husband.

"Give me an example."

"Well, while I was banging you in bed last night, I was thinking about your sister."

❖ The five words a woman wants to hear during sex: "I will always love you."

The five words a man wants to hear during sex: "You can put it anywhere."

❖ Three men were walking along when they came upon a wide, raging river. They needed to get to the other side, but had no idea how to do so.

The first man prayed to God: "Please, God, give me the strength to cross this river." And POOF! God gave him powerful arms and strong legs, and he was able to swim across the mighty river in two hours.

Seeing this, the second man prayed: "Please, God, give me the strength and ability to cross this river." And POOF! God gave him a rowing boat, and he was able to row across the river in an hour.

The third man saw how this tactic worked for the other two, and so he prayed: "Please, God, give me the strength, ability, and intelligence to cross this river." And POOF! God turned him into a woman.

She looked at a map, then walked across the bridge.

❖ What do most men consider a gourmet restaurant?

Any place without a drive-up window.

Eight Signs That Your Partner Is Addicted To Porn
1. Your partner is a guy.

❖ What do you call a magic wand that can make a man disappear?

A home pregnancy-test kit.

❖ A female computer assistant was helping a smug male set up a computer. She asked him what word he wanted to use as a password to log in with. Relishing the chance to embarrass her, he said: "Penis."

Unfazed and without saying a thing, she calmly entered the password and struggled to contain her delight when the computer responded: PASSWORD REJECTED. NOT LONG ENOUGH!!!

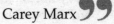

> Whenever I see a man with a beard, moustache and glasses, I think, 'There's a man who has taken every precaution to avoid people doodling on photographs of him.'
>
> Carey Marx

❖ Although no man is an island, you can make quite an effective raft out of six.

❖ What's the difference between men and boys?

The price of their toys.

> Some women say they can tell how good a man is in bed by watching him eat dinner. If he eats quickly and takes large bites, he's probably pretty boring. If he picks at his food like he's a bird, he's probably not very passionate. And if he eats in his underwear over the sink while watching TV, he's probably your husband.
>
> Jay Leno

❖ A man was sick and tired of going to work every day while his wife stayed at home, so he prayed for a change in circumstance. "Dear Lord, I go to work every day and put in eight hours while my wife merely stays at home. I want her to know what I go through, so please allow her body to switch with mine for a day. Amen."

God, in his infinite wisdom, granted the man's wish, and the next morning, sure enough, he awoke as a woman. He got up, cooked breakfast for his partner, woke the kids, set out their school clothes, fed them breakfast, packed their lunches, drove them to school, came home and picked up the dry cleaning, took it to the cleaners, stopped off at the bank to withdraw some cash, went grocery shopping, drove home to put away the groceries, paid the bills, balanced the family accounts, cleaned the cat's litter tray and bathed the dog. By that time it was already one o'clock.

Then he rushed around making up the beds, did the laundry, vacuumed, dusted, swept and mopped the kitchen floor, ran to the school to pick up the kids, got into an argument with them on the way home, set out milk and cookies and got the kids organized to do their homework, then set up the ironing board and watched TV while doing the ironing.

At 5 p.m., he began peeling potatoes and washing and chopping vegetables for dinner. He then cooked and served dinner for his partner and kids. After dinner, he tidied up the kitchen, loaded the dishwasher, folded the laundry, bathed the kids and put them to bed.

By 10 p.m. he was exhausted and even though his daily chores weren't finished, he went to bed where he was expected to make love with a degree of enthusiasm.

The next morning he woke up and immediately knelt by the bed and said: "Lord, I don't know what I was thinking. I was so wrong to envy my wife for being able to stay home all day. Please, please, let us trade back."

The Lord, in his infinite wisdom, replied: "My son, I feel you have learned your lesson and I will be happy to change things back to the way they were. You'll just have to wait nine months, though. You got pregnant last night."

The Qualities of the Sexes

Women are compassionate, loving and caring.

Women are honest and loyal.

Women are always doing little things to show how much they care.

Women will do absolutely anything for their children.

Women bring joy and laughter to the world.

Women have the ability to keep smiling even when they are totally exhausted.

Women know how to comfort a sick friend.

Women know how to turn a simple meal into an occasion.

Women know how to get the most for their money.

Women are easily brought to tears by injustice.

Women have a will of iron beneath that soft exterior.

Women know how to make a man feel like a king.

Women make the world a much happier place to live.

And men?

Men are good at moving heavy things and killing spiders.

Diary of a House Husband

1. Make the beds. What a waste of effort. We're only going to sleep in them again tonight. Forget that. Scratch 1.

2. Mop kitchen floor. The dog licked up that milk spill from breakfast. The floor looks clean to me. Scratch 2.

3. Pick up dog poop in yard. It snowed last night. I don't see any dog poop. Scratch 3.

4. Clean out hallway closet. Take enough out of the closet to close the door. Out of sight, out of mind. This other stuff can go under a bed. Scratch 4.

5. Iron laundry. The creases will probably fall out of these shirts when I wear them. Scratch 5.

6. Feed kids lunch. "Hey, kids, don't you have a friend's house to go to?" Result! Scratch 6.

7. Dust and Hoover. Dust only reappears as soon as you remove it, so why bother? Anyway wife not tall enough to see on top of shelves. Scratch 7.

8. Clean toilet bowl. Whoever looks inside the toilet? A couple of flushes should do the trick. Scratch 8.

9. Remove cobwebs from garage. What, and make families of spiders homeless? Leave them where they are and help the environment. Scratch 9.

10. Clean out the dog kennel. Why? The dog sleeps in our bed. Scratch 10.

11. Pick up the kids. We're talking about my kids here. Parents will usually pay to drop them back off. They'll be back. Scratch 11.

12. Cook dinner. Now how does the microwave work? Scratch 12.

All done. This housework is sooo easy!

❖ What's a man's idea of a romantic night out?
   A candlelit football stadium.

❖ What's the one thing that keeps most men out of college?
   High school.

❖ What does a woman say to a man she has just had sex with?
   She can say whatever she wants . . . he's asleep.

❖ Why don't men eat between meals?
   There is no "between" meals.

❖ Adam said to God: "When you created Eve, why did you make her body so curvy and tender, unlike mine?"
   God replied: "I did that, Adam, so that you could love her."
   "And why," asked Adam, "did you give her long, shiny, beautiful hair, but not me?"
   "So that you could love her," answered God.
   "Then why did you make her so stupid?" asked Adam. "Certainly not so that I could love her?"
   "No, Adam," said God. "I did that so that she could love you."

❖ Men have two emotions: hungry and horny. If you see him without an erection, make him a sandwich.

> ❝ A study says that the number one quality which men find attractive in a woman is her sense of humour. They especially like it when women laugh at a joke and their boobs bounce up and down.
> Jay Leno ❞

❖ Did you hear about the male bodybuilder who won a gold medal at the Olympics?
   He had it bronzed.

❖ Why don't men cook at home?

Because no one's invented a steak that will fit in a toaster.

❖ Two women were talking at a party. One said: "My brother-in-law's a real Renaissance Man."

"Why? Because he has a broad area of knowledge and is an expert in a number of different fields?"

"No. Because he looks as if he was born five hundred years ago."

❖ For a man, what is the downside of a threesome?

He'll probably disappoint two women instead of one.

❖ How do men sort their laundry?

"Filthy" and "Filthy But Wearable".

Why Men Are Like Farts

They shouldn't be let out.

They're all hot air.

A really loud one can empty a room in seconds.

They always pop out at the most inconvenient moment.

They have no sense of direction.

Nobody ever wants to admit responsibility for them.

They create a stink if you give them too many vegetables.

The quiet ones are always the worst.

❖ Here is a fairy story: One day, long, long ago, there was a man who always brought his wife breakfast in the morning, never forgot their wedding anniversary, never wiped his muddy boots on the kitchen floor that she had just cleaned, was kind and considerate towards her mother, didn't leave his dirty clothes in a crumpled heap on the bedroom floor, and always remembered to put the toilet seat down. But this was a long time ago – and it was just one day.

★　　★　　★　　★　　★

MONEY

✳ Two men were discussing ways of making money. One said: "Recently I was asked to invest in buying old Egyptian buildings."

"Really?"

"Yes, but I think it's one of those pyramid schemes."

✳ How do you know that it's difficult living on a submarine captain's pay?

Because they can't keep their heads above water.

✳ Two neighbours living in New York's stockbroker belt were discussing how they had made their respective fortunes.

One said: "When I came here from Mexico three years ago, all I had was the boots on my feet and a sack on my back. Look at me now: a $10 million house, a $3 million penthouse apartment, three classic cars worth $1 million each, a yacht worth $3 million, and $5 million in the bank."

"That's amazing," said his neighbour. "Tell me, what was in the sack?"

"Twenty-four million dollars."

＊ Why did the arthritic contortionist claim state benefits?
  Because he could no longer make ends meet.

＊ A married couple were enjoying a luxury South Sea cruise until their liner was shipwrecked and they were washed ashore on a desert island, the only survivors.

  Day after day, they looked hopefully out to sea in the hope of spotting a passing vessel but none came. As boredom set in, they started to think about their home back in Arizona.

  The wife asked: "Did you remember to pay the final instalment on the Chevrolet before we came away?"

  "No, honey, I clean forgot. Sorry."

  "Did you remember to pay the electric bill before we left home?"

  "No, I completely forgot. Sorry."

  "Did you remember to pay the gas bill?"

  "Do you know, that slipped my mind, too. Sorry."

  "And did you remember to pay the six-monthly tax bill?

  "I knew there was something important I had to do. I'm really sorry, honey."

  "Well, at least there's one good thing," sighed the wife.

  "What's that?"

  "They'll find us."

＊ In 2008, what was the one thing that Wall Street and the Olympics had in common? Synchronized diving.

＊ On his way to work, a businessman regularly passed a beggar on a street corner. The beggar would always hold out one hand, and the businessman would usually give him a few coins. Then one morning, the businessman noticed that the beggar was holding out both hands.

  "Why are you holding out both hands?" he asked.

  "Well, sir," replied the beggar, "business has been so good that I decided to open another branch."

✳ A city guy moved to the country and bought a donkey from a farmer for $100. The farmer agreed to deliver the donkey the next day, but when he drove up in his truck, he had some bad news.

"Sorry," he said. "The donkey has died."

"Well, then just give me my money back."

"Can't do that. I went and spent it already."

"Okay then, just unload the donkey."

"What you gonna do with him?" asked the farmer.

"I'm going to raffle him off."

"You can't raffle off a dead donkey!"

"Sure I can," insisted the city guy. "I just won't tell anyone he's dead."

A month later, the farmer met up with the city guy again and asked: "What happened with the dead donkey?"

"I raffled him off – just like I said I would. I sold five hundred tickets at $2 apiece and made a profit of $998."

"Didn't anyone complain?"

"Only the guy who won. So I gave him his $2 back."

> ❝ I'm not saying our money has lost its value, but today I dropped a $5 bill and was charged with littering.
>
> Jay Leno ❞

✳ A couple who were big spenders had always dreamed of a vacation in Hawaii but had never managed to save up enough money. Then one day they came up with an idea – each time they had sex, they would put a $20 bill into a piggy bank.

After seven months of this, they reckoned there was probably enough money in the piggy bank to pay for their dream vacation, so they smashed it open. The husband was puzzled by what he found. "It's strange," he said. "Each time we had sex, I put a $20 bill into the piggy bank. Yet there are $50 bills and $100 bills in here, too."

The wife replied: "Do you think everybody is as stingy as you are?"

＊ A couple stopped at an English motorway service station for breakfast. They bought two cooked breakfasts, two coffees and two donuts. When the husband reached the cash desk, he said to the cashier: "I'm sorry, I've only got a £50 note."

"That's okay," she said. "Just put the donuts back."

＊ After hearing a church sermon about lies and deceit, a man wrote to the IRS: "I have been unable to sleep, knowing that I have cheated on my income tax. I understand my taxable income and have enclosed a cheque for $900. If I still can't sleep, I will send the rest."

＊ Did you hear about the guy who had a great business plan – he was going to build bungalows for dwarfs? There was just one tiny flaw . . .

＊ Every year at the state fair John entered the $3,000 lottery and lost. Eventually he got so fed up with losing that at the fair he told his friend Mel he wasn't going to bother entering this year.

"That's the wrong attitude," said Mel. "You've got to have faith. Look around you, and see if the good Lord sends a message."

As he strolled around the fair, John became increasingly despondent. With the big draw growing ever nearer, nothing struck him, no divine inspiration, no sign from God.

Just when he was about to give up, he passed old Mrs Brown's pie stand. He happened to glance over just as she was bending down, and noticed that she wasn't wearing any panties. Suddenly her ass began to glow brightly, a finger of flame descended from the skies and etched an orange number seven on each cheek.

Thanking God, John rushed to the raffle booth and played the number 77.

Fifteen minutes later, the draw was held. John lost again. The winning number was 707.

＊ Did you hear about the man who tried looking for gold, but it didn't pan out?

> **❝** How much do you think Senators make? They now make $154,700 a year. But they say it will stimulate the economy because eventually that money will trickle down to the liquor stores, the hookers, the brothels, then it will get back in the community.
>
> Jay Leno **❞**

✳ Seeing a homeless guy begging on the street, a woman took pity on him and gave him a handful of change.

"Thank you," said the homeless man. "Your generosity is much appreciated. You know, my life used to be great but just look at the state of me now."

"How do you mean?" asked the woman.

"Well," he explained, "I was a multi-millionaire. I had bank accounts all over the world with hundreds of thousands of dollars deposited in each."

"So where did it all go wrong?" she asked.

The homeless man sighed: "I forgot my mother's maiden name."

Seeing his shares plummet on a black morning during the recession, the boss called to his secretary: "Get my broker, Miss Wilks."

"Certainly, sir. Stock or pawn?"

✳ A man was sitting at the bar looking dejectedly into his bottle of beer.

"You look pretty down," said the guy on the next stool. "Wanna talk about it?"

"I dunno," sighed the first man. "It's just that this time last year I had a fantastic job. I was making big money."

"So?"

"Well, that was the problem. People started noticing the bills were five millimetres too big!"

✳ A workman went into a rundown public toilet to take a dump. The toilet had two stalls separated by nothing more than a low partition, and there was another man about to step into one of them. The two men briefly acknowledged one another and then set about emptying their bowels.

The workman finished first but as he pulled up his pants prior to flushing the toilet, some coins from his pocket fell into the toilet bowl. He looked at it, thought for a moment and then dropped a $20 bill into the bowl.

The other man, who had heard the commotion, peered over the partition and said: "What the heck did you do that for?"

The workman said: "You don't expect me to put my hand in there for fifty-five cents, do you?"

✳ A millionaire was driving along in his stretch limo when he saw a humble man eating grass by the roadside. Ordering his chauffeur to stop, he wound down the window and called to the man: "Why are you eating grass?"

"Because, sir," he replied, "we don't have enough money for proper food."

"Come with me, then," said the millionaire.

"But sir, I have a wife and seven children."

"That's okay. Bring them all along."

The man and his family climbed gratefully into the limo. "Sir, you are too kind. How can I ever thank you for taking all of us with you, offering a new home to total strangers?"

"No, you don't understand," said the millionaire. "The grass at my mansion is four feet high. No lawn mower will cut it!"

> ❝ The United States has developed a new weapon that destroys people but leaves buildings standing. It's called the stock market. ❞
>
> Jay Leno

* In New York City, a Scotsman and an American were discussing how far each could make a dime go. They agreed to meet up again a few days later to see who had got the most out of a dime.

  The Scotsman revealed how he had bought a cigar with his dime. He had smoked one-third of the cigar the first day and saved the ashes. He smoked another third the second day and saved the ashes. On the third day, he smoked the final third and again saved the ashes, and on the fourth day he gave the ashes to his wife to use as fertilizer on her roses. He told the American proudly: "How's that for stretching a dime!"

  The American said: "Very good, but I got you beat. I bought a Polish sausage for a dime, and the first day I ate half of it. On the second day, I ate the other half. The third day, I used the skin for a condom, and the fourth day I took a shit in the skin and sewed it back up. The fifth day, I took it back to the butcher and told him it smelled like shit. He agreed with me and gave me my dime back!"

* If you had bought $1,000 worth of Lehman Brothers shares in 2007, a year later they would have been worth nothing.

  If you had purchased $1,000 worth of AIG shares in 2007, a year later they would have been worth around $30.

  If you had invested $1,000 in Delta Airlines in 2007, a year later it would have been worth around $49.

  If you had bought $1,000 worth of beer, drunk it all, then taken the empty cans to an aluminium recycling plant, you would have received $214.

  So based on the above statistics, in the current economic climate the soundest investment advice is to drink heavily and recycle.

* A man told his workmate excitedly: "I've just won the jackpot in the Zimbabwe lottery. They tell me that if I hurry, I'll have enough money to buy next week's ticket."

* An antiques expert was walking along a downtown street when he spotted a mangy old cat drinking milk from a saucer in the doorway of a small, rundown store. As soon as he saw the delicate blue and white pattern on the saucer, he knew it was a valuable piece – one that was definitely worth acquiring.

So he walked into the store and said to the owner: "I'll give you five bucks for your cat."

"Sorry," said the owner. "The cat isn't for sale."

"Look," persisted the antiques expert, "I really need a cat around the house to catch mice. I tell you what, I'll pay you $30 for the cat."

"Okay," agreed the owner. "It's a deal." And he handed over the cat.

Disguising it as an afterthought, the expert added: "Hey, for the $30, would you mind throwing in that old saucer? The cat's obviously used to it and it would save me having to buy a dish."

"Sorry, pal," said the store owner. "I can't sell that. It's my lucky saucer. So far this month I've sold fifty-three cats!"

* A woman knocked on the door of a house. "I'm collecting for the local swimming pool," she said.

So the houseowner gave her two buckets of water.

> 66 The government has always warned us that Al-Qaeda planned an attack to damage our economy. Well, I've a feeling someone is sitting in a cave right now going, 'Wasn't me!'
>
> Andre Vincent 99

★   ★   ★   ★   ★

MUSIC AND DANCE

★ The musical director of an orchestra became so annoyed with his lead cellist for playing too fast that he smashed him over the head with the instrument, causing fatal injuries. At his subsequent trial, he was found guilty of murder and sentenced to the electric chair.

As a last meal, he asked for a bunch of green bananas, which he duly ate. The guards then sat him down, plugged him and sent a million volts through his body but when the smoke cleared, he was still sitting there, alive and well. Checking through the statutes, the governor concluded that he had no choice but to release him.

He returned to his job with the orchestra but soon fell out with the lead violinist for not keeping time. After smashing the instrument, he garrotted the violinist with one of the strings. Once again he was found guilty of murder and sentenced to die in the electric chair.

At the prison he again asked for a bunch of green bananas as a final meal. After devouring them, he was placed in the chair and zapped with two million volts, but when the smoke cleared he was still perfectly healthy. The governor had no option other than to release him.

Back with the orchestra, he had a huge row with the trombonist for coming in at the wrong place. He was so angry that he rammed the instrument's slide up the trombonist's butt, causing fatal injuries. Found guilty of murder, he was once more sentenced to death.

As a final meal he again asked for a bunch of green bananas and after wolfing them down, he was seated in the electric chair. Three million volts surged through his body but when the smoke cleared, he remained perfectly healthy.

The executioner was in despair. "How do you keep managing to cheat death in the electric chair?" he asked the musical director. "What's your secret? Is it the green bananas?"

"No," he replied. "I'm just a lousy conductor."

★ A guy picked up a girl in a nightclub and asked her to dance. When it came to a slow dance, he pressed his body close to hers. While they were cheek to cheek, he said: "You smell terrific. What's that you have on?"

"It's Chanel No. 5," she replied, flattered. Wanting to return the compliment, she said: "You smell good, too. What do you have on?"

He said: "Well, I've got a hard-on, but I didn't think you could smell it."

★ Meat Loaf has revealed how he was bullied at school. Apparently one kid took Meat Loaf's dinner money to buy a new Cadillac.

★ A man walked into a record store and asked the assistant: "Have you got anything by The Doors?"

"Yes," she said, "a bucket and a fire extinguisher."

★ Did you know that it took Stevie Wonder eight years to write "Superstition"? He dropped his pencil on the first day.

★ What was Meat Loaf's favourite musical instrument at school?

The dinner bell.

★ A young boy was covering behind the counter of a small music shop while his father, the owner, took a toilet break. No sooner had the father gone than a female customer walked in.

"Excuse me, young man," she said. "Do you happen to have 'Jingle Bells' on a seven-inch?"

"No," he replied, "but I've got dangling balls on a nine-inch."

"That's not a record, is it?" she asked.

He said: "It is for a ten-year-old!"

> Phil Collins is losing his hearing,
> making him the luckiest man at a Phil
> Collins concert.
>
> Simon Amstell

★ A music store was robbed last week. Thieves made away with the lute.

★ A guy kept boring his friends by going on and on about his ideas for a musical based on his life.
  Eventually one of them said to him: "There's no need to make a song and dance about it."

★ The Beach Boys walked into a bar.
  "Round?"
  "Round?"
  "Get a round."
  "I get a round?"
  "Get a round . . ."

★ I conducted an orchestra the other day. It's more fun than you can shake a stick at.

★ Did you hear about the guy who auditioned with a jazz band as a trumpeter? He blew it.

> Without the beat in the background,
> jazz basically sounds like an armadillo
> was let loose on the keyboard.
>
> Bill Bailey

★ Jay Z retired from hip-hop and decided to invest in an ice cream van. Unfortunately, on his first day of trading the supplier didn't show up with the supply of chocolate flakes, leaving Jay Z with 99 problems.

★ What is the name of India's latest karaoke star?
  Gerupta Singh

You Might Be a Drummer If . . .

You tell people at restaurants who sing and clap "Happy Birthday" that they are out of tempo.

You've ever dropped a stick while playing and not noticed.

Your style of dancing involves slapping your thighs and pounding your feet.

You've ever tried to play any other instrument with drumsticks.

You can recognize the world's top guitarists solely by their backsides.

Your drum kit cost more than your car.

You insist on spending an hour tuning your snare, even though no one can hear the difference.

Your girlfriend tells you to stop hitting her in your sleep.

Your house constantly vibrates.

You've ever taken longer than thirty seconds to realize that the rest of the band have stopped playing.

★ The conductor turned to the viola student and said: "You should have taken up the viola earlier."

"Why?" asked the student. "Do you think the practice would have made me really good?"

"No," said the conductor. "But you might have given up by now."

★ A little boy thanked his grandfather for the set of drums he bought him for his birthday. "They're the best present I've ever had," he said. "They've already earned me $80."

"Wow!" said the grandfather. "You must have learned to play them real good!"

"Not really," said the boy. "But Mom gives me $5 not to play them during the day, and Dad gives me $5 not to play them in the evening."

★ Why are harps like elderly parents?

They're both unforgiving and difficult to get in and out of cars.

★ Did you hear about the woman who could only compose music in 3/4 time?
She had waltz timer's disease.

★ A woman answered her front door to find a workman standing on the porch and carrying a box of tools.

"I'm the piano tuner, ma'am," he announced.

"But I didn't send for a piano tuner."

"I know, but your neighbours did!"

★ Following the sad death of Luciano Pavarotti, it has been announced that the three tenors will now be known as twenty quid.

★ A semi-professional singer went for an audition at a local club. The club secretary said: "I hope you're not a hypnotist. We don't want any more hypnotists here."

The man said: "No, I'm not, I'm a singer. But what's the problem with hypnotists?"

The secretary said: "We had one here last week. With twelve people up on the stage in a trance, he tripped over the microphone stand and muttered: 'Shit!' We've been clearing up ever since!"

★   An American tourist visiting the Austrian capital, Vienna, was walking through a graveyard when he suddenly started hearing music. He finally located the source and discovered that it was coming from the grave of Ludwig van Beethoven. Then he realized that the music he was hearing was the Ninth Symphony and that it was being played backwards. Mystified, he left the graveyard but later persuaded a friend to return with him.

By the time the pair had returned to Beethoven's grave, the music had changed. This time it was the Seventh Symphony but, like the previous piece, it was being played backwards. To find an explanation for this bizarre phenomenon, the men decided to consult a music scholar. When they returned with the expert, the Fifth Symphony was playing, again backwards.

The expert noticed that not only were the symphonies being played backwards but also in the reverse order to which they were composed.

By the next day – as word spread throughout the music fraternity – a small crowd had gathered around Beethoven's grave. They were listening to the Second Symphony being played backwards.

After a while the caretaker of the graveyard wandered over to the group, and someone in the crowd asked him if he could explain the reason for the strange music coming from Beethoven's grave.

"Oh, it's nothing to get excited about," said the caretaker. "He's just decomposing."

★   A man went up to the bartender in a music bar and asked: "How late does the band play?"

The bartender replied: "Usually about a half-beat behind the drummer."

★ What does Bjork do when she's feeling horny?

She watches pjorn.

★ A noted television documentary maker spent six years travelling all over the world filming a programme about native dances. His last port of call was Alice Springs, Australia, where, certain that he had now captured on film every single native dance of every indigenous culture in the world, he relaxed in a bar with a well-earned beer. He began chatting to one of the local Aborigines and told him about the project. The Aborigine asked him what he thought of the Butcher Dance.

The documentary maker paled visibly. "Butcher Dance? What's that?"

"What?" said the Aborigine. "You no see Butcher Dance?"

"No, I've never heard of it."

"Oh mate. You crazy. How you say you film every native dance in the world if you no see Butcher Dance?"

"Well, er, I got a corroboree on film just the other week. Is that what you mean?"

"No, no, not corroboree. Butcher Dance much more important than corroboree."

"Oh. Well, how can I see this Butcher Dance then?"

"Mate, Butcher Dance right out there in the bush. Many days' travel to go see Butcher Dance."

"Listen, I've been everywhere from the forests of the Amazon to deepest, darkest Africa and the frozen wastes of the Arctic filming hundreds of dances. Nothing will prevent me from recording this one last dance."

"Okay, mate. You drive north along highway towards Darwin. After you drive 214 miles, you see dirt track off to left. Follow dirt track for 187 miles till you see big dead gum tree – biggest tree you ever see. Here you gotta leave car, because much too rough for driving. You strike out due west into setting sun. You walk three days till you hit creek. You follow this creek to north-west. After two days you find where creek flows out of rocky mountains. Much too difficult to cross mountains here though. You now head south for half a day till you see pass through mountains. Pass very difficult, very dangerous. Take two, maybe three, days to get through rocky pass. When through, head north-west for four days till reach big rock – thirty-foot high and shaped like man's head. From rock, walk due west for a day and a half and you find village. Here you see Butcher Dance."

So the film-maker collected his camera crew and equipment and set off into the wilderness. Despite the scorching heat, the dust and the ever-present flies, he kept his spirits up by thinking about the prospect of capturing on film this mysterious dance that he had never heard mention of before. True to the directions he had been given, he located the dirt track, the tree, the creek and the mountain pass, which was every bit as treacherous as his guide had predicted. It was a back-breaking effort to get all the camera equipment through and the team were near exhaustion by the time they reached the big rock. Having come this far, however, nothing was going to prevent him from realizing his life's dream. By now water was running low and their feet were covered in blisters but bravely they set off on the last leg of their journey. A day and a half later, their minds and bodies shattered by the merciless sun, they finally staggered into the village. Struggling for breath, the film-maker went up to the village chief and said: "We have come to film your Butcher Dance."

"Oh, mate," said the chief. "Very bad you come today. Butcher Dance last night. You too late. You miss dance."

"Well, when do you do the next dance?"

"Not till next year."

"But I've travelled hundreds of miles to see the Butcher Dance. Couldn't you just do an extra dance for me tonight?"

"No way. Butcher Dance very holy. Tradition say only once a year. If do more, gods get very angry and destroy village. You want see Butcher Dance, you come back next year."

The documentary maker was devastated but realized that he had no option but to return to civilization and come back in a year's time.

The following year, he headed back to Australia and, determined not to miss out again, set off from Alice Springs a week earlier than before. But right from the start things went wrong. Heavy rains that year had turned the dirt track to mud and the jeep became bogged down every few miles, finally forcing them to abandon the vehicle and slog through the mud on foot. Then halfway through the mountain pass they were hit by a fierce storm which raged for several days and they had to take refuge in a cave. To make matters worse, when the storm finally subsided the sound man sprained his ankle, reducing their progress to a crawl. By the time they reached the village they had lost all sense of time.

The documentary maker staggered over to the village chief and gasped: "Please don't tell me I'm too late for the Butcher Dance."

The chief recognized him and said: "No, mate. Butcher Dance performed tonight. You come just in time."

Hugely relieved, the crew spent the rest of the day freshening up and then setting up their equipment, preparing to capture this hitherto unseen ritual on film. As dusk fell, the natives covered their bodies in white paint and adorned themselves in all manner of bird feathers and animal skins. Once darkness had settled fully over the land, the natives formed a circle around a huge roaring fire. A deathly hush descended over performers and spectators alike as a wizened old figure with elaborate swirling designs covering his whole body entered the circle and began to chant.

"What's he doing?" asked the documentary maker, figuring that the guy was some sort of witch doctor.

"Hush," whispered the chief. "You first white man ever to see most sacred of our rituals. Must remain silent. Holy man, he asks that the spirits of the dreamworld watch as we demonstrate our devotion to them through our dance and, if they like our dancing, will they be so gracious as to watch over us and protect us for another year."

The chanting of the holy man reached a stunning crescendo before he finally exited the circle. From somewhere the rhythmic pounding of drums boomed out across the village and the natives began to sway to the stirring sounds.

The film-maker was becoming caught up in the excitement. This was the moment. He knew in his heart that the travelling, the hardships and the wait had not been in vain. He was about to become the first outsider to witness the Butcher Dance – the ultimate performance of rhythm and movement ever conceived by mankind.

The chief strode to his position in the circle and, in a loud booming voice, started to sing: "You butch yer left leg in, yer left leg out, in, out, in, out, you shake it all about . . ."

> What kind of dancing takes place on the Internet?
>   Online dancing.

★ It is one of life's ironies that people with club feet generally aren't very good at dancing.

★ Last week I saw a man playing "Dancing Queen" on the didgeridoo. I thought, "That's aboriginal."

★   ★   ★   ★   ★

NATIONALITIES

❖ A boat was shipwrecked in the South Pacific, as a result of which a group of passengers of different nationalities found themselves stranded on a remote but beautiful desert island. The party consisted of:

  Two Italian men and one Italian woman
  Two French men and one French woman
  Two German men and one German woman
  Two Greek men and one Greek woman

Two English men and one English woman

Two Irish men and one Irish woman

Two Bulgarian men and one Bulgarian woman

Two Australian men and one Australian woman

Two Japanese men and one Japanese woman

Two Indian men and one Indian woman

Two American men and one American woman

Two Canadian men and one Canadian woman

One month later, against this idyllic backdrop, the following things had occurred:

One Italian man killed the other Italian man for the Italian woman.

The two French men and the French women were living happily together in a *ménage a trois*.

The two German men tried to invade the French woman before eventually adopting a strict weekly schedule of alternating visits to the German woman.

The two Greek men were sleeping with each other while the Greek woman cooked and cleaned for them.

The two English men were still waiting for someone to introduce them to the English woman.

The two Irish men divided the island into north and south and set up a distillery using a business plan drawn up by the Irish woman.

The two Bulgarian men took one look at the endless ocean, one look at the Bulgarian woman, and started swimming.

The two Australian men tried to sell the Australian woman in return for a recipe for homemade beer.

The two Japanese men had faxed Tokyo and were awaiting instructions.

The two Indian men had opened a corner shop, staffed 24/7 by themselves and the Indian woman.

The two American men were feeling suicidal because the American woman was constantly complaining because there was no fresh bottled water available, she was allergic to seafood, coconut milk was not her preferred moisturizer, and she felt fat standing next to palm trees.

The Canadians were blissfully happy – simply because they knew the Americans weren't having a good time.

★ **Afghan** ★

❖ A guy was walking down a street when he saw an Afghan friend standing on a fifth-floor balcony shaking a carpet.

He shouted up to him: "What's up, Abdul? Won't it start?"

★ **American** ★

❖ An American, a Mexican and an Italian robbed a bank, and escaped with a haul in dollars, pesos and lira. Back at their hide-out, the American distributed the money in three even shares.

"1,000 dollars for me, 1,000 pesos for you, 1,000 lira for you . . . 1,000 dollars for me, 1,000 pesos for you, 1,000 lira for you . . . 1,000 dollars for me, 1,000 pesos for you, 1,000 lira for you . . ."

As the counting continued, the Mexican whispered to the Italian: "I can't stand Americans, but you have to admit they are fair."

> **❝** Americans say this 'ongoing thing in Iraq'. We don't like to call it a war. They never say 'war' on CNN. They say, 'More pockets of resistance were met today.' Sounds like a dry cleaning operation gone bad.
>
> Rich Hall **❞**

❖ **Fifty per cent of Americans don't have a passport. It's not that they don't want to leave their country, it's just that half of them are too fat to fit into a photo booth.**

66 The biggest worry in the US is gas prices getting higher, and if that happens we might see something totally unprecedented in America: people actually walking.

Andre Vincent 99

❖ An American went into a remote bar in Canada, looked around and said: "This place must be the asshole of the world!"

The bartender said: "Just passing through then, are you?"

❖ An English visitor to the United States was taken by a work colleague to his first football game, one that also happened to be being screened live on TV. Afterwards his host family asked him whether he had enjoyed it.

"Not really," he admitted. "I found it boring. It was all very stop-start. Every thirty seconds or so, the referee would blow his whistle, and the game would then take a few minutes to resume."

"Well, you know why that is?"

"No."

"Snack breaks for the audience."

❖ NASA launched a rocket to Mars with an American and two monkeys on board. NASA radioed the first monkey and said: "Adjust oxygen 20 per cent, stop radar and phase to warp factor three."

The first monkey replied: "Okay, roger that."

NASA then radioed the second monkey: "Switch off engine three, start the radiation shield and adjust the anti-gravitation throttle."

"Roger that," said the second monkey.

Then NASA radioed the American: "Feed the monkeys and don't touch a goddamn thing!"

❖ How many American tourists does it take to change a light bulb?

Fifteen. Five to figure out how much the bulb costs in the local currency, four to comment on how "funny-looking" the local light bulbs are, three to hire a local person to change the bulb, two to take pictures, and one to buy postcards in case the pictures don't come out.

★ **Australian** ★

❖ Two Australian bushmen were riding through the outback when they came across a watering hole and saw a guy in the jaws of a crocodile, already half devoured so that only his head and upper torso were visible.

One bushman nodded to the other and said: "He must be one of those flash city types – he's even got a Lacoste sleeping bag!"

❖ An Australian, a chauvinist and a sex maniac walk into a bar. He orders a drink . . .

❖ Three bushmen – one from New Zealand, one from South Africa and one from Australia – were sitting around a campfire in the outback at night boasting about who was the toughest.

The New Zealander said: "Nobody's tougher than me. Only last week, I wrestled and killed a twenty-foot-long crocodile with my bare hands."

"That's nothing," said the South African, exuding bravado. "When a deadly black mamba attacked me, I bit off its head and sucked all the venom out of its body, swallowing it in one gulp."

The Australian remained silent, slowly poking the fire with his penis.

❖ A Chinese guy, an Irishman, an American and an Australian were debating whose country was the best.

   The Chinese guy said: "My country is best because we have the Great Wall."

   The Irishman said: "No, my country is best because we have the greenest grass."

   The American said: "No, my country is definitely the best because we have the most beautiful flag."

   The Australian said: "You're all wrong. My country is best because we have the kangaroo, and that can jump over your Great Wall, crap on your grass and wipe its ass with your flag."

❖ What's the definition of an Australian gentleman?

   One who offers to light his girlfriend's farts before lighting his own.

❖ The United States government funded a study to determine why the head of a man's penis is larger than the shaft. After ten months and at a cost of $450,000 they decided that the head is larger than the shaft in order to give the man greater pleasure during sex.

   The Italian government also funded a study to find out why the head of a man's penis is larger than the shaft. After nine months and at a cost of $360,000, they, too, decided that the head is larger than the shaft so that the man can experience greater pleasure during sex.

   Dissatisfied with these findings, the Australian government conducted their own study. After two weeks and at a cost of $50.35 plus six cases of beer, they concluded that the head of a penis is larger than the shaft to prevent the man's hand flying off and hitting himself in the forehead.

> ❝ I love Australia, I really do. But in the same way I love my parents. They're retarded and I have to.
> Brendon Burns ❞

❖ Backpacking in Australia, a young Englishman found himself with time to kill in a remote outback town before the next leg of his journey. With over two hours until his bus was due, he decided to call into the town's only hotel for a beer and something to eat.

As he walked in, every head at the bar turned to stare out the stranger. The silence was deafening until one of the regulars stood up and announced: "I hope you're not a pervert, because perverts aren't welcome in this town."

"No," said the young man, "I assure you I'm not. I'm just waiting for my bus."

He ordered a beer and a burger, and after his meal needed to use the toilet, particularly with the prospect of a seven-hour bus ride ahead. So he asked the bartender where the toilet was.

"The dunny's out the back," growled the bartender, "and don't make a mess!"

On venturing outside, the young man was horrified to see that the toilets were nothing more than two pits piled high with festering poop. One pile was six feet high, the other four feet high. Bracing himself, he climbed to the top of the smaller pile and did his business. As he climbed down, the guy from the bar appeared and grabbed him around the throat.

"I knew you were a pervert!" he snarled. "You were in the ladies!"

What's the difference between Australians and pigs?

Pigs don't turn into Australians after ten pints of beer.

★ **Canadian** ★

❖ An Englishman, a Canadian and an American were captured
by terrorists. The terrorist leader said: "Before we shoot you,
you will be allowed last words. Tell me what you would like
to talk about."

   The Englishman said: "I want to talk about loyalty and
service to the crown."

   The Canadian said: "Since you are involved in a question
of national purpose, national identity and secession, I wish
to talk about the history of constitutional process in Canada, special status, distinct society and uniqueness within
diversity."

   The American said: "Just shoot me before the Canadian
starts talking."

> ❝ I got drunk in Canada. I was there for
> two days, but I was drunk there for
> four days. I guess it was the time
> difference.
>
> Adam Carolla ❞

❖ Why did the Canadian cross the road?
   To get to the middle.

> ❝ Look at the Canadian flag. It's not a
> symbol of power, it's a leaf. Oh, don't
> screw with Canada, it'll dry up and
> blow away.
>
> Jeremy Hotz ❞

❖ A girl sat sobbing in a police station. "I've been raped by a
Canadian," she wailed.

   "How do you know it was a Canadian?" asked the
officer.

   "Because I had to help him."

★ Chinese ★

❖ A man was walking through Chinatown when he saw a sign saying "Hans Schmidt's Chinese Laundry". Being curious, he went into the shop and was greeted by an elderly Oriental man who introduced himself as Hans Schmidt.

"How come you have a name like that?" inquired the stranger. "You don't look very German!"

"Is simple," said the Oriental shop owner. "Many many year ago when come to this country I stand in immigration line behind big German guy. Immigration lady look at him and go, 'What your name?' He say, 'Hans Schmidt.' Then she look at me and go, 'What your name?' I say, 'Sam Ting.'"

❖ What do you call a Chinese girl with one leg?
Irene.

❖ A Chinese man and a Jewish man were discussing their respective cultures. The Jewish man remarked upon the wisdom of the Chinese.

"Yes," replied the Chinese man. "Our culture is over 4,000 years old. But you Jews are a very wise people too."

"Yes, our culture is over 5,000 years old," said the Jew.

"That's impossible!" exclaimed the Chinese man. "Where did your people eat for a thousand years?"

★ English ★

> ❝ In this country you've got school children dressed as hookers and hookers dressed as school children. It's a nightmare – you don't know whether to carry sweets or money.
>
> Al Murray ❞

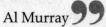

❖ A Geordie was so devoted to his pet dog that when it died, he wanted it commemorated in the form of a gold statue. So he went to a local jeweller's shop and asked: "Can ya make me a gold statue of ma dog?"

"Certainly, sir," said the jeweller. "Would you like it eighteen carat?"

"No, daft lad, I want it chewin' a bone."

❖ A Geordie went into a barber's shop and said: "Can I have a perm, please?"

The barber replied: "I wandered lonely as a cloud . . ."

❖ Three Englishman were standing at the bar when they spotted an Irishman sitting quietly in the corner.

Fortified by alcohol, one of the Englishman went over to the Irishman and said loudly: "Hey, I hear your St Patrick was a drunken loser!"

"Oh really?" said the Irishman. "I didn't know that."

Puzzled, the Englishman walked back to his buddies and said: "I told him St Patrick was a drunken loser, but he didn't seem to care."

The second Englishman said: "You don't know how to wind him up. Watch and learn."

So the second Englishman walked over to the Irishman and announced: "Hey, I hear your St Patrick was lying, cheating, idiotic, low-life scum!"

"Is that so?" said the Irishman. "I didn't know that."

Disappointed at getting no reaction, the second Englishman returned to his buddies. "I told him St Patrick was lying, cheating, idiotic, low-life scum, but he didn't seem at all bothered. I don't understand it."

The third Englishman said: "I know how to get him riled. Watch this."

So the third Englishman went over to the Irishman and yelled: "Hey, I hear your St Patrick was an Englishman!"

The Irishman replied: "Yeah, that's what your buddies were trying to tell me."

> ❝ When the 7/7 bombings happened a few years back, the city reacted in a phenomenally 'London' way. They went: 'Oh my God! There's a bomb on the Piccadilly Line. Well, I can get the Victoria Line and change at Euston.'
>
> Dara O'Briain ❞

❖ Police in Liverpool cordoned off an area of the city following sightings of an unidentified circular object, never seen before. It turned out to be a tax disc.

❖ A Liverpool woman gave birth prematurely to a baby boy. Everyone was so proud of him – he was the first one in the family to have been inside for less than nine months.

❖ **If all the cars in England were lined end to end . . . it would probably be a Bank Holiday.**

❖ The pride of the people of Liverpool took a bit of a knock today when they found out that there's a concert being held for them in Ethiopia.

❖ Why did audiences scream so loudly at Beatles concerts? It was the shock of seeing four Scousers working.

> ❝ Seventy per cent of all people who die in England are cremated, which goes to show that the only thing English people know how to cook is other English people.
>
> Jay Leno ❞

❖ An English aristocrat answered the phone in his stately home. The voice on the other end said: "Hello, Nigel, this is Hermione. We met at a party three months ago."

"Hermione? Three months ago?"

"Yes, it was at Clive's house. After the party you took me home. On the way we parked the Merc and got into the back seat. You told me I was a good sport."

"Oh, yes! Hermione! How are you?"

"I'm pregnant and I'm going to kill myself!"

"I say! You *are* a good sport!"

★ French ★

❖ Why does the French flag have Velcro?

So the blue and red sections can be easily removed in times of war.

❖ An elderly American tourist arrived at French immigration at Paris's Charles de Gaulle Airport and began fumbling for his passport.

The French official quickly grew impatient. "You have been to France before, monsieur?" he asked in an unnecessarily aggressive tone.

"Yes, but it was a while back," replied the old man, still rummaging in his bag.

"In that case," continued the official, "you should know to have your passport ready for inspection."

"But the last time I came to France I didn't have to show my passport or any documents."

"It is not possible," snorted the Frenchman. "I'm telling you, old man, you Americans always have to show your passport on arrival in la belle France."

The American fixed him with an icy stare. "And I'm telling you, young man, that when I came ashore on Omaha Beach in Normandy on D-Day in 1944, there was no damned Frenchman on the beach asking to see my passport!"

❖ Why don't they have fireworks at Euro Disneyland Paris?

Because every time they are set off, the French Army tries to surrender.

❖ A teenage boy was playing in his room on his computer when his grandfather came in and sat on the bed.

"I know you love your computer," said the grandfather, "but you really should get out of the house more and experience life. After all, you're eighteen now. When I was eighteen, I went to Paris, went to the Moulin Rouge, drank all night, had my way with the dancers, pissed on the barman and left without paying! Now that is how to have a good time!"

A week later, the grandfather came to visit again. He found the boy still in his room, but this time with a broken arm in plaster, two black eyes and no front teeth.

"What happened to you?" he asked.

The boy said: "I did what you did. I went to Paris, went to the Moulin Rouge, drank all night, had my way with the dancers, pissed on the barman and he beat the hell out of me!"

"Oh dear!" said the grandfather. "Who did you go with?"

"Just some friends. Why? Who did you go with?"

"The Third Panzer Division."

❖ A Frenchman went into a library in London and asked for a book on war. The librarian said: "No, mate, you'll lose it."

❖ How do you stop a French Army on horseback?

Turn off the carousel.

❖ What's the difference between Frenchmen and toast?

You can make soldiers out of toast.

❖ How were the French relay team knocked out of the Olympics?

They saw a German with a baton and surrendered.

❖ An officer in the United States naval reserve was attending a conference of officers from the US Navy and the French Navy. At a cocktail reception, he found himself in a small group that included personnel from both navies.

A French admiral started complaining that whereas Europeans learned many languages, Americans learned only English. He then asked: "Why is it that we have to speak English at these conferences rather than speak French?"

An American admiral replied caustically: "Maybe it's because the Brits, Canadians, Aussies and Americans arranged it so you wouldn't have to speak German."

❖ What did the mayor of Paris say to the German Army as they entered the city in the Second World War?

"Table for 100,000, monsieur?"

❖ A man walked into a library and asked for a book on French war heroes. The librarian suggested he try the fiction section.

> Why do French tanks have rear-view mirrors?
> So that they can watch the battle.

❖ At the Battle of Waterloo in 1815, the French captured an English major. They took him to their headquarters where a French general began to question him.

The French general asked: "Why do you English officers all wear red coats? Don't you know the red material makes you easy targets for us to shoot?"

The major replied: "English officers wear red coats so that if they are shot, the blood won't show, and the men they are leading won't panic."

"I see," said the French general. "That is an ingenious idea. We might adopt something similar."

And that is why from that day to this, all French Army officers wear brown underpants.

❖ The French government announced after the London bombings that it had raised its terror alert level from Run to Hide. The only two higher levels in France are Surrender and Collaborate. The rise in the alert level was precipitated by a fire which destroyed France's white flag factory, effectively disabling its military.

❖ Barack Obama flew to London to meet Gordon Brown. Halfway through the motorcade along the streets of the English capital, Obama leaned over to Brown and whispered: "I desperately need a pee."

"No problem," said Brown who immediately relayed instructions in the driver's ear. Seconds later, the car drew to a halt outside an impressive building and Brown led Obama inside.

The interior of the building featured a huge marble hall with an ornate fountain and beautiful tapestries hanging on the walls.

"Where is the toilet?" asked Obama.

"Just go right here," advised Brown.

So Obama unzipped himself and peed all over the marble floor, and Brown did likewise. Then both men washed their hands in the fountain before drying them on the tapestries.

"This is a magnificent place," said Obama. "What do we do now?"

"Anything you like," replied Brown. "It's the French Embassy."

❖ What's the difference between a Frenchman and a cow's arse?

There are fewer flies around a cow's arse.

★ **German** ★

❖ How did the Germans invade Poland so quickly?
   They marched in backwards and the Poles thought they were leaving.

❖ How do we know that Hitler was a lousy golfer?
   Because he never did get out of the bunker.

> **" "** According to a new book about Adolf Hitler, he suffered from chronic gas.
> Apparently he had chronic gas so often that he would constantly leave a room if he had a problem. You know Hitler: he didn't want to offend anyone.
>
> Jay Leno **" "**

A German arrived at London's Heathrow Airport. The customs officer said to him:
   "Name?"
   "Kurt Schnellinger."
   "Occupation?"
   "No. Just visiting."

★ **Icelandic** ★

❖ What's the capital of Iceland?
   About $6.50.

❖ What have an Icelandic bank and an Icelandic streaker got in common?
   They both have frozen assets.

★ **Iranian** ★

❖ The Iranian Ambassador to the United Nations met George W. Bush on a recent visit to New York. At the end of his stay, the ambassador turned to Bush and said: "I have just one question about what I have seen in America. My son watches this show called *Star Trek*, and in it there is Chekov, who is Russian, Scottie, who is Scottish, and Sulu, who is Chinese, but there are no Arabs. My son is very upset and does not understand why there are not any Iranians in *Star Trek*.

Bush smiled: "That's because it takes place in the future."

★ **Iraqi** ★

❖ What did Little Miss Muffet and Saddam Hussein have in common?
Both had Kurds in their way.

> If Iraq was so dangerous, how come it only took two weeks to take over? You couldn't take over Baltimore in two weeks!
>
> Chris Rock

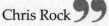

❖ Did you hear about the guy who was half American, half Iraqi?
He was his own worst enemy.

★ Irish ★

❖ Did you hear about the Irish orphanage that held a parents' night?

❖ Two Irishmen went into a bar in Scotland. One asked the bartender: "Is there any good fishing around here?"

"Certainly," said the bartender. "The fish are thick in the water. You don't even need to put the rod in – you just reach in and pull them out! Big salmon! On your way home tonight, get your friend to hold you over the bridge by your legs and you can pull the salmon out of the water."

The two agreed: "Yes, we'll try that when we get to the bridge."

So on their way home they came to the bridge and one held the other upside down by his legs, waiting for the salmon. After three minutes, the guy who was hanging down suddenly shouted: "Quick! Pull me up!"

His friend shouted back: "Have you caught a salmon?"

"No – there's a train coming!"

❖ Paddy's wife was about to give birth, so he rushed her to hospital. On arrival, the nurse asked: "How dilated is she?"

"Oh Jaysus!" beamed Paddy. "We're both over the moon!"

❖ An Irishman walked in to a branch of Home Depot and asked: "Can I order 1,400 bricks please?"

"That's a lot of bricks," said the store assistant. "Are you building a house?"

"No," said the Irishman, "I'm building a barbecue."

"A barbecue? Why do you need 1,400 bricks for a barbecue?"

"Because I live on the eighth floor."

❖ How does an Irishman count his sheep?

He counts the legs and then divides by four.

❖ An Irishman went into a department store and asked the sales assistant: "Do you sell potato clocks?"

"I'm sorry, sir," she replied, "I've never heard of such a thing. We sell digital clocks, alarm clocks, carriage clocks, cuckoo clocks and even grandfather clocks, but what exactly is a potato clock?"

"I don't know either," replied the Irishman, "but I start my new job at nine tomorrow, and my wife said to me: 'You'd better get a potato clock.'"

❖ An Irishman applying for a job as a blacksmith was asked whether he had any experience of shoeing horses.

He said: "No, but I once told a donkey to fuck off."

> 66 Irish people love Muslims. They have taken a lot of the heat off us. Before, we were 'the terrorists' but now we're 'the Riverdance people'.
>
> Andrew Maxwell 99

❖ Murphy and O'Flaherty were standing at the urinals in a public lavatory when Murphy glanced over and noticed that O'Flaherty's penis was twisted like a corkscrew.

"Jesus!" exclaimed Murphy, "I've never seen one like that before."

"Like what?" said O'Flaherty.

"All twisted like a pig's tail."

"Well, what's yours like?"

"Straight and normal."

"Well, I thought mine was normal till I saw yours."

Murphy finished what he was doing and then shook himself before putting it back in his pants.

"What did you do that for?" asked O'Flaherty.

"Shaking off the excess drops," replied Murphy. "Like normal."

"Damn!" said O'Flaherty. "And all these years I've been wringing!"

❖ A woman got into a taxi in Dublin and said: "King Edward's Close."

The taxi driver said: "Don't worry, love. I'll lose him!"

❖ A woman walked into a butcher's shop in Dublin and complained about the lamb chops she had bought there the previous week.

"Those chops were six inches long when I bought them, but by the time I'd finished grilling them, they had shrunk to just three inches!"

"That's funny," said the butcher. "My wife knitted me a sweater recently, and the first time she washed it, the sleeves shrunk by three inches."

"What's your sweater got to do with my lamb chops?" asked the woman indignantly.

"Well," said the butcher, "they must have come from the same sheep."

❖ Did you hear about the Irish farmer who tried fish farming but had to give it up after his tractor kept getting stuck in the lake?

❖ Two Irishmen – Mick and Seamus – went to claim disability benefits by lying about being deaf. Mick walked in and the woman behind the desk said: "Shut the door behind you."

"Okay," he replied and shut the door.

So the woman immediately knew he wasn't deaf and threw him out.

On his way out, Mick whispered to Seamus: "Don't shut the door – it's a trick."

Seamus walked in and again the woman said: "Shut the door behind you."

Remembering what Mick had said, Seamus turned to the woman and replied: "Shut it your bloody self!"

❖ Paddy was appearing on the TV quiz show *Who Wants To Be A Millionaire?* The second question was for £1,000, and it was: "Which of the following was one of the Great Train Robbers – A. Ronnie Biggs; B. Ronnie Barker; C. Ronnie Reagan; or D. Ronnie Corbett?"

Paddy said: "I've had a lovely time and I'm going to take the money and leave."

Question master Chris Tarrant said: "Are you stupid? You've only answered one question and you've still got all three lifelines left!"

Paddy said: "I may be stupid, but I'm not a grass."

❖ A major row broke out among the Irish synchronized swimming team at the Beijing Olympics. Paddy accused Mick of copying him.

> Two Irishmen fell down a well. "It's dark down here, isn't it?" said one.
>
> "I don't know," said the other. "I can't see a thing."

❖ An Englishman, a Scotsman and an Irishman were talking about their families.

The Englishman said: "My son was born on St George's Day, so we called him George."

"What a coincidence!" said the Scotsman. "My son was born on St Andrew's Day, so we called him Andrew."

"That's amazing," said the Irishman. "Wait till I get home and tell our Pancake!"

❖ An Irishman went into a hardware store and asked to buy a bath.

"Would you like one with a plug?" asked the sales assistant.

The Irishman said: "Don't tell me they've gone electric!"

❖ Paddy called a wrong number at three o'clock in the morning. "Is that O'Malley's Bar?" he asked.

"No, it isn't," said the voice at the other end, "this is a private residence."

"Oh, I must have the wrong number. Sorry to have troubled you."

"Ah, it's no trouble. I had to get up to answer the phone anyway."

❖ Mick and Paddy made a promise to their old Uncle Seamus that when he died they would bury him at sea. So when the old sea dog passed away, Mick and Paddy wrapped Uncle Seamus's body in a burial bag and loaded him onto their rowing boat.

After rowing for a while, Mick said to Paddy: "Do you think this is far enough out yet?"

Paddy jumped over the side, but the water only came up to his knees. "This will never do," he said. "We need to row further out to sea."

So they rowed some more, until Mick said: "Do you think this will be deep enough?"

Paddy jumped over the side, but the water only came up to his stomach. "No, Mick, we need deeper water than this," he said.

So they started rowing again, and after a while Mick asked: "How about here?"

Paddy jumped over the side, but the water only came up to his chest. "No, this isn't the right place," he said. "Let's row some more."

So on and on they rowed until Mick asked wearily: "Do you reckon this will be deep enough?"

Paddy jumped over the side and immediately disappeared from view. Mick was becoming really worried when finally, after about ten minutes underwater, Paddy broke the surface, gasping for breath.

"Well, is it deep enough, Paddy?" asked Mick.

"To be sure it is," replied Paddy. "Will you hand me the shovel."

❖ The Irish government has announced that, from 6 January 2010, all cars in Ireland will drive on the right-hand side of the road. If the experiment is successful, all other types of vehicle will follow a week later.

❖ Two Irishmen – Murphy and Flanagan – who had fought for the rebels in a South American republic were captured by government troops and brought before a firing squad.

The army captain said: "Are there any last words you would like to say before you are shot?"

"Yes," shouted Flanagan, "I'd like to say that your president is the biggest idiot on God's earth!"

"Quiet!" snapped Murphy. "Don't cause trouble!"

❖ An Englishman, a Scotsman and an Irishman were travelling through the desert when they became hopelessly lost. They realized that their chances of survival were slim but whilst they weren't afraid of dying in the desert, the one thing that terrified them was the thought of vultures pecking the eyes out of their corpses. So they agreed that if any of them were to die, the others would bury him face down in the sand so the circling vultures couldn't get at his eyes.

A few hours later, the Englishman dropped dead in the baking sun, and the other two buried him face down in the sand as agreed. Shortly afterwards, the Scotsman also died, and the Irishman buried him face down in the sand.

Bravely the Irishman trudged on for a few more miles until he, too, collapsed exhausted in the overpowering heat. Summoning his last ounce of energy, he partially buried himself face down in the sand.

As chance would have it, a few minutes later a camel-riding Arab happened to pass by. Seeing the Irishman's butt protruding from the sand, the Arab remembered how long it had been since he last had sex and proceeded to bang away. But before the Arab could finish, the Irishman stuck his head up and cried: "You can peck my arse all you want, you bastards, but you'll never get my eyes!"

❖ Paddy went onto the TV programme *The Antiques Roadshow*, where experts value items brought in by members of the public, and placed a large metal box on the table.

"Where did you find this?" asked the antiques expert.

"Oh, it's been in the attic for years," said Paddy.

"Have you got insurance?"

"Why do you ask?"

"Because you're going to need it – that's your cold water tank."

❖ O'Reilly said to Murphy: "Set the alarm for five in the morning."

"Why?" said Murphy. "There's only two of us."

❖ A policeman was called out to a farm in County Kerry where the farmer had reported losing 2,033 pigs. The policeman took down the details but when he got back to the station to enter the theft onto the police computer, he decided to double check the exact amount with the farmer.

"Mr O'Flaherty," he said, "are you absolutely sure that you lost 2,033 pigs?"

"Oh yeth, dat ith right," said the farmer.

Satisfied, the policeman put down the phone and typed: "Farmer lost two sows and thirty-three pigs."

❖ Paddy and his wife were lying in bed one night but their chances of sleep were being wrecked by their neighbours' dog barking loudly in the garden.

Eventually Paddy said: "To hell with this!" And he stormed off.

Five minutes later, he came back up upstairs.

"What did you do?" asked his wife.

Paddy said: "I've put the dog in our garden – let's see how they like it!"

★ **Italian** ★

❖ A band at an Italian wedding agreed to take requests. Paulo walked up to them and said: "Hey, do you guys know 'Strangers in Da Night'?"

"Sure we know that one," replied the bandleader.

"Dat's great!" said Paulo. "But I gotta one favour to ask. Could you play it in 5/4 time?"

"Isn't it played in 4/4 time?" asked the bandleader.

"Yeah, but dis here's a special occasion, you know?"

After briefly consulting his fellow musicians, the bandleader said: "Okay, we can do that."

Hearing this, Paulo turned and called out: "Hey, cousin Vincenti! Come up here and sing!"

Cousin Vincenti put down his drink, strolled up to the mike, and as the band started to play, he sang: "Strangers in da fuckin' night . . ."

❖ After their failure in the rowing events at the 2008 Olympics, the Italians decided to send a spy over to the British camp to see if he could pick up any tips. He reported back that the British do things the opposite way to the Italians – the British have eight men rowing and only one man shouting and waving his arms.

❖ Two Italians, Luigi and Antonio, met on the street.

"Hey, Antonio!" shouted Luigi. "Where you been for the past two weeks? No one seen you around."

"Dona talk to me, Luigi. I been inna jail."

"Jail!" exclaimed Luigi. "Why you been inna jail?"

"Wella, Luigi," explained Antonio, "I was lying onna dis beach, and the cops come arrest me and throw me inna jail."

"But dey dona throw you inna jail just for lying onna beach."

"Yeah," said Antonio, "but dis beach was screamin' and akickin' and a yellin'!"

❖ If Tarzan and Jane were Italian, what would Cheetah be?
  The least hairy of the three.

❖ How do you brainwash an Italian?
  Give him an enema.

❖ **Why are most New York Italians called Tony?**
  Because on the boat over to America, they wore a sticker that said: "TO NY".

> My Dad used to say, 'When in Rome, do as the Romans do.' That was just before he got locked up in an Italian prison for murdering 20,000 Christians.
>
> Lee Mack

❖ A New York doctor called in his next patient – an elderly Italian immigrant who sometimes struggled to understand the doctor's instructions.
  The Italian opened his jacket and proudly put a model of Buzz Lightyear on the doctor's desk.
  "I'm sorry. What's this for?" asked the doctor.
  The Italian said: "You tell me bring specimen."

★ Japanese ★

> Where's the safest place to be in the event of a nuclear bomb going off?
> Downtown Hiroshima. I mean, what are the chances . . .?
>
> Jimmy Carr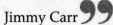

❖   An American businessman went to Tokyo on a business trip but because he didn't like Japanese food, he asked the hotel concierge if there was anywhere he could get American food.

The concierge told him that a new pizza parlour had opened half a mile away and that it did deliveries. Armed with the phone number, the businessman returned to his room and ordered a pizza.

Half an hour later, the delivery guy knocked on the door with the pizza. The businessman took it, but immediately started sneezing uncontrollably. He said to the delivery man: "What the hell did you put on this pizza?"

The delivery man replied: "We put on exactly what you order on phone: pepper only."

❖   On the last day of his visit to New York, a Japanese tourist hailed a taxi to take him to the airport. During the journey, a Honda car overtook the taxi, and the Japanese guy shouted out excitedly: "Honda, very fast! Made in Japan!"

A few minutes later, a Toyota overtook the taxi, and the Japanese guy shouted out excitedly: "Toyota, very fast! Made in Japan!"

Shortly afterwards, the taxi was overtaken by a Mitsubishi, prompting the Japanese guy to shout out excitedly: "Mitsubishi, very fast! Made in Japan!"

The taxi driver had become thoroughly irritated by these outbursts but remained silent until they arrived at the airport. That was when the Japanese guy learned that the taxi fare was $300. "That very expensive," he complained.

The taxi driver replied: "Meter, very fast! Made in Japan!"

Why did Disney World fail in Japan?
Nobody was tall enough to go on the good rides.

★ **Korean** ★

❝ Koreans have recently brought out their own vegetarian version of an instant noodle snack. It's called Not Poodle.

Jack Dee ❞

★ **Mexican** ★

❖ Seeing a man drinking from a stream on his land, an Arkansas farmer shouted: "You don't want to be drinking water from there, it's full of horse piss and cow shit!"

"Sorry, I don't understand," said the man. "I'm from Mexico. Can you speak slower please?"

"Okay," said the farmer. "If you use two hands, my friend, you'll drink it quicker."

❖ Why are Mexicans so short? – Because when they're young, their parents say: "When you grow up, you have to get a job."

❖ Ramona, a Mexican housemaid at a Californian mansion, announced to the lady of the house, Mrs Spicer, that she was quitting.

"But why are you leaving, Ramona?" asked Mrs Spicer.

"I am in the family way," replied Ramona.

Mrs Spicer was shocked. "Who was it?"

"Your husband and your son."

Mrs Spicer was mortified and demanded an explanation. "How did it happen?"

"Well," said Ramona, "I go to the study to clean it and your husband say, 'You are in the way.' I go to the living room to clean and your son say, 'You are in the way.' So I'm in the family way and I quit."

> ❝ According to a new study, there's been
> an increase in the number of illegal
> Mexican immigrants living in Canada.
> You got to hand it to them – that must be
> some tunnel.
>
> Conan O'Brien ❞

❖ Two Americans – Brenda and Kenny – were bungee jumping one day when Brenda suddenly had an idea. She said to Kenny: "You know what, we could make a lot of money running our own bungee-jumping business in somewhere like Mexico."

Kenny thought it was a great idea, so they pooled their money and bought everything they needed for a successful bungee-jumping business: a tower, an elastic cord, insurance, etc. Then they travelled to Mexico and set up on a town square. As they constructed the tower, a crowd began to assemble, and by the time they had finished there were so many people that Brenda decided to give a demonstration.

So she jumped from the tower and bounced at the end of the cord, but when she came back up, Kenny noticed that she had a few cuts and scratches. Unfortunately he was unable to catch her and she fell again, bounced and came back up again. This time she was bruised and bleeding. Sadly Kenny still failed to catch her, with the result that she plunged down once more before bouncing back up. This time she was in a really bad way – she had a couple of broken bones and was almost unconscious.

As Kenny finally caught her, he asked her: "What happened? Was the cord too long?"

Barely able to speak, Brenda gasped: "No, the bungee cord was fine . . . It was the crowd . . . What the HELL is a piñata?"

❖ In times of trouble or stress, I take comfort from enjoying a quiet drink in my back yard while conversing with Jesus. It happened to me only last week when, after a particularly traumatic day, I said: "Jesus, why do I work so hard?"

And a voice came back to me: "It is how man demonstrates his love for his family. He works hard so that he may create a beautiful home for them."

I said: "But I thought money was the root of all evil."

And the reply was: "No, the *love* of money is the root of all evil. Money is a tool; it can be used for good or bad."

I was starting to feel better, but I still had one burning question, so I decided to come straight out and ask it: "Jesus," I said, "what is the meaning of life? Why am I here?"

He replied: "That is a question many men ask. The answer is in your heart and is different for everyone. I would love to chat with you some more, Señor Jones, but for now I have to finish your lawn."

★ **Polish** ★

❖ Two Polish guys were taking their first trip to Warsaw by train. In the course of the journey a vendor came down the corridor selling bananas, a fruit which neither Pole had seen before.

Each bought one. The first man eagerly peeled his banana and bit into it just as the train entered a tunnel. When the train re-emerged into daylight, he looked across to his friend and said: "I wouldn't eat that if I were you. I took one bite and went blind for thirty seconds."

❖ Why did the Polish man quit his job as a restroom attendant?

He couldn't figure out how to refill the hand dryer.

❖ A Polish man complained to one of his fellow workers: "Those bastards in the pub – they told me it would be okay to keep a turkey in the freezer for up to three months. I put one in last night, and when I checked this morning it was dead!"

❖ A Polish guy heard his aged aunt say she had an antique vase that would sell for $10,000 under the hammer. So he smashed it.

❖ Two Polish men met in the street. "Why are you laughing?" asked one.

"It's that stupid dentist," said the other. "He just pulled out one of my teeth!"

"I don't think that's very funny."

"But you don't see! It was the wrong tooth!"

Did you know that the Polish invented vodka?

It takes a Pole to look at a potato and ask, "How do I drink this?"

❖ Two Poles were walking down a street in New York City when a sign in a shop window caught their eye. The sign said: "Suits $10, Pants $5, Shirts $4."

"Hey," said one to the other, "we could clean up at these prices! We could buy all the clothes from this place and sell them at a vast profit back home in Buffalo."

"It sounds like a great idea," agreed the other Pole.

"There's just one thing, though. They might try and con us if they think we're Polish, so when we go into the shop I'll put on my best Noo York accent and you say nothing. Understand?"

The friend nodded in agreement.

Once inside the shop, the first Pole put on an American accent and said: "I'll take fifty suits at $10 each, fifty pairs of pants at $5 each and 100 shirts at $4 each. I'll just back up our truck and . . ."

The shop owner interrupted him. "You're Polish, aren't you?"

"How did you know that?"

"Because this is a dry cleaners."

❖ Did you hear about the Polish electrician who was sacked by the US prison service for refusing to repair an electric chair?
    He said that in his opinion it was a death trap.

❖ Two Polish guys went to London to donate sperm. It was a disaster. One missed the tube and the other came on the bus.

❖ Did you hear about the Pole whose wife gave birth to twins?
    He demanded to know who the other man was.

❖ Did you hear about the ambitious young Polish Army officer who excitedly told his superiors that he thought he had found the mass grave of a thousand snowmen? It turned out to be a carrot field.

⋆ **Russian** ⋆

❝ Russia is a combination of incompetence and evil – like the Post Office with tanks.

Emo Philips ❞

❖ **Did you hear about the new chain of coffee shops in Russia?**
    It's called Tsarbucks.

❖ What's the name of the Russian guy who invented a cure for the common cold?
    Benylin Forchestikov.

❖ At the height of the Cold War, the Americans and the Russians held a secret meeting to determine which nation had the bravest troops. The challenge took place on a cliff in Finland, hundreds of feet above a sheer drop into a raging river.

The American soldier was first to step forward. "Private Miller," barked his platoon commander, "march to the edge of the cliff."

Private Miller saluted, and briskly marched to the very edge of the cliff.

"Private Miller! Jump!" shouted the commander.

But Miller just stood there.

"I said jump!" repeated his commander.

Miller's knees started to shake, but he was otherwise motionless.

"Private Miller, I order you to jump!" yelled the commander.

"I can't," wailed Miller. "I have a wife and a family."

Miller was hurriedly led away for court martial. He had disgraced the American nation.

Now it was the Russian's turn.

"Comrade Ivanevic," barked the Russian commander, "march to the edge of the cliff."

Ivanevic saluted, and briskly marched to the very edge of the cliff.

"Comrade Ivanevic! Jump!" shouted the commander.

Ivanevic jumped off the edge of the cliff, but by some miracle his uniform became snagged on a tree 300 feet down. He was badly injured but was conscious when he was led away on a stretcher. As Ivanevic passed Private Miller, the American soldier asked him: "Ivanevic, how could you do it? How could you jump?"

Ivanevic replied: "I had to. I have a wife and a family."

❖ The President of Indonesia was honoured to receive a special invitation from his Russian counterpart, Vladimir Putin, to visit Moscow. For three days, the Indonesian President was wined, dined and generally granted the full extent of Russian hospitality.

On the final day of the visit, Putin said: "As your stay is coming to an end, it is time for you to play our traditional game, Russian roulette. One of the six chambers of the gun is loaded. You spin the cylinder, point the gun at your head and pull the trigger. You have a five to one chance of living."

The Indonesian President was somewhat startled by the suggestion but knew that his country's pride was at stake. To show fear would bring disgrace upon his people. So he took the gun, spun the cylinder, and then pulled the trigger. To his great relief, the chamber was empty. Nevertheless he had been very impressed by the game and thought of how to match it when Putin visited Indonesia the following year.

It was thirteen months later when Putin set foot in Indonesia. Surpassing even Russian hospitality, the Indonesians plied Putin and his entourage with exotic seafood washed down by generous amounts of alcohol for five days. On the final day, the Indonesian President led Putin to a private room in the palace and announced: "Now at the end of your visit it is time for you to sample our traditional game, Indonesian roulette."

He then took the Russian leader into a room occupied by six beautiful, naked women. The Indonesian President declared: "These women are representatives of our country's tribes. Any one of them will give you a blow job. Take your pick."

Putin's eyes lit up at the prospect but he couldn't see the connection with Russian roulette. "It sounds a great game," he said, "and I can't wait to play, but where is the roulette part? Where is the danger?"

The Indonesian President smiled: "One of them is a cannibal."

❖ While walking down a street in Moscow, a Russian guy was kicking a bottle when suddenly a genie appeared and granted him one wish. The Russian thought for a moment and said: "Well, I love vodka. I wish to drink vodka whenever I want, so make me pee vodka."

The genie granted him his wish, and when the Russian got home he peed into a glass. Although the liquid looked and smelled like vodka, he was still apprehensive about tasting it, but when he summoned up the courage he found that it was the best vodka he'd ever had.

He immediately called his wife. "Natasha! Natasha! Come and see this!" And he then peed into another glass and told her to drink it. She was reluctant at first but when she eventually drank it, she agreed that it was the finest vodka she had ever tasted. They went on to party through the night.

The same thing happened the following night. He peed into two glasses and they drank and partied all night.

On the next night, the guy arrived home from work and said: "Natasha, bring me one glass from the cupboard and we will drink vodka."

She fetched a glass, put it on the table and he peed into it. As he filled the glass, she asked him: "But Boris, why do we need only one glass?"

He raised the glass and said: "Because tonight, my love, you drink from the bottle."

★ Scottish ★

❖ A Scotsman went on his first vacation to Canada. One evening he downed a few whiskies in a local bar and, just as he was about to leave, he noticed a huge stuffed animal head with antlers attached to the wall.

"What the hell is that?" he asked.

"It'a moose," replied the bartender.

"Bugger me!" said the Scotsman. "How big are the cats around here?"

❖ Two Scotsmen – Kenny and Jock – were sitting in a hotel bar discussing Jock's forthcoming wedding.

"How are the preparations going?" asked Kenny.

"They're coming along famously," replied Jock. "The invitations have been printed, the flowers have been ordered, I've sorted out my best man and arranged my stag night. And I've even bought a kilt to be married in."

"A kilt?" said Kenny. "You'll look very smart, I'm sure. What's the tartan?"

"Och," replied Jock, "I imagine she'll just be in white."

❖ A young Scottish lad and lass were sitting on a heathery hill in the Scottish Highlands. They had been silent for a while, when the lass turned to him and said: "A penny for your thoughts."

The lad was a bit embarrassed, but finally he said: "If you must know, I was thinking how nice it would be if you gave me a wee kiss."

So she kissed him.

Afterwards, he once again lapsed into a pensive mood, prompting her to ask him: "What are you thinking now?"

To which the lad grumbled: "Well, I was hoping you hadn't forgotten the penny."

> 66 Nobody thought Mel Gibson could play a Scot but look at him now! Alcoholic and a racist!
> Frankie Boyle 99

❖ A Scotsman was waiting in the queue at the first tee ready to play a round of golf when a small boy approached him and said: "Would you like me to caddie for you, sir?"

The Scotsman eyed him up and down for a moment before asking: "Are ye any good at finding lost golf balls?"

"Oh yes, sir. I'm great at finding lost golf balls."

"Okay, run and search for one. Then we can start!"

❖ Did you hear about the Glasgow advent calendar?

The windows were all boarded up and someone had stolen all the chocolates.

> ❝❝ The Scots invented hypnosis, chloroform and the hypodermic syringe. Wouldn't it just be easier to talk to a woman?
>
> Stephen Brown ❞❞

❖ A Scotsman had recently moved into an apartment in London. One day his mother phoned from Aberdeen and asked him how he was settling in.

"It's not too bad," he said, "but the woman next door keeps screaming and crying all night and the guy on the other side keeps banging his head on the wall."

"Never you mind, son, don't let them get to you. Simply ignore them."

"Aye, that I do. I just keep playing my bagpipes."

> ❝❝ The Beijing Olympics opening ceremony was scary. All those tracksuits and explosions gave me flashbacks to when I was living in Glasgow.
>
> Frankie Boyle ❞❞

❖ Why do Scottish families have double glazing?

So their children can't hear the ice cream van.

❖ An American was visiting Scotland on business. As he stepped off the plane at Prestwick Airport in Ayrshire, he noticed a Scotsman standing beside a long table, on top of which was a selection of human skulls.

"What are these?" asked the American.

"They're the genuine skulls of the most famous Scotsmen that ever lived," came the reply.

"Like who?"

"Rabbie Burns, William Wallace, Bonnie Prince Charlie, Alexander Graham Bell, Arthur Conan Doyle, St Andrew . . ."

"You have the genuine skull of St Andrew himself?" queried the American.

"Aye, I do."

"Hey, I'm part Scottish myself," enthused the American, "so imagine the looks on the faces of my family back home in Maine when I walk in with the skull of St Andrew. I just gotta have it. How much?"

The Scotsman thought for a moment. "Well, laddie," he said, "I was told I'd be a fool to let it go for less than $2,500 but seeing as ye seem so attached to it and it's a beautiful day, I'll let ye have it for $2,499.99."

"It's a deal," said the American, who produced the money in cash and left the airport happy with his purchase.

Back in Maine, the skull proved a real attraction at his local bar where he arranged for it to be hung on the wall. People with Scottish ancestry from all over North America came to gaze at it in wonder.

Five years later, the American returned to Scotland on another business trip and as he got off the plane at Prestwick Airport he noticed the same Scotsman with his table of skulls.

"Hey, what have you got?" asked the American.

"I have the genuine skulls of the most famous Scots in history," came the reply.

"Like who?"

"Rabbie Burns, William Wallace, Bonnie Prince Charlie, Alexander Graham Bell, Arthur Conan Doyle, St Andrew . . ."

"Wait a second," interrupted the American. "Did you say St Andrew?"

"Aye, I did."

"Well, I was here five years ago and you sold me a skull a little bit bigger than that one there, and you told me that skull was St Andrew."

"Aye," said the Scotsman. "I remember you now! You see, this is St Andrew when he was a boy . . ."

> **The scotch egg is such a Scottish food.**
> **It's as though a great Scottish chef said:**
> **'I need a tasty snack. Let's take an egg**
> **. . . and wrap it in meat! Makes it a bit harder.'**
> Bill Bailey

❖ An important time for any young man in Scotland is when he "comes of age" and is allowed to buy and wear his first kilt. A few weeks before his big birthday, wee Kenny went to a tailor's shop and decided on the material he wanted for his first kilt. And while he was there, he also asked the tailor if he could make a pair of underpants in the same material because he had heard that wearing a kilt could be draughty.

A few days later, the tailor called Kenny to say that his order was ready. When Kenny went to collect the items, the tailor handed him the kilt and underpants and told him that there was five yards of the material left over. "You might want to take it home in case you want anything else made of it," he suggested.

So the lad rushed home with his order, and immediately tried on his new kilt. He was so excited that he couldn't wait to show the kilt off to young Fiona next door, but in his haste he forgot to put on the tartan underpants.

When Fiona answered the door, he pointed to the kilt and said: "Well, what do you think?"

"It's very nice," said Fiona admiringly.

"Aye," said Kenny, lifting his kilt in the belief that he was showing her his matching underpants, "and if you think that's good, you'll like what's underneath."

"Oh my!" exclaimed Fiona in shock.

"Aye," he announced proudly, "and if you like what you see, I've got five more yards of it at home!"

> **Where I come from, damp is a colour.**
> Craig Ferguson

❖ A Scotsman took his wife to hospital. She had two black eyes and a broken arm.

"What happened?" asked the doctor.

"She was going through the change," replied the Scotsman.

The doctor was stunned. "Women don't get black eyes and a broken arm when they go through the change!"

The Scotsman said: "They do when it's in my pocket!"

★ Welsh ★

❝ In the Bible, God made it rain for forty days and forty nights. That's a pretty good summer for us in Wales. That's a hosepipe ban waiting to happen. I was eight before I realized you could take a cagoule off.
Rhod Gilbert ❞

❖ Where else but Wales can you get sex, a nice warm jumper and a casserole – all from the same date?

❖ Have you heard about the new online dating site for Welshmen?

EweTube.

❝ Catherine Zeta Jones apparently has bottles of air from Wales in her American mansion to make it smell more like home. If I wanted my house to smell like Wales, I'd just keep kicking my dog until he farted.
Frankie Boyle ❞

NATIVE AMERICANS

* Visiting a Native American reservation for the first time, a US government social worker observed a woman shouting and screaming at a man.

    "That lady sure has your number," said the social worker to the man when the argument had subsided.

    "She no lady," replied the man. "She my wife."

    "Really?" said the social worker. "What's her name?"

    "Wife name Three Horse."

    "Three Horse: that's an unusual name. How did she get it?"

    The man rolled his eyes and said: "Nag, nag, nag."

* As part of the modernization of his tribe and its incorporation into mainstream society, a Native American chief enlisted the services of a church minister to teach him some useful words from the English language.

    As they walked in the forest, the minister pointed to a tree and said to the chief: "Tree." The chief repeated: "Tree."

    A few yards further along, the minister indicated a rock and said: "Rock." The chief repeated: "Rock."

    Shortly afterwards, the minister heard a rustling sound in the bushes and spotted a couple having sex. Embarrassed, he said to the chief: "Riding a bike."

    The chief looked at the couple for a moment, then raised his rifle and shot them both dead.

    The minister was appalled. "We are trying to integrate your people into society. How can we do this when you have just killed two people in cold blood?"

    The chief replied: "My bike."

* When told the reason for Daylight Saving Time, an old Native American said: "Only a white man would believe that you could cut a foot off the top of a blanket, sew it to the bottom of the blanket and have a longer blanket."

On a visit to a reservation, a white US government official asked the Native American chief Running Bear: "You have observed the white man for ninety years. You've seen his wars and his technological advances. You've seen the progress he has made and the damage he has done. In your opinion, where did the white man go wrong?"

The chief considered the question carefully before calmly replying: "When white man find land, Indians running it, no taxes, no debt, plenty buffalo, plenty beaver, clean water, medicine man free. Woman do all work. Indian man spend all day hunting and fishing, all night having sex." Then the chief leaned back in his chair and smiled: "Only white man dumb enough to think he can improve system like that."

＊ A Native American chief and his son were sitting down one day, and the boy asked: "Dad, how do us Indians get our names?"

"It's very simple," replied the chief. "Your oldest brother was born by a river, so we call him Running Brook. Your other brother was born in the early morning, so we call him Rising Sun. Anyway, why do you ask, Broken Rubber?"

＊ When NASA was preparing for the Apollo expedition, they did some training on a Navajo Indian reservation. One day, a Navajo Indian and his son were herding sheep and came across the space crew. The old man, who spoke only Navajo, asked a question which his son translated: "What are these guys in the big suits doing?"

A member of the crew said they were practising for their forthcoming trip to the moon, whereupon the old man became very excited and asked if he could send a message to the moon with the astronauts.

Recognizing a promotional opportunity for the spin

doctors, the NASA people found a tape recorder, and the old man recorded his message. They then asked the son to translate it, but he refused. So NASA took the tape to the reservation where the rest of the tribe listened and laughed but also refused to translate the elder's message to the moon.

Finally, NASA called in an official government translator. He listened to the tape and reported that the moon message said: "Watch out for these guys; they have come to steal your land."

＊ An old Native American Indian lined up all of his ten little Indian sons, stood in front of them and asked solemnly: "Who push port-a-potty over cliff?"

There was no answer, so he asked again: "Who push port-a-potty over cliff?"

There was still no answer, so the old Indian said: "I tell story of Georgie and Georgie father. Georgie chop down cherry tree. Georgie tell truth. Big Georgie no punish."

So the old Indian asked again: "Who push port-a-potty over cliff?"

The smallest boy finally confessed: "I push port-a-potty over cliff."

The old Indian then shook and spanked him as punishment, after which the boy protested: "Georgie tell truth. Georgie no get punished. I tell truth. I get punished. Why you punish, father?"

The old Indian said: "Big Georgie not in cherry tree when it got chopped down."

★　　★　　★　　★　　★

NAVY

★ An Army general and a Naval admiral were sitting in a barber's shop. Both were coming to the end of their shaves when the two barbers reached for some after-shave to slap on their customers' faces.

The admiral shouted: "Don't put that stuff on me! My wife will think I've been in a whorehouse!"

The general turned to his barber and said: "You can put it on me. My wife doesn't know what the inside of a whorehouse smells like."

★ An Army brat was boasting about his father to a Navy brat. "My dad is an engineer. He can do anything. You know the Alps? Well, it was my dad who built them!"

"That's nothing," said the Navy brat. "You know the Dead Sea? Well, it was my dad who killed it!"

★ Why did the Navy change from using bar soap to powder soap?

Because it takes longer to pick up.

★ As a violent storm raged, the captain realized his ship was sinking fast. He called out: "Does anyone here know how to pray?"

One sailor stepped forward: "Aye, captain, I know how to pray."

"Good," said the captain. "You pray while the rest of us put on our life jackets – we're one short."

★ After passing his enlistment physical, a potential recruit was asked by the Navy doctor: "Why do you want to join the Navy?"

"My father said it would be a good idea, sir."

"Oh. And what does your father do?"

"He's in the Army, sir."

★   Two men were walking down the street of a naval port when they saw a drunken sailor on his hands and knees in a large muddy puddle.

"Are you okay, buddy?" they asked.

"I'm looking for something," slurred the sailor, nearly falling on his face. "Can you help me?"

The men looked in the puddle but could see nothing.

Finally the drunk staggered out of the puddle and announced: "I've found it!"

"Found what?" asked the two men.

"The shore!"

My grandfather was in the very first submarine. Instead of a periscope, they had a kaleidoscope. He screamed: "We're surrounded."

★   When an old Navy chief retired to run a chicken ranch, he took with him his long-time companion, his pet parrot.

But the first morning at 4.30, the parrot squawked loudly and said: "Reveille! Reveille! Up all hands! Heave out!"

Roused from his slumbers, the old chief told the parrot: "We are no longer in the Navy. Now go back to sleep."

The next morning, the parrot did the same thing, and the chief told him: "If you keep this up every morning, I'm going to put you in the chicken pen!"

So when the parrot did it again the following morning, the chief kept his threat and put the parrot outside in the chicken pen.

About 6.30 the next morning, the chief was woken by a terrible commotion from the chicken pen. He went outside to investigate and saw that the parrot had about forty white chickens standing at attention in line while on the ground lay three bruised and battered brown chickens.

The parrot was saying: "By heavens, when I say fall out in dress whites, I don't mean khakis!"

★ A Naval admiral and an Army general were fishing together on a lake when a sudden squall blew up and capsized their boat. Both men were left floundering helplessly in the water. Eventually the general managed to right the boat and clamber into it. He then rescued the admiral from drowning by getting him to cling to an oar.

    As the admiral was dragged into the boat, he puffed: "Please don't say a word to anyone about this. If the Navy knew I couldn't swim, I'd be disgraced."

    "Don't worry," said the general. "Your secret is safe. I'd hate my men to find out that I couldn't walk on water."

★ A Navy officer was walking through the crew's quarters of his ship one day and chanced upon a sailor reading a magazine with his feet up on a table.

    "Sailor!" the officer boomed. "Do you put your feet up on the furniture at home?"

    "No, sir," replied the sailor, "but we don't land airplanes on the roof either!"

★ ★ ★ ★ ★

NUNS

❖ An elderly nun was walking home from the convent one night when a young man in a ski mask jumped out from behind some bushes and had his way with her.

    When he had finished, he felt consumed by guilt and begged her not to tell anyone.

    "I cannot keep this quiet," she insisted. "It would be wrong. I have to tell the Mother Superior."

    "And what will you tell her?" asked the young man.

    "I will say I was walking home from the convent when a masked man jumped out of the bushes and raped me twice, unless you're tired."

❖ A priest offered a nun a ride home in his car. She climbed into the passenger seat and crossed her legs, thereby revealing a glimpse of flesh beneath her gown.

The priest was immediately overcome with lust and slyly slid his hand up her lower leg.

"Father!" said the nun, "Remember Psalm 129."

The priest removed his hand but when he next changed gear, he seized the opportunity to slide his hand up her lower leg again.

"Father!" repeated the nun, "Remember Psalm 129."

The priest apologized. "I'm truly sorry, sister, but the temptation was too much. I am only human after all."

Arriving at the convent, the nun sighed heavily and went on her way. When he reached his church, the priest rushed straight to look up Psalm 129. It said: "Go forth and seek, further up, you will find glory."

❖ A priest and several nuns lived in a small rural parish. One day, one of the older nuns noticed that the rugs in the church were beginning to fray. So she went to the priest and said: "Father, I think your rugs need to be replaced soon."

The priest thanked her for bringing it to his attention, and told her that he thought she had been there long enough to refer to church property as "our" instead of "your".

Several days later, the same nun noticed that the church hedge needed trimming. She again went to the priest and told him: "Father, I've noticed that your . . . I mean, our, hedge needs to be trimmed."

The priest thanked her for bringing the matter to his attention and also asked her whether she had seen his watch because it had gone missing. She said she hadn't, but assured him that she would look for it.

A few days later, the bishop paid a surprise visit to the parish. Just as he arrived, the same nun ran into church and called to the priest: "Father, I've found your watch!"

"Bless you, my dear!" said the priest. "Where did you find it?"

The nun replied: "It was under our bed."

❖ What do you call a nun with a washing machine on her head?

  Sistermatic.

❖ Sister Mary Catherine and Sister Mary Elizabeth were walking through the park when they were jumped by two thugs. Their habits were ripped from them, and the men sexually assaulted them.

  Sister Mary Catherine cast her eyes heavenward and cried: "Forgive him, Lord, for he knows not what he is doing!"

  Sister Mary Elizabeth turned to her and said: "Mine does . . ."

❖ What do you call a nun who's had a sex change operation?

  A transister.

Two nuns were in the bath.

  The first one said: "Where's the soap?"

  The other one replied: "Yes, it does, doesn't it?"

❖ A man went into the Sisters of Mercy Hospital for coronary surgery. The operation was successful, and he soon regained consciousness. He came round to find one of the nuns sitting by his bed and gently patting his hand.

  She told him: "Mr Foster, you are going to be just fine. We do have to know, however, how you intend to pay for your stay here. Are you covered by insurance?"

  "No, I'm not," replied the patient.

  "Can you pay in cash?"

  "I'm afraid I can't."

  "Do you have any close relatives who might be able to help?"

  "Just my sister in Colorado, but she's a spinster nun."

  "Nuns are not spinsters, Mr Foster. They are married to God."

  "Okay," said the patient. "Then send the bill to my brother-in-law."

❖ What's the definition of innocence?

A nun working in a condom factory thinking she's making sleeping bags for mice.

❖ A Mother Superior went into a grocery store and said: "I would like to order 120 bananas for the convent."

The grocer suggested: "You'll find that with such large numbers it will work out more economical if you buy 144."

"Oh well," said the Mother Superior, "we could always *eat* the other twenty-four."

❖ A monastery was located right next door to a convent, but the monks and the nuns were not allowed to mix or even to speak to each other.

Early one morning, a group of monks went to take a shower but after they had stripped off, they realized there was no soap. In the belief that the nuns would not yet be up, one of the monks bravely volunteered to nip next door to the convent and steal some soap from the nuns' quarters. So, stark naked, he crept into the convent and quickly found some soap in the washroom. But just as he was about to exit the building, he heard three nuns approaching the front door. He decided that his only course of action was to pose as a new statue and hope that the nuns were taken in by it.

As the nuns entered the convent, they immediately saw the naked "statue" up against the wall in the main corridor. Giggling, they walked up to it and admired it.

"This must be the new figure that the Mother Superior was talking about," said one of the nuns. She then playfully tugged on his penis, forcing the monk to drop two of the bars of soap. "Oh, look! It's a soap dispenser!" she exclaimed.

The second nun also pulled on the statue's penis and the same thing happened.

Then the third nun wanted a turn. She gave the penis an extra hard tug and shrieked: "It dispenses hand cream as well!"

❖ What's black and white and red and has trouble getting through a revolving door?

A nun with a spear through her head.

★ ★ ★ ★ ★

BARACK OBAMA

✳ Barack Obama was seated next to a little girl on an airplane trip back to Washington. He turned to her and said: "Let's talk. I've heard that journeys seem shorter if you strike up a conversation with the person next to you."

The little girl said: "Okay. What would you like to talk about?"

"Oh, I don't know," said Obama. "What about the changes I should make to America?"

"Yeah, that would be an interesting topic," she agreed. "But first let me ask you a question. A horse, a cow and a deer all eat the same stuff – grass. Yet a deer excretes little pellets, while a cow turns out a flat patty, and a horse produces clumps of dried grass. Why do you suppose that is?"

Surprised by the little girl's intelligence, Obama considered the question for a few seconds before finally admitting: "I'm sorry, I have no idea."

The little girl replied: "So do you really feel qualified to change America when you don't know shit?"

> ❝ Barack Obama didn't just appeal to black voters who think he'll change society. He also appealed to white voters who think he's Tiger Woods. ❞
>
> Frankie Boyle

““ I was at a fundraiser for Barack Obama
in Los Angeles and I wanted to have a
really smart question to ask him when I
met him, so I wandered over and said:
'Senator Obama, when you were a student in
Boston, Massachusetts, did you encounter
racism in any form?' And his answer was
really profound. He said: 'I'm Kanye West.'

Sarah Silverman ””

---

* John McCain, Hillary Clinton and Barack Obama all died and went to Heaven. God looked down from his throne and asked McCain: "Do you think you deserve to be in Heaven?"

McCain took a breath and replied: "Well, I think so because I was a great leader and tried to follow the words in your great book."

God looked down and told McCain: "You can sit to my left side."

McCain took his seat, and then God asked the same question to Hillary Clinton: "Do you think you deserve to be in Heaven?"

Hillary thought for a second and then replied: "I think so because I have been fighting for the rights of so many people for so long."

God looked down and told Hillary: "You can sit to my right side."

Finally God turned to Barack Obama and asked him: "Do you think you deserve to be in Heaven?"

Obama smiled and replied: "I think you're in my seat."

““ Barack Obama this week named Nobel
Prize-winning physicist Steve Chu as
his energy secretary, unless he was just
sneezing.

Amy Poehler ””

✳ What do a homeless guy and Barack Obama have in common?

Both are begging for change.

✳ **A lot of voters mistrust Barack Obama because they say he's not a real American. You can see what they mean – after all, he's slim.**

★ ★ ★ ★ ★

OLD AGE

★ A little girl was taking a shower with her grandma when she pointed down and asked: "What's that?"

"That's my beaver," replied the grandma.

The next day the girl was in the shower with her mom and again she pointed down and said: "I know what that is, Mom, it's a beaver."

"How do you know a word like that?" asked her mother, shocked.

"Grandma told me," said the little girl, "but I think hers is dead because its tongue is hanging out."

★ An elderly spinster was so desperate for love that she went to the local newspaper office to put an advertisement in the Lonely Hearts column.

"Well, madam," said the clerk, "we charge a minimum of $1 per insertion."

"You don't say!" exclaimed the spinster. "Here, take $20, and to hell with the advertisement!"

★ Young people aren't cool any more. Instead it's old people who are hip. They're the hip replacements.

★ An old man was telling his friend about the fitness club he had just joined. "I took part in an aerobics class for seniors," he said.

"How did it go?" asked the friend.

"Well, I bent, twisted, turned, jumped up and down, and perspired for an hour, but by the time I'd finally got my leotard on, the class had ended."

> ❝ I'm getting old but at least I can multi-task now. I piss when I sneeze.
> Roseanne Barr ❞

★ Two old ladies were talking at bingo. One said: "Did you come on the bus?"

The other replied: "Yes, but I made it look like an asthma attack."

★ Old people make lovely cakes, but getting their legs in the oven can be a real struggle.

> ❝ Sex is better when you're older, because we don't have to change our sheets. The nurses do it for us.
> Joan Rivers ❞

★ They say that old people are technophobic, but my granddad can't live without his computer – he's on life support.

★ A guy said to his workmate: "I was driving past my grandmother's house today and I saw thirteen pints of milk on her doorstep. I thought, 'She must be thirsty.'"

★ Did you hear about the eighty-three-year-old woman who talked herself out of a speeding ticket by telling the police officer that she had to get there before she forgot where she was going?

Signs That You're Too Old to Trick or Treat

You get winded from knocking on the door.

When the door opens, you shout: "Trick or . . ." and can't remember the rest.

People say, "Great Keith Richards mask!" But you're not wearing a mask.

You ask for high-fibre candy only.

You avoid going to houses where your ex-wives live.

You can strike terror into houseowners just by taking out your teeth.

You have to have a kid chew the candy for you.

You have to choose a costume that won't dislodge your hairpiece.

You're the only Power Ranger in the neighbourhood with a walker.

By the end of the night you have a bag full of restraining orders.

★ A 107-year-old man was asked by a television crew what was the secret of his longevity.

"It's because I gave up sex," he said.

"When did you give up sex?" asked the reporter.

"Fifteen years ago."

"I see," said the reporter. "And why did you give up sex?"

"I had to. I like older women!"

Good Things About Being Elderly

Kidnappers are rarely interested in you.

In a hostage situation you are likely to be released first.

You can sit on the toilet and do the biggest and noisiest evacuation since Dunkirk without the slightest embarrassment.

No one expects you to run – anywhere.

You get plenty of free meals from attending friends' funerals.

People no longer view you as a hypochondriac.

You finally suit a Christmas paper hat.

Things you buy now won't wear out.

You can eat dinner at 4 p.m.

There is nothing left to learn the hard way.

If a sex maniac is on the loose, you are unlikely to be a suspect.

★ An old man was asleep in his chair one afternoon when he was awoken by the sound of the doorbell. He shuffled to the door and when he opened it, he saw a beautiful young woman standing there.
"Oh, dear!" she said. "I'm at the wrong house."
"Sweetheart, you're at the right house," the old guy assured her, "but you're forty years too late!"

Your eyesight won't get much worse.

You no longer have to worry about the shape of your breasts, only whether they touch your toes.

You can jump queues and blame it on being old and confused.

Extortionate dental check-up fees are a thing of the past – you just need to make sure that the glass in which you keep your teeth is clean.

If you don't smell permanently of urine, you are deemed a "catch".

There is no need to worry about losing your looks.

Your investment in health insurance is finally beginning to pay off.

You can have a few drinks too many and merely be labelled a "character".

You can be obnoxious and abusive and merely be labelled a "character".

Your secrets are safe with your friends because they can't remember them either.

★ Two old ladies were discussing their husbands. One said: "I do wish George would stop biting his nails. It's such a horrible habit."

Her friend said: "My Arnold used to do the same. But I eventually cured him of the habit."

"How did you do that?"

"I hid his teeth!"

> ❝ I did a gig at an old people's home.
> Tough crowd. They wouldn't respond
> to my knock-knock jokes until I
> showed ID.
>
> Frank Skinner ❞

★ A man was discussing the problems of caring for elderly people with a colleague at work. He said: "Since my lovely old gran turned senile, all she does all day is stare through the window. I suppose one day I ought to let her in."

★ On a visit to see his grandma, a teenage boy listened while she complained about the high cost of living.

"When I was a girl," she said, "you could go out with twenty cents and come back home with a dozen eggs, two pints of milk, a pound of bacon, half a pound of tea and a fresh chicken."

"That's inflation for you," he said.

"It's nothing to do with inflation," she snapped. "It's all the damn security cameras that shops have nowadays!"

★ A young man told his best friend: "I had sex with a sixty-year-old woman last week and she had skin like a peach."

"Really?"

"Yeah. But have you ever seen a sixty-year-old peach?"

★ Having been playing outside with his friends, a small boy came into the house and asked: "Grandma, what is it called when two people sleep in the same room and one is on top of the other?"

His grandma was surprised to hear such a forthright question from a six-year-old but decided to answer as honestly as she could. "Well," she said hesitantly, "it's called sexual intercourse."

"Oh, okay," said the boy, and he ran outside to carry on playing with his friends.

A few minutes later, he came back in and said angrily: "Grandma, it isn't called sexual intercourse. It's called bunk beds. And Jimmy's mom wants a word with you!"

★ A deaf old lady went to the doctor to find out whether there was any risk of her getting pregnant again.

He told her: "Mrs Hennessey, you're seventy-five. Whilst one can never rule out an act of God, if you were to have a baby it would be a miracle."

When she got home, her husband asked her what the doctor had said.

"I didn't quite catch it all," she admitted, "but it sounded a bit fishy; something about an act of cod, and if I had a baby it would be a mackerel."

★ An old man was sunbathing in the nude when a wasp stung him on his penis. Fortunately he only lived one minute from the doctor's office and was able to get there straight away.

"Can you remove the sting, please, doc?" he asked. "But don't do anything about the swelling."

> ❝ Why do old people pick up the phone and say their number? I know their number, I've just dialled it. Do they open their front door and say their address?
> Michael McIntyre ❞

★ An old man was kneeling by the side of the bed while his wife was lying naked on the sheets. She turned to him and asked: "What are you praying for?"

"Guidance," he replied.

"Pray for stiffness," she said. "I'll guide it in myself!"

★ An old man visited a wizard to see if the curse he had been living with for the past forty years could be removed.

The wizard said: "Before I can do that, I must know the exact words that were used to put a curse on you."

"I can recall them clearly," replied the man. "The words were: 'I now pronounce you man and wife.'"

★ I call my granddad Spiderman. He hasn't got any super powers, he just finds it difficult getting out of the bath.

★ A woman noticed an old man leaving a newsagent's shop carrying a pile of girlie magazines, such as *Penthouse*, *Playboy* and *Mayfair*. Inside the shop, she asked the proprietor what it was all about.

"Oh, him!" laughed the proprietor. "He comes in every week, but I think he must be going blind, because he thinks he's buying comics for his grandchildren."

Catching up with the old man outside, the woman said: "Excuse me, I hate to tell you this, but I think the shopkeeper might be playing a cruel joke on you."

"Oh, him!" laughed the old man. "I've been visiting that shop every week since my wife died. The joke's on him – he only charges me $3 because the fool thinks I'm buying children's comics!"

★ Two sisters were still virgins at the age of eighty-six. Finally in frustration one of them, Ethel, announced: "I'm damned if I'm going to die a virgin. So tonight I'm going out on the town and I'm not coming home until I've been laid!"

Shocked by the outburst, her sister, Betty, warned: "Well, don't be too late. There are some strange people in town on a Saturday night."

All evening Betty waited anxiously to hear the key in the door. At last – at half past one in the morning – Ethel returned and headed straight to the bathroom.

A concerned Betty called through the door: "Are you okay, Ethel?"

There was no answer, so Betty opened the door and saw Ethel sitting there with her panties around her ankles, legs spread, and her head stuck between her legs looking at herself.

"What is it, Ethel?" cried Betty. "What's wrong?"

Ethel said: "Betty, it was ten inches long when it went in and five when it came out. I tell you, when I find the other half, you're gonna have the time of your life!"

★   An elderly couple who still enjoyed an active sex life were shocked when the woman discovered that she had a heart condition which could kill her at any time. Her doctor told her that she had to avoid stress, eat the right foods, and never, ever have sex again because the strain would be too much for her weak heart. Reluctantly the couple agreed to abide by these rules.

However, both got so horny over time that eventually, to guard against temptation, the husband decided he had better sleep downstairs on the couch. That just about worked for a few weeks until, late one night, they met each other on the stairs. She was going downstairs and he was heading up.

"Honey, I have a confession to make," said the woman, her voice quavering. "I was about to commit suicide."

"I'm glad to hear it, sweetie," said the old man, "because I was just coming upstairs to kill you."

★   Three old ladies were sitting in their retirement home reminiscing. The first old lady recalled shopping at the greengrocer's, and demonstrated with her hands the length and thickness of a cucumber that she could once buy for a penny.

The second old lady nodded, adding that onions also used to be much bigger and cheaper. She then used her hands to demonstrate the size of two big onions that she used to be able to buy for a penny each.

The third old lady remarked: "I can't hear a word you're saying, but I remember the guy you're talking about."

★   ★   ★   ★   ★

SARAH PALIN

❖ While tending the hand wound of an old Texas rancher, a doctor struck up conversation with him and pretty soon the topic turned to Sarah Palin and her bid to become Vice-President of the United States.

The old rancher said: "Palin is what I call a post turtle."

Not being familiar with the term, the doctor asked him what a "post turtle" was.

The rancher said: "When you're driving down a country road and you come across a fence post with a turtle balanced on top, that's a post turtle."

The doctor still failed to see the connection with Mrs Palin, so the rancher explained: "You know she didn't get up there by herself, she doesn't belong up there, she doesn't know what to do while she's up there, and you just gotta wonder what kind of dumb ass put her up there in the first place!"

> ❝ Sarah Palin admitted she's smoked marijuana, but she didn't enjoy the experience. Isn't that amazing? Around a hundred million Americans have smoked marijuana, but the only ones who don't seem to like it are the ones who are running for office.
>
> Jay Leno ❞

> ❝ The governor of Alaska is so dumb she thinks the capital of China is Chinatown and that soy milk is Spanish for 'I am milk.'
>
> Wyatt Cenac ❞

❖ Sarah Palin's chief adviser burst excitedly into her office one morning.

"Governor," he beamed. "Some great news at last. Have you seen today's newspapers?"

"I saw that there was a sale on at Bloomingdale's."

"No, even better than that. According to a new post-election survey, people want you to run for President in 2012."

The news was music to her ears. She stood up proudly and announced: "You mean I am the chosen one, the woman of the people? You say that thousands of Republicans have been pleading with me to run for the Presidency in 2012?"

The adviser looked sheepish. "Er, I didn't say they were Republicans . . ."

❝ In Boca Raton, Florida, a woman who looked like Sarah Palin caused a near riot when she walked into a diner for breakfast. After a minute or two, people finally realized it wasn't her when she started answering questions.

Jay Leno ❞

❝ President Obama met with former political rival John McCain. And both men said it was a relief to put their differences aside, sit down, and really make fun of Sarah Palin.

Conan O'Brien ❞

★   ★   ★   ★   ★

PARTIES

* A student decided to hold a party where his guests came as different emotions – fear, happiness, misery and so on. The first guest turned up covered in green paint with the letters N and V painted on his chest.

  "What have you come as?" asked the host.

  "I'm green with envy," came the reply.

  "Hey, that's brilliant! Come in and have a drink."

  A few minutes later, a woman showed up, wearing a pink body-stocking with a feather boa wrapped around her private parts.

  "Wow, great outfit!" laughed the host. "And you've come as . . .?"

  "I'm tickled pink," she said.

  "That's great! Come in and have a drink."

  Shortly afterwards, the doorbell rang again, and this time there were two naked Irish guys standing there. One was standing with his penis in a bowl of custard while the other had a pear on the end of his dick.

  "What emotions are you two supposed to represent?" asked the host.

  "Well," said one of the guys, "I'm fucking dis custard and he's come in dis pear!"

> 66 I went to a party dressed as sodium chloride. Someone threw hydrochloric acid over me. I didn't know how to react.
>
> Tim Vine 99

* On the way home from a party, a wife said to her middle-aged husband: "Have I ever told you how sexy and irresistible to women you are?"

  "I don't believe you have, dear," he replied, flattered.

  "Then what in hell's name gave you that idea at the party?"

✳ A man called over to his neighbour one morning: "That must have been a hell of a party you had last night. Didn't you hear me thumping on the wall?"

"No," said the neighbour, "but don't worry about it. We were making a fair bit of noise ourselves."

> 66 My girlfriend and I went to a dinner party the other night and we ended up playing charades. There was another couple there who were deaf. They were so good.
>
> Zach Galifianakis 99

✳ At a big cocktail party, an obstetrician's wife noticed another guest – a large, oversexed woman – making overtures to her husband. She tried to ignore it until they disappeared into a bedroom together.

Immediately she rushed into the room, pulled the two apart and yelled: "Look, lady! My husband just delivers babies, he doesn't install them!"

✳ As the guest of honour at a high-society dinner party, the speaker was about to deliver his speech when his wife, who was sitting at the other end of the table, sent him a piece of paper with the word "KISS" scribbled on it.

A guest seated next to the speaker said: "Your wife has sent you a KISS before you begin your speech. She must love you very much."

"You don't know my wife!" answered the speaker. "The letters stand for 'Keep It Short, Stupid.'"

✳ A guy said to his friend: "I went to a dyslexic rave last night. Everyone was taking Fs and a guy in the corner was trying to inject a heron."

✳ A bitter divorced guy bumped into his ex-wife's new husband at a party. After a few drinks, he sauntered arrogantly over to him and sneered: "So, how do you like using second-hand goods?"

"It doesn't bother me," said the new husband. "Once you get past the first three inches, it's all brand new."

✳ At a party, an attractive woman was asked by the host whether she would like another drink. "No, I mustn't," she replied. "My husband limits me to one drink."

"Why's that?" asked the host.

"Because," she replied, "after one drink I can feel it; and after two drinks, anyone can!"

✳ A wealthy lady had hired a band, a caterer and a clown for her granddaughter's birthday party.

Shortly before the party was due to start, two bums showed up looking for a handout. Feeling sorry for them, the lady promised them a free meal if they would chop some wood out back. Gratefully, they went to the rear of the house.

The guests arrived, the party got under way, and all of the children were having a wonderful time. The only problem was that the clown hadn't arrived, and soon he phoned to say that he was stuck in traffic and wouldn't be able to get there in time.

Disappointed, the lady tried valiantly to entertain the children herself but she was a poor substitute. Just then she happened to look out of the window and saw one of the bums doing cartwheels across the back lawn. She watched in awe as he swung from tree branches, did midair flips, and jumped high in the air.

So she went outside and said to the other bum: "What your friend is doing is absolutely marvellous. I have never seen such a thing. Do you think he would consider repeating this performance for the children at the party? I would pay him $75."

"I don't know," said the bum. "Let me ask him. Hey, Willie! For $75, would you chop off another toe?"

Did you hear about the guy who went to a fancy dress party as oxygen?

He was in his element.

POLICE

★ Cop: "We arrested this man beating the living daylights out of some poor guy for no reason at all. What should we charge him with?"

Desk sergeant: "Impersonating a police officer."

★ A man was complaining to his friend: "I'm sick of the police telling me how to drive when they themselves are even worse drivers."

"How do you mean?" asked the friend.

"Well, just look at how many signs you see by the side of the road saying, 'Police Accident'."

★ It was the first day of Christmas and all police celebrations in the town were put on hold when they had to investigate a shooting in a park. Officers combed the ground in search of evidence relating to the gun but could find nothing until one keen young detective suddenly started looking in the only deciduous tree in the park – a huge oak that, because it was winter, had lost all its leaves. Sure enough, within a couple of minutes he had found the spent bullet casing from the shooting – crucial evidence that would enable forensics to identify the make of gun.

"How did you know where to look?" asked his senior officer.

"It was obvious when you think about it," replied the young detective. "What do you associate with the first day of Christmas? A cartridge in a bare tree."

Real-life Speeding Excuses

My shoes have just been resoled and I'm not used to the extra weight on the pedal.

I needed to get to the gas station before the fuel ran out.

I was in a complete daze because I've got a new air freshener in my car.

I'm a member of the Royal Family.

I was hurrying to the gas station before they ran out of free glasses.

Thank heavens, officer. I thought the blue flashing light chasing me was a UFO.

I was trying to get away from the car following me.

These "go faster" stripes really do work, then.

I was trying to make up the hour we lost when the clocks went forward.

★ A police officer stopped a motorist for driving too fast in poor visibility. He asked the driver: "What would you do if Mr Fog came down suddenly?"

The driver replied sarcastically: "I'd put Mr Foot on Mr Brake."

"Let me start again," sighed the policeman. "What would you do if mist or fog came down suddenly?"

★ How do you join the police?
Handcuff them together.

★ A police officer knocked on the door of a man's house and said: "Excuse me, sir, have you driven your car at all this morning?"

"No, officer," replied the man. "I've been in bed all morning."

"I see, sir," said the officer suspiciously. "It's just that your car was reported as having been involved in an accident, and I've just felt the hood, and it's warm, so we know you've been using it."

The man said angrily: "Well, why don't you put your hands down your pants and touch your dick?"

"Why?" asked the officer.

Slamming the door in the cop's face, the man yelled: "Just because it's warm doesn't mean you've been using it!"

★ A young woman phoned the police late one night and reported a sex maniac in her apartment.

"We'll be right over," said the officer.

"Oh," she said. "Can you wait till morning?"

★ A policeman came up to me yesterday and said: "Where were you between four and six?"

I said: "Primary school."

★   ★   ★   ★   ★

POLITICS

❖ Politicians may think they're like God, and in some ways they're right: no one believes in them, they haven't done anything for ages and they give jobs to their immediate family.

❖ The 2008 US presidential election was too close to call. Neither the Republican nor the Democrat candidate had enough votes to win. There was talk about ballot recounts and court challenges, but finally both parties decided on a week-long ice-fishing competition, at the end of which whoever caught the most fish would be declared President.

The contest was to take place on a frozen lake in North Minnesota. There were to be no observers present and both John McCain and Barack Obama were to go out separately and return at 6 p.m. each day for the catch to be counted.

At the end of the first day, Obama had caught ten fish but McCain had caught none. The Republicans were certain that their man's greater experience would count in time but at the end of the second day, Obama had a total of twenty-five fish while McCain still had none.

Suspecting a dirty tricks campaign, McCain asked running mate Sarah Palin to spy on his opponent.

Palin duly reported back and said: "You're right, John, Obama is cheating. You're not going to believe this, but he's been cutting holes in the ice!"

> ❝ What I liked about John McCain was that he was always an optimist. He always saw the glass as half full . . . of his teeth.
>
> David Letterman ❞

❖ Why did God give Republicans one more brain cell than a horse?

So they wouldn't shit during the parade.

❖ A lifelong Republican supporter suddenly announced that he was switching to the Democrats on his deathbed.

"I can't believe you're doing this," said his friend. "For your entire life you've been a staunch Republican. Why would you now want to become a Democrat?"

"Because I'd rather it was one of them that died than one of us."

> " The only way you can ever accuse a
> Conservative of hypocrisy is if they
> walk past a homeless person without
> kicking him in the face.
>
> Jeremy Hardy "

What do you get when you ask a politician to tell "the truth, the whole truth, and nothing but the truth"?

Three different answers.

❖ A son in his late twenties was still living with his parents, who worried that he seemed unable to decide on a profession. Even they were unsure what path he should follow, so in the hope of providing some career guidance, they set up a secret test.

They took a $10 bill, a Bible and a bottle of whisky and put them together on the hallway table. The couple then hid from view in the nearby closet. The father explained to his wife: "If our son takes the money, he will be a businessman; if he takes the Bible, he will become a priest; but if he takes the bottle of whisky, then I'm afraid he will end up a drunkard."

Peering through the closet keyhole, they saw their son arrive home and look at the items on the table. First he took the $10 bill, held it up to the light, and slipped it into his pocket. Next he picked up the Bible, leafed through the pages, and put it in another pocket. Then he grabbed the bottle of whisky, had a quick swig, and took it with him. Seeing his son disappear up to his room carrying all three items, the father whispered: "Damn! Our son is going to be a politician!"

> 66 I like Groundhog Day. It's nice to see something coming out of a hole in the ground that's not running for President.
>
> Jay Leno 99

❖ Campaigning in Amish country, a politician stopped outside a homestead, where he saw a young man milking a cow. He casually strolled over to the young man and prepared to make a lengthy pitch for his vote.

But just as he was getting started, an old man called from inside: "Luke, get in the house! And who's that you're talking to?"

"He says he's a politician, Pop."

"In that case," added the old man, "you'd better bring the cow inside with you."

> 66 The Tory Conference are not an attractive lot, are they? I mean, if all those people were born in the same village, you'd blame pollution, wouldn't you?
>
> Jeremy Hardy 99

❖ As the band started to play at an embassy function, a drunken politician asked: "Beautiful lady in red, will you waltz with me?"

"Certainly not," came the reply. "First, you are drunk. Second, it is not a waltz but the Venezuelan national anthem. And third, I am not a beautiful lady in red, but the papal nuncio."

❖ A woman was having a new kitchen fitted, so she rang the council and said: "Can I have a skip outside my house?"

The guy from the council said: "You can cartwheel around the block for all I care!"

❖ In North London, a staunch Conservative man married a woman who came from a Labour-supporting family. The reception was in full swing and everyone was having a great time until the groom climbed on to a table and proposed a toast, "To the Conservative Party!"

Hearing this, the wife's family stormed out, and she herself immediately stopped talking to her new husband.

Later that night, when they got to bed in the honeymoon hotel, he tried to instigate sex with her but she pretended to be asleep and did not respond. After another two futile attempts, he gave up.

However the wife then started to feel guilty and decided that perhaps she had been a little harsh on him. So in a tactical climbdown, she whispered: "Darling, there's a split in the Labour Party and if the Conservative candidate would like to stand, there's a good chance he'll get in!"

The groom replied: "Too bloody late! The Conservative candidate has stood three times already but failed to get in, so he went independent and lost his deposit!"

> You English are a freaky-looking lot. Gordon Brown? Shouldn't he be bashing his head against a bell somewhere?
>
> Brendon Burns

> We all hate paying taxes, but the truth of the matter is that without our tax money, many politicians would not be able to afford prostitutes.
>
> Jimmy Kimmel

> A president doesn't have to be smart. All he has to do is point the army and shoot.
>
> Homer Simpson

❖   Arriving at church one morning, a preacher discovered a dead donkey in the church grounds. He called the police, but since there was no indication of foul play, the police referred him to the public health department. They said that as there was no obvious health threat, he should call the sanitation department. The manager there said he could not collect the dead donkey without authorization from the mayor. The preacher was reluctant to call the mayor, who was notoriously bad-tempered, but he realized that in this instance he had little choice.

The mayor was every bit as irascible as the preacher had feared. "What are you ringing me for?" he raged. "I've got better things to do with my time than worry about donkeys. Anyway I thought it was your job to bury the dead."

Unable to resist the temptation to retaliate, the preacher replied calmly: "Yes, mayor, it is indeed my job to bury the dead, but first I always like to notify the next of kin!"

❖   A travelling salesman got a flat tyre out in the country. Since the spare also turned out to be flat, he knew his only hope was to flag down a passing motorist and get a ride into the nearest town.

The first vehicle to stop was a pickup truck driven by an old man.

"Need a lift?" he asked.

"Yes, please," replied the salesman.

"What are you, Republican or Democrat?"

"Republican."

"Up yours!" growled the old man, and he drove off.

The next car to stop was driven by a factory worker. "Republican or Democrat?" he asked.

"Republican," said the salesman.

"Forget it!" said the factory worker, and he drove off.

Concluding that this probably wasn't a Republican area, the salesman decided to change his story. So when the next car – a convertible driven by a beautiful young woman – stopped, he told her he was a Democrat.

"Jump in," she said, and they sped off down the road.

Soon he found himself unable to take his eyes off her.

He gazed at the wind blowing through her hair, her perfect breasts and her short skirt that rode higher and higher up her thighs. Finally he yelled: "Stop the car!"

She slammed on the brakes and he jumped out.

"What's the problem?" she asked.

"I can't stand this any more," he cried. "I've only been a Democrat for five minutes and already I want to screw somebody!"

★   ★   ★   ★   ★

PRISON

* An American, an Englishman and a Polish guy were on death row at the state penitentiary. The prison governor gave them a choice of three ways to die – be shot, hung, or injected with the AIDS virus.

The American said: "Shoot me in the head." The guards did, and the American fell to the floor, dead.

The Englishman said: "Hang me." The guards did, and the Englishman slumped to the floor, dead.

The Polish guy said: "Give me the AIDS virus." So the guards injected him with the AIDS virus, but the Polish guy just fell about laughing.

"Why are you so happy?" asked the guards.

"Because you guys are so stupid," said the Pole. "I'm wearing a condom!"

> Why do they put alcohol on the arm of a death row inmate before they give him the needle? Are they afraid he might get an infection?
>
> George Carlin

* A man who robbed a number of banks and building societies, disguised as a woman, has finally been convicted. Handing him a fifteen-year prison sentence, the judge warned him that his career as a female impersonator was probably not over just yet.

* The prison governor agreed to listen to the pleas of a woman who was desperate for her husband to be released from jail.

  "What was he convicted of?" asked the governor.

  "Stealing milk," said the woman.

  "I see. And is he a good husband?"

  The wife shifted awkwardly in her seat. "To be frank, no, he's not a very good husband. He's lazy, he hits the kids, he swears at me when he's drunk, and he's had at least four affairs."

  "Well," said the governor, "it sounds to me as if you're better off without him. Why on earth do you want him out of jail?"

  She said: "We've run out of milk."

* An inmate at a tough, maximum-security jail said to a new prisoner: "I've got two tickets for the warden's ball. Do you want to buy one?"

  "No thanks," replied the newcomer. "I can't dance."

  "It's not a dance, it's a raffle!"

* Thrown into prison, a stockbroker was nervous when he discovered that his cellmate was a burly, bearded guy with a big scar down the side of his face and a body covered in tattoos.

  Sensing the newcomer's unease, the cellmate said: "Don't worry, I'm in here for white-collar crime, too."

  The stockbroker let out a huge sigh of relief. "I'm really glad to hear that," he said. "I was dreading being locked up with some homicidal maniac. I was convicted of fraud and insider trading. So what was your white-collar crime?"

  The cellmate said: "I murdered three priests."

* Why is it that prison walls are never built to scale?

* * * * *

PSYCHIATRISTS

* A man made an appointment with a clinical psychologist and explained his problem. "I think I'm a schizophrenic with multiple-personality disorder. Some days I believe I'm a temptress in a Bizet opera, others days I'm convinced that I am the head of the German Luftwaffe in the Second World War."

   The psychologist listened patiently before concluding: "Well, it seems to me that you don't know if you're Carmen or Goering."

* A man went to see a psychiatrist and said: "Doctor, you've got to help me. I just can't stop having sex!"

   "How often do you have sex?" asked the psychiatrist.

   "Well, twice a day I have sex with my wife," said the man. "Twice a day!"

   "That's by no means unusual," replied the psychiatrist.

   "But that's not all," continued the man. "Twice a day I also have sex with my secretary. Twice a day!"

   "Well, I must say that is somewhat excessive," mused the psychiatrist.

   "But that's not all," added the man. "Twice a day I also have sex with a prostitute. Twice a day!"

   "Well, that's definitely too much," concluded the psychiatrist. "You've got to learn to take yourself in hand."

   "I do," said the man. "Twice a day!"

* Psychiatrists and rectal surgeons: they deal with odds and ends.

★   A woman went to see a psychiatrist. "Doctor, I want to talk to you about my husband. He thinks he's refrigerator."

"That's not so bad," said the psychiatrist. "It's a fairly harmless contraption."

"Well maybe," she said. "But he sleeps with his mouth open and the light keeps me awake."

★   What happens when a psychiatrist spends the night with a hooker?

In the morning each of them says: "That'll be $250 please."

★   A psychiatrist congratulated his patient on making such good progress.

"You call this progress?" snapped the patient. "Six months ago, I was Abraham Lincoln. Now I'm nobody!"

A schizophrenic went to see a psychiatrist but was kept waiting for an hour and a half. He was beside himself.

★   A man went to a psychiatrist to say that he had a phobia about answering the phone. The psychiatrist listened patiently to the man's fears, gave him some advice and asked him to come back in two weeks.

A fortnight later the man returned as arranged.

"So how are your problems with the phone?" asked the psychiatrist.

"I think you've cured me," said the man. "Now I answer it whether it rings or not."

★   A new receptionist started work in a psychiatrist's office, but at the end of her first day he felt he had to have a quiet word with her.

"Your general approach is fine," he said, "but try saying, 'We're very busy' rather than 'It's a madhouse.'"

★ A young man was visiting a psychiatrist, hoping to cure his eating and sleeping disorder.

"Every thought I have turns to my mother," he told the psychiatrist. "As soon as I fall asleep and start to dream, I wake up so upset that all I can do is go downstairs and eat a slice of toast."

The psychiatrist said: "What, just one slice of toast for a growing boy like you?"

★ Stan was a fairly good golfer but he always had a problem with the fourteenth hole on his local course. It was a short hole but there was a large lake between the tee and the green, and without fail Stan would drive his ball into the water. It reached the point where he dreaded playing that hole because he knew he would end up in the lake. Eventually one of his regular playing partners suggested Stan consult a therapist to rid him of his phobia.

So Stan booked ten sessions with the therapist who, by hypnotizing him, was able to plant thoughts in his mind. The idea was that whenever Stan stood on the fourteenth tee, he would not see the dreaded lake ahead, but instead a plush velvet fairway leading all the way down to the green.

Six months later, a group of golfers were sitting in the clubhouse when one asked: "Whatever happened to Stan? I haven't seen him around lately."

Another replied: "Didn't you know? He drowned at the fourteenth six months ago."

★ A woman took her young son to a psychiatrist. "He's got attention deficit disorder, doctor."

"Right," said the psychiatrist to the boy. "How long have you had it?"

The boy said: "I'm going bowling tonight."

★ Concerned about his heavy drinking, a man went to see a psychiatrist who told him: "You use alcohol as a crutch."

The man said: "So how come I fall over when I'm drunk?"

★ A man told a psychiatrist: "I can't stop deep-frying things in batter. I've deep-fried my laptop, I've deep-fried my mobile phone, I've deep-fried my DVD player, and battered my jeans. What's wrong with me?"

The psychiatrist took a deep breath and said: "It appears to me that you're frittering your life away."

★ My psychotherapist thinks I have an obsession with revenge ... We'll see about that.

★ ★ ★ ★ ★

PSYCHICS

❖ Driving along the road, a man saw a fortune teller sitting at a table on the grass verge. She was smiling and laughing. Incensed, the man climbed out of his car, ran over to the woman and started hitting her.

As luck would have it, a police car happened to be passing, and seeing the assault, two officers jumped out and quickly handcuffed the attacker.

"What do you think you're doing?" they asked the man.

"I'm sorry," he replied, "but I'd always wanted to strike a happy medium."

❖ Six months after a waiter died, his widow went to see a medium who promised she would contact him in the great beyond.

In the course of the séance, the widow was sure she could see her husband standing in the corner, dressed in his waiter's uniform.

"Maurice!" she cried. "Come closer and speak to me!"

A ghostly voice drifted from the corner: "I can't. It's not my table."

❖   A woman visited a fortune teller who told her that a lot of money was coming her way. That afternoon she was hit by a Securicor truck.

❖   For months, Mrs Rapuchka implored her husband to accompany her to the séance parlour of Madame Helga. "She's a real gypsy, Solly, and she brings the voices of the dead into our world. We all talk to them. Last week, I spoke with my mother, may she rest in peace. For $20 you can talk to your grandfather whom you miss so much."

So Solly went along to Madame Helga's next séance. He sat under a coloured light at a green table, holding hands with the person on either side. They all made a low humming noise while Madame Helga, lost in a trance, ran her hands over a crystal ball.

After a few minutes, Madame Helga called out: "I am in contact with the dead! It is a man, an old man . . . I'm getting a name . . . No, wait . . . He says he is Mr Rapuchka's grandfather."

"Zayde?" said Solly, swallowing the lump in his throat.

"Ah, Solly," a thin voice quavered. "It is good to speak to you after all this time. I am so happy in the other world. I am with your grandmother and we spend all our time laughing and joking."

Solly went on to ask his grandfather half a dozen questions, and he answered each one until saying: "Now, Solly, I must go. The angels are calling. I can only answer one more question. So ask away."

"Zayde," said Solly hesitantly, "when did you learn to speak English?"

❖   A young woman went to see a fortune teller who told her: "You will be broke and unhappy till you are fifty."

"What happens when I'm fifty?" asked the young woman.

"Nothing," said the fortune teller. "But you'll be used to it by then."

❖   A ventriloquist set up a stall in a shopping mall, selling dummies and books about his art, but business was desperately slow. After three months he had hardly made any money and feared that he would have to close down as he could no longer afford the rent. Eventually he confided in his accountant, who suggested: "Why don't you try something completely different? Another client of mine is making a fortune as a psychic, conducting séances. That's where the money is these days."

So the ventriloquist changed his stall and set up business as a psychic, offering three different rates for séances – $30, $50 and $100.

On his first day, a woman asked him about conducting a séance to contact her dead husband.

"Certainly, madam. As you can see there are three different prices of séance – $30, $50 and $100."

"What do you get for $30?" she inquired.

"For $30 you get to talk to your dead husband."

"And for $50?"

"For $50 you get to talk to him and he talks back."

"And what do you get for a $100?"

"For $100, you talk to him and he talks back to you while I drink a glass of water."

❖   A woman went to a séance. "Is there anybody out there?" asked the medium, and a small voice replied in the affirmative.

"Is that you, Bert?" asked the woman.

"Yes," he replied.

"Are you all right?"

"Yes, I'm fine," replied the voice.

"What's it like where you are?"

"It's great," he said. "Today I went swimming and did a bit of fishing."

"You never did any of that while you were alive."

"No. But I wasn't a duck then."

❖   A medium was performing on stage before a handful of people. The theatre descended into darkness, the medium entered a trance-like state and after a couple of minutes of eerie silence, he called out plaintively: "Does the name Old Forge mean anything to anyone here?"

"Well, I'll be damned!" cried a woman on the front row. "That was the name of my grandmother's house!"

The medium said: "Well, my dear, I think I can contact her for you."

The woman said: "So can I. She's sitting next to me!"

You Might Need a New Psychic If . . .

He looks suspiciously like the guy who fixed your leaking tap last week.

His idea of an "out of body experience" involves whipped cream and women's clothing.

His spoon bending requires a pair of pliers.

He says your astrological sign is "those balancing thingies".

He tries to read your tea leaves while they're still in the bag.

Psychics Magazine rates him just below fortune cookies and just above your mom.

He keeps trying to read your palm with his genitalia.

He shakes his crystal ball, then predicts a severe snowstorm.

PUNS

* William Penn, the founder of Philadelphia, had two aunts, who were renowned for their skill as bakers. One day Penn was petitioned by concerned citizens after the four bakeries in Philadelphia had raised the price of pies to the point where only the wealthy could afford to buy them. Not wanting to confront the bakeries, Penn instead approached his aunts, who were so angered by the situation that they offered to bake ten dozen pies themselves and to sell them for five cents less than the bakeries were charging. The old ladies' initiative was a triumph. Their pies sold like hot cakes, and the competition they created succeeded in bringing down the price of pastry in Philadelphia. The two women were feted across the city and their story was subsequently set to music as the Pie Rates of Penn's Aunts.

* After months of excavating a site, an archaeological dig in Scandinavia unearthed an imposing statue of the ancient Norse god of thunder. It was an exciting find, and everyone associated with the dig gathered round to admire the figure's rippling muscles and famous giant hammer. But what really set it apart from similar statues were the dramatic eyes – two dazzling, blood-red rubies that shone menacingly from his warrior-like face.

  Knowing that the stunning eyes in particular would make headlines around the world, the two leading archaeologists on the dig were naturally keen to claim the remarkable discovery as their own and, much to the amusement of the assembled throng, squabbled long into the night as to whose name should be put forward. The bickering finally ceased when they reluctantly agreed to a proposal that the statue be listed as a joint discovery. As their colleagues dispersed, one junior digger turned to his friend and remarked "Well, that was a fight for Thor eyes."

✳ Two geologists were staring at a huge fissure in a rock face. One turned to the other and said: "It's not my fault."

✳ NASA decided to send a team of astronauts to the moon to investigate once and for all whether or not it was made of cheese. They deliberately landed on a part of the moon not visited by previous missions and set about taking samples from the moon's surface.

At first the rugged terrain offered no evidence of cheese but as they ventured further from their spacecraft, they came across an area of outstanding natural beauty where the ground was pure brie. They reported back the exciting news to mission control who immediately ordered them to dig up a large sample. No sooner had they done this than mission control told them to dig up another large sample. The astronauts thought it was fairly pointless and that it might spoil the environment but nevertheless they obeyed the instructions.

Then their radio crackled into life again: "Mission control to lunar landing. Please dig up a third large sample of this brie and bring it back to Earth."

The astronauts protested. "This is an area of outstanding natural beauty, and if we do as you request, we're going to leave three huge holes in it. The place will be ruined. After all, did you ever see such a thing in your life as brie mined thrice?"

✳ After their ship went down, four sailors were able to escape to safety in a lifeboat. Relieved just to be alive, they decided to light a relaxing cigarette. However, although their cigarettes were dry, their matches were wet and so they had no way of lighting the cigarettes.

Eventually one of the sailors came up with a solution. He threw a cigarette overboard, and they were all able to smoke because . . . the lifeboat had become a cigarette lighter.

＊ A young man was walking down a deserted street late at night on his way home from a club. It was raining steadily, so he turned up the collar of his jacket. Just then he heard a strange noise. Bump, bump, bump.

It seemed to be coming from behind, so he turned round and through the rain was able to make out the faint outline of a box following him down the street. Bump, bump, bump.

As the box got closer, he could see that it was a coffin. Bump, bump, bump.

By now he was getting a little spooked, so he decided to walk faster, but the coffin kept gaining on him. Bump, bump, bump.

So he started jogging, only for the coffin to speed up too. Bump, bump, bump.

He was now seriously frightened and accelerated into a sprint as he turned the corner into his street. The coffin started sprinting too. Bump, bump, bump.

Still the coffin appeared to be gaining with every step, but his house was now in sight. Would he be able to make it in time? The coffin pursued him relentlessly. Bump, bump, bump.

He raced up the drive of his house and fumbled for his keys. He could hear the coffin right behind him. Bump, bump, bump.

Sweating heavily, he finally managed to open the door and quickly slammed it behind him, but the coffin just burst through the glass pane. Bump, bump, bump, crash.

Fleeing for his life, he ran up the stairs. Surely the coffin wouldn't be able to climb stairs, but to his horror it could. Bump, bump, bump.

With nowhere to hide, he took refuge in the bathroom. The coffin approached the door. Bump, bump, bump.

Desperately searching for a weapon, he reached into the medicine cabinet and threw a bar of Imperial Leather soap at the coffin. It had no effect, so he grabbed a sachet of Alberto VO5 shampoo and threw that at the coffin. Still the coffin advanced menacingly towards him. Bump, bump, bump.

In a last, defiant gesture, his hand darted back into the cabinet and this time he threw a bottle of Robitussin. And the coffin stopped.

＊ Two young women went into a hairdresser's. One had a mass of curls, the other had straight hair. Both asked the hairdresser for a perm but he said he could only accommodate one, because he was running low on solution.

"Please let me have it," begged the girl with the curls.

"No, let it be me," pleaded the girl with straight hair.

After a moment's deliberation, the hairdresser chose the girl with the curls.

"Why are you giving her the treatment?" demanded the girl with straight hair. "You can see that I need it more than her."

"Ah yes," he said, "but remember the proverb: the curly bird gets the perm."

＊ One Christmas Eve a burglar broke into the home of a prominent local lawyer. He took the lawyer's Christmas gifts from under the tree but left behind those packages intended for the lawyer's wife and children.

As he was leaving the house, the burglar was apprehended by a police officer. Caught red-handed, he had little choice other than to confess to what he had done but he maintained that he couldn't be arrested for it.

"Why not?" asked the officer.

"Because," replied the burglar, "the law states that I'm entitled to the presents of an attorney."

＊ A man told his wife: "If interfering was an Olympic sport, you'd win the gold meddle!"

Why did the medieval queen insist that her personal musicians play in rotation?

It was her minstrel cycle.

✳ Count Dracula had thoroughly enjoyed his night on the town, drinking Bloody Marys in clubs and biting the necks of unsuspecting women. Shortly before sunrise he was making his way home when he was suddenly hit on the back of the head. Looking round, he saw nothing, but on the ground was a small sausage roll.

A mystified Dracula continued on his way until a few yards further along the road he felt another blow to the back of his head. Again he turned around quickly but could see nothing except, lying on the ground, a chicken drumstick. More puzzled than ever, Dracula resumed his journey, only to feel another bang to the back of his head. He turned around instantly but there was no sign of the culprit. Furious, he looked down and saw a cocktail sausage lying on the sidewalk. He stood motionless for a few seconds, peering into the darkness, but could see nothing untoward.

He had walked only a short distance further along the road when he felt a tap on the shoulder. With a swirl of his cape, he turned as fast as he could. Just then he felt a sharp stabbing pain in the heart. He fell to the ground clutching his chest, which had been punctured by a small cocktail stick laden with a chunk of cheese and a pickle. As he lay dying on the sidewalk, Dracula looked up and saw a young woman.

"Who the hell are you?" he gasped.

She replied: "I'm Buffet the Vampire Slayer."

✳ For a display on the walls of their school classroom, a kindergarten teacher asked her young students to cut out and paint pictures of clouds. To make the clouds more interesting and colourful, she decided that they should all have a face and told the children to paint a sulphur yellow lion's face in the middle of each cloud.

The children loved painting the yellow lion faces in the clouds and the end result was stunning, except that one little girl forgot to include the face and just drew an ordinary cloud.

"What did I tell you?" said the teacher. "Every cloud has a sulphur lion in."

* A man was trying to carry out repairs to the edge of the roof of his house. It was a tricky operation, which required delicate balance. Gingerly he crept along the roof until the damaged area was within reach, but just then the roof gave away beneath him and he plunged to the ground, landing right next to three women who were deep in conversation.

As he lay bloodied and bruised on the ground, one of the women turned to him and said: "You've been eavesdropping."

* A woman baked two cakes to sell at her village fete – one for $5, the other for $10. A man soon expressed an interest in buying one and, pointing at the $10 cake, asked her: "What type of cake is that?"

The woman replied: "That's Madeira cake."

* Did you hear about the German vampire who became a poet?
He went from bat to verse.

* One day all the vegetables took a day off from the supermarket and went on a boat trip down the river. But they couldn't decide which of them should navigate the craft along the tricky waterway.

First, a stick of celery tried to steer the boat but failed miserably, nearly running aground. "It's not my fault," he wailed. "I'm only a stick of celery."

Next a potato took a turn at steering the boat but in spite of all his eyes, he got into a terrible tangle. "It's not my fault," he cried. "I'm only a potato."

Just then they glanced across to see another vegetable guiding his vessel effortlessly down river. "Who's that little fat guy in the turban?" they asked. "How come he can steer a boat so well?"

"Ah," replied a passing courgette, "that's the onion bargee."

✳ A farmer who cared for baby animals was stunned by the brutal murder of a piglet. He was determined to find the culprit but the only witness to the killing was a hare from an adjoining field. Since the hare was unable to speak, the farmer lined up his four prime suspects – a cow, a horse, a young goat and a duck – and staged an ID parade. "Right, hare," he said, "I want you to pick out the animal that killed my piglet."

The hare hopped up and down the line, checking each animal, before finally hopping forward two paces and stopping in front of the young goat.

"It wasn't me! It wasn't me!" protested the goat.

The farmer shook his head and said: "Hare's looking at you, kid."

✳ A man walked into Starbucks and ordered a coffee. But when he tried to drink it, he found that instead of coffee, his cup contained a pair of beige cotton trousers.

"Excuse me," he said to the waiter. "This isn't what I ordered."

"It must have been," said the waiter, shrugging his shoulders and walking away.

Seething with indignation, the customer summoned the manager and said: "This isn't what I ordered. I want coffee, not trousers."

"I'm sorry, sir," replied the manager. "It is exactly what you ordered – a cup o' chinos."

✳ Compact disc manufacturers were worried about music industry plans to phase out CDs and bring back LPs. Defending the threat to their livelihood, the CD manufacturers took their case to court, where the judge listened patiently to a lengthy debate about the relative merits of CDs and LPs.

After weighing up the various arguments, the judge ruled in favour of LPs.

The CD manufacturers were furious. "Do we have no right of appeal?" they demanded.

"I'm afraid not," said their lawyer. "The judge's decision is vinyl."

* A little-known fact about William Tell is that apart from being an expert with the crossbow, he was also an accomplished chef. One day he had prepared a new dish for his Swiss friends but, ever the perfectionist, he felt there was something missing from the sauce.

   "Do you think the sauce needs more berries?" he suggested.

   "No, no," they said. "I think you have just the right amount of berries."

   "More salt, then?"

   "No, the amount of salt is perfect," they insisted.

   "Herbs, that's it," he said triumphantly. "I should have put in more herbs. What do you think?"

   "Hmmm," they pondered, tasting the sauce. "Perhaps only thyme, Will Tell."

Two Englishmen were comparing notes on their summer vacations.

   "I stayed at a hotel in Lyme Regis," said one.

   "In Dorset?"

   "Certainly. I'd recommend it to anyone."

* The world of golf has been hailing a new invention that will make carrying a bag full of clubs a thing of the past. The new device that has been attracting so much attention is called the "bee-nut". It is a simple, metal fastener, which, when attached to a golf club, allows the player to adjust the club head to any angle. Thus, for example, a player can use the same club to putt with as he uses to get out of a bunker. Golf clubs with this modification are selling quickly, and players everywhere are taking golfing picnics so that they can try their new bee-nut putter sand wedge.

* Why did the man keep getting back on his bike every time he fell off?

   He was a firm believer in recycling.

❋ A botanist was trying to conduct research into a particular type of fern, so he sent a request to all his colleagues, asking them to forward to him any information they had about it.

Unfortunately, his request was not worded very well, as a result of which all the botanists he had contacted thought he was looking for details about any ferns, rather than just the one species. Consequently, within hours of sending out the request, his fax machine was buzzing with piles of useless documents relating to all manner of ferns – tree ferns, wood ferns, cinnamon ferns, ostrich ferns – but precious few about the particular type he wanted.

In despair, he sent another message to his colleagues: if it ain't bracken, don't fax it.

❋ A woman ran a thriving pet shop in the south of France that specialized in selling exotic breeds of bird. Her supplier was always keen to interest her in unusual species and over the course of several months had managed to persuade the shopkeeper to stock bitterns, storks, cranes and herons.

Then one day the supplier turned up with a wooden crate and said: "Edith, I've got a lovely bird for you here: it's a little egret. Look at the plumage. You stock a few of these, and they'll fly off the shelves."

"No, I don't think so," she said. "I still haven't sold those storks you brought in last month."

The supplier was nothing if not persistent and two days later, he returned to the shop with the wooden crate. "Edith," he said, "have you changed your mind about the egret? Beautiful plumage."

"No," said the shopkeeper. "I am not interested."

Two days later the supplier was back again, carrying that same wooden crate. "Edith," he said, "this is your last chance, because if you won't take this delightful bird, I'll have to try elsewhere. And you know I don't want to do that. So come on, Edith. Won't you reconsider?"

"For the last time," said Edith, suddenly bursting into song, "no, no egrets, no, we will have no egrets . . ."

* A man walked into a butcher's shop and bet him $50 that he couldn't reach the meat on the top shelf.

    "No," said the butcher, "the steaks are too high."

* After spending the night on a park bench, a tramp decided to stretch his legs the following morning. As he was shuffling past the park lake, he heard a cry for help and turned to see a small girl struggling in the water. Without hesitation, he dived into the lake, swam out to the little girl and carried her back to the safety of dry land. There, he wrapped his shabby coat around the girl and was about to ask a passer-by to summon an ambulance when the girl's father appeared.

    "Thank you so much for saving my little girl's life," said the father. "How can I ever repay you?"

    "Well," stammered the tramp, "in case you hadn't noticed, I'm a little short of cash, so a small reward would be much appreciated."

    The father looked in his wallet and pulled out $20, adding apologetically: "I'm afraid this is the only cash I have on me at the moment, but if you can wait until I get to the bank . . ."

    "No, no," said the tramp. "Twenty dollars is more than I've seen in my whole life. It is ample reward for saving your daughter's life."

    The tramp was overcome with excitement and immediately started thinking how he could spend the money. Since he had never been on vacation in his life, he decided to call into a travel agent's.

    "I have $20," he told the travel agent, "and I would like to book a vacation."

    "Any particular destination you had in mind?" sneered the sales assistant. "Australia perhaps, the Bahamas . . ."

    "I don't mind," said the tramp, oblivious to her sarcastic tone, "as long as it's not more than $20."

    "Well," said the sales assistant curtly, "I can tell you now that you won't get a vacation for $20."

"Could you at least look?" asked the tramp. "It would mean so much to me."

"Very well," she sighed, "but you're wasting your time."

The assistant went to the back of the shop and unlocked an old filing cabinet. From the bottom drawer, she pulled out a file that was covered in a two-inch layer of dust. Leafing through the yellowing pages, she suddenly stopped and called out in amazement: "I don't believe it! I've found a sub-economy class, round-the-world cruise for $20!"

"Wonderful!" exclaimed the tramp. "I'll take it!"

A few days later he arrived at the port of departure and saw the most luxurious ocean liner he had ever set eyes upon. But as the tramp headed up the gangplank, the irate ship's captain came running towards him, shouting: "Get off my ship, you filthy bum!"

"But I've got a ticket," protested the tramp. "Sub-economy class."

The captain inspected the ticket and, seeing that it was valid, relented. "Okay," he said, "you can come on board, but not now. I don't want my first-class passengers seeing you. Come back at midnight when it's dark and I'll show you to your quarters."

So the tramp returned at midnight and the captain gave him a tour of the ship – past the ornate state cabins, casinos and ballrooms, through the first-class lounge with its imposing crystal chandeliers and luxurious carpets, descending into second class, which was scarcely less majestic, then down into third, fourth, fifth class, down through the crew's quarters, down through the galleys and the engine rooms until, finally, at the lowest point in the ship, wedged against the hull, the captain opened a watertight door to reveal a tiny, sparse cabin with a hammock, a bedside table and an alarm clock.

"Sheer luxury!" exclaimed the tramp. "A room of my very own."

"I'm glad you like it," said the captain. "There's just one thing. Your sub-economy ticket only allows you to use the ship's facilities at night – when all the other passengers are asleep. That's what the alarm clock is for, so you're not out and about at the wrong time. Enjoy your cruise."

The cruise began, and the tramp had the time of his life. He slept by day and went up on deck at night, playing tennis against a wall, trying his hand at clay-pigeon shooting, and swimming in the pool. Then one night he climbed to the highest diving board and executed a perfect, Olympic-standard dive, hitting the water without causing so much as a ripple. Unbeknown to the tramp, the dive was witnessed by the captain, who had become quite fond of his unusual passenger.

"That was amazing," enthused the captain. "Where did you learn to dive like that?"

"Well, actually it's the first time I've ever dived in my life," replied the tramp.

"Incredible!" said the captain. "I've never seen anything like it! And it's given me an idea. How would you feel about training for a week or so and then putting on a diving display for the other passengers? We could have you perform the highest dive in history and enter it in the Guinness Book of World Records. In return, I'll let you travel first class for the rest of the cruise."

"It's a deal," said the tramp.

So for the next week the tramp honed his diving skills at night while by day the ship's crew erected the highest diving board known to man. The whole ship was abuzz with the record attempt and the identity of the mystery diver.

Come the big day and the tramp, wearing a pair of swimming trunks provided by the captain, emerged from his hideaway and for the first time walked on to the deck in sunshine. The watching crowd gasped in astonishment. The tramp gazed up at the diving board – a slender column of metal that stretched higher than the eye could see.

"Well, tramp," said the captain, shaking him warmly by the hand, "let's see what you can do." And with that, he handed him a walkie-talkie and the tramp started to climb.

Up and up he went. Below him the ship grew smaller. On and on, past seagulls in flight, and still higher until the ship was just a speck on the ocean below. On still further until his head was in the clouds, miles above the ocean. Finally he reached the platform, climbed on to the precarious perch and radioed the captain.

"I'm ready to dive now, captain," he announced.

"Right you are," replied the captain. "Good luck!"

Hearing those words, the tramp put down the walkie-talkie and dived. Down he went, through the clouds, picking up speed as he went. Soon the ocean came into view, then the ship, growing larger by the second, past the seagulls in flight.

"I can see him! I can see him!" cried a hundred voices from the ship's deck, pointing at a tiny dot in the sky.

Faster and faster the tramp descended, hurtling down towards the pool. The crowd was hushed with anticipation. Finally he hit the water without causing so much as a ripple and carried on down . . .

. . . Smashing through the bottom of the pool . . .

. . . Through the first deck . . .

. . . Through the second deck . . .

. . . Through the third deck . . .

. . . Through the fourth deck . . .

. . . Through the fifth deck . . .

. . . Through the crew's quarters . . .

. . . Through the galleys . . .

. . . Through the engine rooms . . .

. . . Through his own little cabin . . .

. . . Through the huge, double-strength steel hull of the mighty ship.

He smashed through the lot, finally coming to rest on the sea bed. Gasping for air, he immediately swam up to the surface, where he was hauled aboard the ship to a hero's welcome.

The captain was beaming from ear to ear. "Well, tramp," he said, "that was the most amazing dive I've ever seen – a world record without doubt."

The tramp blushed modestly.

"But tell me," continued the captain, "the most remarkable thing of all is how you survived smashing through this boat after you dived. How did you do it?"

The tramp looked at the captain and the dozens of well-wishers and replied quietly: "Well, you see I'm just a poor tramp, so you must understand I've been through many a hard ship in my life."

> " Someone left a piece of plasticine in my dressing-room. I didn't know what to make of it.
>
> Tim Vine "

* **Did you hear about the woman who entered a contest for most prominent veins?**
  She didn't win, but she came varicose.

* Tidying her ten-year-old son's room one day, a mother was shocked to find a dozen photographs hidden under his bed, each photo showing frogs mating. She decided not to say anything to him, but instead she waited to see whether the pictures were still there the following week.

  A week later, she discovered that the pile had increased to over twenty pictures of frogs mating, including photos of bullfrogs in high states of arousal and two poison arrow frogs in the actual act of copulation. She was becoming increasingly alarmed by her son's bizarre fascination, but again decided not to say anything for the time being.

  The following week, she looked under her son's bed once more and, to her horror, found that the pile of photos depicting the sexual activities of frogs had increased to over a hundred.

  That evening when he came home from school, she finally challenged him about the pictures. "Son," she said, "why have you got more than a hundred pictures of frogs mating? Don't you think it's a bit weird?"

  "What's the problem?" he asked indignantly. "It's the most natural thing in the world for boys to collect frog's porn."

✳ Trying to sneak back on board ship at three o'clock in the morning following a heavy drinking session ashore, a sailor was dismayed to find the chief petty officer waiting for him. With the sailor unable to provide an acceptable excuse for his tardiness, he was issued with an immediate punishment. "Take this broom," ordered the CPO, "and sweep every link on this anchor chain by daybreak."

The sailor picked up the broom and started to sweep but as he did so, a tern landed on the broom handle. The sailor gestured at the bird to leave, but it refused to move. So he picked the tern off the broom handle and tossed it out of the way. However a few minutes later, the tern returned, once again alighting on the broom handle, and again the sailor was obliged to toss the bird overboard.

This battle of wills continued throughout the night. Each time the tern landed on the broom handle, the sailor tossed it aside, only for it to come back a couple of minutes later. He was so distracted by the bird that he was unable to get much cleaning done as he could only sweep at the chain's links once or twice before the bird reappeared.

As dawn broke, the CPO arrived to check up on the sailor's progress. He was not impressed: "What have you been doing all night?" he barked. "This chain is no cleaner than when you started! What do you have to say for yourself, young man?"

"I'm sorry," said the sailor, "but I tossed a tern all night and couldn't sweep a link."

✳ On his first day at work, an apprentice butcher was ordered to chop up some rabbit carcasses for display in the shop window. He was able to slice through the baby rabbits without any problem but found that the blade was not strong enough to force its way through the adult animals.

After struggling for half an hour, he relayed his concerns to his boss who smiled knowingly and replied: "Remember what they say, son: old rabbits are hard to break."

★   ★   ★   ★   ★

QUESTIONS

★ What would a chair look like if our knees bent the other way?

★ Do deaf people have a sign for "Talk to the hand"?

★ Pencils could be made with erasers at both ends, but what would be the point?

★ If tennis players get tennis elbow and squash players get squash knees, do gynaecologists get tunnel vision?

★ If Jesus was so smart, why didn't he think to turn water into gas?

★ Why is it that when you hang something in your closet for a few months, it automatically shrinks two sizes?

★ Is there another use for multi-purpose compost, other than growing plants in it?

★ Why do protons have mass? I didn't even know they were Catholic.

★ Why do they call it an asteroid when it's outside the hemisphere, but a haemorrhoid when it's in your butt?

★ Does a shepherd get a staff discount?

★ Why doesn't Viagra junk mail come with pictures of naked women so that you can see whether you need it or not?

★ At what stage do you tell a highway it was adopted?

★ Why is it called "after dark" when it is really "after light"?

★ If God had intended us to go metric, why did he give Jesus twelve disciples?

★ If actions speak louder than words, then why can't you hear mime artists?

★ Is it okay to order a club sandwich when you're not even a member?

★ How would a dyslexic person dance the YMCA?

★ Why is "phonics" not spelled the way it sounds?

> I've just been offered eight legs of venison for $100. Is that two deer?

★ Persistent truants: when will they ever learn?

★ Wouldn't it be ironic if everyone went blind in the year 2020?

★ If electricity comes from electrons, does morality come from morons?

★ When the salt said hello to the pepper, was it an example of seasonings' greetings?

★ Why does aspirin come with a childproof cap and yet bullets come in a cardboard box?

★ What does the word for "dots" look like in Braille?

★ A newspaper ad read: "Large unboxed mirror for sale, never used." So how did they know it was a mirror?

REDHEADS

❖ What's the difference between a ginger guy and a brick?
   A brick will get laid.

❖ The council told a man that he had to get his dog neutered. There was no way he could afford to have this done by a veterinary, so he simply dyed its fur ginger.

❖ A man was depressed because his newborn son was ginger and yet neither parent had ginger hair. He just couldn't work out how he had been that unlucky.
   "There must be a simple explanation," said a friend. "If it's not too personal a question, how often do you and Jenny have sex?"
   "Only about once a year."
   "Well, there's your explanation – it's just rust."

❖ Why do ginger people get sunburnt easily?
   It's Nature's way of telling us they should be locked indoors.

❖ What is every ginger's wish?
   To go prematurely grey.

❖ A guy went to a singles bar to look for a bedmate for the night. He sat at the bar and had a few drinks while surveying the possibilities. He finally decided on a cute redhead who seemed to be dancing with a succession of different guys. So he quickly downed another drink, and made sure that he was in position to ask her for the next dance.
   He got it, but it was a fast dance that left him feeling light-headed after all the drinks.
   "How many drinks does it take to get you dizzy?" he asked the redhead afterwards.
   "Oh, only two or three," she answered, adding: "And don't call me Dizzy."

❖ Why didn't Indians scalp redheads?
  Because the hair from a buffalo's butt was more manageable.

❖ Why can't gingers do trigonometry?
Because they can't get a tan.

❖ Why are ginger kids bald for the first six months?
  To allow time for bonding.

❖ Those Harry Potter films are so unrealistic. Honestly: a ginger kid with two mates!

❖ A friend of mine's just had a ginger baby. I told her to keep its head shaved and say it's having hospital treatment.

❖ What do you call a redhead with friends?
  Rich.

❖ A husband went to the doctor and said: "I feel like killing my wife. She's a redhead and she's driving me crazy. Please help me."

  The doctor thought for a moment and said: "Look, here are some pills. Take these twice a day and they'll allow you to fuck your wife six times a day. If you do this for thirty days, you'll finally screw her to death, and the autopsy will simply show that she died of heart failure during sex."

  "Thanks, doctor," said the husband, grabbing the bottle of pills. "I'll start right away."

  Almost a month later, the doctor saw the husband coming down the sidewalk in a wheelchair. His face was haggard and gaunt, he looked to have aged about twenty years and he could hardly move his body.

  "What happened?" asked the doctor. "And what happened to your redheaded wife?"

  "Don't worry, doc," wheezed the husband, struggling for breath. "Two more days and she'll be dead!"

❖ How do you know when your redhead has forgiven you?
   She stops washing your clothes in the toilet bowl.

❖ How do you get a redhead to argue with you?
   Say something.

❖ What do you call a woman who knows where her husband is every night?
   A redhead.

❖ Two sailors on shore leave were walking down the street when they noticed a beautiful blonde.
   The first sailor asked his friend: "Have you ever slept with a blonde?"
   "Yes, I have," said the second sailor
   A little further on, they spotted a gorgeous brunette.
   "Have you ever slept with a brunette?" asked the first sailor.
   "Yes, I have," said the second sailor.
   A few hundred yards further on, they saw a stunning redhead.
   "Have you ever slept with a redhead, then?" asked the first sailor.
   "Not a wink," smiled his friend.

❖ The sun: burning gingers so we don't have to.

❖ **What's safer, a redhead or a piranha?**
   A piranha; they only attack in groups.

❖ What's the difference between dating a redhead and putting your hand into a blender?
   There's a fifty-fifty chance that the blender isn't on.

❖ Why aren't there more redhead jokes?
   Someone told them to a redhead.

❖ How do you know that a guy at the beach has a redhead for a girlfriend?

She has scratched STAY OFF MY TURF on his back with her nails.

★   ★   ★   ★   ★

REDNECKS

✳ To solve a recruitment crisis, the chief of staff of the US Air Force decided to invite all the local young men and women along to an open day at an Arkansas airfield. As he and his staff were standing near a brand new jet fighter plane, two brothers walked over to them.

The chief of staff held out his hand, introduced himself and, addressing the first brother, said: "Tell me, son, what skills can you bring to the Air Force?"

The young man replied: "I pilot."

"Great!" enthused the chief of staff, turning to his aide. "He's just what we're looking for. Get him in straight away to complete all the paperwork."

With that, the aide hustled the first brother away.

Then the chief of staff turned to the other brother and asked: "So, what skills do you bring to the Air Force?"

"I chop wood," he said.

"Sorry, son," said the chief of staff. "We don't need wood choppers in the Air Force. Is there anything else you can do?"

"I chop wood!" repeated the young man.

"Son, you're not listening to me. We don't need wood choppers in the Air Force, not in the twenty-first century."

"But you hired my brother," protested the young man.

"Of course we did. He's a pilot."

"Well, I have to chop it before he can pile it!"

✳ A half-dressed redneck couple were fondling each other on the couch while watching TV. "Look at them homosexuals," complained the man. "They're ruining the sanctity of marriage. We oughta go to San Francisco and show those darned liberals that marriage means one man and one woman. Ain't that right, darlin'?"

The woman replied: "That's right, Daddy."

✳ Billy-Bob and Bubba were sitting in the back of their trailers, drinking beer and talking about life.

Billy-Bob said: "If I snuck over to your house while you were out fishing and screwed your wife, and she got pregnant, would that make us kin?"

Bubba scratched his head for a bit and then said: "I don't think so . . . but it sure would make us even."

✳ A redneck had just been served in a Las Vegas cocktail lounge when he called the young female bartender back and said: "Miss, right now ah really could do with a piece of ass."

"Hell, the most direct proposition I've ever had!" she exclaimed. Then she smiled and added: "Sure, why not? It's pretty slow here just now. There's a room we can use upstairs."

When the pair returned half an hour later, the redneck sat down at the same table and the girl asked cheekily: "Will there be anything else?"

"Sure," replied the redneck. "Where ah come from in Arkansas, we like our bourbon in water cold, so ah still need a piece of ass for mah drink."

Two newlyweds were driving from Dallas to a motel in Austin for their honeymoon. As they arrived on the outskirts of Austin, Jim-Bob reached over and put his hand on Charlene's knee.

Charlene smiled: "Oh, Jim-Bob, now that we're married, you can go further than that!"

So he drove on to Laredo.

You Know You're in a
Redneck Church If . . .

In a congregation of over 500, there are only seven surnames in the church directory.

The collection plates are hubcaps from a 1956 Chevy.

A member of the congregation requests to be buried in his four-wheel drive truck because "It ain't never been in a hole it couldn't get out of."

The opening day of deer season is recognized as an official church holiday.

When they learn that Jesus fed the 5,000, the congregation asks whether the two fish were bass or catfish, and what bait was used to catch 'em.

The baptismal pool is a rusty washtub on wheels.

The communion wine is Billy-Bob's home brew.

The minister and his wife drive matching pickup trucks.

Instead of a bell, you are called to service by a duck call.

The choir is known as the "OK Chorale".

The finance committee refuses to provide funds for the purchase of a chandelier because none of the members knows how to play one.

"Thou shalt not covet" applies to hunting dogs too.

> The choral robes bear the logo "Billy-Bob's Spicy Chicken Diner".
>
> The final words of the benediction are, "Y'all come back now, ya hear."

* Ma was busying herself in the kitchen when she hollered out: "Pa, you need to go and fix the outhouse!"

Pa replied: "There ain't nothing wrong with the outhouse!"

Ma yelled back: "Yes, there is. Now get out there and fix it!"

So Pa strolled over to the outhouse, looked around and yelled back: "Ma, there ain't nothing wrong with the outhouse!"

Ma shouted: "Stick your head in the hole!"

Pa yelled: "I ain't sticking my head in that hole!"

Ma said: "You have to stick your head in the hole to see what to fix."

So Pa stuck his head in the hole, looked around and shouted: "I'm telling you, woman, there ain't nothing wrong with the outhouse!"

Ma hollered back: "Now take your head out of the hole!"

Pa proceeded to pull his head out of the hole, then started yelling: "Ma! Help! My beard is stuck in the cracks in the toilet seat!"

To which Ma replied: "Hurts, don't it?"

★   ★   ★   ★   ★

RELIGION

★ Henry and Ethel attended the same small-town church, where every week Ethel taught Sunday school. After admiring her from afar for years, Henry finally plucked up the courage to ask Ethel out to dinner. To his delight, she accepted and he booked them a table at his favourite restaurant.

At the restaurant he asked her: "Would you like some wine with dinner?"

"Oh no, Henry," said Ethel. "What would I tell my Sunday school class?"

Henry was taken aback and didn't say much more until the end of the meal when he pulled out a packet of cigarettes and said: "Would you like a smoke, Ethel?"

"Oh no, Henry," said Ethel. "What would I tell my Sunday school class?"

By now Henry was totally hacked off. He drove Ethel home in virtual silence but on the way they passed a motel. Figuring he had nothing to lose after two setbacks, he asked her if she wanted to spend the night at the motel with him.

"That would be nice, Henry," she said.

Henry was amazed by her response and quickly checked them both in to the motel where they enjoyed a night of raw passion.

The next morning he asked her: "What are you going to tell your Sunday school class?"

"The same as I always tell them: you don't have to drink or smoke to have a good time."

> " Just saw the Pope on TV. Anyone else get nervous watching a German guy on a balcony addressing a crowd of 200,000?
>
> Nick DiPaolo "

★ **The church janitor was also the organist, so he had to watch his keys and pews.**

★ Whenever a new Pope is elected, a little-known tradition is performed whereby the Chief Rabbi is granted an audience with His Holiness. The Chief Rabbi presents the Pope with a silver tray bearing a velvet cushion, on top of which is an ancient, shrivelled parchment envelope. The Pope responds by symbolically stretching out his arm in a gesture of courteous but firm rejection. The Chief Rabbi then retires, taking the envelope with him, and does not return until the next Pope is elected.

Upon his election in 2005, Benedict XVI was intrigued by this curious ritual, the origins of which were unknown to him. He instructed the Vatican's most eminent scholars to research it, but they were unable to shed any light on the matter. When the time came and the Chief Rabbi was shown into his presence, Pope Benedict faithfully enacted the traditional rejection but, as the Chief Rabbi turned to leave, he called him back.

"My brother," whispered the Pope, "I must confess that we Catholics are ignorant of the meaning of this ritual, performed for centuries between our two faiths. I have to ask you, what is it all about?"

The Chief Rabbi shrugged and replied: "We have no more idea than you do. The origin of the ceremony has been lost with the passage of time."

"Very well," said the Pope. "Let us retire to my private chambers and enjoy a glass of wine together, then with your agreement, we shall open the envelope and finally reveal the secret contents."

The Chief Rabbi agreed, and, fortified in their resolve by the wine, they gingerly opened the ancient parchment envelope. With trembling fingers, the Chief Rabbi reached inside and extracted a folded sheet of yellowed paper.

As the Pope peered over his shoulder, the Chief Rabbi slowly opened out the paper. They both gasped with shock – it was the bill for the Last Supper.

★   The other day I visited a local Christian bookstore and saw a "Honk if you love Jesus" bumper sticker. Having just come from a powerful prayer meeting, I felt particularly spiritual that day, so I bought the sticker and put it on my bumper.

On my way home, while waiting at a red light at a busy intersection, I became lost in thought about the Lord and how good He is, and I didn't notice that the light had changed. It is a good thing someone else loves Jesus, because if he hadn't honked, I'd never have noticed. In fact, at that moment I discovered that lots of people love Jesus. While I was sitting there, the nice man behind started honking like crazy, and he leaned out of his window and screamed: "For the love of God, go!" What an exuberant cheerleader he was for the Lord.

Everyone started honking! I just leaned out of my window, waving and smiling at all these loving people. I even honked my own horn a few times to share in the love. There must have been a man from Florida back there, because I heard him yelling something about a sunnier beach.

I saw another man waving in a funny way with only his middle finger stuck up in the air. When I asked my teenage grandson in the back seat what that meant, he said it was a Hawaiian good luck sign or something. Touched by this act of kindness from a complete stranger, I leaned out the window and gave him the good luck sign back. My grandson burst out laughing; even he was enjoying this religious experience.

A couple of the drivers were so caught up in the joy of the moment that they got out of their cars and started walking towards me. I bet they wanted to ask what church I attended, but that was when I noticed the light had changed. So I waved to all my sisters and brothers, smiled at them all, and drove on through the intersection. I realized I was the only car that had got through the intersection before the light changed again, and I felt kind of sad that I had to leave them after all the love we had shared, so I slowed the car down, leaned out of the window, and gave them all the Hawaiian good luck sign one last time as I drove away.

★ Mother Teresa died and went to Heaven. She found God waiting for her at the Pearly Gates.

"Are you hungry?" God asked.

"Yes, I could eat something," replied Mother Teresa.

So God opened a can of tuna, reached for a chunk of rye bread, and they began to share it. While eating this humble meal, Mother Teresa glanced down into Hell and saw the inhabitants devouring huge steaks, chickens, lobsters and pastries. She was curious but said nothing.

The next day, God again invited her to join him for a meal. Again it was tuna and rye bread and, just like the previous day, when Mother Teresa looked down into Hell, she saw everyone tucking into lamb, turkey, venison and delicious desserts. Still she said nothing.

The following day, mealtime in Heaven arrived, and another can of tuna was opened. This time Mother Teresa could contain herself no longer. Meekly she asked: "God, I am deeply grateful to be in Heaven with you as a reward for the pious, selfless life I led. But all I get to eat here is tuna and rye bread while down in Hell they eat like emperors and kings. I just don't understand it."

God sighed. "Let's be honest, Teresa," he said, "for just two people, it doesn't pay to cook."

★ A man lay dead in the street, surrounded by a small group of people. He was immaculately attired in a top hat, black tail suit, bow tie and patent leather shoes.

"How did he get here?" asked the police officer who had been called to deal with the grim discovery.

"He threw himself off the roof," said a bystander.

"Do any of you know him?" asked the officer.

"I do," said one man in the crowd.

"What religion is he?" asked the officer. "Protestant, Catholic, Jewish, Muslim?"

"None at all, he was an atheist."

"What a shame!" said the officer. "All dressed up and nowhere to go!"

★ God summoned Jesus for a paternal chat. "Have you found any work yet, my son?" he asked.

"Yes," replied Jesus. "I've been offered two jobs – one as a carpenter on Mars at $25,000 a year and one on Earth at $30,000 a year."

"So, which one will you choose?" said God.

"I think I'm going to take the job on Mars," replied Jesus.

God was mystified. "But you've been offered 30K on Earth and only 25K on Mars. I don't understand your reasoning."

"Yes," said Jesus, "but last time I was on Earth I was hammered with tax."

> " I was surprised how British Muslims reacted to the Danish cartoons. How can you get this worked up about a cartoon? But then I remembered how angry I was when they gave Scooby Doo a nephew.
> Paul Sinah "

Leaving church one Sunday, a middle-aged woman said to her husband: "Do you think that Flanagan girl is dyeing her hair?"

"I didn't even see her," replied the husband.

"And that skirt Mrs Fitzgerald was wearing," continued the wife. "Don't tell me you thought that was appropriate attire for a mother of four?"

"I'm afraid I didn't notice that either," said the husband.

"Huh!" scoffed the wife. "A lot of good it does you going to church!"

★   A priest approached a small boy in the street and said: "Could you tell me where the Post Office is, please?"

The boy gave him directions, and the priest said: "Thank you. If you come to my sermon tonight, I will tell you how to get to Heaven."

"I don't think so," said the boy. "You don't even know how to get to the Post Office!"

★   A young woman went to confession. She said: "Bless me, Father, for I have sinned. Last night my boyfriend made love to me seven times."

The priest said: "You must go home and suck the juice of seven lemons."

"And will that absolve me?" asked the young woman.

"No," replied the priest, "but it will take that smug look off your face."

★   Jesus saw a crowd of vigilantes chasing a woman, ready to stone her. "What's going on?" he asked.

The head of the vigilantes answered: "This woman was found committing adultery, and the law says we should stone her."

"Wait!" said Jesus. "Let he who is without sin cast the first stone."

Suddenly a stone descended from the sky and hit the woman on the head.

"Aw, c'mon, Dad!" cried Jesus. "I'm trying to make a point here!"

> " I can't help thinking that Last Supper must have been a bit tense, with Jesus relating the bread to his broken skin and the wine to his own blood. I bet no one touched the meatballs.
>
> Danny Bhoy "

✳ An Irish cop in New York was called to a disturbance in the street. A crowd had gathered to watch a young man who was threatening to jump from the roof of a twelve-storey building.

The cop yelled up to the man: "Don't jump! Think of your father!"

"I haven't got a father," the man shouted back. "I'm going to jump!"

"No, don't jump!" pleaded the cop. "Think of your mother!"

"I haven't got a mother either," said the man. "I'm going to jump!"

"No, don't jump!" yelled the cop. "Think of your children!"

"I don't have any children. I'm going to jump!"

"No, please don't jump! Think of the Blessed Virgin!"

"Who?"

The cop shouted: "Jump, Protestant! You're blocking the traffic!"

✳ A man was struck by a bus on a busy city street. As he lay dying, a crowd gathered around him.

"A priest! Somebody fetch me a priest!" gasped the dying man. A policeman checked the crowd, but there was no priest, minister or man of God of any kind.

"A priest, please!" the dying man repeated.

Then out of the crowd stepped a little old man. "Officer," he said, "I'm not a priest, I'm not even a Catholic, but for the past forty-two years I have lived behind St Mary's Catholic Church, and every night I overhear the Catholic litany. Perhaps I can be of some comfort to this poor man."

The policeman thought it was a good idea and took the old man over to where the accident victim lay dying. The pensioner knelt down gingerly, leant over the man and announced in a solemn voice: "One little duck, number two; doctor's orders, number nine; two fat ladies, eighty-eight . . ."

★ Toward the end of Sunday service, the minister asked the congregation: "How many of you have forgiven your enemies?"

Eighty per cent held up their hands.

The minister then repeated his question, and all held up their hands except one little old lady.

"Miss Carey," said the minister, "are you not willing to forgive your enemies?"

"I don't have any," she replied, smiling sweetly.

"Miss Carey, that is very unusual," said the minister. "How old are you?"

"Ninety-eight," she replied.

"Wonderful!" gushed the minister. "Miss Carey, would you be so kind as to come down out front and tell the rest of our congregation how a person can live ninety-eight years and not have an enemy in the world?"

The sweet little old lady tottered down the aisle, faced the congregation and said: "I outlived the bitches!"

> 66 I phoned up the spiritual leader of Tibet and he sent me a goat with a long neck. It turned out I'd phoned Dial-a-Llama.
>
> — Milton Jones 99

A woman who lived next door to a preacher was puzzled by his personality change in the pulpit. At home he was shy, quiet and retiring but in church he was a real fire-and-brimstone orator, rousing the masses in the name of God. It was as if he were two different people.

One day she asked him about the dramatic transformation that came over him whenever he preached.

"Ah," he said, "that's my altar ego."

★ A woman met a preacher in the street and asked him: "Does your church welcome all denominations?"

"Yes," he replied, "but we prefer tens and twenties."

★ A priest was celebrating the twentieth anniversary of his arrival in the parish. To mark the occasion, the church had staged a special event at the town hall, to be attended by various local dignitaries.

Invited to make a little speech of his own, the priest admitted: "When I first came here, all those years ago, my immediate thoughts were what a terrible town this was. For example, although obviously I cannot reveal his identity, the very first person who entered my confessional told me how he had stolen money from the school charity box, thrown a brick through an old lady's window while drunk, and had been having an affair with the wife of the chief of police. But thankfully I soon discovered that he was an isolated case, and that this town has many warm-hearted souls."

As others then paid tribute to the priest's service to the community, the mayor, who was making the main speech, apologized for arriving late. Taking to the stage, the mayor then began his speech. "I well remember Father O'Riordan's arrival in this town twenty years ago. As a matter of fact, I had the honour of being the first person to go to him in confession . . ."

> ❝ The Church of England recently brought out prayers for Monday morning. It has a prayer you can say if you're on a train and can't find a seat. When I'm on a train, I pray loudly to Allah and I generally get the whole carriage.
> Frankie Boyle ❞

★ A Sunday school teacher was talking to her class of kindergarten students about Heaven. She said: "If I sell my house and my car and give all the money to poor people, will I go to Heaven?"

"No," chorused the children.

"What if I quit my job and spend all my time helping orphans, then do I get to go to Heaven?"

"No," answered the children in unison.

"Okay, so just how do I get to go to Heaven?"

One little boy shouted out: "You gotta be dead first."

★ A priest and a rabbi arrived at the Pearly Gates. St Peter said: "Can I help you, gentlemen?"

"I hope so," said the priest. "Father Feherty and Rabbi Michaels – we've just died and we would like to be welcomed into Heaven."

St Peter studied his clipboard for their names. "I'm afraid not," he said. "You're not on my entry list."

"But we must be," they chorused. "We're pillars of our respective faiths."

St Peter scratched his head. "I'll tell you what I'll do: I'll send you down to Hell for the time being and if Satan is happy to transfer you up here, I'll accept you into Heaven."

So St Peter sent them on their way, chuckling to himself because he knew full well that Satan never lets anyone go to Heaven. But fifteen minutes later, the priest reappeared at the Pearly Gates.

"I don't believe it!" said St Peter. "Satan let you come back?"

"Yes," said the priest. "He was in a good mood and said that for twenty bucks each we could escape from Hell and enjoy an eternal afterlife in Heaven."

"So where is the rabbi?" inquired St Peter.

"I don't know," said the priest. "But when I left, he had got Satan down to $19.50."

★ Two hundred years ago, the Pope decreed that all the Jews had to leave the Vatican. Inevitably the Jewish community was in uproar over the decision and the sheer force of their opposition forced the Pope to agree to something of a compromise. He suggested taking part in a public, religious debate with a member of the Jewish community. If the Jew won the debate, his people could stay; if the Pope won, the Jews would have to leave.

The Jews chose as their representative an elderly man by the name of Moishe who asked for one additional rule to the debate: neither man would be allowed to talk. Despite considering it a strange request, the Pope agreed to this extra condition.

Come the day of the great debate, the Pope and Moishe sat opposite each other on a raised platform, watched intently by their respective supporters. At first, the two men simply studied each other but then the Pope suddenly raised his hand and showed three fingers. Moishe looked back at him and raised one finger.

The Pope then waved his fingers in a circle around his head. Moishe responded by pointing to the ground beneath his feet

Immediately the Pope pulled out a wafer and a glass of wine. Moishe pulled out an apple. Seeing this, the Pope rose to his feet and announced, to gasps from the audience: "I give up. This man is too good. The Jews can stay."

Half an hour later, the inquest was in full swing among the cardinals, who wanted to know why the Pope had suddenly surrendered. The Pope said: "First I held up three fingers to represent the Holy Trinity. He responded by holding up one finger to remind me that there was still one God common to both our religions. Then I waved my finger around me to show him that God was all around us. He responded by pointing to the ground and showing that God was right here with us. I pulled out the wine and the wafer to show that God absolves us from our sins. He pulled out an apple to remind me of original sin. He had an answer for everything. What could I do?"

Meanwhile the jubilant Jewish community had crowded

around Moishe. "What happened?" they asked.

"Well," explained Moishe, "first he said to me that the Jews had three days to get out of here. I told him that not one of us was leaving. Then he told me that this whole city would be cleared of Jews. I let him know that we were staying right here."

"And then?" asked a woman.

"I don't know," said Moishe. "He took out his lunch and I took out mine!"

★ Two women were talking about their experiences of the Catholic Church. One said: "We had a lovely parish priest, Father O'Hara, and because of his compassion and sincerity, I have remained a committed Catholic."

"You've been lucky," said the other. "When my brother was younger, a priest bent him over the altar and took him from behind. The priest called it 'the will of God' but we call it 'the wedding we'll never forget'."

> 66 God must be in prison, because that's where everyone finds him.
> Robert Hawkins 99

★ A priest was walking along the street when he was accosted by a Turk.

"Pictures of leetle boys?" said the Turk.

"Go away," said the priest. "I'm not interested."

But the Turk was persistent. "Go on – pictures of leetle boys?"

"I'm a man of God," said the priest. "Now will you please go away!"

"Last chance," said the Turk. "Pictures of leetle boys?"

"Oh, okay then," sighed the priest. "How many do you want?"

★ On the first day, God created the dog and said: "Sit all day by the door of your house and bark at anyone who comes in or walks past. For this, I will give you a life span of twenty years."

The dog said: "That's a long time to be barking. How about only ten years and I'll give you back the other ten?"

So God agreed.

On the second day, God created the monkey and said: "Entertain people, do tricks, and make them laugh. For this, I will give you a life span of twenty years."

The monkey said: "Do monkey tricks for twenty years? That's a long time to perform. Why don't I give you back ten years like the dog did?"

And God agreed.

On the third day, God created the cow and said: "You must go into the field with the farmer all day long and suffer under the sun, have calves and give milk to support the farmer's family. For this, I will give you a life span of sixty years."

"Hold on," said the cow. "That's an exhaustive lifestyle to keep up for sixty years. Why don't we make it twenty, and I'll give you back the other forty?"

And God agreed.

On the fourth day, God created Man and said: "Eat, sleep, play, marry, and enjoy your life. For this, I will give you a life span of twenty years."

But Man said: "Only twenty years? That's not long to pack in all those things you want me to do. How about you add my twenty to the forty the cow gave back, the ten the monkey gave back and the ten the dog gave back so that I have a life span of eighty years?"

"Very well," sighed God. "If that's what you definitely want."

So that's why for the first twenty years we eat, sleep, play and enjoy ourselves; for the next forty years we slave in the sun to support our family; for the next ten years we do monkey tricks to entertain the grandchildren; and for the last ten years we sit on the front porch and bark at everyone.

✳ A Southern preacher was busy masturbating in the bathroom. As he finished and pulled up his pants, he was horrified to see the window cleaner staring at him.

Two minutes later, the doorbell rang and the preacher, still red-faced, rushed downstairs to answer it.

"I've done your windows, reverend," smirked the window cleaner. "That'll be $100."

The preacher hurriedly paid him and shut the door.

The preacher's wife, who had been listening from the kitchen, said: "A hundred dollars for six small windows! He must have seen you coming!"

✳ Two guys were talking. One said to the other: "I don't understand it. I'm Church of England and you're Catholic; I'm allowed to practise birth control but you, as a Catholic, are not. Yet I have eight kids and you have none. How come?"

The Catholic said: "It's because I only do it during the safe period."

"Really? When's that?"

"When you're out at work."

> ❝ Two guys came knocking at my door and said: 'We want to talk to you about Jesus.' I said: 'Oh, no, what's he done now?'
>
> Kevin McAleer ❞

✳ A little boy was spending the weekend with his grandmother who decided to take him to the park. Admiring the beautiful landscape, she remarked: "Doesn't it look like an artist painted this scenery? Did you know God painted this just for you?"

The boy said: "Yes, God did it, and he did it left-handed."

His grandmother was confused. "What makes you say God did this with his left hand?"

"Well," said the boy, "we learned at Sunday School last week that Jesus sits on God's right hand!"

Three Good Arguments . . .

There are three good arguments that Jesus was black:
1. He called everyone "Brother".
2. He liked gospel music.
3. He didn't get a fair trial.

There are three equally good arguments that Jesus was a Native American:
1. He was at peace with nature.
2. He ate a lot of fish.
3. He talked about the Great Spirit.

There are three equally good arguments that Jesus was Jewish:
1. He went into his father's business.
2. He lived at home until he was thirty-three.
3. He was sure his mother was a virgin, and his mother was sure he was God.

★ Seeking to boost church attendance, a new Baptist minister began making personal calls to the homes of his parishioners. One man, who had not been to church for several months, was implored to join the congregation the following Sunday. It so happened that he was a producer of fine peach brandy and he said that he would attend church, but only on condition that the pastor drank some of his brandy and, more importantly, admitted to doing so in front of his congregation. The pastor agreed and drank up.

That Sunday, as promised, the man attended the service and waited expectantly for the pastor to fulfil his part of the deal. After a few minutes, the pastor recognized him from the pulpit and declared with a visible smile: "I note with pleasure that Mr Finnegan is here with us this morning. I want to thank him publicly for his hospitality this week and especially for the peaches he gave me and the spirit in which they were given."

There are three equally good arguments that Jesus was Mexican:

1. He was born in a barn.
2. He walked around in flip-flops.
3. If he ever did anything, it was a miracle.

There are three equally good arguments that Jesus was Italian:

1. He talked with his hands.
2. He had wine with his meals.
3. He used olive oil.

But the most compelling argument of all is that Jesus was a woman:

1. She fed a crowd at a moment's notice when there was virtually no food.
2. She kept trying to get her message across to a bunch of ignorant men.
3. And even when she was dead, she had to get up because there was still work to do.

★ **What do a pint of Guinness and a Catholic priest have in common?**

Black coat, white collar and you have to watch your arse if you get a dodgy one.

★ When a priest was pulled over for speeding, the police officer noticed an empty wine bottle in his car and could smell alcohol on his breath.

"Father, have you been drinking?" asked the officer.

"Only water, my son," replied the priest.

"Then why can I smell wine?"

The priest looked at the wine bottle and exclaimed: "Oh my Lord! He's gone and done it again!"

★   A priest, a Pentecostal preacher and a rabbi all served as chaplains to the students at a university in Georgia. They met up on a regular basis in the university coffee shop to discuss theology, both among themselves and with any passing students. One day, one of the students voiced the opinion that preaching to people wasn't that hard and that a real challenge would be to preach to a bear.

Although it initially seemed a ridiculous proposition, the three religious men gradually warmed to the idea and decided to put it into practice. They would head off into the woods separately, find a bear, preach to it, and attempt to convert it.

Two weeks later, they all met up again to compare notes as to how they had fared with their respective bear conversions.

Father O'Reilly was first to speak. He had his arm in a sling, was on crutches and was heavily bandaged around the head. "Well," he said, "I went into the woods to find me a bear. And when I found him, I began to read to him from the Catechism. At first, that bear was not at all receptive and began slapping me around with his huge paws, but when I sprinkled him with holy water, he became as gentle as a lamb. The bishop is coming out next week to give him first communion and confirmation."

Reverend Joe Bob Pearson spoke next. He was in a wheelchair, with an arm and both legs in casts and he was connected to an intravenous drip. "Well, brothers," he began, "I went out and found me a bear and began to read to him from God's holy book. But that bear wanted nothing to do with me, and started snarling and growling. But let me tell you brothers, I was not prepared to let that bear reject the word of God, so I grabbed hold of him and we wrestled – my, how we wrestled – down one hill, up another, and down another until we came to a creek. And when we came to that creek, brothers, I quickly pushed his head under the water and baptized his hairy soul. And just like you said, he became as gentle as a lamb. We spent the rest of the day praising Jesus."

They both turned to Rabbi Goldblum, who was lying in

a hospital bed. He was in a full body cast and traction with intravenous drips and tubing connected to at least a dozen parts of his body. He was in a really bad way. Barely able to speak, the rabbi looked up plaintively at the other two and gasped: "Looking back on it, circumcision may not have been the best way to start things off . . ."

> ❝ I know that Abu Hamza's a hate preacher but it must be terrible to go through life with two hooks for hands.
> Luckily, he likes corn on the cob.
>
> Frank Skinner ❞

★ A preacher was winding up his temperance sermon with tremendous fervour. "If I had all the beer in the world," he roared, "I'd take it and throw it into the river."

And the congregation cried, "Amen!"

"If I had all the wine in the world," continued the preacher, "I'd take it and throw it in the river."

And the congregation cried, "Amen!"

"If I had all the whisky and rum in the world, I'd take it and throw it in the river."

And the congregation cried, "Hallelujah!"

With that, the preacher sat down. The song leader then stood up very tentatively and announced: "For our closing song, let us sing hymn number 365, 'Shall We Gather at the River . . .'"

> ❝ I like Jesus, but he loves me, so it's awkward.
>
> Tom Stade ❞

★ A Catholic boy was lying in the road seriously injured after being hit by a car outside a church. A passer-by ran over to him and asked: "Would you like me to fetch a priest?"

The boy replied: "Can't you see I've just been hit by a car? Sex is the last thing on my mind!"

★ Christianity: one woman's lie about having an affair that got seriously out of hand.

> ❝ I like the Ten Commandments but I have a problem with the Ninth. It should be: 'Thou shalt not covet thy neighbour's ox, except in Scrabble.'
> David O'Doherty ❞

★ For years, two brothers had used their wealth to hide their evil ways from the community. On the face of it, they were devoted Christians, even attending the same small-town church, but the truth was that they were crooked and corrupt.

When a new pastor joined the church, attendances rose markedly, prompting a fund-raising campaign to be launched to build a new, larger place of worship. The straight-talking pastor loved interacting with his parishioners but he had no time for the brothers and could see them for what they really were.

Then one of the brothers died suddenly. The day before the funeral, the surviving brother sought out the pastor and handed him a cheque for the amount needed to finish paying for the new church. "I have only one condition," he said. "At his funeral, you must say my brother was a saint."

The pastor gave his word and deposited the cheque in the bank. The next day at the funeral, he did not hold back. "He was an evil man," he declared from the pulpit. "He cheated on his wife, abused his family and bribed local officials. He lived a life of greed, dishonesty and deception. But compared to his brother, he was a saint."

> ❝ What if God is a woman? Not only am I going to Hell, but I'll never know why.
> Adam Ferrera ❞

★ A huge beech tree stood next to a cemetery fence on the outskirts of town. One day, two boys filled up a bucket with nuts that had fallen from the branches and sat down next to the tree, out of view from the path that ran alongside the graveyard, to divide up the nuts.

"One for you, one for me. One for you, one for me," said one of the boys, sharing out the nuts equally. The bucket was so full that several nuts rolled out towards the fence.

Cycling along the path adjacent to the cemetery was a third boy. As he passed, he heard voices from within and stopped to investigate. Pressing his ear to the fence, he heard: "One for you, one for me. One for you, one for me." He was immediately stricken with horror. "Oh no!" he shuddered. "It's Satan and St Peter dividing the souls at the cemetery!"

He cycled down the path as fast as he could until he met an old man hobbling along with a cane. "Come quick!" gasped the boy. "You won't believe what I just heard: Satan and St Peter are up at the cemetery dividing the souls."

"What nonsense!" said the old man. "Don't waste my time with such silly stories. Can't you see I'm struggling to walk as it is?"

But the boy persisted and eventually the old man relented and hobbled up to the cemetery. Standing by the fence, they heard: "One for you, one for me. One for you, one for me."

The old man whispered: "Boy, you've been telling the truth. Let's see if we can see the devil himself."

Quaking with fear, they peered through the fence in the hope of catching a glimpse of Satan. Tighter and tighter they gripped the wrought iron bars, but still they were unable to see anything.

Finally they heard: "One for you, one for me. And one last one for you. That's all. Now let's go and get those nuts by the fence and we'll be done."

It is said that the old man made it back to town five minutes before the boy.

★ A vicar, notorious for his lengthy sermons, watched as a man got up and left halfway through his message. The same man returned just before the finish.

Afterwards the vicar asked him where he had gone.

"I went to get a haircut," said the man.

"Why didn't you do that before the service?" asked the vicar.

"I didn't need one then!"

★ A young woman travelling home on a flight from France to the United States turned to the priest sitting next to her and said: "Father, I wonder if I could ask you a favour?"

"Certainly, my dear," he replied.

"You see," she said, "in Paris I bought an expensive electronic hairdryer that is well over customs limits, and I'm worried they'll confiscate it. Could you possibly carry it through customs for me – under your robes, perhaps?"

"I'd love to help you," said the priest, "and I will do what I can but I must warn you: I will not lie."

"Very well, Father. I understand. And thank you."

When they arrived at customs, she let the priest go through first. The customs official asked: "Father, do you have anything to declare?"

The priest answered: "From the top of my head down to my waist, I have nothing to declare."

Puzzled by this response, the official asked: "And what do you have to declare from your waist to the floor?"

The priest said: "I have a marvellous little device designed to be used on a woman, but which is, to date, unused."

The official smiled knowingly and said: "Very good, Father. Go through . . . Next!"

> ❝ Bishops tried to take a step forward by introducing female bishops. It failed. Everyone knows bishops can only move diagonally.
>
> Jimmy Carr ❞

★ A priest and a pastor stood by the side of a road holding up a sign that said: "The End Is Near! Turn yourself around now before it's too late!"

They planned to hold the sign up to each passing car, but as the first driver sped by, he yelled: "Leave us alone, you religious nuts!"

Seconds later, from around the corner they heard a screech of tyres followed by a loud splash.

The priest turned to the pastor and said: "Do you not think that instead we should just put up a sign that says "Bridge Out"?"

★ ★ ★ ★ ★

RIDDLES

❖ What's the difference between PMS and BSE? – One attacks the poor cow's brain and sends it mental. The other is an agricultural problem.

❖ Why do seagulls have wings? – To beat tramps to the dumpster.

❖ How do you stop your mouth from freezing? – Grit your teeth.

❖ What gets longer when pulled, fits between breasts, inserts neatly into a slot and works best when jerked? – A seat belt.

❖ What was Beethoven's favourite fruit? – "Bananana."

❖ What's pink and fluffy? – Pink fluff.

❖ What's blue and fluffy? – Pink fluff holding its breath.

❖ What do you get if you add two apples and three apples? – A high-school math problem.

❖ What's the best thing about fingering a gypsy when she's on her period? – You get your palm red for free.

❖ What's the difference between a unicorn and a lettuce? – One is a funny beast, the other is a bunny feast.

❖ What did one palm tree say to the other? – Let's have a date.

❖ Did you hear about the frog that broke down? – He got toad away.

❖ What's the difference between stress, tension and panic? – Stress is when your wife is pregnant, tension is when your girlfriend is pregnant, and panic is when both are pregnant.

❖ How do you get even with a blind guy? – Leave a plunger in the toilet.

❖ Why do journalists wear shirts that don't need ironing? – Freedom of the press.

❖ What's the height of suspicion? – Seeing the coalman leaving your house with one clean finger.

❖ When isn't it a good time to ask someone to cut you some slack? – When you're bungee jumping.

❖ What do you call a person who keeps on talking when people are no longer interested? – A teacher.

❖ How do you make antifreeze? – Steal her rug.

❖ What's red and white and sits in trees? – A sanitary owl.

❖ What's the difference between Noah's Ark and Joan of Arc?
– Noah's Ark was made of wood and Joan of Arc was Maid
of Orleans.

❖ What is the blood type of all pessimists? – B negative.

❖ What's the difference between mayonnaise and sperm? –
Mayonnaise doesn't hit the back of a girl's throat at thirty
miles an hour.

What do you call a hippie's wife? – Mississippi.

❖ What are the three fastest forms of communication? –
Telephone, television, tellawoman.

❖ Why do deaf women wear tight panties? – So you can read
their lips.

❖ What did Speedy Gonzales say to his wife on their
honeymoon? – This won't hurt, did it?

❖ What's black and white and goes round and round? – A
penguin in a revolving door.

❖ Why did the admiral decide against buying a new hat? – He
was afraid of cap sizing.

❖ What is the difference between a well-dressed man on a
tricycle and a badly dressed man on a bicycle? – A tire.

❖ Why was there no room at the inn for Joseph and Mary?
– Because it was Christmas.

❖ What is red and has seven dents? – Snow White's cherry.

❖ What's long, yellow and fruity? – An apple in disguise.

❖ What do you call seafood in a cement mixer? – Hardcore prawn.

❖ Everyone knows that two wrongs don't make a right, but what did two rights make? – The first airplane.

❖ Why did the poop commit suicide? – Because its life was going down the pan.

❖ What does DAM stand for? – Mothers Against Dyslexia.

❖ What's hairy on the outside, wet on the inside, starts with "c', ends with "t", and has a "u" and an "n" in the middle? – A coconut

❖ What's the difference between a photo-copier and the flu? – One makes facsimiles and the other makes sick families.

❖ How can you tell when Barbie has her period? – Your Tic Tacs are missing.

❖ Why is it hard for a ghost to tell a lie? – Because you can see right through him.

❖ What do you have if you have one large green ball in your left hand and one large green ball in your right hand? – The undivided attention of the Jolly Green Giant.

❖ What's the hardest thing about eating vegetables? – The life-support equipment.

❖ Why don't prawns give to charity? – Because they're shellfish.

❖ Who was the greatest financier in the Bible? – Noah. He was floating his stock while everyone else was in liquidation.

❖ Why did the boa constrictors get married? – They had a crush on each other.

❖ If there is H_2O on the inside of a fire hydrant, what is on the outside? – K_9P.

❖ How did the woman feel after having a joss stick shoved up her butt by a hippie? – She was incensed.

❖ Why was the guitarist nervous? – Because he was always fretting about something.

❖ What's grey, lifeless and comes from Antarctica? – A melted penguin.

❖ Why are photographers so depressed? – Because they always focus on the negatives.

❖ What did the tampon say to the other tampon in school? – I'll see you next period.

❖ How can you get four suits for a dollar? – Buy a pack of cards.

❖ Why did the eagles grow their claws extra long? – To take part in a talon contest.

❖ What's the definition of perfect balance? – A pregnant hunchback.

❖ What do you call someone who can't tell the difference between a spoon and a ladle? – Fat.

★   ★   ★   ★   ★

ROYALTY

✳ For her wedding to Prince Charles, Camilla bought new shoes, which got increasingly tight around her feet as the wedding day wore on. That night, when the festivities were finally over and the newlyweds were able to retire to their room, Camilla flopped on the bed and said: "Charles, be a dear. Take my shoes off – my feet are absolutely killing me."

Her ever-obedient Prince of Wales worked vigorously on her right shoe, but it would not budge.

"Harder!" yelled Camilla.

Charles shouted back: "I'm trying, my darling! But it's just so blooming tight!"

"Come on, my prince!" she cried. "Give it all you've got!"

At last the shoe was released from her foot, prompting Charles to let out a loud groan and Camilla to exclaim: "Ooooh, God! That feels sooo good!"

In their bedroom next door, the Queen said to Prince Philip: "See? I told you, with a face like that, she would still be a virgin!"

Just then, as Charles tried to remove Camilla's left shoe, he cried: "Oh, bloody hell, darling! This one's even tighter!"

To which Prince Philip said to the Queen: "That's my boy: once a Navy man, always a Navy man!"

✳ It's a good thing King Cnut wasn't dyslexic.

✳ A man parked his car outside Buckingham Palace, and immediately a parking attendant ran over and told him: "You can't park there."

"But I'm here to cut Prince Charles' hair," said the man.

"Have you got a permit?"

"No, I've gotta take a bit off the back and sides."

> ❝ Prince Charles and Camilla went on tour to a really rural area of India. The locals must have thought, 'Diana's let herself go a bit.'
> Frankie Boyle ❞

✳ Once upon a time, a beautiful, independent, self-assured princess happened upon a frog in a pond.

The frog said to the princess: "I was once a handsome prince until an evil witch put a spell on me. One kiss from you and I will turn back into a prince and then we can marry, move into the castle with my mom and you can cook my meals, clean my clothes, give birth to my children and forever feel happy doing so."

That night, while the princess dined on frogs' legs, she kept laughing and saying: "I don't *think* so!"

> ❝ In 1926, the Queen Mother laid the first block of stone in our tenement. After a month or so the council realized she was going to take forever so they had to let her go, and get the builders in.
> Sean Lock ❞

✳ Prince Charles arrived in Iran on a state visit and asked the President: "Where's the Shah?"

The President looked puzzled. "What do you mean, sir? There is no Shah. We got rid of the Shah years ago."

"Very well," said Prince Charles. "In that case I'll take a bath."

* Prince Charles was being shown around a Scottish hospital. At the end of his visit, he was led into a ward where there were a number of patients displaying no obvious signs of injury. He went over to talk to the man in the first bed, and the patient proclaimed:

"Fair fa' yer honest, sonsie face
Great chieftain e' the puddin' race!
Aboon them a' ye tak your place, painch tripe or thairm:
Weel are ye wordy o' a grace as lang's my arm."

Somewhat taken aback, Prince Charles smiled politely and moved onto the next bed, where the patient immediately launched into:

"Some hae meat, and canna eat,
And some wad eat that want it,
But we hae meat and we can eat,
And sae the Lord be thankit."

Prince Charles was completely lost for words and simply hurried on to the next patient who declared loudly:

"Wee sleekit cow'rin tim'rous beastie,
O what a panic's in thy breastie!
Thou need na start awa sae hasty, wi' bickering brattle.
I wad be laith to run and chase thee, wi' murdering prattle!"

"Very nice," said Prince Charles before whispering to the hospital manager: "I see you saved the psychiatric ward until last."

"Oh no," said the manager, "this is the Serious Burns Unit."

* Prince Philip and the Queen were dining in one of London's top restaurants. The waiter asked Prince Philip what he would like to order.

"We'll have two rare steaks, my good fellow," said Prince Philip.

"Does sir mean two bloody steaks?" queried the waiter.

"Yes, that's right," said Prince Philip. "Two bloody steaks!"

The Queen added: "And plenty of fucking chips!"

* Camilla confided to the Queen: "Every time I suck Charles' penis, I get acid indigestion."

The Queen said: "Have you tried Andrews?"

* Prince Charles was reversing his Land Rover out of the garage when he ran over the Queen's favourite corgi. He quickly got out but it was too late: the corgi was dead, squashed to a pulp. Just then a genie popped up and said: "Your highness, I can give you one wish. What would you like?"

The Prince said: "This is Mummy's favourite dog. Can you bring it back to life?"

The genie examined the corgi. "I'm sorry," he said, "but this dog can't be saved. He's way beyond repair. This dog is very, very dead. I'm afraid there's nothing I can do."

"But you must be able to do something," pleaded Charles. "It's Mummy's favourite."

"I'm really sorry," repeated the genie, "but there's no way I can bring it back to life."

"Very well," sighed Charles. "But do I still have a wish?"

"Yes," said the genie.

"Well, I would like you to make my new wife Camilla as beautiful as my first wife Diana was."

The genie thought for a moment, then said: "Let's have another look at the dog."

★　★　★　★　★

SALESPEOPLE

> ❝ My first job was selling doors, door-to-door. That's a tough job. Ding dong. 'Can I interest you in a . . . oh, shit, you've got one already, haven't you?' ❞
> Bill Bailey

★ A cold-caller from a double glazing company phoned a man's home one evening.

"Hello, sir, this is Superseal Double Glazing," he began. "I was just wondering if you might be interested in—"

"Hold it right there," said the homeowner. "Before you start your sales pitch, can I ask you a question?"

"Uh, okay."

"What has a one-inch dick and hangs down?"

"I don't know," said the salesman.

"A bat. And what has a seven-inch dick and hangs up?"

Then he put the phone down before the salesman could answer.

> ❝ I answered the phone to a cold-caller today. It was my nan, asking that I pay her heating bill.
>
> Jimmy Carr ❞

★ Walking up to a department store's fabric counter, a pretty young woman said to the salesman: "I'd like this material for a dress. How much does it cost?"

"Just one kiss per metre," grinned the smooth-talking salesman cheesily.

"That's fine," said the girl. "I'll take ten metres."

With anticipation written all over his face, the salesman quickly measured out the cloth, wrapped it, and then teasingly held it out.

The girl grabbed the package, pointed to the wizened old man standing next to her and smiled: "Grandpa here will pay the bill."

A travelling salesman was trapped in his hotel in Washington State by torrential storms and floods. So he emailed his office in New York to say that he would be delayed by a few days.

His boss emailed back: "Start vacation immediately."

★ A salesman was lying in his motel room, flicking through the Gideon Bible. Suddenly he had had a flash of inspiration and walked along to reception, where the girl on the desk was a pretty little redhead. He stopped and talked with her for a while.

"What time do you finish?" he asked eventually.

"Nine o'clock," she replied.

"How about coming round to my room after work for a few drinks?"

"Well, I'd like to, but I don't know whether I should."

"It'll be okay. It says so in the Bible."

"Oh, well all right then. See you at nine."

Just after nine o'clock, she knocked on the door of his room. He let her in, sat her on the bed and reached into the minibar for some drinks.

"How about a brandy and dry?" he suggested.

"I'd like to," she said, "but I'm not sure if I should."

"It'll be fine," he insisted. "It says so in the Bible."

"Well, in that case, all right."

They had a few drinks, and then he suggested that they get into bed for a cuddle.

"I'd like to," she said, "but I'm not sure if it would be okay."

"Of course it would. It says so in the Bible."

So they climbed into bed, and one thing led to another. Afterwards, as she got dressed, she asked him: "Exactly whereabouts in the Bible does it say that all this is okay?"

He reached for the Gideon Bible beside the bed, and opened the front cover where someone had written: "The redhead on the reception desk is a sure thing."

★ A sales representative for a condom company was on her way to an international condom convention. Hurrying through the busy airport, she dropped her briefcase carrying her samples, scattering dozens and dozens of condoms all over the terminal floor.

She noticed fellow travellers staring at her as she tried to put the condoms back into her briefcase. "It's okay," she explained. "I'm going to a convention."

* A salesman was cold-calling door-to-door, trying to sell double glazing. When he called at one house, the woman householder told him in no uncertain terms that she was not interested in his product and slammed the door in his face. But to her surprise, the door didn't close and instead bounced back open. So she tried for a second time, with more force, but the door still wouldn't close and bounced back open again.

    Convinced that the salesman was deliberately putting his foot in the door to prevent her shutting it, she reared back to give the door an almighty slam that would finally teach him a lesson.

    But as she went to do so, the salesman interrupted: "Ma'am, before you do that again, you ought to move your cat."

* A man realized he needed to purchase a hearing aid, but didn't want to spend a lot of money. "How much do they cost?" he asked the salesman.

    "Anything from $2 to $2,000."

    "Can I see the $2 model?" said the customer.

    The salesman put the device around the man's neck, and said: "You just stick this button in your ear and run this little string down to your pocket."

    "How does it work?" asked the customer.

    "For $2, it doesn't work," said the salesman. "But when people see it on you, they'll talk louder!"

* A man was disturbed from a Saturday afternoon in front of the TV by a door-to-door salesman.

    "Good afternoon, sir," said the salesman cheerily. "I'm from BettaGardens. Now let me make it clear right away that I'm not trying to sell you anything – it just so happens that we are working in this area at the present. Having said that, I can't help noticing that your garden gate has probably seen better days. It's a bit old and rusty and is hanging there on one hinge: not every secure either in terms of the gate itself or in terms of protecting your property. So I am delighted to tell you that we at BettaGardens will be able to supply you with a free, yes, free, top-of-the-range replacement gate."

And with that he handed the householder a glossy catalogue.

The householder was suspicious. "A free gate?" he mused. "Where's the catch?"

"There isn't one," beamed the salesman.

"Well, it's not much bloody use then, is it?" the householder said, and slammed the door.

★　★　★　★　★

SCHOOL

❖ The pretty teacher was concerned about one of her eight-year-old students. Taking him aside after class one day, she asked: "Johnny, why has your school work been so poor lately?"

"I'm in love," replied Johnny.

Holding back an urge to smile, the teacher asked: "With whom?"

"With you," he said.

"But Johnny," she said gently, "don't you see how silly that is? It's true that I would like a husband of my own someday, but I don't want a child!"

"Oh, don't worry," said the boy reassuringly, "I'll use a rubber."

❖ Teacher: "I hope I didn't see you looking at Timmy's test paper."

Johnny: "I hope you didn't see me either!"

❖ A group of third, fourth and fifth graders accompanied by two female teachers went on a field trip to the local racecourse to learn about thoroughbred racehorses. In the course of the tour some of the children wanted to go to the toilet, so it was decided that the girls would go with one teacher while the boys went with another.

As the teacher assigned to the boys waited outside the men's toilet, one of the boys came out and told her that he couldn't reach the urinal. Reluctantly the teacher went inside and began hoisting the little boys up by their armpits, one by one. As she lifted one up by the armpits, she couldn't help but notice that he was unusually well-endowed for an elementary schoolchild.

"I guess you must be in the fifth?" she said.

"No, ma'am," he replied. "I'm in the seventh, riding Lucky Charm. Thanks for the lift anyway."

The teacher at an English school stood in front of a map of the world. "Jack," she said, "can you show me where on this map America is?"

Jack pointed correctly to America.

"Now, Jenny," continued the teacher, "can you tell me the name of the person who discovered America?"

Jenny said: "Jack just did, Miss."

> When I was at school, all the boys used to go and snog Julie Miller in the art cupboard. And you know, they don't make teachers like Julie Miller any more.
>
> Jason Manford

❖ A small boy complained to his teacher: "The other kids keep throwing gold bars at me."

"I see," said the teacher. "It seems to me that you're a victim of bullion."

❖ A teacher was walking along the school corridor when he saw three boys peeing up against a wall of the science block.

"What do you think you're doing?" he demanded.

"We're having a contest, sir. Whoever can pee the highest gets $10."

In a rage, the teacher rushed straight to the principal. "Mr Grimes," he said, "I've just stumbled across three boys urinating up the wall of the science block. Apparently whoever could get the highest would win $10."

"So what did you do?" asked the principal.

"I hit the roof!"

"Cool! Did you get your money?"

❖ The schoolteacher asked her class of young children to name one thing they needed at home but didn't yet have.

"Jimmy?"

"A Nintendo Wii."

"Very good, Jimmy. How about you, Anna?"

"A Super Barbie doll's house," said Anna.

"That sounds nice, Anna. Eric?"

Eric remained silent.

"Surely there must be something you can think of, Eric?"

"No, nothing."

"Really, Eric? You do surprise me."

"I know it's true for a fact," insisted Eric. "Because last week my dad came home drunk, was sick all over the carpet, and my mom said it was the last thing we needed."

❖ A woman answered the phone one afternoon and the voice on the other end said: "This is Daybury School, I'm afraid to have to tell you that your son's been telling lies."

The woman replied: "Well, tell him he's bloody good at it, because I haven't got any kids!"

❖ Teacher: "How do you spell crocodile?"

Johnny: "K-R-O-K-O-D-I-A-L"

Teacher: "No, that's wrong."

Johnny: "Maybe it is wrong, but you asked how *I* spell it!"

❖ Teacher: "Why weren't you at school yesterday, Johnny?"
Johnny: "My grandpa got burnt."
Teacher: "I'm sorry to hear that. He wasn't burnt too badly, was he"?
Johnny: "Oh, yes. They really know what they're doing at those crematoriums."

❖ The teacher noticed that little Johnny had arrived for school wearing only one glove.

"Why have you only got one glove?" she asked.

"Well, Miss," explained Johnny, "I was watching the weather forecast on TV last night, and it said it was going to be sunny but on the other hand it could get quite cold."

❖ A young class were enjoying the first day of first grade. The teacher said: "Now that we're all grown up, we aren't going to use baby talk any more. Instead we're going to use grown-up words. Now who would like to start by telling us about what they did in summer vacation?"

A little girl called Jenny put up her hand and said: "This summer vacation I rode a choo-choo."

"No, Jenny," interrupted the teacher. "We don't say 'choo-choo' any more. We say 'train'. Remember to use grown-up words. Now, who's next?"

Little Johnny raised his hand. "This summer vacation I went to Disneyland and saw Winnie the Shit."

❖ A teacher was giving a lesson about the circulation of the blood. He said: "Now boys, as you know, if I stood on my head, the blood would run into it and I would turn red in the face."

"Yes, sir," they chorused.

"So why is it," asked the teacher, "that while I am standing upright, the blood doesn't run into my feet and make them turn red, like my head?"

A young voice from the back called out: "Because your feet aren't empty!"

School Answering Machine Message

To lie about why your child is absent, press 1

To make excuses why your child did not do his/her homework, press 2

To swear at staff members, press 3

To ask why you didn't get information that was already enclosed in your newsletter and several other letters posted to you, press 4

To request another teacher, for the third time this year, press 5

To complain about not being able to park your 4x4 directly outside the school gates, press 6

To shop your child, press 7

To complain that your child has got food poisoning from school lunches, press 8

To apologize for your behaviour at parents' evening, press 9

If you want us to bring up your child, press 0

❖ One day at school, the teacher decided to play an animal game. She held up a picture of a giraffe and asked if any of the class knew what it was. "See its long neck?" she said. "What animal has a long neck?" And Jenny answered: "It's a giraffe."

"Very good, Jenny," said the teacher.

Then the teacher held up a picture of a zebra, and when no answers were forthcoming, she said: "See the stripes on this animal? What animal has stripes?" And Timmy answered: "It's a zebra."

"Well done, Timmy," said the teacher.

Next the teacher held up a picture of a deer. None of the children recognized the animal, so the teacher said: "See the big antlers on this animal? What animal has horns?"

Still nobody put up their hand, so the teacher offered a further clue: "It's something your mother calls your father."

Little Johnny immediately shouted out: "I know what it is. It's a horny bastard."

Math Test for State Schools

Name:
Nickname:
Gang name:

1. Leroy has 0.5 kilos of cocaine. If he sells an eight-ball to Kevin for $500 and 100 grammes to Wayne for $100, what is the street value of the rest of his stash?

2. The Bad Blood Gang have 72 juvenile convictions between them. The Crazy Hoods have 120. Express the Crazy Hoods' criminal superiority as a percentage.

3. If an average can of spray paint covers twenty-two square metres and the average letter is one square metre, how many letters can be sprayed with eight fluid ounce cans of spray paint with 20 per cent extra paint free?

4. Jules got nine years for murder. He also got $750,000 for the hit. If his common-law wife spends $60,000 a year, how much money will he have left when he gets out two-thirds of the way through his sentence?

5. Damon pimps four bitches. If the price is $50 a ride, how many tricks per day must each bitch perform to support Damon's $800-a-day coke habit?

6. Liam steals Jordan's skateboard. As Liam skates away at a speed of 35mph, Jordan loads his brother's Armalite. If it takes Jordan twenty seconds to load the gun, how far will Liam have travelled before he is taken out?

Math Test for Public (i.e. Private) Schools

1. Ben smashes up his old man's car, causing x amount of damage and killing three people. Ben's father uses his influence with the chief of police to intervene in the court system, forges his insurance claim and receives a payment of y. The difference between x and y is three times the life insurance settlement for the three dead people. What kind of car is Ben driving now?

2. Fiona's personal shopper decides to substitute generic and own-brand products for the designer goods favoured by her employer. In the course of a month she saves the price of a return ticket to Fiji, and Fiona doesn't even notice the difference. Express Fiona's stupidity on a scale of 1 to 10.

3. If Verity throws up four times a day for a week, she can fit into a size 8 Versace. If she throws up three times a day for two weeks, she has to make do with a size 10 Dolce & Gabbana. Which is her better option?

4. Hermione wants a boob job but Daddy will only pay one-third of the $12,000 price. Given that Hermione earns $500 a week as a soft-porn model, how long will it be before Daddy's little princess gets her 36Ds?

5. If Jasmine marries property developer Miles, she will immediately receive a lump sum of $3 million. If she marries celebrity lawyer Simon, she will receive a guaranteed $120,000 per annum plus two Ferraris, worth $70,000 each, and a country retreat valued at $900,000. Which is her better option, or should she marry for love?

6. Jeremy is being blackmailed by a rent boy for 45 per cent of Jeremy's annual earnings as a banker. As Jeremy earns $80,000 (without bonuses), how much will he have to cough up to keep out of the papers?

❖ The teacher asked little Johnny if he knew his numbers.
  "Yes," he said. "My dad taught me."
  "Good. So what comes after eight?"
  "Nine," answered Johnny.
  "And what comes after nine?"
  "Ten."
  "And what comes after ten?"
  "The jack."

> 66 I read about that kid who had sex with
> his teacher – he just died from
> high-fiving.
>   Zach Galifianakis 99

❖ **Teacher: "Johnny, your essay on 'My Dog' is exactly the same as your brother's. Did you copy his?"**
Johnny: "No, Miss, but it's the same dog."

❖ Did you know that after school 35 per cent of teenagers go back to an empty house . . . break a window, steal a DVD player and then go home?

❖ A small boy was performing in a school play when he suddenly fell through a large crack in the floorboards.
  The audience gasped, but the boy's mother calmly turned to her friend and said: "Don't worry, it's just a stage he's going through."

❖ Teacher: "Mary, give me a sentence starting with 'I'."
  Mary: "I is . . ."
  Teacher: "No, Mary. Always say 'I am . . .'"
  Mary: "Okay, miss. I am the ninth letter of the alphabet."

❖ A first-grade teacher was having trouble with one of her students. She asked the boy: "Michael, what is the matter with you these days? Your attitude stinks."

Michael answered: "I'm too smart for first grade. My sister is in third grade, and I'm smarter than she is, so I should be in third grade too."

In a bid to resolve things, the teacher took Michael along to the principal's office and while Michael waited in the outer office, she explained the situation to the principal. He told the teacher that he would give Michael a test and if he failed to answer any of the questions correctly, he would have to return to first grade and behave himself.

Michael was then taken to the principal's office for the test.

"What is four times four?" asked the principal.

"Sixteen," answered Michael.

"What is eleven minus seven?" said the principal.

"Four," replied Michael instantly.

And so it went on. Every third-grade standard question the principal asked, Michael answered. Eventually the principal said to the teacher: "I think Michael can move up to third grade."

"Let me ask him a few questions," suggested the teacher.

"Very well," agreed the principal.

"Okay, Michael," began the teacher. "What does a cow have four of that I only have two of?"

"Legs," answered Michael.

The teacher continued: "What is in your pants that you have but I do not have?"

The principal raised his eyebrows.

"Pockets," replied Michael.

Teacher: "What does a dog do that a man steps into?"

Michael: "Pants."

Teacher: "What goes in hard and pink then comes out soft and sticky?"

Michael: "Bubblegum."

The principal wiped a few beads of perspiration from his brow.

Teacher: "What does a man do standing up, a woman do sitting down and a dog do on three legs?"

Michael: "Shake hands."

Teacher: "Now I am going to ask some 'Who am I' questions."

Michael: "Okay."

Teacher: "You stick your poles inside me. You tie me down to get me up. I get wet before you do."

Michael: "Tent."

Teacher: "A finger goes in me. You fiddle with me when you're bored. The best man always has me first."

The principal was growing increasingly nervous.

Michael: "Wedding ring."

Teacher: "I come in many sizes. When I'm not well, I drip. When you blow me, you feel good."

Michael: "Nose."

Teacher: "I have a stiff shaft. My tip penetrates. I come with a quiver."

Michael: "Arrow."

Teacher: "And finally. What word starts with an 'F' and ends in 'K' and means a lot of excitement?"

Michael: "Firetruck."

The principal breathed a huge sigh of relief and told the teacher: "Put Michael in third grade. He's obviously very smart. I got the last nine questions wrong myself."

 My parents made us take Latin. It comes in handy if someone in the family gets possessed.

Kathleen Madigan

❖ The teacher had asked each child to bring one electrical appliance into school for "show and tell".

"What did you bring, Mary?" asked the teacher.

"I brought a kettle."

"And what is it for?"

"It's for boiling water."

"That's very good, Mary," said the teacher. "Now, Billy, what have you brought for us?"

"I brought an electric can opener," said Billy. "It opens cans, miss."

"Well done, Billy," said the teacher, "but I see that Johnny hasn't brought anything."

"Yes I have, Miss," said Johnny. "It's in the corridor."

The whole class looked out into the corridor.

"What's that, Johnny?" asked the teacher.

"It's a heart/lung machine," replied Johnny. "They use it in hospitals to keep your heart going."

"I see. And what did your father say about it?"

"Aaaaaaaahhhhhhh!"

★ ★ ★ ★ ★

SCIENCE AND TECHNOLOGY

* A man bought a camera phone and suggested to his wife that they should use the video feature and make a saucy video.

"The one problem, though," he said, "is that the facility is thirty seconds."

"Yes, that is a problem," agreed his wife. "If we're recording our foreplay, how are we going to fill the other ten seconds?"

> 66 There are too many cameras right now. You go to buy something, and it's also a camera. And I say, 'I just wanted a grapefruit.'
>
> Mike Birbiglia 99

﹡ A techno-geek was working late at the office when his friend dropped by to see him.

"How you doing, buddy?" asked the friend.

"Yeah, I'm good. Did you see my new secretary on the way in?"

"Yeah, she's gorgeous. How did you persuade her to work late?"

"Easy, and I'm glad you like her, because – believe it or not – she's a robot! She does everything I tell her."

"A robot?" queried the friend. "No way!"

"She's the latest model from Japan. Let me tell you how she works. If you squeeze her left boob, she takes dictation; if you squeeze her right boob, she takes a letter. And that's not all – she can have sex, too!"

"You're kidding, right?"

"No, she's something else, I tell you! Why don't you borrow her for ten minutes or so while I finish off a few things here?"

So the friend took the robot secretary into the restroom. At first there was silence but after a couple of minutes terrible screams could be heard.

"Damn!" thought the geek. "I forgot to tell him her ass is a pencil sharpener!"

> What do you call a robot that always takes the longest route round?
> R2 detour.

﹡ A female chemistry student wanted to make some potassium hydroxide solution and proposed to throw a large lump of potassium into a bucket of water. The professor listened to her plan but suggested that she stir the water for five minutes before adding the potassium.

"Why?" she asked.

He replied: "Because it will give me time to get away!"

❋ Dennis was a gadget freak. Whenever some new piece of technology came into the shops, he was always the first to buy it, regardless of whether or not he needed it. His wife Helen had grown to tolerate his foibles, so it came as no great surprise to her when one day he arrived home with his latest must-have toy, a robot.

"If it's not a silly question," she asked, "why do we need a robot?"

"Ah," he said excitedly, "this is no ordinary robot: it's actually a lie detector. You watch. I'll try it out on Kenny when he gets home."

Kenny, their ten-year-old son, eventually got home from school around 6 p.m. – nearly two hours later than usual.

"Where have you been?" demanded Helen.

"Several of us went to the library to work on a science project," said Kenny.

With that, the robot walked around the table and slapped Kenny, knocking him off his chair.

"Son," said Dennis, "this robot is a lie detector. Now tell us where you really were after school."

"Okay," said Kenny, his head bowed. "We went to Robbie's house and watched a movie."

"What did you watch?" asked Helen.

"*The Lion King*," said Kenny cautiously.

The robot went over to Kenny and slapped him again, sending him tumbling from his chair once more.

"The truth!" demanded Dennis.

His lip quivering, Kenny got up, sat down and confessed. "I'm real sorry I lied," he said. "We watched a tape called *The Sex Goddess*."

"I am ashamed of you, son," said Dennis. "When I was your age, I never lied to my parents."

The robot immediately walked over to Dennis and delivered a whack that nearly knocked him out of his chair.

Seeing this, Helen creased up with laughter and with tears streaming down her face she cried: "You really asked for that! You can't be too mad with Kenny. After all, he is your son!"

With that, the robot walked straight over to Helen and slapped her three times.

> **❝** I notice that there are no 'B' batteries. I think that's to avoid confusion. Because if there were, you wouldn't know when someone was stuttering.
>
> Demetri Martin **❞**

> **❝** The man who invented the taser has passed away at the age of eighty-eight. I understand his relatives were stunned.
>
> Conan O'Brien **❞**

★ ★ ★ ★ ★

SEX

★ A man went to his doctor and asked for an urgent prescription of Viagra. The doctor said: "Very well, but remember it takes at least half an hour before it becomes effective."

"That's no good," said the man. "She'll probably have wriggled free by then."

★ A wife was standing in the kitchen one morning, preparing soft-boiled eggs and toast for breakfast, and wearing only the T-shirt she had slept in. As her husband walked in, she turned to him and said: "You've got to make love to me right now, here, across the kitchen table."

His eyes lit up. He could hardly believe his luck, and before she could change her mind, he had sex with her on the kitchen table.

Afterwards, she hurriedly thanked him and returned to the stove, with her T-shirt still around her neck.

Happy but puzzled, he asked her: "What was all that about?"

"Oh," she said. "The egg timer's broken."

★ A guy wandered over to a beautiful woman in a bar and started chatting to her. Soon he said: "Do you mind if I ask you a personal question?"

"That depends on how personal it is," she replied.

"Okay," he said tentatively. "How many men have you slept with?"

"No way am I going to tell you that!" she snapped. "That's my business!"

"Oh, sorry," he said. "I didn't realize you made a living from it."

★ **A guy said to his friend: "Have you ever been to bed with an ugly woman?"**

The friend said: "No, but I've woken up with plenty."

★ Two male friends met up in a bar. "You're looking very pleased with yourself," said one.

"Yes," said the other, "I had one of the best nights of my life last night – and it was with my ex-wife."

"Really? The woman who left you penniless after running off with another man? How come?"

"Well, I read on the Internet that a restricted air supply can heighten your sexual enjoyment, so I thought I'd give it a try. And it's true. Seeing her face turn purple gave me a real buzz."

★ A guy was in bed with his Thai girlfriend. After having great sex, she spent the next hour tenderly stroking his penis. Enjoying the sensation, he eventually turned to her and lovingly asked her: "Why do you like doing that?"

She said: "Because I really miss mine."

> ❝ I don't see the problem with premature ejaculation. I mean, sex AND an early night.
>
> Frankie Boyle ❞

> **❝** I don't understand the whole concept of a massage. You get a woman to rub every single part of your body except the one part you really want rubbed.
>
> Rodney Carrington **❞**

★ A man said to his wife: "When I die, I'd like to die having sex."

She said: "Well, then at least we know it will be quick."

★ A worried nineteen-year-old girl told her mother that she had missed her period for the last two months. The mother immediately went to the drugstore to buy a pregnancy-test kit, the results of which confirmed that the girl was pregnant.

"Who was the pig that did this to you?" shrieked the mother. "I demand to know! He must answer for his actions."

The girl made a phone call and forty-five minutes later a Rolls-Royce pulled up outside the family house. Out stepped a mature, distinguished man, impeccably dressed from head to toe. He sat in the living room with the father, the mother and the girl and outlined his intentions. "Your daughter has informed me that she is pregnant and that I am the father. I am sorry to have caused you all any distress, but I intend to behave honourably in this matter. Unfortunately my personal situation dictates that I cannot marry her but I shall provide for the child.

"If a girl is born, I will bequeath her two retail stores, a townhouse, a beach villa and a $1,000,000 bank account. If a boy is born, I propose to give him two factories and a $2,000,000 bank account. If it is twins, a factory and $1,000,000 each. However, if there is a miscarriage, what do you suggest I do?"

At this point the father, who had remained silent, placed a hand firmly on the man's shoulder and told him: "Then you try again."

★ A girl said to her new boyfriend: "I'm going to call your penis a weapon of mass destruction."

"Hey, I like that," he smiled. "It sounds kinda big, powerful and scary."

"Yes," she said, "but I'm calling it that because it's so hard to find."

> 66 If size doesn't matter, how come my girlfriend's vibrator isn't three inches and crooked?
>
> Doug Stanhope 99

★ A man was sitting in a bar peering gloomily into the bottom of his glass.

"What's up?" asked the bartender.

"It's my girlfriend. You see, we had sex last night but I only lasted just over a minute. As I rolled off her, she said: 'I want you to finish me off.'"

"And what's the problem?" asked the bartender.

"I haven't yet decided what to do with the body."

I've always had this fantasy of making love to two women. Like in the same year.

★ A drugstore was broken into and all the Viagra tablets were taken. Police later arrested two men for being in possession of swollen goods.

★ There was a fire at the Viagra factory last night. It went up in no time.

★ Jim and Jake were stranded in the desert, dying of thirst. As they staggered along beneath the blazing sun, they spotted a small shack. They knocked on the door and it was answered by the ugliest, smelliest, hairiest woman they had ever seen. Jim told the woman that they were desperate for water, and she said: "Sure you can have water – if you have sex with me."

Jim was horrified: "I would rather die in this desert", he announced, "than have sex with such a repulsive creature as you."

However, Jake valued his life and agreed to do the deed, leaving Jim waiting outside the shack.

The hideous woman dragged Jake into her private room and demanded that he make love to her. He said he would, on condition that she closed her eyes. The woman shut her eyes and Jake, looking around the room, noticed a table full of corn on the cob. Thinking quickly, he fucked her with a piece of corn on the cob and threw it out of the window before she opened her eyes again.

But the woman wanted more and demanded to be pleasured a second time. Jake reluctantly agreed, provided she closed her eyes again. When she had done so, he picked up another piece of corn on the cob, rammed it into her a few times and threw it out of the window before she re-opened her eyes.

Finally satisfied, the woman agreed to give Jake and Jim some water. Jake shouted outside to relay the good news to his friend.

"Never mind the water," said Jim. "I want some more of that buttered corn."

> **“** Butt sex is a lot like spinach: if you're forced to have it as a child, you won't enjoy it as an adult.
>
> Daniel Tosh **”**

★ Did you hear about the dyslexic pervert who went into an S&M shop and came out with a nice cardigan?

★   A guy met an older woman in a bar. They drank and flirted and he decided she was pretty hot for a fifty-five-year-old. As they exchanged a passionate kiss, she whispered in his ear: "Have you ever had a mother and daughter together?"

"No," he answered. "But it's something I've always fantasized about."

"Well, tonight could just be your lucky night," she said, knocking back another double vodka.

Scarcely able to contain himself, he went back to her place. She turned the key in the door, put the hall light on and shouted upstairs: "Mom, you still awake?"

> " As I've got older, I've found that sex from behind has been a godsend. Because with sex from behind you don't have to look interested.
>
> Frank Skinner "

★   A man took his wife to bed and pleasured her with a large, thick cucumber. They enjoyed great sex and after she had experienced a multiple orgasm, they both fell asleep exhausted.

A few hours later, he was woken by the bed shaking violently and her screaming: "Oh God, I'm coming! Yes, yes, yes!"

"What is it, darling?" he asked. "Are you okay?"

When she had recovered, she said: "Don't worry, I'm fine. It's just the cucumber repeating on me."

★   A couple got into an argument over who enjoys sex more: men or women.

The man said: "Guys clearly enjoy sex more than women. That's why we're so obsessed with it."

"That doesn't prove a thing," the woman countered. "Think about it: when your ear itches and you put your little finger in and wiggle it around, then pull it out, which feels better – your ear or your finger?"

A Year's Sex Diary

TO MY DEAR WIFE:

During the past year I have tried to make love to you 365 times. I have succeeded 36 times, which is an average of once every 10 days. The following is a list of why you rejected my advances on the other occasions:

49 times you were too tired
38 times you had a headache
31 times you said you weren't in the mood
26 times the sheets were clean on that day
20 times it was too hot
20 times it was too cold
19 times you had to get up early
17 times it was too late
16 times you were afraid of waking the baby
15 times you said you were too sore
14 times you pretended to be asleep
13 times you wanted to finish the book you were reading instead
12 times it was the wrong time of the month
9 times you said your mother would hear us
8 times you were sunburnt
7 times you didn't want to mess up your new hairdo
5 times you were worried about your irritable bowel
4 times you had just painted your fingernails
3 times you said the neighbours would hear us
2 times you had run out of lubricant jelly
1 time the dog got there first

Of the 36 times I did succeed, the activity was not satisfactory because:

9 times you just laid there
8 times you were still reading your book
7 times you reminded me there's a crack in the ceiling

5 times you told me to hurry up and get it over with

4 times I had to wake you and tell you I was finished

2 times you asked whether I had remembered to lock the back door

1 time I was afraid I had hurt you because I felt you move

TO MY DEAR HUSBAND:

I think you have things a little confused. Here are the reasons you didn't get more than you did:

95 times you were watching sport on TV

51 times you worked too late

37 times you came home drunk

28 times you didn't come home

20 times you had to get up early to play golf

18 times you came too soon.

18 times you didn't come at all

14 times you were soft before you put it in

12 times you were exhausted because you had been thinking about it all day

10 times you got cramp in your toes

9 times you got it caught in your zipper

6 times you came in your boxers while watching Internet porn

5 times you had man flu

3 times you had a splinter in your finger

2 times you had a nosebleed

1 time you were worried because you had found a grey hair down below

Of the times we did get it together:

The reason I laid still was because you missed and were screwing the pillow. I wasn't talking about the crack in the ceiling, what I said was, "Do you want me on my back or kneeling?" The time you felt me move was because you farted and I was trying to breathe.

★ A young couple had just enjoyed great sex. When they were finished, she looked in the box of condoms but was surprised to see there were only three left from the box of twelve.

"What happened to the other eight?" she asked.

"Uh, I masturbated with them," replied her boyfriend nervously.

The next day, she related the story to one of her male friends in the office and asked him: "Have you ever done that?"

"Yeah, once or twice," he replied.

"Really?" she said incredulously. "You have masturbated while wearing a condom?"

"Oh," he said, "I thought you were asking if I'd ever lied to my girlfriend."

★ After nine years of marriage, a wife suddenly announced: "I'm bored with our sex life. It's always the same. Why don't we try the 'other hole'?"

"Yuk! No way!" exclaimed her husband. "And risk you getting pregnant?"

★ A guy was complaining to his buddy about a new girl he had just started dating. "She's really weird," he said. "All she ever wants me to do is screw her in the ear."

"That is weird."

"Yeah, every time I go to stick my dick in her mouth, she turns her head."

> ❝ I'm very romantic when I masturbate. I light some candles. Then I try to shoot them out when I'm done. Never invite me to a birthday party.
>
> Dave Attell ❞

★ There's been a new addition to the *Kama Sutra*. It's called the gas board position: you stay in all day and nobody comes.

★ A rooster was walking along one day when he came to a riverbank with a big bag of cat food beside it. Uninterested in the bag, he looked over to the other side of the river and saw a huge bag of chicken food, which immediately made his mouth water. Next to the bag of feed was a cat that was hungrily eyeing the cat food on the rooster's side of the river.

The two looked at each other and wondered what to do. Eventually the rooster called across to the cat and said: "If we take a run at it and jump high enough, we should be able to make it to the other side of the river."

The cat replied: "Okay. Let's give it a try."

The rooster walked back about twenty feet, took a long run-up and soared into the air, flapping his wings frantically. To his delight, he landed on the far side of the river and immediately started devouring the chicken feed.

Now more motivated than ever, the cat walked back about twenty-five feet, took a long run-up and leaped into the air, but SPLASH! he landed right in the middle of the river.

The moral of the story is: for every satisfied cock, there's a wet pussy.

> 66 A company has started selling a vibrator that responds to a woman's vocal commands, including slower, harder, and faster. Women say it's not so much what the vibrator does, but just the fact that it listens.
>
> Conan O'Brien 99

★ A guy was standing glumly at the bar.

"What's up?" asked his friend.

"My wife suggested we should play some sex games to spice up our love lives."

"Yeah, what's wrong with that?"

"Well, unfortunately 'Guess who I shagged last night?' didn't go down too well."

★ With his wife eight months' pregnant, a guy was becoming increasingly desperate for sex. One night as he gazed longingly at her, she finally took pity on him, reached into a drawer and said: "Here, take this $50 bill to the woman at number 136. She will let you sleep with her. But remember, this is a one-off. Don't even think about trying it again."

"Thanks, honey," he said, and rushed out of the door before she changed her mind.

A few minutes later, he returned, handed the bill back to his wife and said dejectedly: "It's not enough. She says she wants sixty."

"That bitch!" raged the wife. "When she was pregnant and her husband came over here, I charged him only fifty!"

A guy said to his college buddy: "I'm going to organize a group sex session in my apartment tonight. Do you want to come?"

"Sure," he said. "How many people are coming?"

"Three, if you bring your girlfriend."

★ "How are you doing?" said a young guy bumping into his buddy at the bar.

"I was fine . . . until last night."

"Why? What happened?"

"My girlfriend and I were talking about how many people we had slept with."

"Oh. What did she say?"

"She said she could count the number of guys she's slept with on one hand."

"That's good, surely?"

"Yeah, I was relieved . . . but then I saw that she was holding a calculator."

★ A truck driver in California picked up a young female hitchhiker who was wearing a really short skirt.

Introducing himself, he said: "My name's Jerry Snow."

"Hi," she smiled. "I'm June Anderson."

As he drove along the highway, she asked: "Why do you keep sizing me up with those sidelong glances?"

He answered: "I'm imagining what it would be like to have eight inches of Snow in June."

> 66 You know what you get for donating your eggs, ladies? Five thousand bucks.
> Guys, you know what we get for our sperm? Fifty bucks. I got a towel at home that's worth $200,000.
>
> Nick DiPaolo 99

★ A guy picked up a woman in a nightclub and took her home. While they were walking, he didn't say a word.

Later as they undressed, she said: "You're not the communicative type, are you?"

"No," he replied, pulling his dick from his underpants. "I do all my talking with this."

The woman looked at it disconsolately and said: "You really *don't* have much to say, do you?"

★ Every night, a customer went into a cafe and chatted up the waitress. He kept pestering her for sex until eventually he wore down her resistance.

"Okay," she said, "I'll have sex with you, but only if you can promise me that bells will ring and lights will flash."

"I can guarantee it!" he said. Then he screwed her on top of the pinball machine.

★ Two guys were discussing their sex lives. One said: "Last week my girlfriend complained that our sex life was getting dull and that I should try and think outside the box."

"So what did you do?"

"I poked her up the ass instead!"

★ A little girl accidentally saw her father getting dressed one morning and, pointing to his dick, asked him what it was. Not wanting to explain sex to her just yet, he told her that it was a secret.

Inquisitive, she then asked her mother: "What's that long thing between Daddy's legs?"

Equally evasive, the mother replied: "I don't know. He hasn't told me."

A couple of days later, the little girl proudly told her mother: "I finally figured out what that thing between Daddy's legs is. It's a toothbrush."

"Why do you think that?" asked her mother, amused.

"Because," said the little girl, "this morning I saw the maid sliding it in and out of her mouth and she had toothpaste dripping down her chin."

66 When you have sex with a glow-in-the-dark condom, it's kind of like being in a lighthouse. It's light, it's dark. It's light, it's dark. It's light, it's dark.

Frank Skinner 99

★ Two girlfriends – Jenny and Jo – were chatting about their love lives over coffee.

Jenny said: "I have to be really careful not to get pregnant."

Jo said: "But I thought Tony recently had a vasectomy."

"He did," said Jenny. "That's why I need to be really careful."

★ A guy arrived home late in the evening from a hard day's work and collapsed exhausted on the bed. However, his wife was feeling amorous and whispered in his ear: "What would you do if I said you had a sexy, horny, raving nymphomaniac lying next to you?"

Half-asleep, he replied: "Don't worry, darling, I'd stay faithful."

★ A man bought some flavoured condoms and suggested to his wife in bed: "Let's play a game. I put one on and you have to guess what flavour it is."

So she closed her eyes, dived under the duvet and said: "Cheese and onion flavour."

He said: "Give me a chance to put one on!"

★ A guy was desperate to have sex with a girl from the office but she was already engaged to someone else. One day he became so frustrated by her unavailability that after a few drinks he issued a brazen proposition: "Have sex with me and I'll pay you $200."

"No way," she said. "What sort of girl do you think I am?"

"Listen," he persisted, "it will all be over before you know it. I'll throw the money on the floor, you bend down, and I'll be finished by the time you've picked it up."

She began to waver – if only because $200 would help towards the wedding costs – but said that she would have to consult her boyfriend first. So she called her boyfriend, told him about the offer and asked him what he thought.

To her surprise, her boyfriend said: "It sounds like easy money. All you have to do is ask him for the $200, then pick it up as fast as you possibly can. He won't even have time to get his pants down."

She agreed that it sounded foolproof and accepted the proposal.

The boyfriend then waited anxiously for her to call back when it was all over. Half an hour passed, but there was no news. Finally after three-quarters of an hour he rang her and asked: "How did it go?"

She replied tearfully: "The bastard used pennies."

> ❝ I've got a friend whose nickname is 'Shagger'. You might think that's pretty cool. She doesn't like it.
> Jimmy Carr ❞

★   A man longed to wed a maiden with her virtue intact but after searching high and low for a true virgin, he resigned himself to the fact that every girl in town over the age of twelve had enjoyed sexual relations. He decided the only solution was to adopt a baby girl from an orphanage, raise her until the age of five, and then send her away to a monastery for safekeeping until she was old enough to become his bride. Sure enough, after many years away, she finally reached maturity and he retrieved her from the monastery and married her.

After the wedding, they made their way back to his house and into the bedroom where they prepared themselves for the consummation. As they lay down together in bed, he reached across for a jar of petroleum jelly.

"Why the jelly?" she asked him.

"So I don't hurt your most delicate parts during the act of lovemaking," he replied tenderly.

She said: "Why don't you just spit on your cock like the monks did?"

★   ★   ★   ★   ★

SHOPPING

❖   A man went to a store to buy a chimney. "How much is this one?" he asked.

The sales assistant replied: "Oh, it's on the house."

❖   A woman went into a hardware store and asked the sales clerk for two AA batteries. The clerk gestured with his fingers, said, "Come this way," and headed towards the back of the store.

"If I could come that way," she said, "I wouldn't need the batteries."

❖ A rough, ugly woman walked into Wal-Mart with her bratty kids in tow. Straight away, they ran riot, racing up and down the aisles while she yelled obscenities at them. Finally, after several complaints from shoppers, the manager sent over the official Wal-Mart greeter to deal with the situation.

"Good morning, ma'am," he said in his most charming tone, "and welcome to Wal-Mart. Nice children you've got there. Are they twins?"

Wiping her nose on her sleeve, the woman answered gruffly: "'Course they're not twins. One's eight and the other's six. What the hell makes you think they're twins? Do they look alike?"

"No," replied the greeter. "It was just beyond my imagination to think you had been laid more than once."

❖ A woman went to a furniture store and bought a new self-assembly wardrobe for her bedroom. She took it home and painstakingly put it together. She was very pleased with her efforts until a train passed by close to her house and caused the wardrobe to collapse. Thinking it was a freak accident, she re-assembled the wardrobe but once again it collapsed when the next train rattled past.

So she went back to the store to complain, and the store sent out a repair man to investigate the problem. He arrived just in time to see the wardrobe collapse once more as a train passed by. Puzzled by the malfunction, he decided to rebuild the wardrobe and sit inside it to see if he could stop it from collapsing.

Seconds after the repair man climbed inside, the woman's husband arrived home. Seeing the wardrobe door half open, he peered in and saw the repair man crouching inside.

"What the hell are you doing here?" he boomed angrily.

The repair man replied: "You're probably not going to believe this, but I'm waiting for a train."

Have you heard about the new shampoo for hobos?

It's called Go and Wash.

❖ A woman was telling her neighbour about the supermarket that had opened recently on the outskirts of town.

"It's very state of the art and designed to make shopping a natural and relaxing experience. It has an automatic water mister to keep all the fruit fresh. Just before it switches on, you hear the sound of distant thunder and smell the aroma of fresh rain. As you approach the milk aisle, you hear cows mooing and there's the scent of fresh hay. As you approach the eggs, you hear hens clucking and the air is filled with the delicious smell of bacon and eggs frying. And the vegetable department features the aroma of fresh buttered corn."

"It sounds wonderful," enthused the neighbour.

"Yes, but I don't buy toilet paper there any more."

> ❝ My mother is the kind of woman you don't want to be in line behind at the supermarket. She has coupons for coupons.
>
> Chris Rock ❞

❖ As part of his weekly supermarket shop, a man went to the meat counter to buy a pack of boneless chicken breasts but was disappointed because they were all too small. So he complained to the butcher and she promised to pack up some more and to have them ready for him by the time he had finished his shopping.

He continued with the rest of his shopping until a few aisles further on, he heard her voice boom out over the public address system: "Will the gentleman who was looking for bigger breasts please meet me at the back of the store."

❖ A man went into a shop and bought a self-help tape. It was called "How to Handle Disappointment". When he opened the box, it was empty.

❖ A man went into a discount shop and asked the woman at the cash desk if everything in the shop really was $1.

"That's right," she said. "Every item in the shop."

So he gave her a dollar and asked for the cash register.

❖ A woman arrived at the cash desk of a clothes store and reached into her handbag for her purse. As she did so, the clerk couldn't help noticing that there was a TV remote in the woman's handbag.

"Excuse me," said the clerk. "Do you always carry your TV remote with you when you're shopping?"

"No," replied the woman. "But my husband refused to come shopping with me, so I figured this was the most evil thing I could do to him."

> 66 I have no problems with buying tampons. I am a fairly modern man.
> But apparently they're not a 'proper' present.
>
> Jimmy Carr 99

❖ A married couple were shopping in the supermarket when the husband picked up a crate of Budweiser and put it in the trolley.

"What do you think you're doing?" asked the wife.

"They're on offer – only $25 for twelve cans," he explained.

"Put them back," she demanded. "We can't afford it."

A few aisles later, she picked up a $50 jar of face cream and put it in the trolley.

"What do you think you're doing?" asked the husband indignantly.

"It's my face cream," she said. "It makes me look beautiful."

He said: "So do twelve cans of Bud and they're half the price!"

❖ Did you hear about the dyslexic man who went out to buy maps?

He came back with a tin of Spam.

❖ On a trip to a shopping mall, a couple agreed to split up, visit their favourite shops and meet up again in an hour and a half. So while he visited the bike shop and the sports outfitters, she concentrated on the big clothes store. When he met up with her ninety minutes later as arranged outside the clothes store, she was carrying a dozen bags filled with clothes.

"I don't believe it!" he exclaimed. "Have you really bought all that?"

"Well, yes," she replied. Then gesturing towards the interior of the shop, she added: "But look at all the stuff I'm leaving behind."

> ❝ I bought a clock, and then the big hand fell off. But I didn't want to throw it out so I added 'ish' to the end of each number.
> Demetri Martin ❞

❖ With his wife ill in bed, a man did the weekly supermarket shop, and by the time he reached the checkout his trolley was overflowing. Behind him in the queue was a little old lady with just a loaf of bread and a packet of butter in her basket.

He turned to her and said: "Is that all you've got, love?"

Her face lit up. "Yes, dear," she said.

"Well," he said, "if I were you, I'd have a sit down, because I'm going to be ages here."

> ❝ I went to buy a duvet. I asked the shop assistant what filling I should have. She said: 'Get down.' So I hit the deck.
> Rhod Gilbert ❞

❖ **Did you hear about the man who nearly bought an origami belt but then realized it would just be a waist of paper?**

❖ A man received a phone call from his wife at work one lunchtime, asking him to pick up some groceries on his way home. Reminding her that this was his golf league afternoon, he said he would be happy to go to the store after his round of golf.

After playing his round, he stopped at the store and collected two bags of groceries. He then carried the bags to his Rolls-Royce in the car park, but on getting to the car he struggled to reach into his pocket for his keys because his arms were full.

He happened to spot a pretty young woman walking past, and so he called out to her: "Excuse me, could you do me a favour? I can't reach into my pocket to get my car keys out so that I can open the trunk and put these groceries away. Do you think you could reach into my pocket for my keys?"

"Sure. No problem," she said.

So she pulled the keys out of his pocket but with them came two golf tees, which fell to the ground.

"Gee, what are these for?" she asked.

"Oh," he replied, "those are to keep my balls in the air while I'm driving."

"Boy!" she exclaimed. "Those Rolls-Royce people think of everything!"

❖ Shopping at a supermarket, a guy noticed a pretty blonde woman waving at him and mouthing "hello". But he was puzzled because he couldn't place her. So when he caught her up, he asked her: "Do you know me?"

"I think you're the father of one of my kids," she replied.

He started to panic. His mind raced back to the only time he had ever been unfaithful to his wife and he blurted out: "My God, are you the stripper from my bachelor party that got me so aroused I had to lay you right there and then on the pool table while all my buddies sprayed whipped cream on us?"

"No," she replied calmly. "Actually I'm your son's math teacher."

SPORTS

* An owner had a racehorse that had never won a race. Finally the owner lost patience and warned the horse: "Either you win this afternoon or you'll be pulling a milk wagon tomorrow morning."

  That afternoon, the horse was lined up with the others in the starting gate. As the stalls opened, the rest of the field raced away, but as the gate was removed, the owner saw his horse fast asleep on the track.

  Angrily he ran over, kicked the horse and yelled: "Why are you sleeping?"

  The horse wearily lifted its head and replied: "I have to get up at three in the morning."

> " I don't believe for a second that weightlifting is a sport. They pick up a heavy thing and put it down again. To me, that's indecision.
>
> Paula Poundstone "

* Before a gymnastics event at the Beijing Olympics, an American athlete was sitting next to a Chinese athlete in the locker room. The American said: "Everyone in the States says China has a human rights problem. Is that true?"

  "I'm afraid so," replied the Chinese athlete. "In our legal system, it is hard to get a fair trial. The judges decide who has won before the trial even takes place."

  "That's terrible," said the American. "What a way to live!"

  In an attempt to lighten the mood, the Chinese athlete asked: "So, do you think you will do well in your floor routine today?"

  "I know I will," answered the American. "We've paid off the Spanish and French judges, and the Russians are trading votes with us."

✳ Did you hear about the man who dreamed someone was shouting: "On your marks, get set, go!?"

He woke up with a start.

✳ A Russian oil baron who had six children – all girls – began to despair because he had no son and heir. Imagine his joy when one of his wives finally presented him with a son.

Just before the boy's sixth birthday, the baron took him to one side and said: "Son, I am very proud of you. Anything you want, I shall get for you."

The son replied: "Daddy, I would like to have my own airplane." Not wanting to do anything by halves, his father bought him United Airlines.

Just before his son's seventh birthday, the baron took him to one side. "Son, you are my pride and joy. Anything you want, I shall get for you."

The son replied: "Daddy, I would like a boat." Since only the best was good enough, his father bought him Princess Cruise Lines.

Just before his son's eighth birthday, the baron took him to one side. "Son, you bring so much happiness into my life. Anything you want, I shall get for you."

The son replied: "Daddy, I would like to be able to watch cartoons." Not wanting to look a cheapskate, his father bought him Disney Studios and their theatres, where the boy watched all his favourite cartoons.

Just before his son's ninth birthday, the baron took him to one side. "Son, you are an inspiration to us all. Anything you want, I shall get for you."

The son, who by now was really into the Disney cartoons, replied: "Daddy, I would like a Mickey Mouse outfit." Not wishing to appear mean with his money, his father bought him Chelsea Football Club.

✳ A guy put a thousand pounds on a horse. The horse collapsed.

＊ You have to congratulate swimmer Michael Phelps for winning a record eight medals at the Beijing Olympics, but isn't it strange seeing a white man wearing that much gold?

> 66 We were playing the Olympics on the PlayStation and out of respect for the Paralympics, we broke two of the buttons.
>
> Jason Manford 99

＊ A racehorse owner was furious with his jockey after the horse trailed in last. "Could you not have raced any faster?" he raged.

"Sure I could have," replied the jockey, "but you know we are supposed to stay on the horse."

> 66 Rugby, posh man's sport, fifteen men on a team, because posh people can afford to have more friends.
>
> Al Murray 99

＊ Three women were sitting around boasting about their sons. One said: "My son graduated first in his class from Stanford. He's now a doctor, making $250,000 a year in Seattle."

The second woman said: "My son graduated first in his class from Harvard. He's now a lawyer, making $500,000 a year in San Francisco."

The third woman said: "My son never did too well in school. He never went to any university but he now makes a $1,000,000 a year in New York working as a sports repairman."

"What's a sports repairman?" asked the other two.

"He fixes games," replied the woman. "You know, hockey games, football games, baseball games."

＊ I went bobsleighing last night. I killed twenty-one people called Bob.

> ❝ Put all your money on the Italian in the Olympic swimming final. I don't know his name but apparently he's a postman in Venice.
>
> Mark Lawrenson ❞

✳ Four jockeys were travelling home from the Kentucky Derby when their car smashed into a truck and burst into flames, killing all four outright.

One of the jockeys' trainers was informed of the tragedy and was asked to go to try and identify him, but was warned that all four men were badly burnt and hardly recognizable.

Inside the morgue, the sheet was pulled back on the first body.

"No, that's not him," said the trainer.

The sheet was pulled back on the second.

"No, that's not him either," said the trainer.

The sheet was pulled back on the third charred body.

"No, that's definitely not him," insisted the trainer.

Then the sheet was pulled back on the fourth corpse.

"Yes, that's him, all right," said the trainer.

The mortician said: "I'm amazed. These bodies are burnt to a crisp yet you were able to identify your jockey instantly. How can you be so sure?"

The trainer said: "That useless son-of-a-bitch has been my jockey for five and a half years, and, trust me, he's never in the first three."

✳ What time does Andy Murray go to bed?
Tennish.

✳ Did you hear about the guy who met up with his tennis partner to play doubles?

It took them ages to find two other men who looked like them.

London Olympics 2012

With the 2012 Olympic Games being held in the East End of London, a number of the events have been altered to reflect the local population.

Opening Ceremony
The flame will be ignited by a petrol bomb thrown by a native of the area in the traditional dress of balaclava and shell suit. The flame will be contained in a large overturned police van situated on the roof of the stadium.

Men's 100 Metres
Competitors will have to hold a DVD player and microwave oven (one under each arm) and on the sound of the starting pistol, a police dog will be released from a cage ten metres behind the athletes.

Men's 100 Metre Hurdles
As above, but with added obstacles – car bonnets, walls, hedges, garden fences, etc.

Women's 100 Metres
All competitors are to run in short skirts and white stilettos.

Hammer
Competitors may specify the type of hammer they wish to use (claw, sledge, etc), the winner being the one who can cause the greatest physical damage in three attempts.

Fencing
Entrants will be required to dispose of as many stolen goods as possible in five minutes.

Modern Pentathlon
Amended to include mugging, breaking and entering, arson and joyriding.

Shooting

A strong challenge is expected from the local men in this event. The first target will be a moving police van. In the second round, competitors will aim at a convenience store clerk, bank teller or security guard.

Boxing

The boxing competition will be restricted to husband and wife teams, and will take place on a Friday night. The husband will be given fourteen pints of lager while the wife will be told not to make him any tea when he comes home. The bout will then commence.

Cycling Time Trials

Competitors will be asked to break into the university bicycle shed and take an expensive mountain bike owned by some unsuspecting student on his first trip away from home – all against the clock.

Cycling Pursuit

As above, but the bike will be owned by a visiting member of the Australian rugby team who will witness the theft.

Swimming

All waterways are currently being tested for toxicity levels in the hope of finding one that can support human life.

Men's 50km Walk

Unfortunately this event will have to be cancelled as the police cannot guarantee the safety of anyone walking the streets of East London, especially someone that appears to be mincing.

The Closing Ceremony

Following a display of synchronized rock throwing, the Olympic flame will be extinguished by riot police water cannon. After the Games, the stadium itself will be boarded up and used only by local entrepreneurs wishing to remove the copper piping.

* A middle-aged couple were in the audience at the World Snooker Championships when, in the darkness, they spotted a pair of young lovers caressing each other passionately.

   "I don't know whether to watch them or watch the game!" remarked the husband.

   "Watch them," advised the wife. "You already know how to play snooker."

* Three disabled athletes – a blind man, an amputee and a guy in a wheelchair – were flying back with the US team from the 2008 Paralympics when their plane crashed in the Nevada Desert. The trio were the only survivors and faced an anxious wait hoping that someone would rescue them.

   After two days there was still no sign of help, so, feeling really thirsty, they decided to set off in search of water. The amputee led the way, with the blind man pushing the guy in the wheelchair, and soon they found an oasis.

   The amputee waded into the water first, drank freely, and when he came out the other side, lo and behold, he had a new leg.

   Excited, he immediately encouraged his friends to do the same. The blind man offered to push the guy in the wheelchair, but the latter wanted to be independent and insisted that the blind man went ahead first.

   So the blind man walked into the water, drank liberally, and when he emerged the other side, lo and behold, he could see.

   By now the guy in the wheelchair was eagerly anticipating his dip in the oasis. So he wheeled himself in, drank copious amounts of water, and when he wheeled himself out the other side, lo and behold, he had new tyres.

* A guy took his girlfriend to her first football game. Afterwards he asked her what she thought about it.

   "I liked it," she said, "but I couldn't understand why they were killing each other just for twenty-five cents."

   "What do you mean?" he asked.

   "Well, everyone kept yelling, 'Get the quarter back!'"

✳ Two aliens were visiting Earth to research local customs. They split up so that they could learn more in the time allowed, and one happened to stumble across a game of cricket but mistook it for a strange religious ceremony. Afterwards, he met up with his fellow alien and described what he had seen.

"I went to a large green field shaped like a meteorite crater. Around the edges, several thousand worshippers gathered. Then two priests walk to the centre of the field to a rectangular area and hammer six spears into the ground, three at each end. Then eleven more priests walk out, clad in white robes. Then two high priests wielding clubs walk to the centre and one of the other priests starts throwing a red orb at the ones with the clubs."

"Gee," said the other alien. "What happens next?"

"Then it begins to rain."

★　★　★　★　★

TELEVISION AND RADIO

★ A CNN reporter covering the Middle East heard a story about an elderly Jew who had been going to the Wailing Wall in Jerusalem to pray twice a day, every day, for a number of years. So she went to the Wailing Wall and, after waiting around for an hour or so, she spotted him. When he had finished his prayers, she approached him for an interview.

"Sir," she asked, "how long have you been coming to the Wailing Wall and praying?"

"Forty years."

"Tell me, what do you pray for?"

"For peace between Jews and Arabs; for all the hatred to stop; for all of our children to grow up as friends."

"And how do you feel after doing this for forty years?"

"Like I'm talking to a wall!"

★ While his wife was enjoying a night out with her friends, a husband took the opportunity to relax and watch some TV. But he was interrupted when their twelve-year-old son, who had been watching his own TV in his room, appeared in the doorway and asked: "What's love juice?"

Choking on his beer, the dad decided that perhaps it was time to explain a few things to the boy. "Well, son," he said, "one day – maybe soon – you'll meet a girl you really like and you'll get aroused and your penis will get hard. You will touch the girl all over and when you reach the top of her leg it will feel wet. This is her love juice coming out of her vagina, which means that she is ready for sexual intercourse."

The son looked puzzled and said: "Okay, Dad, thanks."

As the boy was about to leave the room, the dad said: "Hang on, son, what are you watching up there to make you ask such a question?"

The son replied: "Wimbledon."

★ Batman hit Penguin over the head with a vase and said: "T-Pau!"

Penguin said: "Don't you mean 'Kerpow!'?"

Batman said: "No, I had china in my hand!"

★ What do you call a Teletubby that's been burgled?
A Tubby.

> ❝ The only reality show I want to see is 'Find Osama'. Twelve minor celebrities are sent to Afghanistan to track down Bin Laden. We'll either find Osama or lose some minor celebrities. Either way, we're up!
> Andy Parsons ❞

★ Did you hear about the new TV talent show for dogs?
It's called *Bone Idol*.

★ Conducting a vox pop, a TV news reporter asked a man in the street? "Do you support GM food?"

The man said: "Not really. I think they should stick to making cars."

★ Bob had finally made it through to the last round of *The $64,000 Question*. He was going to answer a question on American history.

The show's host said: "You know that if you answer this question correctly, you walk away with $64,000?"

"Yes," replied Bob.

"Okay, Bob, this is a two-part question, and you may answer either part first. As a rule, the second half of the question is generally easier. Which part would you like to answer first?"

"I'll try the easier part first."

The audience hushed in expectation. Bob had been the show's best contestant for months, astounding everyone with his remarkable knowledge. Acres of news print had been devoted to his appearances. The whole nation was willing him to win.

"Here we go then, Bob," said the host. "I will ask you the second part of the question first. The very best of luck."

The host took the big money question from an envelope. "Bob, here is your question: 'And in what year did it take place?'"

The government of Dubai have banned *The Flintstones*. They won't let it be screened anywhere in the country, which is strange because . . . Abu Dhabi do.

★ An elderly lady phoned her local TV station to complain about the weather forecaster.

"What's the problem?" asked the TV station press officer.

The old lady said: "Your weather forecaster said there would be six inches of snow last night, but when I woke up this morning there was miles of it!"

★ A woman rang the Shopping Channel.
   The girl who answered the phone said: "Can I help?"
   "No thanks," said the woman. "I'm just browsing."

★ **Having bought a new flat-screen plasma TV, a young woman asked her brother how to change channels.**
   "I haven't the remotest idea," he said.

★ A radio station in Sydney, Australia, ran a competition called "Mate Match" where the DJ called someone at work who was in a serious relationship. The contestant was then asked three highly personal questions and if their partner then gave the same answers to those three questions, the couple would win a fabulous prize.
   One morning the DJ rang a number and said: "Have you ever heard of Mate Match?"
   "Yes, I have," laughed a male voice on the other end of the line.
   "Great! Then you know we're giving away a trip to the Gold Coast if you win. What's your name? First name only please."
   "Brian."
   "Okay, Brian. Are you married, or what?"
   "Yes, I am married."
   "Right. Now what's your wife's name? First name only please."
   "Sara."
   "Is Sara at work, Brian?"
   "Yes, she's at work."
   "Okay, first question, Brian. When was the last time you had sex?"
   "About eight o'clock this morning."
   "Atta boy, Brian. Question two: how long did it last?"
   "About ten minutes," answered Brian sheepishly.
   "Wow! You really want that trip, huh? No one would ever have said that if a trip wasn't at stake."

"Yeah, that trip sure would be nice."

"Okay," continued the DJ. "Final question: where did you have sex at eight o'clock this morning?'"

"Sara's gonna kill me," laughed Brian.

"This sounds good, Brian. Where was it?"

"Well, her mum is staying with us for a couple of weeks, and the mother-in-law was in the shower at the time."

"Atta boy, Brian."

"So we did it on the kitchen table."

The DJ then put Brian on hold and called his wife's work number. Sara answered the phone.

"Hi, Sara," said the DJ. "We're live on air right now playing Mate Match. Do you know the rules?"

"No," said Sara.

"Well, all you have to do is answer three questions honestly. Be completely honest, remember. And if your answers match Brian's answers, then the both of you will be off to the Gold Coast for five days on us."

"Wow!"

"Right. First question: when did you last have sex, Sara?"

"Oh God! Uh, this morning before Brian went to work."

"What time?" asked the DJ.

"Around eight o'clock."

"Very good. Next question: how long did it last?"

"Twelve, fifteen minutes maybe."

"That's close enough," said the DJ. "I'm sure you're trying to protect his feelings. Now we've got one last question, Sara. You are one question away from a trip to the Gold Coast. Are you ready?"

"Yes."

"Where did you have it?"

"Oh my God, Brian!" shrieked Sara. "You didn't tell them that, did you?"

"Just tell him, honey," said Brian.

"Sara, what's bothering you so much?" asked the DJ.

"Well," giggled Sara.

"Come on, Sara," pressed the DJ. "Where did you have it?"

"Up the arse."

TRANSPORT AND TRAVEL

❖ After spending his entire life in the desert, a man decided to visit a cousin in the city. It was a whole new experience for him – for a start, he had never before seen a train or train tracks.

While standing in the middle of some railroad tracks one day, he heard a loud whistle but had no idea what it was and so failed to move out of the way in time. Luckily he received nothing worse than a glancing blow and escaped with a few broken bones and minor internal injuries.

Following three weeks in hospital, he recovered at his cousin's house. While in the kitchen, he suddenly heard the teakettle whistling. He immediately grabbed a baseball bat from the nearby closet and proceeded to batter the teakettle into an unrecognizable lump of metal.

Hearing the commotion, his cousin rushed into the kitchen, and seeing what had happened, wanted to know: "Why have you ruined my perfectly good teakettle?"

"Man," replied the desert guy, "you gotta kill these things while they're small."

❖ **I went off the rails when I was younger; I guess I wasn't cut out to be a train driver.**

❖ A man was sick of his two-and-a-half-hour drive to work every day.

"You should try the train," suggested a neighbour.

"I did once, but I couldn't drive the thing to save my life!"

> ❝ At least it's comfortable on Eurostar. It's murder on the Orient Express.
> Tim Vine ❞

You Know You're a Biker When . . .

Your best friends are all named after animals.

Your idea of jewellery is chains and barbed wire.

You have motorcycle parts in the dishwasher.

Your family photo album is a series of tattoos on your back.

You can tell what kind of bugs they are by their taste.

Your best shoes have steel toes.

You carry a picture of your bike in your wallet.

You wake up next to your girlfriend and your first thought is whether your bike will start.

You would rather become a vegetarian than ride in a car.

Your kids take a motorcycle chain to "Show and Tell".

Your idea of a good party is one where someone rides his bike in and does donuts in the living room.

Your coffee table collapses under the weight of motorcycle magazines.

Your garage is bigger than your house.

❖ Sometimes when you cry, no one sees your tears. Sometimes when you are worried, no one sees your pain. Sometimes when you are happy, no one sees your smile. But you try lighting a cigarette on a bus and see how much attention you get!

> The New York City subway system announced it will hire 350 more workers to clean up the subway. So this brings the number of workers cleaning the subway to . . . 350.
>
> Conan O'Brien

❖ A young man was travelling on a train when he let out a loud, involuntary fart. In an attempt to cover his embarrassment, he tried to make conversation with the elderly lady sitting opposite him and asked her: "Do you happen to have today's paper?"

"No," she replied, "but at the next station I'll try and grab you a handful of leaves."

❖ A man had been shipwrecked alone on a remote desert island for two years when he suddenly noticed that a bottle had been washed ashore. And inside the bottle was a message on a piece of paper.

With trembling hands, the man reached into the bottle and pulled out the piece of paper, his first contact with the outside world in twenty-four months. The message on it read: "Due to lack of activity, we regretfully inform you that we have cancelled your email account."

> I had a mate whose dream was to be run over by a steam train. It happened last week. Chuffed to bits, he was.
>
> Tim Vine

❖ A mother was anxiously awaiting her twenty-year-old daughter's return home from a year of overseas travel. As the passengers came through the door into the airport arrivals lounge, the mother noticed that right behind her daughter was a man dressed in feathers with exotic markings all over his body, and carrying a shrunken head. Seeing her mother, the daughter ran up to her, flung her arms around her and then introduced the strange-looking man as her new husband.

The mother threw up her hands in horror. "You never listen to me, darling!" she screamed. "You never listen! I said for you to marry a RICH doctor. A RICH doctor!"

❖ When astronaut Neil Armstrong walked on the moon, he not only gave his famous speech about "one small step for man, one giant leap for mankind", he also made a number of barely heard remarks, either to his fellow astronauts or to Mission Control. Just before he entered the landing craft, for example, he was heard to say: "Good luck, Mr Gorsky."

Many people at NASA thought it was a casual greeting to one of the Soviet cosmonauts, but a check through records showed nobody by the name of Gorsky linked to the Soviet space programme. Over the ensuing years, a number of people quizzed Armstrong as to what "Good luck, Mr Gorsky" meant, but he simply smiled enigmatically and refused to elaborate.

Then in 2006, while Armstrong was taking part in a question-and-answer session following a speech, a reporter brought up the old riddle of Mr Gorsky. This time Armstrong finally revealed the origins of the story as, in the intervening period, Mr Gorsky had died.

Apparently when he was a kid, Armstrong was playing baseball with a friend in the backyard. His friend hit a fly ball that landed by the front of his neighbours' bedroom windows. The neighbours were Mr and Mrs Gorsky. As young Neil bent down to retrieve the ball, he heard Mrs Gorsky shouting at Mr Gorsky: "Oral sex? You want oral sex? You'll get oral sex when the kid next door walks on the moon!"

❖ Did you hear about the astronaut who broke the law of gravity?

   He got a suspended sentence.

★   ★   ★   ★   ★

DONALD TRUMP

✳ Donald Trump went to the doctor and said: "Can you give me something to boost my esteem?" The doctor handed him a huge pair of stick-on ears.

   "Will these make me more attractive and powerful?" asked Trump.

   "No," said the doctor, "but they'll stop people laughing about your hair."

✳ What's the difference between an astronaut and Donald Trump's hairdo?

   One amazes mankind by defying the laws of gravity, and the other is a spaceman.

   How can you tell that Donald Trump's hairdo believes in God?

   Because it's dyed and ascending to Heaven.

✳ Why did aliens try to land on Donald Trump?

   They thought his comb-over was a crop circle.

✳ A man walked into a barber shop, handed him a picture of Donald Trump and said: "I'd like to look like that."

   "I'm sorry, sir," came the reply. "I'm a hairdresser, not a taxidermist."

> 66 Here's a sure sign that spring is around the corner: Donald Trump has just evicted a family of robins out of his hair.
>
> David Letterman 99

* Donald Trump does a lot to help the less fortunate people in society. For a start, he lets a blind man cut his hair.

* What does Melania Knauss see in Donald Trump?
  A billion dollars and high cholesterol.

★ ★ ★ ★ ★

VACATION AND LEISURE

★ A man and his wife were vacationing on their yacht off the coast of Australia. After they had sailed out to sea a few miles, he asked her: "Do you want to go swimming?"
   "I can't," she said. "I'm on my period."
   "Damn!" he moaned. "You always take the fun out of shark fishing."

> 66 My parents went on vacation last week. I mean, I assume they made it. You'd think I'd at least get a text . . . plane went down ☹.
>
> Matt Kirshen 99

★ A skydiving instructor was answering questions from a group of first-time jumpers. A nervous beginner asked: "So, if my chute doesn't open and the reserve doesn't open either, how long have I got until I hit the ground?"
   The instructor said: "You have the rest of your life."

★ A tour guide was showing a tourist around Washington, DC. The guide pointed out the spot where George Washington supposedly threw a dollar across the Potomac River.

"That's impossible!" said the tourist. "No one could throw a dollar that far."

"You have to remember," replied the guide, "that a dollar went a lot further in those days."

★ Two guys were sitting in a bar, talking about their summer vacations. The first said: "My wife was so excited about going to the Grand Canyon, but when she eventually saw it, her face dropped a mile. I guess it was my fault really for pushing her over the edge."

★ A couple who holidayed regularly in Spain spent many of their days apart because he was a sun worshipper whereas she always stayed in the shade. So at lunchtimes she would sit in their hotel room with a sandwich while he sat outside a local bar and enjoyed a few beers.

One lunchtime he stayed away a little longer than usual and when he returned to the room, she was furious.

"Where have you been?" she moaned. "I've been dying of thirst here. What do you think I am, a bloody camel?"

"Why didn't you go to the pool bar and buy some water?" he said. "It's only a hundred yards over there."

"You know I can't go out in the sun in the middle of the day. Anyway, now you're finally here, I want you to go and get me a bottle. But remember, it must be still water. I don't want any of that sparkling stuff."

"Okay my sweet. Still water it will be."

So he headed off to the pool bar and returned a few minutes later carrying a bottle of water.

"Is it still water?" she demanded.

"Of course it's still water," he replied wearily. "Who do you think I am, bloody Jesus?"

> ❝ I was walking in the park and this guy waved at me. Then he said: 'I'm sorry, I thought you were someone else. I said:
> 'I am.'
>
> Demetri Martin ❞

★ An American tourist in Africa was admiring a necklace worn by a local tribesman. "What is it made of?" she asked.

"Crocodile's teeth," replied the tribesman.

"I guess," said the tourist, "that they mean as much to you as pearls do to us?"

"No," said the tribesman. "Anyone can open an oyster."

★ A neighbour wondered why a woman was wearing black. "My husband died last week," she explained.

"Oh, I'm so sorry to hear that."

"Yes, he was taken ill on our recent alpine vacation suffering from shock because someone attached a rocket to his skis."

"My, how terrible!"

"Yes, after that he went downhill very fast."

★ A woman had been walking in the park for some time when she decided to sit down on a bench. To rest her aching feet for a few moments, she took off her shoes and stretched out her legs on the bench.

Just then a wino appeared and asked her with a leer: "Are you up for it then, love?"

"How dare you!" said the woman. "I'm not one of your cheap pickups!"

"Well then," said the wino, "what are you doing in my bed?"

★ On an African safari, a native guide was asked how to keep from being attacked by wild animals at night.

"Just carry a lighted torch," he suggested.

"Does that really work?" asked one of the tourists.

"It depends," said the guide, "on how fast you carry it."

★ Two young lovers went up into the mountains for a romantic winter vacation. On arrival, the guy went out to chop some wood, but when he got back he complained that his hands were icy cold.

"Okay," said his girlfriend, "put them here between my thighs and that will warm them up." So he did.

After lunch, he went out to chop some more wood and again he came back complaining that his hands were freezing.

"Just put them between my thighs," said his girlfriend, "and that will warm them up." So he did.

After dinner, he went out to chop some more wood to get them through the night. When he came back, he said: "Honey, my hands are really, really freezing!"

She looked at him and said: "For crying out loud, don't your ears ever get cold?"

> ❝ I'll tell you what I love doing more than anything: trying to pack myself in a small suitcase. I can hardly contain myself.
>
> Tim Vine ❞

★ As a coach load of American tourists on a visit to England drove through Wiltshire, the guide was busily pointing out places of interest.

When they approached Stonehenge, the guide announced: "This is Stonehenge, a megalithic monument dating from about 2,800 BC. It consisted originally of thirty upright stones, their tops linked by lintel stones to form a continuous circle about a hundred feet across. The uprights were built from local sandstone, and each stone weighs around twenty-six tons."

At the back of the coach, one tourist turned to his wife and said: "Pretty impressive, huh?"

"Yes," she agreed. "But wouldn't you think they'd have built it further back from the main road?"

★ Ted and Mike were out walking in the country when Ted turned to Mike and said: "I really need to take a crap."

"There's a tree," said Mike. "Why don't you go behind that?"

Ted looked at the tree and said: "But I don't have any toilet paper."

"You've got a dollar, haven't you?" asked Mike. "You can wipe yourself with that."

Reluctantly Ted took his advice, disappeared behind the tree and did his business. Minutes later, he came back with crap all over his hands.

"What happened?" asked Mike. "Didn't you use the dollar?"

"Yes," said Ted. "But have you ever tried to wipe with three quarters, two dimes and a nickel?"

★ A middle-aged married couple were members of a party that went snorkelling off Hawaii. After spending an hour in the water, everyone got back on the boat except for the wife and a handsome young man. As she continued to explore underwater, she noticed that wherever she swam, he did, too. She continued snorkelling for another forty minutes, and so did he.

She felt really flattered by his attention, and as she took off her fins, she coyly asked him why he had remained in the water for so long.

"I couldn't get out until you did," he replied matter-of-factly. "I'm the lifeguard."

> 66 I want to hang a map of the world in my house. Then I'm going to put pins into all the locations that I've travelled to. But first I'm going to have to travel to the top two corners of the map so that it won't fall off the wall.
>
> Steven Wright 99

Genuine Holiday Complaints

A tourist at an African game lodge overlooking a waterhole complained that the sight of a visibly aroused elephant ruined his honeymoon by making him feel "inadequate".

A woman threatened to call police after claiming she had been locked in her hotel room by staff. In fact, she had mistaken the "do not disturb" sign on the back of the door as a warning to stay in the room.

"The beach was too sandy."

"I was bitten by a mosquito – no one said they could bite."

"Topless sunbathing on the beach should be banned. The holiday was ruined as my husband spent all day looking at other women."

"We bought Ray-Ban sunglasses for $5 from a street trader, only to find out they were fake."

"It took us nine hours to fly home from Jamaica to England; it only took the Americans three hours to get home."

"We had to queue outside with no air conditioning."

"No one told us there would be fish in the sea. The children were startled."

★ An American and his wife were driving around Ireland on vacation when one of the rear tyres on their car developed a slow puncture. He managed to find a small local garage where he asked the owner if he had an air line.

"An air line?" replied the owner. "You must be joking! We don't even have a bus station!"

★ I met the guy who invented crosswords today. I forget his name. It was P something T something R.

★ **A man complained to his friend: "We go on vacation in eight days and my wife has just broken her wrist. Bloody typical, isn't it! Now I'll have to carry my own suitcase!"**

★ A scoutmaster was teaching his scouts about survival. "What are the three most important things", he asked, "that you should bring with you in case you get stranded alone in the desert?"

Hands were raised to suggest food, matches, distress flares and so on, but one boy said: "A compass, a canteen of water and a deck of playing cards."

"Why those items?" asked the scoutmaster.

The boy replied: "The compass is to find direction, and the water is to prevent dehydration."

"Yes, I understand that," said the scoutmaster, "but why would a deck of playing cards be of any use if you were stranded alone in the desert?"

"Well, you know how it is," said the boy. "As soon as you start playing solitaire, someone is bound to come up behind you and say, 'Put that red six on top of the black seven.'"

> 66 I phoned the local ramblers' club today, but the bloke who answered just went on and on.
> Tim Vine 99

★　A young man arrived home in a state of exhaustion.

"Are you okay?" asked his mother. "How did your day out with grandma go?"

"Never again!" he said. "I've never been so embarrassed in my life. I couldn't believe some of the things she said, things like: 'What are you doing here? We don't want your sort in this country! Go on, get back to Africa, get back to India!' Everybody was staring at us. Eventually I had to tell her: 'Gran, it's a zoo.'"

★　★　★　★　★

WEDDINGS

❖　A bride said to her mother: "I've got something new and something borrowed, but I still need something old and blue."

"Don't worry," said the mother. "Your grandma's coming to the wedding, and she can't afford to pay her heating bills."

❖　Leaving their wedding reception, a honeymoon couple hailed a cab to take them to their romantic hotel destination in the hills. The driver wasn't too sure how to get there but said he would ask them for directions when they got nearer.

Meanwhile the newlyweds started getting amorous on the back seat, and before long they had stripped off and were having sex.

Seeing a fork in the road, the driver said: "I take the next turn, right?"

"No way, get your own!" said the groom breathlessly. "This one's all mine!"

Two young boys were attending a wedding. One asked the other: "How many men can a woman marry?"

"Sixteen," came the reply.

"How do you know that?"

"Easy. All you have to do is add it up, like the preacher said: 'Four better, four worse, four richer, four poorer.'"

❖ On their wedding night, the bride and groom were just about to climb into bed when she said to him nervously: "Honey, you know I'm a virgin and I'm ignorant about sex. Before we do it, can you explain it to me?"

"Okay, sweetheart," he said. "To make things easier, we will call your private place 'the prison' and call my private thing 'the prisoner'. And what happens is, I put the prisoner in the prison. Do you understand?"

"Yes," she said, and they made love for the first time.

Afterwards, he was lying on the bed basking in the satisfaction of a job well done when she nudged him and giggled: "Honey, the prisoner seems to have escaped!"

Taking the hint, he turned to face her and smiled: "Then we will have to re-imprison him."

And they had sex for a second time.

At the end, he flopped down on the bed, totally satisfied, but she still wanted more and, with a suggestive smile, purred: "Honey, the prisoner is out again!"

Somehow he managed to rise to the occasion for a third time, but the exertion left him completely exhausted. However she was so enjoying the new experience that a few minutes later she nudged him again and whispered: "Honey, the prisoner escaped again!"

He just about had the energy to turn his head and sigh: "Sweetheart, it's not a life sentence, you know!"

❖ A worried young woman went to her doctor and said: "Doctor, I'm getting married this weekend and I've led my fiancé to believe that I'm still a virgin when in fact I'm not. Is there anything you can do to help me?"

The doctor said: "Medically, there's nothing I can do but there is a little trick you might like to try. On your wedding night, when you're getting ready for bed, take an elastic band and slide it to your upper thigh. When your husband inserts his penis, snap the elastic band and tell him it's your virginity snapping."

Deciding that her husband was gullible enough to fall for the ruse, she put the plan into action. After a beautiful, romantic wedding, the happy couple retired to the honeymoon suite. There, she went into the bathroom, slipped the elastic band up her leg, finished preparing and climbed into bed with her new husband.

Wasting no time, her husband slid the end of his penis into her, whereupon she snapped the elastic band.

"Ow!" he yelled. "What the hell was that?"

"Oh, nothing, honey," she replied. "It was just my virginity snapping."

"Well snap it back again," he cried. "It's wrapped around my balls!"

A nervous young bride became irritated by her husband's lusty advances on their wedding night and told him: "I demand proper manners in bed, just as I do at the dinner table."

Amused by his wife's formality, the groom smoothed his tousled hair and climbed quietly between the sheets.

"Is that better?" he asked.

"Yes, much better," she replied.

"Very good, darling," he continued. "Now would you please be so kind as to pass the pussy?"

❖ A young couple rushed into a city church and said to the minister: "We want to get married right away. Here are all our papers, and these people are our witnesses. Can you do a quick service?"

The minister conducted a short service and pocketed his fee, but afterwards couldn't help saying to the groom: "Isn't there a proverb about marrying in haste? Why are you two in such a hurry?"

Dragging his bride after him, the groom ran out into the street and shouted back to the minister: "We're double-parked!"

❖ "How did your wedding go?" Phil asked his friend Mark when they met in the pub two weeks later.

"Yeah, it was fine, I guess," shrugged Mark.

"You don't sound too convinced . . ."

"Well, it was just that Carrie couldn't wait to get home after the reception. I was hoping it was for a wild night of passionate sex, but it turned out she just wanted to change her relationship status on Facebook from 'Engaged' to 'Married'."

❖ A brawl broke out at a wedding reception, as a result of which the groom ended up in court on a charge of assault.

The first witness was the best man, who began his testimony by explaining that it was traditional for the best man to have the first dance with the bride.

"I understand," said the judge.

"Well," continued the best man, "after we had finished the first dance, the music kept on going, so we carried on dancing to the second song, and when the music kept on going after that, we carried on dancing to the third song. Then all of a sudden the groom jumped over a table, came running towards us, and kicked the bride hard in her privates."

"That must really have hurt!" exclaimed the judge in horror.

"Hurt?" said the best man. "He broke three of my fingers!"

❖ A shy white couple decided to save their first sexual encounter until their wedding night. And because the wife didn't want to get pregnant, she sent her husband out to buy some condoms while she prepared herself for the challenge ahead by drinking liberally from the hotel room mini bar. To add to the atmosphere, she switched the room lights off and left the door slightly ajar.

When a few minutes later she heard someone pushing the door open, she naturally thought it was her husband, unaware that it was in fact the black bellhop bringing the complimentary bottle of champagne. Asking no questions, she dragged him onto the bed in the gloom, had wild sex with him and fell asleep straight afterwards through a combination of alcohol and exhaustion.

Meanwhile the husband was struggling to find a shop that sold condoms, and when he did finally find one, he realized that he only had one twenty-cent coin. So he asked the shop owner if he could buy just an individual condom, and the owner asked him which quality he wanted. "The white condom, lowest quality, is fifteen cents," explained the shop owner. "The black condom, average quality, is twenty cents, and the purple condom, best quality, is twenty-five cents."

The husband chose the black condom as he had only twenty cents.

Returning to the hotel, he found his wife fast asleep. Without a warning, he put on the condom, jumped on her and started making love. She was surprised that he still had the energy after the first session.

Nine months later, she gave birth to a baby boy. When the boy was able to talk, he asked his father: "Dad, why am I black when you and Mom are white?"

"Think yourself lucky, son," replied the father. "If I'd have had five cents more, you'd have been purple!"

❖ Preparing for her wedding, a young woman asked her mother to go out and buy a nice long black negligee and to place it carefully in her suitcase so that it wouldn't wrinkle. Unfortunately the mother forgot all about it until the last minute, and by that time all she could find was a short pink nightdress. Thinking that it was better than nothing, she bought it and hurriedly threw it into the daughter's suitcase.

After the wedding, the bride and groom went back to their hotel room. He was rather shy, so he asked her to change in the bathroom and not to look while he got ready for bed. In the bathroom, she opened her suitcase and saw the negligee that her mother had thrown in there.

"Oh no!" she exclaimed. "It's short, pink and wrinkled!"

And the groom cried out: "I told you not to look!"

❖ A Japanese bride was getting married in Indonesia. On her big day, she was preparing to walk down the aisle when she glanced down and behind at her outfit and whispered something in her father's ear. Suddenly he started panicking and shouting, and all of the guests ran screaming from the chapel.

Ten minutes later, a jeep pulled up and three bush rangers carrying rifles and nets jumped down from the vehicle. They went up to the bride's father and said: "Right, where's the giant lizard?"

The bride looked bewildered. "What giant lizard?" she asked.

Her father said: "The one you told me about just as we were about to walk down the aisle."

"No, father," said the bride, raising her eyes to the heavens. "Your hearing is getting worse. What I said was: 'Is my kimono draggin'?'"

❖ As the groom walked down the aisle of the church to take his place at the altar, the best man could not help noticing that he was wearing a huge grin from ear to ear.

The best man said: "Hey, I know you're happy to be getting married, but you look absolutely thrilled."

The groom whispered: "That's because I've just had the best blow job of my entire life, and I'm marrying the wonderful woman who gave it to me."

A few moments later, the bride came walking down the aisle, and she, too, was wearing a big, radiant smile.

The maid of honour noticed this and said: "Of course you're pleased to be getting married, but I've never seen anyone look so happy and excited."

The bride whispered: "That's because I've just given the last blow job of my entire life!"

On their wedding night, the young bride turned to her husband and said: "I know it can be difficult for men to read women's moods, so here are a few pointers: in the evening, if my hair is neat and tidy, that means I don't want sex at all; if my hair is a little dishevelled, that means I may or may not want sex; and if my hair is wild and untamed, that means I want sex."

"Okay, sweetheart," replied the groom. "Just remember that when I come home from work, I usually like a drink. If I have only one drink, that means I don't want sex; if I have two drinks, I may or may not want sex; and if I have three drinks, the state of your hair becomes irrelevant."

❖ A man was playing golf when a ball hit him right in the groin, leaving him writhing in agony. Next day at the doctor's office, he asked: "How bad is it, doc? Because I'm getting married next week and my fiancée is still a virgin."

The doctor said: "I'll have to put your manhood in a splint so that it will heal and keep straight. It should be okay in about two to three weeks."

The doctor then took four tongue depressors, made them into a neat little four-sided splint and wired the contraption together. The groom deliberately avoided mentioning his little mishap to his bride before their wedding day.

On their honeymoon night, his wife opened her blouse to reveal a gorgeous pair of breasts and told him lovingly: "You'll be the first. No one has ever touched these before."

Determined to outdo his wife, the husband dropped his pants and said: "Well, check this out – it's still in its crate!"

❖ A ninety-five-year-old man married a twenty-three-year-old girl, prompting fears for his health from the wedding guests. They were afraid that the wedding night might prove fatal because he was a frail old man and she was a vivacious young woman.

But the next morning everyone was surprised to see the bride come down the main stairwell of the hotel very slowly, step by step, and painfully bow-legged. Eventually she managed to hobble to the front desk.

The clerk looked very concerned, and asked the bride: "What happened to you? You look as if you've gone ten rounds with Evander Holyfield?"

"It's my husband!" she gasped. "Oh, my God! When he told me that he'd been saving up for seventy-five years, I thought he meant his money!"

❖ A young couple were planning to get married, but as the big day approached they became increasingly apprehensive. For each had a problem they had never shared with anyone, not even each another.

Finally overcoming his embarrassment, the groom decided to confide in his father. "Dad," he said, "I am really worried about this marriage."

"Why?" asked his father. "Are you not sure that you love her?"

"Of course I love her," replied the son, "more than anything else in the world. It's just that I've got horribly smelly feet, and I'm afraid they will put her off."

"No problem," said the father. "All you have to do is wash your feet as often as possible, and always wear socks, even to bed."

The son thanked him for his advice, and promised to follow it.

Meanwhile the bride-to-be had finally plucked up the courage to confide in her mother. "Mom," she said, "when I wake up in the morning, my breath is truly awful."

"But honey," said her mother comfortingly, "everyone has bad breath in the morning."

"No, you don't understand," said the daughter. "My

breath in the morning is so horrendously rancid that I'm afraid my husband won't want to sleep in the same room as me."

Her mother thought for a moment about the problem and then said: "Try this. In the morning, get straight out of bed and head for the kitchen to make breakfast. While your husband is busy eating, slip into the bathroom and brush your teeth. The important thing is not to say a word until you have brushed your teeth."

"I shouldn't even say good morning?" queried the daughter.

"No, not a word," the mother affirmed.

So the daughter promised to give it a try.

Two weeks later, the couple were married and, remembering the advice each had received – he with his perpetual socks and she with her morning silence – they managed quite well.

But then four months into their married life, disaster struck when the husband woke just before dawn one morning to find that one of his socks had come off. Fearful of the consequences, he frantically searched the bed, and in doing so woke his wife.

Without thinking, she asked: "What are you doing?"

"Oh my God!" he replied in horror, recoiling from her breath. "You've gone and swallowed my sock!"

★ ★ ★ ★ ★

WEIGHT

✳ Have you heard about the garlic diet?

You don't actually lose any weight, but from a distance, your friends will think you look thinner.

* A young woman, Chelsea, said to her friend Kelly: "I'm going to the doctor today, Kel."

  "Why's that?" asked Kelly. "Is something the matter?"

  "I dunno," said Chelsea. "I want to ask the doctor how many calories there are in sperm."

  "Why worry?" said Kelly. "If you're swallowing that much, no guy is going to care if you're a bit chubby."

* My girlfriend suffers from depression brought on by anorexia. I told her she should lighten up.

* A young man was talking to a girl on an Internet chatroom. She sent him a photo of herself and, realizing she looked a bit chunky, wrote: "The camera adds ten pounds."

  He wrote back: "Well, stop eating cameras, then."

* A man and his wife were working in their garden one day when he remarked: "Your butt is getting really big. I bet you're bigger than the barbecue grill."

  To prove his point, he fetched a tape measure and measured first the grill, then his wife's bottom. "Yeah, I'm right," he said triumphantly, "your butt is two inches wider than the barbecue grill!"

  Although hurt by his comments, she decided to remain silent.

  That night in bed, he started to get amorous but she simply pushed him away.

  "What's wrong?" he asked.

  She replied: "Do you really think I'm going to fire up this big-ass grill for one little sausage?"

> " I'm the fluffy one – that's the politically correct term for 'fat'. I'm tired of hearing about women getting rejected by handsome, good-looking, slim guys. Give a fluffy guy a chance. The worst we're gonna do is have dinner without you.
>
> Gabriel Iglesias "

* Becoming anxious about her ballooning weight, a woman went to see a therapist. The woman told him that no matter how hard she tried, she had never been able to stick to diets. He told her: "The key to a happy and successful life is: always finish what you start."

  The woman took his advice on board and when she returned for her next appointment, she had a much more optimistic outlook.

  "I feel better already," she told the therapist. "So far today I've finished a giant bag of chips, a packet of biscuits and a chocolate cake."

* My aunt reckoned smoking would help her lose weight. It did – one lung at a time.

* A guy told his buddy: "I've got a new girlfriend and she's anorexic."

  "Oh, right. How's it going?"

  "Not too well. Each week, I'm seeing less and less of her."

Apparently 72 per cent of American women are now overweight. Shocking figures!

* A heavily overweight man had tried all kinds of exercise to slim down – swimming, running, aerobics, but nothing seemed to work. As a last resort, his doctor suggested that he take up golf, adding: "There's no finer game."

  So the man went and out bought a set of golf clubs but a few weeks later he was back at the doctor's asking if he could take up some other sport.

  "Why? What was wrong with golf?" asked the doctor.

  "Well," explained the patient, indicating his vast stomach, "the trouble is that when I put the damn ball where I can see it, I can't hit it. And when I put it where I can hit it, I can't see it!"

✳ A middle-aged woman queued at the drugstore for almost half an hour. Eventually the girl behind the counter served her and said: "I'm really sorry about your wait."

The woman snapped: "Well, you're not exactly skinny yourself!"

✳ A husband was standing on the bathroom scales, desperately holding his stomach in.

Thinking that he was trying to reduce his weight, his wife remarked: "I don't think that will help."

"It does," he said. "It's the only way I can read the numbers!"

✳ My wife got upset last night because I mentioned that her butt looked a little big in the picture I was looking at . . . on Google Earth.

Did you hear about the woman who was so thin and frail that when she bent over to pick up a sieve, she strained herself?

✳ A woman was laughing to herself as she waited at the school gates to collect her daughter. Eventually one of the other mothers said to her: "You're in a good mood today. What's tickling you?"

"My husband's been on a diet for the past four days and he's lost five pounds already."

"That's really good. But what's so funny about it?"

"Well, I've worked out that in six months he will have disappeared completely."

✳ A large wife was watching a James Bond movie at home with her husband. After a while she drooled: "Cor! I could do him some damage!"

"How's that then?" asked her husband. "By going on top?"

Signs That You're Carrying a Few Extra Pounds

Your clothing size is your age, or older.

One of your legs is as big as a person.

Your boobs touch your back when you lie down.

You bump into things that you never did before.

Chairs make rude noises when you sit in them.

You realize the rolls on your arms aren't muscles.

You don't fit on the toilet seat.

The car seat belt won't expand any further.

You've forgotten what it was like to be able to cross your legs.

It only takes four shirts for a large load in the washer.

When you go up the stairs, the house shakes.

The bed appears to have shrunk.

Your favourite clothing store has the name "tents" in the title.

✳ A woman at a diet club was lamenting the fact that she had put on weight. "I made my family's favourite cake over the weekend," she told the group, "and they ate half of it at dinner. The next day, I kept staring at the other half until I finally weakened and cut myself a thin slice. Well, I'm ashamed to say that once I got the taste there was no stopping me. One slice led to another and soon the whole cake was gone. I was totally dismayed by my lack of willpower, and I knew that my husband would be bitterly disappointed in me."

"What did he say when he found out?" asked the group leader gently.

"Oh, he never found out," said the woman. "I made another cake and ate half!"

✳ A man was sitting on the bus when a large woman called across to him: "If you were a gentleman, you would stand up and let someone else sit down."

He replied: "And if you weren't so fat, at least four people could sit down!"

✳ How do you get a fat girl into bed? – Piece of cake.

✳ In fact, doctors say there are seven million people who are overweight. Of course, that's just round figures.

✳ How can you tell when your girlfriend is getting fat? – When she can fit into your wife's clothes.

✳ A large, elderly woman was waiting at the side of the road. When a young man approached, she asked him: "Can you see me across the road?"

He said: "I can see you half a mile away."

> ❝ I broke up with a girl once because she lied about her weight. I say that, she died in a bungee-jumping accident.
> Jimmy Carr ❞

* On a visit to his parents' house, a young man was asked by his mother to set the table for dinner. When he opened the refrigerator, he saw taped to the inside of the door a picture of a scantily-dressed, super slim model.

"What's the picture all about?" he asked.

His mother explained: "I put it up there to remind me not to over-eat."

"Is it working?"

"Yes and no. I've lost fifteen pounds, but your dad has gained twenty."

* A large girl told her boyfriend that she wanted to end their relationship. Trying to break the news gently to him, she said: "You'll get over me one day."

He said: "Not without scaffolding."

* Sitting up in bed one night, a wife said: "I think it would be really romantic if when I die, I could be buried in my wedding dress."

Without looking up from his book, the husband replied: "Then you'd better hope you die of some wasting disease."

* A guy said to his friend: "My wife is the double of Kate Moss. Kate is eight stone and my wife is sixteen stone."

* * * * *

WOMEN

* Why are there so few women superheroes?

Because by the time they'd got changed, the entire world would be wiped out.

★ Two guys were discussing the merits of women drivers. One said: "I hate women drivers. They shouldn't be allowed on the road. And whenever they do something stupid, I let them know my feelings in no uncertain terms!"

The other said: "I'm not so sure that's a good idea. I was driving into work this morning when I saw a woman cut in front of a pickup truck, causing him to brake sharply to avoid hitting her. The truck driver was obviously angry because he immediately hung his arm out of the window and gave the woman the finger. I thought to myself: "That guy is stupid." You see, I always smile nicely and wave politely whenever a female does anything to me in traffic, and here's why:

"I drive forty-eight miles each way to work every day. That's a total of ninety-six miles. Of these, sixteen miles each way is bumper-to-bumper. Most of the bumper-to-bumper is on an eight-lane highway. There are seven cars every forty feet for thirty-two miles. That works out at 982 cars every mile, or 31,424 cars. Even though the rest of the thirty-two miles is not bumper-to-bumper, I figure I pass at least another 4,000 cars. That brings the number to something like 36,000 cars that I pass every day. Statistically, females drive half of these. That's 18,000 women drivers.

"In any given group of females, one in twenty-eight has PMS. That's 642.

"According to *Cosmopolitan*, 70 per cent describe their love life as unsatisfactory. That's 449.

"According to the National Institute of Health, 22 per cent of all females have seriously considered suicide or homicide. That's ninety-eight.

"And 34 per cent describe men as their biggest problem. That's thirty-three.

"According to the National Rifle Association, 5 per cent of all females carry weapons, and this number is increasing.

"That means that every single day, I drive past at least one female that has a lousy love life, thinks men are her biggest problem, has seriously considered suicide or homicide, has PMS, and is armed.

"Give her the finger? I don't think so!"

Women like jewellery. They're like raccoons: show them some shiny stuff and they'll follow you home.

Alonzo Bodden

★ Two guys were standing at a bar, discussing the state of their relationships. "When my girlfriend drinks red wine," said one, "she gets really turned on and will do anything to please me."

The other guy sighed: "If my girlfriend drinks red wine when she has PMS, we both agree on one thing: we both wish I was dead."

★ A woman was told she had to have a colostomy. She immediately burst into tears, sobbing: "It's terrible news, absolutely terrible!"

Her husband put his arm around her and said comfortingly: "Hey, darling, it's not the end of the world. There are worse things that could have happened."

"You don't understand," she yelled. "Where the hell am I going to find shoes to match the bag?"

★ To a woman, why is a car like a hysterectomy? – She can't reverse either of them.

Having a woman as a friend is about as useless as having $19 in the bank and wanting to use your ATM card.

Alonzo Bodden

★ A woman said to her husband one day: "Show me your feminine side."

"Okay," he replied, and walked out the door.

When he returned forty-five minutes later, she moaned: "Where have you been?"

He said: "I've been parking the car."

> They say a woman's work is never done. Maybe that's why they get paid less.
>
> Sean Lock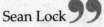

★ What's long and hard and makes women groan? – An ironing board.

> I love women, but I feel like you can't trust some of them. Some of them are liars. I was in the park and I met this girl, she was cute and she had a dog. I went up to her, we started talking, and she told me her dog's name. Then I said: 'Does he bite?' She said: 'No.' And I said: 'Oh yeah? Then how does he eat?' Liar!
>
> Demetri Martin

★ Scientists have discovered that most women will, at some time, contain intelligent DNA. Unfortunately, 95 per cent of them spit it out.

> Women have no feelings. It's actually men who are the more romantic. Men are the people you will hear say: 'I've found somebody. She's amazing. If I don't get to be with this person, I can't carry on. I have a job, I have a flat, but they mean nothing. I have to be with her. Because if I can't, I'm going to end up in some bedsit, I'll be an alcoholic, and I won't be able to walk the streets any more.' That is how women feel about shoes.
>
> Dylan Moran

Good Girls vs. Bad Girls

Good girls say: "Thanks for a wonderful dinner."
Bad girls say: "What's for breakfast?"

Good girls never go after another girl's man.
Bad girls go after him AND his brother.

Good girls wax their floors.
Bad girls wax their bikini lines.

Good girls loosen a few buttons when it's hot.
Bad girls make it hot by loosening a few buttons.

Good girls wear white cotton panties.
Bad girls don't wear any.

Good girls blush during bedroom scenes in movies.
Bad girls know they could do better.

Good girls always make their own bed in the morning.
Bad girls never sleep in their own bed.

Good girls only own one credit card and rarely use it.
Bad girls only one own bra and rarely use it.

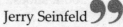

Looking at cleavage is like looking at the sun. You don't stare at it – it's too risky. You get a sense of it and then you look away.

Jerry Seinfeld

Good girls love Italian food.
Bad girls love Italian waiters.

Good girls paint their bedroom pink.
Bad girls paint the town red.

Good girls prefer the missionary position.
Bad girls do too, but only for starters.

Good girls wear high heels to work.
Bad girls wear high heels to bed.

Good girls say: "No."
Bad girls say: "When?"

Good girls believe that you're not fully dressed
without a strand of pearls.
Bad girls believe that you are fully dressed with just a
strand of pearls.

Good girls stay in and play Scrabble.
Bad girls go out and play the field.

Good girls never consider sleeping with the boss.
Bad girls never do either, unless he's very, very rich.

Good girls make chicken for dinner.
Bad girls make reservations.

A magazine top ten of the most painful
things women have to endure says
number one is having your nipples
clamped. Surely having them towed away is
worse.

Dave Spikey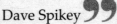

★ One day, God decided to make a companion for Adam. He told St Peter of his decision, adding that he wanted to make a being who was similar to Man, yet was different – someone who could offer Man comfort, companionship and pleasure. God said he intended calling this being Woman. So St Peter set about creating this being and thought of ways in which she would be appealing and could provide physical pleasure to Man. When he had finished, he showed God his ideas.

God was mightily impressed. "You have done an excellent job, Peter, and now all that remains is for you to provide the brain, nerve endings and senses to Woman."

"I could actually use your input on this, Lord," said St Peter. "Have you had any thoughts about how you want Woman to behave?"

"Yes, I have," replied God. "I want you to make her brain slightly smaller, yet more intuitive, more feeling, more compassionate, and more adaptable than Man's."

"How many nerve endings shall I put in her hands?" asked St Peter.

"How many did we put in Adam?"

"17,000."

"Then we shall do the same for Woman."

"And how many nerve endings shall we put in her feet?"

"How many did we put in Adam's?"

"9,500."

"Ah yes, these beings are constantly on their feet, so they benefit from having fewer nerve endings there. Do the same for Woman."

"How many nerve endings shall we put in Woman's genitals?" asked St Peter.

"How many did we put in Adam?"

"520."

"Yes, we did want Adam to have a means of receiving extra pleasure in life, didn't we? Do the same for Woman."

"Certainly, Lord."

"No, wait," said God. "Damn it, give her 12,000 – I want her to scream out my name!"

★ What do you show a woman who has been driving accident-free for five years? – Second gear.

★ A group of guys and a girl were watching a baseball game. The guys were impressed by her knowledge of the rules and eventually asked: "How come you know so much about baseball?"

"Well," she explained, "I used to be a man until I had a sex change."

The guys had never met a transsexual before and were immediately curious. "What was the most painful part of the whole procedure?" they asked. "Was it when they cut off your penis?"

"That was very painful," she replied. "But it wasn't the most painful part."

"Was it when they cut off your balls?"

"That was also very painful, but it wasn't the most painful part."

"So what was?"

"The part that hurt most was when they cut my salary in half."

★ You tell a man something, and it goes in one ear and out the other. You tell a woman something, and it goes in both ears and comes out of the mouth.

> A woman's like a pack of cards. You need a heart to love her. You need a diamond to win her. You need a club to smash her head in. And a spade to bury the bitch.
>
> Jack Dee

✶ A guy and his girlfriend had just got into bed one night. With her encouragement, he soon became aroused but then suddenly she announced: "I don't feel like it. I just want you to hold me."

"What?" he protested.

She went on: "You're simply not sufficiently in touch with my emotional needs as a woman for me to satisfy your physical needs as a man. Can't you just love me for who I am and not what for what I do for you in the bedroom?"

Realizing that he had drawn a blank that night, he went to sleep.

The next day, he decided to take time off work to spend more time with her. He bought her a nice lunch and then took her shopping at an exclusive department store, accompanying her while she tried on a number of very expensive outfits. She couldn't decide which one to buy, so in the end he said he'd buy them all for her. Then she wanted new shoes to match her new clothes, so he said: "Let's buy a pair for each outfit." Next she moved on to the jewellery department and chose a pair of sparkling diamond earrings. By now, she was nearing sexual satisfaction at the prospect of having so much bought for her. "I think that's everything, honey," she smiled. "Let's go to the cashier."

But suddenly he said: "No, darling, I don't feel like it."

"What?" she protested.

"Darling," he continued, "I just want you to HOLD this stuff for a while. You're simply not sufficiently in touch with my financial needs as a man for me to satisfy your shopping needs as a woman. Why can't you just love me for who I am and not for the things I buy you?"

They didn't have sex that night either.

> ❝ Her long tan legs. Those dark bedroom eyes. Her deep, sexy voice. Her huge protruding Adam's apple . . . hey, wait a minute.
>
> Jeffrey Ross ❞

★ "Good afternoon, ladies," said Sherlock Holmes to three women sitting on a bench in a London park.

"Do you know those women?" asked his faithful companion, Dr Watson.

"No," said Holmes as the pair continued walking. "I don't know the spinster, the prostitute and the new bride."

"Good heavens, Holmes!" exclaimed Watson. "If you don't know them, how can you be so sure that they are what you say?"

"Elementary, my dear Watson," explained Holmes, glancing back. "Observe how they are eating their bananas."

"So?"

"Well, Watson, the spinster holds the banana in her left hand and uses her right hand to break the banana into small pieces which she then puts in her mouth."

"I see what you mean, Holmes. That's amazing! What about the prostitute?"

"She holds the banana in both hands and crams it into her mouth."

"Holmes, you've surpassed yourself! But how do you know that the other woman is a new bride?"

"Simple," replied Holmes. "She holds the banana in her left hand and uses her right hand to push her head towards the banana."

Doing the rounds at a singles night, a woman said sarcastically to a grossly obese guy: "How come a handsome hunk like you hasn't been snapped up yet?"

Without appreciating the irony in her remark, he replied arrogantly: "I guess I slipped through the net."

To which the woman commented: "Must have been one hell of a net!"

Philosophy of a Lazy Wife

I don't wash the windows because I love birds and I don't want one to fly into a clean window and get hurt.

I don't cook because if I helped put the manufacturers of supermarket ready meals out of business, I would feel guilty about all those people losing their jobs.

I don't disturb cobwebs because I don't like the thought of making a spider homeless.

I don't wax floors because I am terrified a guest will slip and get hurt and maybe even sue me.

I don't put things away because my husband would never be able to find them again.

I don't iron because I choose to believe the labels when they say "Permanent Press".

I don't hoover because by cutting down on electricity I'm helping to save the planet.

I don't weed the garden because I don't want to destroy God's work.

WORDS OF WISDOM

❖ No matter how much you push the envelope, it will still be stationery.

❖ Those who flee temptation usually leave a forwarding address.

❖ A problem shared is attention gained.

❖ A problem shared is a buck passed.

❖ Advent calendars: their days are numbered.

❖ **Friendship is like incontinence: everyone can see it, but only you can feel its true warmth.**

❖ One-armed butlers: they can take it, but they can't dish it out.

❖ It's a fact: taller people sleep longer in bed.

❖ There's no "I" in team, unless you're dyslexic.

❖ Wrestlers don't like to be put on hold.

❖ When travelling between Russia and Alaska, you must first get your Bering Strait.

❖ **Opening a new funeral parlour can be quite an undertaking.**

❖ Acupuncture: a jab well done.

❖ There's always light at the end of the tunnel unless you're agoraphobic.

❖ If we don't conserve water, we could go from one ex-stream to another.

❖ # Criticism is not nearly as effective as sabotage.

❖ Be true to your teeth, or they will be false to you.

❖ The only thing you ever get free of charge is a dead battery.

❖ Statistically, six out of seven dwarfs aren't happy.

❖ Every two in one people are schizophrenic.

❖ You're only young once, but you can be immature forever.

❖ # Reincarnation is making a comeback.

❖ Humpty Dumpty had a great fall – and a pretty good spring and summer, too.

❖ Two needles of different length will never see eye to eye.

❖ Ideas are like gold dust – they often get panned.

❖ Procrastination is the art of keeping up with yesterday.

❖ Gardening tip: if you water your lawn with beer, the grass will come up half cut.

❖ Bungee jumping is for suicidal people who are indecisive.

❖ If you can keep your head while others around you are losing theirs, you may want to land your helicopter somewhere else.

❖ Always go the extra mile – especially if what you want is a mile away.

❖ Life not only begins at forty, it begins to show.

❖ Hangmen always keep their customers in the loop.

❖ A clean house is the sign of a broken computer.

❖ When you are arguing with an idiot, make sure the other person isn't doing the same thing.

❖ Chasing the American Dream does not count as exercise.

❖ Pheasant and plum jam: the preserve of the upper classes.

❖ Those who like to do the ironing find their pleasure in creases.

❖ Never lie to an X-ray technician. He will see right through you.

❖ The first day at the nudist colony is always the hardest.

❖ A bachelor is a man who is footloose and fiancée-free.

❖ www.conjunctivitis.com – a site for sore eyes.

❖ If a judge loves the sound of his own voice, expect a long sentence.

❖ The nice part of living in a small town is that when you don't know what you're doing, someone else does.

❖ If it really were the thought that counted, more women would be pregnant.

❖ Good health is merely the slowest possible rate at which one can die.

❖ When the wheel was invented, it caused a revolution.

To get sincere personal advice and the correct time, try calling a random telephone number in the early hours of the morning.

❖ Dermatologists often make rash statements.

❖ I'm not addicted to cocaine. I just like the way it smells.

❖ Teamwork means never having to take all the blame yourself.

❖ Exit signs: they're on the way out.

❖ He who hogs the blankets is usually very wrapped up in himself.

❖ The easiest time to add insult to injury is when you're signing somebody's plaster cast.

❖ A bird in the hand makes blowing your nose difficult.

★   ★   ★   ★   ★

WORK

* After thirty years as a sewer worker, Jim's record was acknowledged by a visit from the town's mayor who wanted to see for himself the valuable service that Jim performed. So the mayor climbed down into the sewer and asked Jim why he liked his job so much.

  "Well," said Jim, "my job is fascinating. You see that big poop floating past us now? That's from the carpenter. I can tell because you can see sawdust in it. Now this next poop, that's from the gardener. I can tell because it's got grass clippings in it. And this big poop coming into view now is from my wife."

  The mayor was amazed. "Jim, I can understand the logic behind the carpenter and the gardener, but how on earth do you know that that poop out of all the millions of poops in the sewer is from your wife?"

  "Easy," said Jim. "It's got my lunch tied to it."

* A chief executive of a major company was scheduled to address an important convention, so he asked the press officer to write him a punchy, twenty-minute speech. But when the chief executive returned from the convention, he was furious.

  "What's the idea of writing me an hour-long speech?" he raged at the press officer. "Most of the audience walked out before I was even halfway through!"

  The press officer was mystified. "I wrote you a twenty-minute speech," he said. "I also gave you the two extra copies you asked for."

* Two guys met up in a bar. "How did the job hunting go?" asked one.

  "I struck lucky," said the other. "I've been offered a job, $800 a week, working for the Brittle Bone Society."

  "Did you accept?"

  "I snapped his hand off."

✳ Did you hear about the woman whose husband got her a job as a human cannonball? – She went ballistic.

✳ A wife had long suspected that her husband was having an affair with his pretty young PA, so one day she decided to try and catch him out by calling in at his office unannounced. She marched in through the door to find the PA sitting on the husband's lap.

Without hesitating, he dictated: ". . . and in conclusion, gentlemen, regardless of shortages, I cannot continue to operate this office with just one chair."

✳ Did you hear about the archaeologist whose career was in ruins?

✳ Jim was telling a friend that he had been fired from his factory job.

"Why did the foreman fire you?" asked the friend.

"Oh," said Jim, "you know what foremen are like. They stand around with their hands in their pockets all day, watching other people do the work."

"We all know that," replied the friend, "but why did he let you go?"

"Jealousy," said Jim. "All the other workers thought I was the foreman."

✳ A guy in an office revealed to his co-workers that in a moment of tender romance, he had asked his girlfriend to marry him.

"What did she say?" asked one.

"I don't know," he said. "She hasn't emailed me back yet."

✳ A man arrived home from the office and told his wife: "What a day I've had! All the computers went down, and we had to do everything manually. It took me twenty minutes to shuffle the cards for solitaire!"

✳ Did you hear about the guy who got a job at a paperless office? – Everything was great until he needed a shit.

> 66 A guy gave me a job at an information booth, no questions asked.
> Jay London 99

✳ A pretty young secretary marched into her boss's office and said: "I'd like to get something off my chest."
"Yes. What?"
"Your eyes."

✳ On leaving school, a boy got a job with a telegram company but on his first day he was hauled over the coals by his boss. "I've just had a complaint from the firm you sent that telegram to," raged the boss. "They say they could hardly understand it because there's no punctuation – it's just one long continuous sentence. Why?"
"Because you told me to send it like that," said the boy.
"What are you talking about?"
"Just before I sent it, you said to me: 'This telegram is urgent, so I want you to pull out all the stops.'"

Did you hear about the guy who used to work at Starbucks until he got fed up with the daily grind?

✳ At an interview for a job with a large company, a woman asked if the firm had a fitness programme.
"Our employees don't need one," smiled the human resources manager. "They are routinely jumping to conclusions, flying off the handle, beating around the bush, running down the boss, going around in circles, dragging their feet, dodging responsibility, passing the buck, pulling strings, throwing their weight around, stretching the truth, bending the rules, stabbing others in the back and pushing their luck!"

Signs That You're Living and Working in the Noughties

You've sat at the same desk for four years and worked for three different companies.

Your supervisor doesn't have the ability to do your job.

You try to enter your password on the microwave.

You haven't played solitaire with real cards in years.

You email your colleague who works at the next desk to you.

When your computer crashed, your biggest loss was your collection of jokes.

Your reason for not staying in touch with friends is that they don't have email addresses.

When you make phone calls from home, you automatically insert a "9" to get an outside line.

To qualify for sick leave, you must be at least in traction.

---

* The manager of a retail clothing store was reviewing a potential employee's application and noticed that the man had never worked in retail before.

The manager said: "For someone with no experience, you are certainly asking for a high wage."

"Well," replied the applicant, "the work is so much harder when you don't know what you're doing."

✳ A young man complained to his friend: "I was sacked from my job today for asking the customers if they wanted 'Smoking or Non-Smoking'. The funeral director told me the correct phrase was 'Cremation or Burial'."

> 66 Receptionists are just secretaries who can't type.
>
> Al Murray 99

✳ Two dyslexic men were working in the kitchen of a restaurant.
  The first said: "Can you smell gas?"
  The second replied: "I can't even smell my own name."

✳ A young job seeker was being shown around a latex factory by the manager. Firstly, he was shown the machine that made the teats for babies' feeding bottles. It went hiss, pop, hiss, pop – the hissing noise being the sound of the latex poured into the mould and the popping noise occurring as the hole was put into the end of the teat.
  Next he was shown the machine that made condoms. It went hiss, hiss, hiss, pop.
  "Right," he said, eager to impress. "I know that the hissing sound is the latex being poured into the mould. But what's the popping noise?"
  The manager explained: "We put a hole in every fourth condom."
  "Why would you do that?" asked the young man. "It can't be very good for the condom industry."
  "No," said the manager, "but it's brilliant for the baby bottle teat business!"

✳ A guy said to his friend: "What do you call a tall guy who can masturbate successfully nine times in a single day?"
  "I don't know," said the friend. "I give up."
  "No, it's not a joke. I need to know what to put on my CV."

New Office Terminology

Blamestorming – Sitting around in a group, discussing why a deadline was missed or a project failed, and determining who was responsible.

Seagull manager – A manager who flies in, makes a lot of noise, craps on everything and then leaves.

Assmosis – The process by which people seem to absorb success and advancement by sucking up to the boss rather than by working hard.

Salmon day – The experience of spending an entire day swimming upstream, only to get screwed and die.

Mouse potato – The online answer to the couch potato.

Prairie dogging – In an office filled with cubicles, when someone yells or drops something loudly, and people's heads pop up over the partition walls to see what's happening.

Percussive maintenance – The art of whacking the hell out of an electronic device to get it to work again.

Stress puppy – Someone who seems to thrive on being stressed out and whiny.

404 – Someone who is utterly clueless, from the World Wide Web error message "404 Not Found."

Testiculating – Waving your arms around and talking bollocks.

> A while back I got a job doing colonic irrigations. That takes it out of you.
>
> Tim Vine

* What did the guillotine operator receive when he was made redundant? – Severance pay.

How to Place New Employees in Your Company

1. Put 400 bricks in a closed room.
2. Put the new employees in the room and close the door.
3. Leave them alone and come back six hours later.
4. Then analyse the situation:
a. If they are counting the bricks, put them in the Accounting Department.
b. If they are recounting them, put them in Auditing.
c. If they have messed up the whole place with the bricks, put them in Engineering.
d. If they are arranging the bricks in some strange order, put them in Planning.
e. If they are throwing bricks at each other, put them in Operations.
f. If they are sleeping, put them in Security.
g. If they have broken the bricks into pieces, put them in Information Technology.
h. If they are sitting around idly, put them in Human Resources.
i. If they claim to have exhausted every different combination, yet not a single brick has been moved, put them in Sales.
j. If they are staring out of the window, put them in Strategic Planning.
k. If they have already left for the day, put them in Marketing.

✳ A new girl started at work today and I offered her instant promotion in return for sex. I'd love to see her face when she finds out I'm not the boss!

✳ A muscular young man was boasting about his physique on the building site where he worked. He claimed he could beat anyone on the site in a trial of strength and took particular delight in mocking one of the older workers. Eventually the older man became irritated by the taunts.

"Okay," said the older man, "put your money where your mouth is. I'll bet you a week's wages that I can haul something in a wheelbarrow over to that outbuilding that you won't be able to wheel back."

"You're a weak old man!" said the cocky young upstart. "This will be like taking candy from a baby. But if you don't mind losing a week's wages, off you go."

With that, the older man grabbed the wheelbarrow by the handles. Then, nodding to the young man, he said: "Okay, get in."

> ❝ Jesus was a carpenter. A tradesman. You can tell he was a tradesman because he disappeared off the face of the Earth for three days with no rational explanation.
>
> Al Murray ❞

✳ Worker: "You said you'd give me a pay rise if you were happy with me."
Boss: "That's true, I did. But how can I be happy with someone who wants more money?"

✳ A man came home and told his wife: "I got fired at work today. My boss said my communication skills were awful."
"What did you say?"
"I didn't know what to say."

* A houseowner complained to a workman he had hired: "I gave you a list of eight jobs to do around the house, but you've only done numbers one, three, five and seven."

   The workman replied: "That's because I'm an odd-job man."

* A boss and his young assistant marched onto a noisy factory floor. None of the workers paid them the slightest attention until the boss yelled out: "Tequila, schnapps, bourbon!"

   And suddenly there was silence apart from two guys at the back who carried on talking amongst themselves.

   Impressed by his boss's ability to get the workers' attention and ever eager to impress, the young assistant directed his voice at the chattering pair and also shouted out: "Tequila, schnapps, bourbon!"

   Hearing this, the boss turned to him and said: "Hey, what do you think you're doing? I call the shots around here!"

> ❝ Before I got into comedy, I was a plumber for 150 years – although that's just an estimate.
>
> Gordon Southern ❞

* Delicate negotiations between union members and their employer were in danger of breaking down, with the union refusing to admit that its workers were blatantly abusing the sick leave provisions set out under the terms of their contract.

   The talks dragged on for three days, until one morning at the bargaining table, the company's chief negotiator held up a newspaper. "This man", he announced, "called in sick yesterday. But here on the sports page is a photo of this supposedly ill employee after he had won a golf tournament yesterday with a score of five under par!"

   Everyone present waited for a response from the union negotiator. After a moment or two he broke the silence by saying: "But just think of the score he could have made if he hadn't been sick."

Employee Review

John Watts, the chief executive of a company, asked his manager to write a detailed employment review describing Ken Stewart, one of his programmers.

1. Ken Stewart, my assistant programmer, can always be found
2. hard at work in his cubicle. Ken works independently, without
3. wasting company time talking to colleagues. Ken never
4. thinks twice about assisting fellow employees, and he always
5. finishes given assignments on time. Often Ken takes extended
6. measures to complete his work, sometimes skipping coffee
7. breaks. Ken is an individual who has absolutely no
8. vanity in spite of his high accomplishments and profound
9. knowledge in his field. I firmly believe that Ken can be
10. classed as a high-calibre employee, the type which cannot be
11. dispensed with. Consequently, I duly recommend that Ken be
12. promoted to executive management, and a proposal will be
13. executed as soon as possible.

A memo was sent immediately after the letter.

John,

That idiot Ken was reading over my shoulder while I wrote the report sent to you earlier today. Kindly read only the odd numbered lines above (1, 3, 5 etc) for my true assessment of him.

Regards,

Keith

Genuine Notes to Milkmen

Dear milkman, I've just had a baby, please leave another one.

Please leave an extra pint of paralysed milk.

Milkman, please could I have a loaf but no bread today.

Sorry not to have paid your bill before, but my wife had a baby and I've been carrying it around in my pocket for weeks.

Please send me details about cheap milk as I am stagnant.

Milk is needed for the baby. Father is unable to supply it.

My daughter says she wants a milkshake. Do you do it before you deliver or do I have to shake the bottle?

Please send me a form for cheap milk, for I have a baby two months old and did not know about it until a neighbour told me.

Please leave no milk today. When I say today, I mean tomorrow, for I wrote this note yesterday.

Milkman, please close the gate behind you because the birds keep pecking the tops off the milk.

When you leave the milk, please put the coal on the boiler, let dog out and put newspaper inside the screen door. PS. Don't leave any milk.

* I take my work extremely seriously, which is why the circus says I'm a lousy clown.

* Knock knock.
  Who's there?
  Doorbell repairman.

* A man walked into the human resources department of a large company and handed in his job application. As the HR executive scanned the CV, he noticed that the applicant had been fired from every post he had ever held.

  "If you don't mind me saying so, your employment history is appalling," said the executive. "You've been dismissed from all twelve jobs you've had."

  "I know," agreed the applicant.

  "Well, I'm afraid it's not much of a recommendation. Can you think of one good reason why we should take you on in view of your employment record?"

  "Well," said the applicant, "at least it shows I'm not a quitter!"

* ## Did you hear about the unemployed dwarf who did a bit of casual work?
  ### He asked to be paid under the table.

* My brother is forever getting hold of the wrong end of the stick, which is a problem when you work on a sewage farm.

* Did you hear about the guy who quit his job at the helium gas factory because he didn't like being spoken to in that tone of voice?

★   ★   ★   ★   ★

ZOOS

★ A zookeeper needed some extra animals for his zoo, so he decided to write a letter. But unfortunately he didn't know the plural of "mongoose".

He started the letter: "Dear sir, I need two mongeese." But that didn't sound right, so he tried again. "Dear sir, I need two mongooses." But that didn't sound right either. Then he had an idea. "Dear sir, I need a mongoose, and while you're at it, send me another one."

★ A zookeeper spotted a visitor throwing $10 bills into the elephant enclosure.

"Don't do that," shouted the zookeeper. "You'll make the animals sick."

"But the sign says it's okay," replied the visitor.

"No it doesn't."

"Yes it does. It says: 'Do not feed. $10 fine.'"

★ While cleaning out the aviary at a rundown zoo, a keeper noticed that one of the finches had died of old age. So he put it in a sack and continued with his rounds.

When he reached the primate cage, he saw to his horror that two chimpanzees had also died of natural causes, so he put them in the sack with the finch.

His next stop was the insect house where the Amazonian honey bees lived. As he entered their cage to see how much honey they had produced, he accidentally trod on three of the bees, squashing them to a pulp. So he put the dead bees in the sack.

Since money was tight, he decided to use the dead creatures as food for the zoo's only lion. That afternoon he emptied the sack into the lion's cage. The lion took one look at his meal and groaned: "Oh no! Not finch, chimps and mushy bees!"

Signs That You're at a Bad Zoo

The stripes on the zebra peel away in the heat.

The lion in the cage doesn't move and bears an uncanny resemblance to the one from *The Lion King*.

The miniature Vietnamese pot-bellied pig has a coin slot in the middle of its back.

When a child throws a peanut at the gorilla, the ape shouts: "Will you stop that, it hurt!"

The snake is a draught excluder with two eyes painted on.

The camel is a horse with a flower pot strapped to its back.

The ostrich has "Property of Bernie Clifton" stamped on its side.

The back legs of the elephant don't move in co-ordination with its front legs.

The elephant has a zip leading from its front legs to its trunk.

Most of the animals eat in the zoo cafeteria.

★ On their first visit to the city, two country guys went to the zoo. As they entered the big cat house, the lion let out a spine-tingling roar.

"Come on," said one of the guys nervously. "Let's get out of here."

"You go if you want," said the other, "but I'm staying for the whole movie!"

★ What did the polar bear eat after the zoo dentist fixed its tooth?
    The zoo dentist.

★ A zoo guide was telling visitors about the elephant. "Ladies and gentlemen, this is the elephant, the largest animal to roam the lands. Every day the elephant eats three dozen bunches of bananas, six tons of hay and two thousand pounds of assorted fruits. Madam, please don't stand near the elephant's backside ... Madam, PLEASE don't stand near the elephant's backside ... MADAM ... MADAM ... Too late. George, dig her out."